T0202431

Lecture Notes in Computer Science 13853

Founding Editors

Gerhard Goos
Juris Hartmanis

Editorial Board Members

Elisa Bertino, *Purdue University, West Lafayette, IN, USA*
Wen Gao, *Peking University, Beijing, China*
Bernhard Steffen , *TU Dortmund University, Dortmund, Germany*
Moti Yung , *Columbia University, New York, NY, USA*

The series Lecture Notes in Computer Science (LNCS), including its subseries Lecture Notes in Artificial Intelligence (LNAI) and Lecture Notes in Bioinformatics (LNBI), has established itself as a medium for the publication of new developments in computer science and information technology research, teaching, and education.

LNCS enjoys close cooperation with the computer science R & D community, the series counts many renowned academics among its volume editors and paper authors, and collaborates with prestigious societies. Its mission is to serve this international community by providing an invaluable service, mainly focused on the publication of conference and workshop proceedings and postproceedings. LNCS commenced publication in 1973.

Essaid Sabir · Halima Elbiaze ·
Francisco Falcone · Wessam Ajib ·
Mohamed Sadik
Editors

Ubiquitous Networking

8th International Symposium, UNet 2022
Montreal, QC, Canada, October 25–27, 2022
Revised Selected Papers

Springer

Editors
Essaid Sabir ⓘD
University of Quebec at Montreal
Montreal, QC, Canada

Halima Elbiaze ⓘD
University of Quebec at Montreal
Montreal, QC, Canada

Francisco Falcone ⓘD
Public University of Navarre
Pamplona, Spain

Wessam Ajib ⓘD
University of Quebec at Montreal
Montreal, QC, Canada

Mohamed Sadik ⓘD
Hassan II University of Casablanca
Casablanca, Morocco

ISSN 0302-9743 ISSN 1611-3349 (electronic)
Lecture Notes in Computer Science
ISBN 978-3-031-29418-1 ISBN 978-3-031-29419-8 (eBook)
https://doi.org/10.1007/978-3-031-29419-8

This Springer imprint is published by the registered company Springer Nature Switzerland AG
The registered company address is: Gewerbestrasse 11, 6330 Cham, Switzerland

Preface

The International Symposium on Ubiquitous Networking (UNet) is an international scientific event that highlights new trends and findings in hot topics related to ubiquitous computing/networking. UNet'22 was held in a hybrid mode on October 25–27, in the fascinating city of Montréal, Canada.

Ubiquitous networks sustain development of numerous paradigms/technologies such as distributed ambient intelligence, Internet of Things, Tactile Internet, Internet of Skills, context-awareness, cloud computing, wearable devices, and future mobile networking (e.g., B5G and 6G). Various domains are then impacted by such a system: security and monitoring, energy efficiency and environment protection, e-health, precision agriculture, intelligent transportation, homecare (e.g., for elderly and disabled people), etc. Communication in such a system has to cope with many constraints (e.g., limited-capacity resources, energy depletion, strong fluctuations of traffic, real-time constraints, dynamic network topology, radio link breakage, interference, etc.) and has to meet the new application requirements. Ubiquitous systems bring many promising paradigms aiming to deliver significantly higher capacity to meet the huge growth of mobile data traffic and to accommodate efficiently dense and ultra-dense systems. A crucial challenge is that ubiquitous networks should be engineered to better support existing and emerging applications including broadband multimedia, machine-to-machine applications, Internet of Things, sensors and RFID technologies. Many of these systems require stringent Quality of Service including better latency, reliability, higher spectral and energy efficiency, but also some Quality of Experience and Quality of Context constraints.

The UNet conference series is a forum that brings together researchers and practitioners from academia and industry to discuss recent developments in pervasive and ubiquitous networks. This conference series provides a venue to exchange ideas, discuss solutions, debate identified challenges, and share experiences among researchers and professionals. UNet aims also to promote adoption of new methodologies and to provide the participants with advanced and innovative tools able to catch the fundamental dynamics of the underlying complex interactions (e.g., game theory, Mechanism Design theory, Learning theory, SDR platforms, etc.). Papers describing original research on both theoretical and practical aspects of pervasive computing and future mobile computing (e.g., 5G, 6G, AI-driven communications, IoT, TI, etc.) were invited for submission to UNet'22.

Message from the General Chairs

On behalf of the organizing committee, it is our great pleasure to welcome you to the proceedings of the 2022 8th International Conference on Ubiquitous Networking (UNet'22), which was held in a hybrid mode, on October 25–27, 2022.

The UNet conference series is a forum that aims to bring together researchers and practitioners from academia and industry to discuss recent developments in pervasive systems and ubiquitous networks. This conference series provides a venue to exchange ideas, shape future systems, discuss solutions, debate identified challenges, and share experiences among researchers and professionals. UNet aims also to promote adoption of new methodologies and provide the participants with advanced and innovative tools able to catch the fundamental dynamics of the underlying complex interactions (e.g., artificial intelligence, game theory, mechanism design, learning theory, SDR platforms, etc.). Papers describing original research on both theoretical and practical aspects of pervasive computing and future mobile computing (e.g., 5G, 6G, AI-driven communications, IoT, TI, etc.) were invited for submission to UNet'22.

Technically sponsored by Springer Nature, and co-organized by LATECE Laboratory, NEST Research Group, STARACOM, and Université de Québec à Montréal, the 2022 UNet follows seven successful events held virtually, and in-person in France, Tunisia, and Morocco. Over the past editions, the reputation of UNet has rapidly grown and the conference has become one of the most respected venues in the field of ubiquitous networking and pervasive systems.

The conference would not have been possible without the enthusiastic and hard work of a few colleagues. We would like to express our appreciation to the Technical Program Chairs, Essaid Sabir, Francisco Falcone, and Wessam Ajib, for their valuable contribution in building the high-quality conference program. We also thank the track Chairs and all the organizing committee members. Such an event relies on the commitment and the contributions of many volunteers, and we would like to acknowledge the efforts of our TPC members for their invaluable help in the review process. We are also grateful to all the authors who contributed to the conference with their work.

Special thanks to our Keynote Speakers, the best in their respective fields, Carla Fabiana Chiasserini, Halim Yanikomeroglu, Muriel Médard, Mérouane Debbah, Gerhard Fettweis, and Francisco Falcone, for sharing their expert views on current hot research topics. We also would like to thank Hamidou Tembine for the outstanding tutorial he delivered at UNet 2022.

We hope that you enjoyed the rich program we have built this year, that you made the most out of your participation, and that you will come back to UNet for many years to come!

October 2022

Halima Elbiaze
Mohamed Sadik

Message from the TPC Chairs

It is with great pleasure that we welcome you to the proceedings of the 2022 International Conference on Ubiquitous Networking (UNet'22), held in hybrid mode. You will find an interesting technical program of 5 technical tracks reporting on recent advances in ubiquitous communication technologies and networking; tactile internet and internet of things; mobile edge networking and fog-cloud computing; artificial intelligence-driven communications; and data engineering, cyber security, and pervasive services.

UNet 2022 featured 6 keynote speeches delivered by world-class experts, shedding light on the future 6G mobile standard, novel 6G enablers, global connectivity, AI-driven communications for 6G, Internet of everything, and smart cities. Moreover, an exciting tutorial covering the new trends of data-driven mean-field theory for ultra-dense networks and ubiquitous systems was also delivered.

In this edition, the UNet conference received 43 submitted manuscripts from 24 countries, out of which 17 papers were selected to be included in the final program with an acceptance rate of 39%. The proceedings also include 4 invited papers from experts in ubiquitous computing. The selection of the program of UNet'22 was possible in the first place thanks to the thorough review performed by our TPC committee members. Overall, the average quality of the submission has respected the fairly high standards of the event. The selection process, we believe, has been conducted in a rigorous and fair manner. More specifically, each paper received at least 2 independent reviews made by TPC members, taking into consideration the quality of presentation, the technical soundness, the novelty, and the originality of the manuscripts. The evaluation scale for each aspect of the evaluation was set to range from 1 to 5.

Building this excellent program would not have been possible without the dedication and the hard work of the different Chairs, the Keynote Speakers, the Tutorial Speakers, and all the Technical Program Committee members. We grasp the opportunity to acknowledge their valuable work, and sincerely thank them for their help in ensuring that UNet'22 will be remembered as a high-quality event.

We hope that you enjoyed this edition's technical program, and we were pleased to e-meet you during the conference.

October 2022

Essaid Sabir
Francisco Falcone
Wessam Ajib

Organization

Honorary Chair

Christian Agbobli   University of Quebec at Montreal, Canada

General Chair

Halima Elbiaze   University of Quebec at Montreal, Canada

Co-chair

Mohamed Sadik   Hassan II University of Casablanca, Morocco

TPC Chairs

Essaid Sabir	University of Quebec at Montreal, Canada
Francisco Falcone	Universidad Pública de Navarra, Spain
Wessam Ajib	University of Quebec at Montreal, Canada

Track Chairs

Oussama Habachi	Univ. of Limoges XLIM-SRI, France
Elmahdi Driouch	University of Quebec at Montreal, Canada
Manzoor Ahmed Khan	UAE University, UAE
Elarbi Badidi	UAE University, UAE
Diala Naboulsi	University of Quebec at Montreal, Canada
Tembine Hamidou	University of New York, USA
Alexandre Reiffers	IMT Atlantique, Brest, France
Slim Rekhis	University of Carthage, Tunisia

Publicity Chairs

Antonio Jara	HOPU, Spain
Safaa Driouech	Orange Labs, France
Wissal Attaoui	Inwi, Morocco
Sujit Samanta Kumar	National Institute of Technology, Raipur, India

Steering Committee

Mohamed-Slim Alouini	KAUST, Saudi Arabia
Eitan Altman	Inria Sophia Antipolis, France
Francesco De Pellegrini	University of Avignon, France
Rachid El-Azouzi	University of Avignon, France
Halima Elbiaze	University of Quebec at Montreal, Canada
Mounir Ghogho	International University of Rabat, Morocco & University of Leeds, UK
Marwan Krunz	University of Arizona, USA
Essaid Sabir	Hassan II University of Casablanca, Morocco
Mohamed Sadik	Hassan II University of Casablanca, Morocco

Technical Program Committee

Abdelkrim Abdelli	USTHB, Algeria
Wessam Ajib	University of Quebec at Montreal, Canada
Brahim Alibouch	Ibn Zohr University, Morocco
Imran Shafique Ansari	University of Glasgow, UK
Elarbi Badidi	UAE University, UAE
Paolo Bellavista	University of Bologna, Italy
Asma Ben Letaifa	SupCom, Tunisa
Yann Ben Maissa	INPT, Morocco
Salah Benabdallah	University of Tunis, Tunisia
Mustapha Benjillali	INPT, Morocco
Yahya Benkaouz	Mohammed V University of Rabat, Morocco
Fatma Benkhelifa	Imperial College London, UK
Hassan Bennani	Mohammed V University of Rabat, Morocco
Olivier Brun	Laboratoire d'Analyse et d'Architecture des Systèmes, France
Stefano Chessa	Universita' di Pisa, Italy
Domenico Ciuonzo	University of Naples Federico II, Italy
Deepak Dasaratha Rao	Sysintel Inc, USA

Sabrina De Capitani di Vimercati	Università degli Studi di Milano, Italy
Yacine Djemaiel	University of Carthage, Tunisia
Elmahdi Driouch	Université du Québec à Montréal, Canada
Schahram Dustdar	Vienna University of Technology, Austria
Loubna Echabbi	INPT, Morocco
Hajar El Hammouti	KAUST, Saudi Arabia
Mohamed El Kamili	Hassan II University of Casablanca, Morocco
Halima Elbiaze	University of Quebec at Montreal, Canada
Moez Esseghir	University of Technology of Troyes, France
Francisco Falcone	Universidad Pública de Navarra, Spain
Dieter Fiems	Ghent University, Belgium
Rosa Figueiredo	University of Avignon, France
Giancarlo Fortino	University of Calabria, Italy
Alexandros Fragkiadakis	Institute of Computer Science, FORTH, Greece
Miguel Franklin de Castro	Federal University of Ceará, Brazil
Vasilis Friderikos	King's College London, UK
Yacine Ghamri-Doudane	University of La Rochelle, France
Alireza Ghasempour	ICT Faculty, USA
Hicham Ghennioui	University of Sidi Mohammed Ben Abdellah, Morocco
Majed Haddad	University of Avignon, France
Ridha Hamila	Qatar University, Qatar
José Luis Hernandez Ramos	European Commission - Joint Research Centre, Belgium
Amal Hyadi	McGill University, Canada
Khalil Ibrahimi	University of Ibn Tofail, Morocco
Tawfik Ismail	Cairo University, Egypt
Carlos Kamienski	Universidade Federal do ABC, Brazil
Vasileios Karyotis	Ionian University, Greece
Donghyun Kim	Georgia State University, USA
Hyunbum Kim	Incheon National University, South Korea
Jong-Hoon Kim	Kent State University, USA
Mohamed Koubaa	Université Tunis El Manar, Tunisia
Mohammed-Amine Koulali	Mohammed I University, Morocco
Udhaya Kumar Dayalan	Trane Technologies, USA
Samson Lasaulce	University of Lorraine, France
Shancang Li	University of the West of England, UK
Marco Listanti	University of Rome "La Sapienza", Italy
Michael Losavio	University of Louisville, USA
Bala Krishna Maddali	GGS Indraprastha University, India
Zoubir Mammeri	Paul Sabatier University, France
Wojciech Mazurczyk	Warsaw University of Technology, Poland

Natarajan Meghanathan	Jackson State University, USA
Amitava Mukherjee	Globsyn Business School, India
Francesco Palmieri	Università degli Studi di Salerno, Italy
Al-Sakib Khan Pathan	Independent University, Bangladesh
Shashikant Patil	SVKM's NMiMS Mumbai, India
Marcin Piotr Pawlowski	Expeditus, Poland
Nancy Perrot	Orange Labs, France
Tom Pfeifer	IoT Consult Europe, Germany
Miodrag Potkonjak	UCLA, USA
Luis Quesada	Insight Centre for Data Analytics, Ireland
Khalid Rahhali	Mohamed V University of Rabat, Morocco
Mounir Rifi	Hassan II University of Casablanca, Morocco
Domenico Rotondi	FINCONS SpA, Italy
Giuseppe Ruggeri	University of Reggio Calabria, Italy
Walid Saad	Virginia Tech, USA
Dhananjay Singh	Hankuk University of Foreign Studies, South Korea
Maha Sliti	University of Carthage, Tunisia
Razvan Stanica	INSA Lyon, France
Bruno Tuffin	Inria Rennes Bretagne-Atlantique, France
Om Vyas	Indian Institute of Information Technology, Allahabad, India
Wei Wei	Xi'an University of Technology, China
Konrad Wrona	NATO Communications and Information Agency, The Netherlands
Sherali Zeadally	University of Kentucky, USA
Ping Zhou	Apple Inc., USA

UNet'22 Keynote Speakers

Making Machine Learning Sustainable

Carla Fabiana Chiasserini

Abstract. While Machine Learning has become pervasive as an essential component of many network services and user applications, its energy cost is often difficult to cope with. It is thus critical to improve the sustainability of Machine Learning by reducing its resource demand. This talk tackles this issue while focusing on the emerging approach of Distributed Machine Learning. In particular, we will discuss both the benefits and the challenges posed by Distributed Learning, and the solutions to minimize the energy cost of this approach while fulfilling the performance requirements of a learning process, in terms of learning quality and time. The talk will also discuss Machine Learning model compression as a promising solution to energy saving as well as to the need for the reuse of computing resources. By leveraging model compression, it is indeed possible not only to tune the network and computing resources to the learning requirements, but also to tailor a Machine Learning model around the available resources.

Dr. Carla Fabiana Chiasserini is Full Professor at Politecnico di Torino, Italy, and a Research Associate with the Italian National Research Council (CNR) and the National Inter-University Consortium for Telecommunications (CNIT). She was a Visiting Researcher at UC San Diego (1998–2003), and a Visiting Professor at Monash University (2012 and 2016) and at Technische Universität Berlin (2021 and 2022). She is a Fellow of the IEEE and a Senior Member of ACM. Her research interests include NextG Networks, Edge Computing, Networking for Machine Learning, and Connected Vehicles. She has published over 350 journal articles and refereed conference papers, and she has received several awards for her scientific work. Currently, she serves as Editor-in-Chief of the Computer Communications journal and as Editor-at-Large of the IEEE/ACM Transactions on Networking. Carla is also a member of the Steering Committee of the IEEE Transactions on Network Science and Engineering and of the ACM MobiHoc conference. She has served for several years on the Editorial Board of such journals as the IEEE Transactions on Wireless Networks and the IEEE Transactions on Mobile Computing, and she has been Co-Guest Editor of a number of journal special issues. Carla is/has been involved in many national and international research projects, either as a coordinator or a PI. For more information, please refer to:

https://www.det.polito.it/personale/scheda/(nominativo)/carla.chiasserini
https://scholar.google.com/citations?user=np0OO24AAAAJ&hl=en

Stratospheric Networks of the Future: It Is More than Connectivity

Halim Yanikomeroglu

Abstract. In this talk, a forward-looking wireless infrastructure will be presented which includes a new stratospheric access & computing layer composed of HAPS (high-altitude platform station) constellations positioned in the stratosphere, 20 km above the ground, in addition to the legacy terrestrial layer and the emerging satellite layer. With its bird's-eye and almost-line-of-sight view of an entire metropolitan area, a HAPS is more than a base station in the air; it is a new architecture paradigm with access, transport, and core network functionalities for integrated connectivity, computing, sensing, positioning, navigation, and surveillance, towards enabling a variety of use-cases in an agile, smart, and sustainable manner for smart cities and societies of the future.

Dr. Halim Yanikomeroglu (FIEEE, FEIC, FCAE) is a Professor at Carleton University. He received his Ph.D. from the University of Toronto in 1998. He contributed to 4G/5G technologies and standards; his research focus in recent years includes 6G/beyond-6G, non-terrestrial networks (NTN), and future wireless infrastructure. His extensive collaboration with industry resulted in 39 granted patents. He supervised or hosted in his lab around 170 postgraduate researchers. He co-authored IEEE papers with faculty members in 80+ universities in 25 countries. He has given around 110 invited seminars, keynotes, tutorials, and panel talks in the last five years. He is a Fellow of IEEE, Engineering Institute of Canada (EIC), and Canadian Academy of Engineering (CAE), and an IEEE Distinguished Speaker for Communications Society and Vehicular Technology Society. Dr. Yanikomeroglu serves as the Chair of the Steering Committee of IEEE's flagship wireless event, Wireless Communications and Networking Conference (WCNC). He has served as the General Chair and Technical Program Chair of several leading international IEEE conferences. He has received several awards for his research, teaching, and service, including IEEE ComSoc Fred W. Ellersick Prize (2021), IEEE VTS Stuart Meyer Memorial Award (2020), IEEE ComSoc Wireless Communications Technical Committee Recognition Award (2018), and a number of best paper awards.

Guessing Random Additive Noise Decoding (GRAND) or How to Stop Worrying About Error-Correcting Code Design

Muriel Médard

Abstract. To maintain data integrity in the face of network unreliability, systems rely on error-correcting codes. System standardization, such as has been occurring for 5G, is predicated on co-designing these error-correcting codes and, most importantly, their generally complex decoders, into efficient, dedicated and customized chips. In this talk, we show that this assumption is not necessary and is has been leading to significant performance loss. We describe "Guessing Random Additive Noise Decoding," or GRAND, by Duffy, Médard and their research groups, which renders universal, optimal, code-agnostic decoding possible for low to moderate redundancy settings.

Moreover, recent work with Yazicigil and her group has demonstrated that such decoding can be implemented with extremely low latency in silicon. GRAND enables a new exploration of codes, in and of themselves, independently of tailored decoders, over a rich family of code designs, including random ones. Surprisingly, even the simplest code constructions, such as those used merely for error checking, match or markedly outperform state-of-the-art codes when optimally decoded with GRAND. Without the need for highly tailored codes and bespoke decoders, we can envisage using GRAND to avoid the issue of limited and sub-optimal code choices that 5G encountered, and instead have an open platform for coding and decoding.

Muriel Médard is the Cecil H. and Ida Green Professor in the Electrical Engineering and Computer Science (EECS) Department at MIT, where she leads the Network Coding and Reliable Communications Group in the Research Laboratory of Electronics. She obtained three Bachelor's degrees (EECS 1989, Mathematics 1989 and Humanities 1991), as well as her M.S. (1991) and Sc.D (1995), all from MIT. She is a Member of the US National Academy of Engineering (elected 2020), a Fellow of the US National Academy of Inventors (elected 2018), American Academy of Arts and Sciences (elected 2021), and a Fellow of the Institute of Electrical and Electronics Engineers (elected 2008). Muriel was elected president of the IEEE Information Theory Society in 2012, and served on its board of governors for eleven years. She holds an Honorary Doctorate from the Technical University of Munich (2020).

She was co-winner of the MIT 2004 Harold E. Egerton Faculty Achievement Award and was named a Gilbreth Lecturer by the US National Academy of Engineering in 2007. She received the 2017 IEEE Communications Society Edwin Howard Armstrong Achievement Award and the 2016 IEEE Vehicular Technology James Evans Avant Garde Award. She received the 2019 Best Paper award for IEEE Transactions on Network Science and Engineering, the 2018 ACM SIGCOMM Test of Time Paper Award, the 2009 IEEE Communication Society and Information Theory Society Joint Paper Award, the 2009 William R. Bennett Prize in the Field of Communications Networking, the 2002 IEEE Leon K. Kirchmayer Prize Paper Award, as well as eight conference paper awards. Most of her prize papers are co-authored with students from her group.

She has served as technical program committee co-chair of ISIT (twice), CoNext, WiOpt, WCNC and of many workshops. She has chaired the IEEE Medals committee, and served as member and chair of many committees, including as inaugural chair of the Millie Dresselhaus Medal. She was Editor in Chief of the IEEE Journal on Selected Areas in Communications and has served as editor or guest editor of many IEEE publications, including the IEEE Transactions on Information Theory, the IEEE Journal of Lightwave Technology, and the IEEE Transactions on Information Forensics and Security. She was a member of the inaugural steering committees for the IEEE Transactions on Network Science and for the IEEE Journal on Selected Areas in Information Theory.

Muriel received the inaugural 2013 MIT EECS Graduate Student Association Mentor Award, voted by the students. She set up the Women in Information Theory Society (WithITS) and the Information Theory Society Mentoring Program, for which she was recognized with the 2017 Aaron Wyner Distinguished Service Award. She served as undergraduate Faculty in Residence for seven years in two MIT dormitories (2002–2007). She was elected by the faculty and served as member and later chair of the MIT Faculty Committee on Student Life and as inaugural chair of the MIT Faculty Committee on Campus Planning. She was chair of the Institute Committee on Student Life. She was recognized as a Siemens Outstanding Mentor (2004) for her work with High School students. Since 2015 she has served on the Board of Trustees of the International School of Boston, for which she is treasurer.

She has over fifty US and international patents awarded, the vast majority of which have been licensed or acquired. For technology transfer, she has co-founded two companies, CodeOn, for which she consults, and Steinwurf, for which she is Chief Scientist.

Muriel has supervised over 40 masters students, over 20 doctoral students and over 25 postdoctoral fellows.

Exploring the Union of AI and 6G

Mérouane Debbah

Abstract. Fueled by the availability of more data and computing power, recent breakthroughs in cloud-based machine learning (ML) have transformed every aspect of our lives, from face recognition and medical diagnosis to natural language processing. However, classical ML exerts severe demands in terms of energy, memory and computing resources, limiting their adoption for resource-constrained edge devices. The new breed of intelligent devices requires a novel paradigm change calling for distributed, low-latency and reliable ML at the wireless network edge. This talk will explore the potential of the Mobile AI paradigm to unlock the full potential of 5G and beyond.

Dr. Mérouane Debbah is Chief Researcher at the Technology Innovation Institute in Abu Dhabi. He is a Professor at CentraleSupélec and an Adjunct Professor with the Department of Machine Learning at the Mohamed Bin Zayed University of Artificial Intelligence. He received the M.Sc. and Ph.D. degrees from the Ecole Normale Supérieure Paris-Saclay, France. He was with Motorola Labs, Saclay, France, from 1999 to 2002, and also with the Vienna Research Center for Telecommunications, Vienna, Austria, until 2003. From 2003 to 2007, he was an Assistant Professor with the Mobile Communications Department, Institut Eurecom, Sophia Antipolis, France. In 2007, he was appointed Full Professor at CentraleSupélec, Gif-sur-Yvette, France.

From 2007 to 2014, he was the Director of the Alcatel-Lucent Chair on Flexible Radio. From 2014 to 2021, he was Vice-President of the Huawei France Research Center. He was jointly the director of the Mathematical and Algorithmic Sciences Lab as well as the director of the Lagrange Mathematical and Computing Research Center. Since 2021, he has led the AI & Digital Science Research centers at the Technology Innovation Institute. He has managed 8 EU projects and more than 24 national and international projects. His research interests lie in fundamental mathematics, algorithms, statistics, information, and communication sciences research. He is an IEEE Fellow, a WWRF

Fellow, a Eurasip Fellow, an AAIA Fellow, an Institut Louis Bachelier Fellow and a Membre émérite SEE. He was a recipient of the ERC Grant MORE (Advanced Mathematical Tools for Complex Network Engineering) from 2012 to 2017. He was a recipient of the Mario Boella Award in 2005, the IEEE Glavieux Prize Award in 2011, the Qualcomm Innovation Prize Award in 2012, the 2019 IEEE Radio Communications Committee Technical Recognition Award and the 2020 SEE Blondel Medal. He has received more than 20 best paper awards, among which the 2007 IEEE GLOBECOM Best Paper Award, the Wi-Opt 2009 Best Paper Award, the 2010 Newcom++ Best Paper Award, the WUN CogCom Best Paper 2012 and 2013 Award, the 2014 WCNC Best Paper Award, the 2015 ICC Best Paper Award, the 2015 IEEE Communications Society Leonard G. Abraham Prize, the 2015 IEEE Communications Society Fred W. Ellersick Prize, the 2016 IEEE Communications Society Best Tutorial Paper Award, the 2016 European Wireless Best Paper Award, the 2017 Eurasip Best Paper Award, the 2018 IEEE Marconi Prize Paper Award, the 2019 IEEE Communications Society Young Author Best Paper Award, the 2021 Eurasip Best Paper Award, the 2021 IEEE Marconi Prize Paper Award, the 2022 IEEE Communications Society Outstanding Paper Award, the 2022 ICC Best Paper Award as well as the Valuetools 2007, Valuetools 2008, CrownCom 2009, Valuetools 2012, SAM 2014, and 2017 IEEE Sweden VT-COM-IT Joint Chapter best student paper awards. He is an Associate Editor-in-Chief of the journal Random Matrix: Theory and Applications. He was an Associate Area Editor and Senior Area Editor of the IEEE Transactions on Signal Processing from 2011 to 2013 and from 2013 to 2014, respectively. From 2021 to 2022, he serves as an IEEE Signal Processing Society Distinguished Industry Speaker.

Thoughts and Possible Advancements on 4 Thrusts for 6G

Gerhard Fettweis

Abstract. Even though 6G is 8 years away, many seem to try to pin down exact features and specifications already today. This leads to some interesting statements, also made by large corporate players. Just one example is the statement that 6G will require a $10\times$ improvement in spectral efficiency while simultaneously achieving at least a $10\times$ improvement in energy efficiency. No theory is yet known to show how this could be achievable. In the end, operators will need to earn money providing a new level of services at a cost-level which makes these services affordable for mass market consumers. Therefore, here we rather want to ask the question which thrust of improvement could make sense, and why. We then give some possible ways forward. The 4 thrusts for improvements discussed are: trustworthiness, energy efficiency, cost, and new functionality. If we truly believe that 6G will provide an infrastructure for Tactile Internet remote-controlled personal mobile robotic and XR applications, we need lower-cost, energy efficient, and trustworthy networks that integrate joint communications & sensing. Can this be realistically achieved without infringing physics or theoretic bounds?

Dr. Gerhard Fettweis coordinates the 5G Lab Germany, and 2 German Science Foundation (DFG) centers at TU Dresden, namely cfaed and HAEC. In Dresden, his team has spun out 16 start-ups, and set up funded projects in volume of close to 500 million Euros

Fettweis is an IEEE Fellow, a member of the German Academy of Sciences (Leopoldina) and the German Academy of Engineering (acatech), and has received multiple IEEE recognitions as well as the VDE ring of honor. He is also co-chair of the IEEE 5G Initiative, and has helped organize IEEE conferences, most notably as TPC Chair of ICC 2009 and TTM 2012. And, he was General Chair of VTC Spring 2013 and DATE 2014.

Fettweis earned his Ph.D. under H. Meyr's supervision from RWTH Aachen in 1990. After one year at IBM Research in San Jose, CA, he moved to TCSI Inc., Berkeley, CA. Since 1994, Fettweis has been Vodafone Chair Professor at TU Dresden, Germany, with 20 companies from Asia/Europe/US sponsoring his research on wireless transmission and chip design.

The Role of Communications as Enablers for Achievement of Sustainable Development Goals

Francisco Falcone

Abstract. In order to cope with global challenges humanity is facing in terms of climate change, sustainability and governance, the UN has established the roadmap for years to come on the pillars of the Sustainable Development Goals (SDG). Among the different aspects and specific goals specified within the SDGs, providing resilient and adaptive communication technologies is key towards their achievement. In this presentation, an overview of capabilities and challenges related to communication technologies with a specific focus on wireless communications will be discussed, with applications related to the scope of implementing context aware environments in Smart Cities and Smart Regions, thus enabling the advancement of several SDGs.

Dr. Francisco Falcone is a Telecommunications Engineer (January 1999) and Doctor in Communications (September 2005), both from UPNA. From 1999 to 2000, he was a Microwave Network Engineer, Siemens-Italtel, Málaga. From 2000 to 2008, he was a Mobile Access Network Engineer, Telefónica Móviles, in Pamplona. In 2009 he co-founded Tafco Metawireless, a spin-off of the UPNA (with EIBT national label), of which he was its first manager. In parallel, from 2003 to 2009 he was Assistant Lecturer (profesor asociado) in the Department of Electrical and Electronic Engineering, UPNA. In June 2009 he became Associate Professor (PCD) at UPNA. From May 2011 to August 2022 he was Associate Professor (TU) at UPNA and since September 2022, Full Professor. From 2011 to 2012 he was secretary of the Department of Electrical, Electronic and Communication Engineering of UPNA. From January 2012 to July 2018 and from July 2019 to November 2021 he was Head of the Department of Electrical, Electronic and Communication Engineering of UPNA. In 2018 he was Visiting Professor at Kuwait College of Science and Technology, Kuwait, for three months. He is also affiliated with the Smart Cities Institute of the Public University of Navarra, a multidisciplinary research institute with over 100 researchers, being Head of the Institute since May 2021, working on contextual and interactive environments solutions, through the integration of heterogeneous wireless communications networks, based on HetNet and IoT. Since June 2022, he is Distinguished Visiting Professor in the Telecommunications School of Engineering and Science, Tecnologico de Monterrey, Mexico.

He specializes in applied and computational electromagnetics, more specifically in: analysis and design of complex electromagnetic media, artificial materials and metamaterials, with special attention to the design of devices applicable to communication systems (filters, diplexers, couplers, antennas), device implementation in flexible/paper substrates, wireless power transfer systems, implementation of computational electromagnetic code and hybrid code, and developing in-house code such as FDTD, 3D Ray Launching and Radar RCS, applied to the analysis of communication systems and contextual intelligence environments. His current lines of research are linked to the implementation of devices applicable to various communication systems (fundamentally PLMN, WSN, LPWAN and Radar systems), as well as radioelectric analysis, both at the physical layer and at the system level, in order to optimize their operation in terms of energy consumption, interference handling and capacity/coverage relationships.

The work carried out has resulted in over 200 articles in ISI-WOK indexed journals, 400 contributions in international and national conferences, 2 books, 6 book chapters and participation in 89 public- and private-funded projects. His citation metrics are h-index: 39 (Clarivate-Publons), 45 (Scopus), 52 (Google Scholar).

He has been Associate Editor of the IEEE Transactions on Wireless Communications (2014-15) and is currently Associate Editor of IEEE Antennas and Wireless Propagation Letters (since 2016), Associate Editor of IEEE Sensors Letters (since 2017) and Associate Editor of Scientific Reports (since 2021).

He has been awarded several research awards: CST Best Paper Award 2003 and 2005, Prize of the Official Association of Telecommunications Engineers 2005 for the Best Doctoral Thesis, UPNA PhD Award 2004-2006 in Experimental Sciences, 1st Prize Juan López de Peñalver 2010 to the best young researcher, Real Academia de Ingeniería de España, XII Talgo Foundation Award for Technological Innovation with the proposal "Implementation of an Environment for the Railway Ecosystem", ECSA-2 Best Paper

Award (2015), Best Paper Award IISA (2015), ECSA-3 Best Paper Award (2016), ECSA-4 Best Paper Award (2018), Best Paper Award ISSI (2019) and IIoT 2020 Best Paper Award. He is a Senior Member of IEEE (2009).

Data-Driven Mean-Field Game Theory (Tutorial)

Hamidou Tembine

Abstract. Breakthroughs in machine learning (ML) and particularly deep learning have transformed all aspects of our lives, including face recognition, medical diagnosis, and natural language processing. This progress has been fueled mainly by the availability of more data and more computing power. However, the current premise in classical ML is based on a single node in a centralized and remote data center with full access to a global dataset and a massive amount of storage and computing. Nevertheless, the advent of a new breed of intelligent devices ranging from drones to self-driving vehicles, makes cloud-based ML inadequate. This talk will present the vision of distributed edge intelligence featuring key enablers, architectures, algorithms and some recent results.

Dr. Hamidou Tembine (Senior Member, IEEE) graduated in applied mathematics from the École Polytechnique, Palaiseau, France, and received the Ph.D. degree from Inria and University of Avignon, France, and the master's degree in game theory and economics. His main research interests are learning, evolution, and games. He has been a Visiting Researcher with the University of California at Berkeley, Berkeley, CA, USA; McGill University, Montreal, Quebec, Canada; University of Illinois at Urbana-Champaign (UIUC), Champaign, IL, USA; École Polytechnique Fédérale de Lausanne (EPFL), Switzerland; and University of Wisconsin-Madison, Madison, WI, USA. He is a prolific researcher and has over 150 scientific publications, including magazines, letters, journals, and conferences. He is the author of the book on "Distributed Strategic Learning for Wireless Engineers" (CRC Press, Taylor and Francis 2012), and a coauthor of the book "Game Theory and Learning for Wireless Networks" (Elsevier Academic Press). He has been the co-organizer of several scientific meetings on game theory in networking, wireless communications, and smart energy systems. He has been a TPC member and reviewer for several international journals and conferences. He is a Next Einstein Fellow, Class of 2017. He is a Simons participant and a Senior Fellow at IPAM, UCLA. In 2014, he received the IEEE ComSoc Outstanding Young Researcher Award for his promising research activities for the benefit of the society. He was a recipient of over 10 best paper awards in the applications of game theory.

Contents

Internet of Things and Vehicular Communications

Artificial Intelligence-Driven Communications

Pervasive Services and Cyber Security

Spectrum Management and Channel Prediction

On the Influence of Microscopic Mobility in Modelling Pedestrian Communication

Lars Wischhof[(✉)] [iD], Maximilian Kilian [iD], Stefan Schuhbäck [iD], and Gerta Köster [iD]

Munich University of Applied Sciences HM, Munich, Germany
{lars.wischhof,maximilian.kilian,stefan.schuhbaeck,gerta.koester}@hm.edu

Abstract. In the recent past, wireless network simulations involving pedestrians are getting increasing attention within the research community. Examples are crowd networking, pedestrian communication via Sidelink/D2D, wireless contact tracing to fight the Covid-19 pandemic or the evaluation of Intelligent Transportation Systems (ITS) for the protection of Vulnerable Road Users (VRUs). Since in general the mobile communication depends on the position of the pedestrians, their mobility needs to be modeled. Often simplified mobility models such as the random-waypoint or cellular automata based models are used.

However, for ad hoc networks and Inter-Vehicular Communication (IVC), it is well-known that a detailed model for the microscopic mobility has a strong influence – which is why state-of-the-art simulation frameworks for IVC often combine vehicular mobility and network simulators. Therefore, this paper investigates to what extent a detailed modelling of the pedestrian mobility on an operational level influences the results of Pedestrian-to-X Communication (P2X) and its applications.

We model P2X scenarios within the open-source coupled simulation environment CrowNet. It enables us to simulate the identical P2X scenario while varying the pedestrian mobility simulator as well as the used model. Two communication scenarios (pedestrian to server via 5G New Radio, pedestrian to pedestrian via PC5 Sidelink) are investigated in different mobility scenarios. Initial results demonstrate that time- and location-dependent factors represented by detailed microscopic mobility models can have a significant influence on the results of wireless communication simulations, indicating a need for more detailed pedestrian mobility models in particular for scenarios with pedestrian crowds.

Keywords: pedestrian communication · wireless network simulation · coupled simulation · mobility model

We thank the research office (FORWIN) of the Munich University of Applied Sciences for supporting the research collaboration. The authors gratefully acknowledge the support by the Faculty Graduate Center CeDoSIA of TUM Graduate School at Technical University of Munich, Germany. The authors also acknowledge the financial support by the Federal Ministry of Education and Research of Germany in the framework of roVer (project number 13FH669IX6).

E. Sabir et al. (Eds.): UNet 2022, LNCS 13853, pp. 3–18, 2023.
https://doi.org/10.1007/978-3-031-29419-8_1

1   Introduction

For wireless communication in general, the local situation of a node, such as the attenuation of the signal or interference, depends on time and position, i.e. the channel is time-variant and location-dependent. Simulations of wireless networks must therefore model the position of a wireless node. For mobile wireless networks, such as networks based on Inter-Vehicle Communication (IVC), this is usually achieved by applying a suitable mobility model. Since modelling the mobility at a sufficiently high level of detail is often not trivial, a commonly used approach is to couple a wireless network simulation modelling the communication aspects with a mobility simulator. In case of vehicular networks, it often is a traffic simulator such as SUMO [15].

Motivated by new application areas such as crowd sensing and networking, wireless contact tracing to fight against the Covid-19 pandemic or Intelligent Transportation Systems (ITS) protocols for the protection of Vulnerable Road Users (VRUs), wireless network simulations of scenarios involving pedestrians are getting more attention within the research community. For example, for VRU protection, suitable message formats such as the VRU Awareness Messages (VAM) [6] were recently standardized and are considered in industry forums such as the 5G Automotive Association (5GAA). As a consequence, also the research in this area gained momentum, e.g. to evaluate the impact of VAM generation rate adaptation on the awareness of VRUs [14]. In order to evaluate the potential of these new message formats and protocols, wireless network simulations are the typical method.

In all these simulations, the mobility of pedestrians needs to be modeled. Traditionally, very simplified mobility models such as the linear mobility model or the random-waypoint model [10] have been used, e.g. for the evaluation of communication in cellular networks. However, these simplified models do not model the movement of individual pedestrians in detail. Therefore, in order to be able to model the interaction among pedestrians or between pedestrians and vehicles, traffic simulators such as SUMO model pedestrian mobility more precisely, so that the situation at a crossing can be simulated [4].

However, in the research field of pedestrian dynamics, much more detailed mobility models are known. These models, which are also called *pedestrian locomotion models* in pedestrian dynamics, are able to model typical movement patterns of pedestrians and their behavior more realistically but usually at a higher computational cost. Examples are the gradient navigation model [3], the Social Force Model (SFM) [7] or the Optimal Steps Model (OSM) [21]. These are applied in research using dedicated simulators such as JuPedSim or Vadere[1] [12].

The main motivation for this paper is therefore, to investigate to what extent results of pedestrian communication simulations – such as the number of received packets or communication delays – are influenced by a more detailed modelling of the pedestrian mobility on a microscopic level based on models from pedestrian dynamics.

---

[1] https://www.jupedsim.org/; https://www.vadere.org/.

The main contributions of this paper are:

1. Based on metrics such as the number of received packets and the observed Signal-to-Interference-and-Noise Ratio (SINR), we present wireless network simulations for a simple and a more complex pedestrian communication scenario, applying mobility models with varying level of detail. The results provide insights on the influence of microscopic pedestrian mobility models in these scenarios.
2. The scenarios are furthermore evaluated in a server-based variant applying 5G New Radio (NR) and a direct-communication (sidelink) variant. The results indicate that the influence of the mobility model also depends on the application and the underlying pedestrian communication paradigm.
3. In our simulative evaluation, we illustrate how open-source components can be used to implement pedestrian communication simulations with detailed pedestrian mobility models, such as OSM or SFM. The simulation framework as well as the settings for reproducing the presented results ares publicly available and can serve as a basis for future research in related areas.

The rest of the paper is structured as follows: First, we give an overview of related work in pedestrian communication, microscopic pedestrian mobility models and simulator coupling in Sect. 2. Afterwards, the simulation concept, scenarios and metrics are presented in Sect. 3. A detailed description of the simulation parameters and the coupled simulation framework follows in Sect. 4. Sect. 5 presents the simulation results. Sect. 6 concludes the paper with a short summary.

2 Related Work

It is a well-established fact that performance results of wireless communication system simulations can change drastically when the mobility model is varied [2,9]. For example, already two decades ago, Camp et al. [2] presented a survey of mobility models for ad hoc networks including simulation results demonstrating the influence of simple mobility models such as the Random Waypoint or Random Walk models. For pedestrian mobility, this was confirmed by Helgason et al. in [8] where the commercial mobility simulator Legion Studio was used to model pedestrian mobility at the operational level. They also showed that often accurately capturing the scenario is more important than a detailed estimation of the input mobility parameters. However, it has to be noted that [8] first assumes a very generic model of the physical layer using abstract performance metrics such as contact time and rate that is later-on extended to a simplified Bluetooth model but never models higher networking layers. Therefore, it is not clear if their findings would also apply to metrics on higher layers or pedestrian communication applications.

Hess et al. present a detailed survey on human mobility modeling in [9] that also takes models from pedestrian dynamics such as the Social Force Model

(SFM) [7] into account. The survey includes recommendations for engineering new mobility models but does not consider the influence of different mobility models on wireless networks and their metrics.

A specific application of pedestrian communication is content distribution within a local area, for which a pedestrian mobility model is presented in [25]. However, it does not take interaction among pedestrians into account and concludes that for higher densities the assumption of uncorrelated speeds of pedestrians does not hold. To overcome this limitation, it suggests to use a model from pedestrian dynamics, such as SFM [7], for future work.

A number of other works consider pedestrian mobility on higher levels, such as the tactical level. For example, Vogt et al. [24] consider the aspect of destination selection and path finding in their model. More recently, deep learning approaches have also been applied to model pedestrian flows and trajectories. An overview can be found in [16]. These higher levels of pedestrian mobility are out-of-scope for our paper since we focus on the influence of the operational level of pedestrian mobility.

Regarding the practical aspect of including detailed microscopic mobility models in wireless network simulations, as required for the simulative evaluation in this paper, related work exists mainly in the area of vehicular communication: Realistically modelling the microscopic mobility of vehicles is complex and not feasible in typical simulators for wireless networks such as ns-3 or OMNeT++. Therefore, state-of-the-art frameworks such as veins [23] couple network simulators with dedicated vehicular mobility simulators such as SUMO via the Traffic Control Interface (TraCI) [26].

Recently, SUMO has been extended to model pedestrian mobility [4]. Furthermore, dedicated pedestrian dynamics simulators such as Vadere [12] are available. Therefore, an approach for coupling pedestrian mobility and network simulation has been proposed in a previous paper [19] and since then has been significantly extended, as described in Sect. 4.

3   Scenarios

In order to evaluate the influence of detailed microscopic mobility models on cellular 5G NR and sidelink communication simulations, we define two scenarios where several pedestrians are closely located: a crowded sidewalk and a bottleneck scenario. The underlying assumption is that a microscopic mobility model becomes more relevant when the mobility of a person is influenced by others, e.g. in a blocking situation. In contrast, in a situation where a single person walks alone on a sidewalk, the mobility model has a low influence since in this case the person simply moves with the desired velocity.

Pedestrian Mobility in SUMO. [13] The traffic simulator SUMO models sidewalks as a special type of lane where only pedestrians are allowed. A lane is a polyline with a specific width. SUMO supports a *nonInteracting* and a *striping* pedestrian model: In *nonInteracting* pedestrians walk at a fixed speed and are not influenced by other pedestrians, whereas in *striping* the lane is divided in stripes of a predefined width (default in SUMO: 0.65 m). Pedestrians try to occupy the rightmost stripe. In case a stripe is occupied by a slower or oncoming person, a pedestrian changes to a different stripe if sufficient space is available. Otherwise, i.e. if all stripes are occupied, the pedestrian slows down. In the following, *striping* is used in order to take interaction among pedestrians into account.

Pedestrian Mobility in Vadere. [11] In contrast to SUMO, the focus of Vadere is pedestrian dynamics. Thus, it supports a wider range of detailed pedestrian mobility or locomotion models, e.g. behavior heuristics, gradient navigation or SFM. A popular and well-established locomotion model, which is used in the following, is the Optimal Steps Model (OSM) [11,22]. It models pedestrian mobility as a series of discrete footsteps. The model chooses the next footstep of a person by optimizing the utility within a circle around its current position. The radius of the step circle is correlated to the free-flow speed of the pedestrian. Utility values are based on floor fields which combine attraction (i.e. getting closer to a target location) with repulsion (obstacles, other pedestrians). Thus, in crowded situations pedestrians decrease their step-length and thereby decelerate. Furthermore, virtual pedestrians in OSM try to maintain a certain distance to others. The strength of this desire is regulated through parameters [11], such as the intimate space width.

3.1 Scenario A: Crowded Sidewalk

This scenario models a crowded sidewalk: At simulation time $t_0 = 0s$, a group of pedestrians starts walking on a straight sidewalk towards a destination 400 m away. An example for this situation would be a bus stop where a group of people gets out of the bus or sidewalk next to a subway station where a train arrived. The simulation ends at $t_e = 600$ s, a time at which all pedestrians have reached the destination. The rationale why this scenario was chosen is that in this crowded situation, the way in which inter-action among pedestrians is handled in the different microscopic mobility models is suspected to be relevant. Furthermore, the different degrees of freedom which a pedestrian has in the mobility models could be relevant. Both could lead to differences in pedestrian mobility and, as a consequence, on the observed pedestrian communication.

Due to the different ways in which the local environment is modeled in SUMO and Vadere, the sidewalk is represented by specific structures in each mobility simulator. Figure 1a shows the sidewalk in Vadere: On the floor field, the area in which pedestrians can move (i.e. the sidewalk itself) is limited by one obstacle on the left and one on the right side. The starting point is represented by the green square and the destination by the orange square. The distance between the obstacles is 2.50 m and the width of what a persona considers as intimate space is set to 0.65 m.

The corresponding model in SUMO is shown in Fig. 1b. As pedestrians move in SUMO only on roads or sidewalks, there is no need to limit their degree of freedom additionally by using obstacles. The starting point is the top red dot and the exit point the bottom red dot. The length and width of the sidewalk are set to the same values as in Vadere. For the width of a single stripe of the sidewalk, the default value of 0.65 m is kept since it is already identical to the intimate space configured in Vadere.

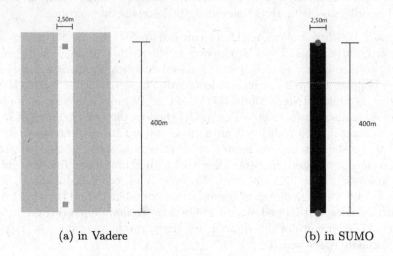

(a) in Vadere   (b) in SUMO

Fig. 1. Sidewalk model (Scenario A).

3.2   Scenario B: Bottleneck

The second scenario models a situation, where a group of pedestrians needs to go through a narrow entrance, as it occurs, for example, when entering a soccer stadium, metro station or theater. The scenario covers a distance of 370 m, the narrow entrance is located at a distance of 280 m (measured from the starting point, see Fig. 2). (We choose a cone shaped bottleneck, because SUMO's stripe model limits the type of structures that can be captured. While the shape of the bottleneck is a little unusual, it still covers the characteristics that we want to investigate: a crowd of pedestrians who are funneled through a small opening and thus have to interact.)

After passing the narrow entrance, the pedestrians spread out to five different target locations at a distance of 190 m measured from the entrance. Since the total number of modeled pedestrians is chosen to be a multiple of five, the same number of pedestrians walks towards each target location. Hereby, we model the fact that usually after passing the entrance of a location, the different groups of persons will walk to different locations inside.

In Vadere, this bottleneck scenario is modeled as follows (see Fig. 2a): At each of the five pedestrian source locations (green), the same number of pedestrians is generated at the start time of the simulation. Each pedestrian is also assigned one of the target locations (orange) which it walks towards. Narrowing obstacles (grey walls) limit the horizontal space from 20.0 m at the start to 2.5 m at the narrow entrance. As a result, Vadere generates a floor field which first attracts the pedestrians to the narrow entrance (single orange square in the middle), afterwards each pedestrian is attracted by the corresponding target location.

In SUMO, due to the completely different approach for modeling pedestrian mobility, a different way of modeling the scenario needs to be used (Fig. 2b): As pedestrians in SUMO are only moving on roads or sidewalks (and not freely as they do in Vadere), the bottleneck is modeled through road segments getting thinner in their width. The narrow entrance, modeled with the same position and width as within Vadere, is created by using five road segments which stepwise reduce the width from 20.0 m at the start to 2.5 m at the narrow entrance. At the end of the bottleneck, the pedestrians are routed to five different target locations, analogously to the model in Vadere.

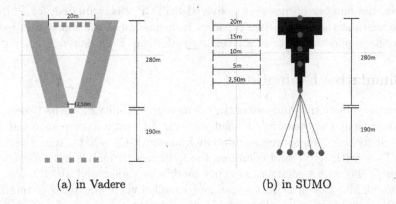

(a) in Vadere   (b) in SUMO

Fig. 2. Bottleneck model (Scenario B). (Color figure online)

3.3 Pedestrian Communication

From the technical point of view, a wide range of options is available in order to implement the information dissemination among pedestrians: Different radio access technologies such as GSM, UMTS, LTE, 5G can be applied. Communication can be performed via a server on the Internet (as it is done for typical smartphone apps today), via WLAN and in near future also via Sidelink of the 4G/5G cellular standards [1], just to name a few. In the paper, a typical centralized, server-based and a direct, decentralized variant are evaluated.

Centralized, Server-Based Pedestrian Communication via 5G NR (P2P-CS): In this variant, we model information dissemination via HTTP, TCP, IP with a backend server - as it is typical for mobile applications today. For the wireless communication, a 5G Standalone (SA) cellular network with New Radio (NR) is assumed (refer to Sect. 4 for parameters).

Direct Pedestrian-to-Pedestrian Communication via Sidelink (P2P-SL): P2P-SL assumes a completely different communication pattern, as it would occur in future for example mobile sensing or cooperative awareness applications [5]. Applications on the smartphone of a pedestrian send multicast data packets with (sensor) data via Sidelink to all other pedestrians in the local area. Neither a communication infrastructure nor a centralized server is required, since multicast data transmission via UDP and Sidelink (PC5 interface) is applied.

Metrics: The mobility model possibly influences the behavior on all layers of the protocol stack. However, in order to limit the complexity of this study, we need to restrict ourselves to a very limited subset in this paper. As a typical metric on the lower network layers, the average number of received MAC packets and the observed Signal-to-Interference-and-Noise Ratio (SINR) on the uplink is selected. As a metric on transportation/application layer, the average number of messages and the per-packet delay is measured: in case of P2P-CS communication, the number of messages delivered by TCP was evaluated; for P2P-SL communication, the delay between packet transmission at the source and reception at the application layer of a receiving pedestrian is measured.

4   Simulative Evaluation

In order to evaluate the influence of the microscopic mobility model on pedestrian communication, the scenarios defined in Sect. 3.1 and 3.2 were modeled and evaluated in the open-source simulation framework CrowNet[2]. It is based on OMNeT++ with INET and combines the system-level mobile network models of Simu5G [17] with pedestrian mobility models in Vadere and SUMO.

Since SUMO as well as Vadere can be controlled via Traffic Control Interface (TraCI) [19,26], CrowNet allows us to run exactly the same communication models with different microscopic mobility models. For the unified integration of the mobility simulation in CrowNet, the V2X simulation framework Artery [18] was extended to support pedestrian simulation based on Vadere.

Wireless communication is modeled in OMNeT++ with INET and Simu5G frameworks identically and independently of the microscopic mobility model that is used. The eNB/gNB is placed at position (300 m; 300 m) for all scenarios. For P2P-SL (sidelink), a cellular eNB and a core network consisting of PGW and a router is modeled. In the P2P-CS variant which assumes 5G NR communication, the gNB and a minimal core network with UPF, iUPF, a router and a HTTP server is modeled. All modifications as well as the simulation scripts to reproduce our results are available in the CrowNet repository.[3]

4.1   Simulation Parameters

Running the combined simulations requires setting the parameters for the communication and mobility models. Table 1 lists the parameters for the micro-

---

scopic pedestrian mobility models. For Vadere (middle in Table 1), the pedestrian potential intimate space width models the size of the space that virtual pedestrians consider as intimate and reserved to family. The potential personal space width models the size of the space that virtual persons consider als personal and reserved to friends. The intimate space factor is used to calibrate the strength of the desire to keep personal space free. Whenever a parameter relevant for both models, we set it to the same value (Table 1, top). Table 2 lists the most relevant parameters for the communication models in INET and Simu5G.

Table 1. Parameters for pedestrian mobility models: in both models (top), specific for Vadere (middle), specific for SUMO (bottom).

Symbol	Value	Description
N_{ped}	30	number of pedestrians in scenario
μ_s	1.34 ms^{-1}	mean of ped. speed-distribution [20, 27]
σ_s	0.26 ms^{-1}	std. dev. of ped. speed-distribution [20, 27]
s_{min}	0.5 ms^{-1}	minimum speed of pedestrian [27]
s_{max}	2.5 ms^{-1}	maximum speed of pedestrian [27]
r_{ped}	0.2 m	pedestrian radius
w_{int}	0.65 m	ped. potential intimate space width
w_{pers}	1.2 m	ped. potential personal space width
f_{int}	1.2	intimate space factor
w_{stripe}	0.65 m	stripe width (sidewalk)

Varied Parameters. Since we assume that the effect of the microscopic mobility model on the metrics defined in Sect. 3.3 is likely to increase with the intensity of pedestrian communication, we vary the communication load. For sidelink communication (P2P-SL) in the scenarios, we therefore vary the inter-transmission interval $S_{p,app}$ in the range of 10 ms (i.e. high load) to 100 ms (i.e. low load) while keeping the packet size constant. Since for the server-based HTTP communication (P2P-CS), setting the packet (segment) size on the application layer would have no effect since it is a result of the TCP model, we vary the HTTP response size S_{res} in the range of 10 kB to 100 kB. Usually, increasing S_{res} leads to more traffic and a higher load – however, the congestion control mechanisms implemented in TCP will adapt the rate in congested situations.

For each of the two scenarios and the two mobility models, ten different parameter settings with ten repetitions each were simulated, i.e. 2x2x10x10 = 400 simulations were run. For each simulation, a new random seed was chosen. Since a simulation with $N_{ped} = 30$ pedestrians takes approx. 4.5 h to simulate the scenario duration of 600 s, this is a compromise between accuracy and run time.

Table 2. Parameters for communication model.

Symbol	Value	Description
B	7	EUTRA FDD Band
		(UL 2500-2570 MHz MHz, DL 2620-2690 MHz MHz)
N_{RB}	6	number of resource blocks (P2P-SL)
c_{cqi}	7	Channel Quality Indicator (P2P-SL only)
D_{RLC}	UM	RLC type (UM: unacknowledged mode)
S_{MAC}	5 MB	max. queue size on MAC layer of eNB/gNB
$S_{p,app}$	300 B	UDP payload (P2P-SL)
$T_{p,app}$	10..100 ms	inter-transmission time (P2P-SL)
S_{req}	350 B	mean request size (exp. dist, P2P-CS)
S_{res}	10..100 kB	mean response size (exp. dist, P2P-CS)

5   Results

In the following, we present results for the two mobility scenarios (Sect. 3) in combination with the two communication variants (P2P-SL and P2P-CS, see Sect. 3.3) regarding the metrics defined in Sect. 3.3. If not mentioned otherwise, plots show the arithmetic mean of all nodes in all simulation repetitions and error bars indicate the standard deviation.

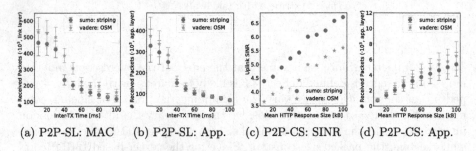

(a) P2P-SL: MAC   (b) P2P-SL: App.   (c) P2P-CS: SINR   (d) P2P-CS: App.

Fig. 3. Results for Sidewalk (Scenario A) with $N_{ped} = 30$ persons.

Figure 3 shows the results for the Sidewalk (Scenario A): For multicast sidelink communication, the number of received packets on the MAC layer is similar for both microscopic mobility models as long as the packet inter-transmission time $T_{p,app}$ is larger than 50 ms (Fig. 3a). With decreasing $T_{p,app}$ (i.e. increasing load), the difference is more significant. For $T_{p,app} = 40$ ms, the number of received packets differs by more than 25%. This is likely to be caused by the fact that in this case the network is near an overload condition (where network behavior changes), making the positions of the pedestrians (and thus the influence of the mobility model) more relevant. In general, the number of received packets is higher when pedestrian mobility is modeled by OSM (Vadere) compared to striping (SUMO) in this scenario. At the application layer (see Fig. 3b), the impact of the mobility model is much less visible – in particular for low load ($T_{p,app}$ exceeding 40 ms).

For server-based pedestrian communications via TCP, the observations are similar: In this case we use the average Signal-to-Interference-plus-Noise (SINR) as a metric on the lower layer, since the number of transmitted packets is dynamically controlled by TCP. Again, while metrics on the lower layer differ (Fig. 3c), the influence of the mobility model is low on the application layer (Fig. 3d) – in particular for low load (e.g. S_{res} less than 60 kB). Furthermore, the average number of received data packets on the application layer is higher in case of OSM although the SINR is lower. This seems counterintuitive at first. However, investigating the positions of pedestrians in detail for an example simulation (Fig. 5), it becomes visible that for OSM the pedestrians have a tendency to move slower to the end of the corridor compared to striping. This could be caused by the additional degrees of freedom in OSM (persons can make steps in different directions within the corridor of 0.65 m whereas in striping they move always straight to the end of the corridor). Therefore, the pedestrians are within range of the base station for a longer time allowing them to receive more packets – overcompensating the lower SNIR.

In order to confirm the assumption that the differences in the results are caused by the different approaches for modelling pedestrian interaction in crowded situations (e.g. choosing the next step in OSM/Vadere vs. being on a stripe in SUMO), we simulate the same scenario with only $N_{ped} = 2$ pedestrians. In this case, almost no mobility interaction between pedestrians occurs and the applied microscopic model should have less influence on our metrics. This is confirmed by the results in Fig. 4. Neither the metric on the link layer (Fig. 4a) nor on the application layer (Fig. 4b) show a significant influence of the pedestrian mobility model when only two pedestrians are present in the scenario.

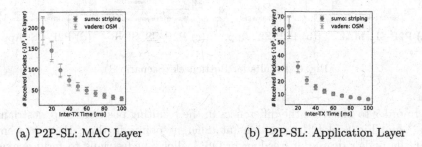

(a) P2P-SL: MAC Layer   (b) P2P-SL: Application Layer

Fig. 4. Sidewalk (Scenario A) with $N_{ped} = 2$ persons.

For the Bottleneck scenario (Scen. B, see Sect. 3.2), the results in Fig. 6 confirm the effects observed in Scenario A: The impact of the microscopic mobility model is higher on lower networking layers (Fig. 6a, 6c) compared to the effects

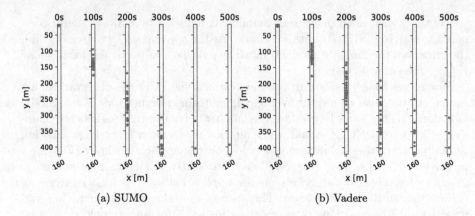

(a) SUMO   (b) Vadere

Fig. 5. Example for pedestrian positions (Scen. A, Smp. 1).

on the application layer (Fig. 6b, 6d). However, compared to the crowed Side-walk scenario, the influence seems to be slightly reduced, in particular in the P2P-CS variant on the application layer (Fig. 6d). A possible explanation is that for the bottleneck itself the inter-action between pedestrians is similar for both models: the pedestrians are standing in front of the bottleneck, with a distance corresponding to the intimate space width (OSM/Vadere) or stripe width (strip-ing/SUMO).

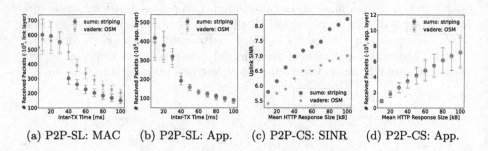

(a) P2P-SL: MAC   (b) P2P-SL: App.   (c) P2P-CS: SINR   (d) P2P-CS: App.

Fig. 6. Results for Bottleneck (Scenario B).

In order to illustrate the differences in the resulting positions of pedestrians, Fig. 7 and Fig. 8 plot the positions at different points in time. Here, it seems that the higher degree of freedom in OSM allows pedestrians to form a more compact group (at $T = 100\,\text{s}$), to pass the bottleneck more quickly and to spread in a wider range of directions after passing the bottleneck (at $T = 300\,\text{s}$).

Figure 9 additionally shows results for the end-to-end delay of device-to-device communication (D2D via sidelink, P2P-SL) measured on the application layer. This delay can vary over several orders of magnitude: In situations with low communication load when sufficient resources on the sidelink are available

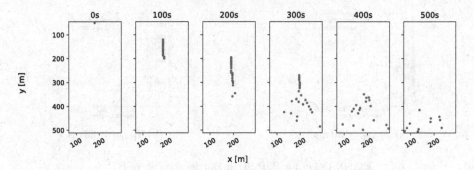

Fig. 7. SUMO: Example for positions in Bottleneck scenario (Scen. B, Smp. 1).

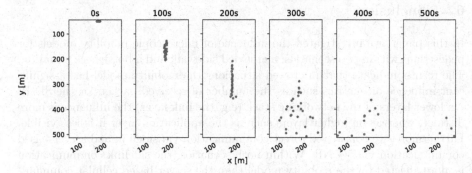

Fig. 8. Vadere: Example for positions in Bottleneck scenario (Scen. B, Smp. 1).

(Fig. 9b), whenever the mobile device of a pedestrian has data to transmit, it requests resources on the sidelink at the eNB, receives a corresponding grant with low delay and transmits its data. Thus, the resulting delay is dominated by the delay for getting the resource grant and transmitting the data. Queuing only rarely occurs and thus the resulting delay is in the order of milliseconds. On the other hand in overload conditions (Fig. 9a, $T_{p,app} = 30$ ms), the mobile device does not get sufficient resources to transmit all available data packets - the packets are queued and due to the queuing delay the total delay can increase up to the order of tens of seconds. While this basic effect is visible for both microscopic mobility models and the total end-to-end delay is similar for $T_{p,app} = 30$ ms as well as for $T_{p,app} \geq 60$ ms, the delays for situations where overload only partially occurs (inter-TX time $T_{p,app} \in \{40$ ms, 50 ms$\}$) varies significantly for the two microscopic mobility models. A likely reason is that due to the differences in modelling interaction between pedestrians, in striping/SUMO the overload conditions occurs earlier at more locations within the network compared to OSM/Vadere.

(a) $T_{p,app} \geq 30\,ms$ (b) $T_{p,app} \geq 50\,ms$

Fig. 9. Delay for P2P-SL in Bottleneck (Scen. B).

6 Conclusion

In this paper, we investigated the influence of microscopic mobility models for pedestrians within two scenarios: a crowded sidewalk and a bottleneck situation. The results indicate that in crowed situations the mobility model has a significant influence on metrics such as the number of received packets or the SINR. On lower layers of the networking stack (e.g. the link layer) the influence is more distinct, whereas on higher layers such as the application layer it is less visible. Furthermore, we considered direct communication via sidelink and server-based communication via 5G NR. Within both scenarios, the sidelink communication is more affected by the mobility model than the server-based cellular communication.

While the results of these two example scenarios cannot be generalized, they illustrate the need for detailed pedestrian mobility models when evaluating protocols and applications for pedestrian communication. This does not necessarily mean that these models have to be implemented within the communication simulator – a coupling as already know from inter-vehicular communication is also an option and open-source frameworks for this are available. In future work, we will investigate a wider range of scenarios including vehicles and public transport.

References

1. Bazzi, A., Berthet, A.O., Campolo, C., Masini, B.M., Molinaro, A., Zanella, A.: On the design of sidelink for cellular v2x: a literature review and outlook for future. IEEE Access **9**, 97953–97980 (2021). https://doi.org/10.1109/access.2021.3094161
2. Camp, T., Boleng, J., Davies, V.: A survey of mobility models for ad hoc network research. Wirel. Commun. Mob. Comput. **2**(5), 483–502 (2002). https://doi.org/10.1002/wcm.72
3. Dietrich, F., Disselnkötter, S., Köster, G.: How to get a model in pedestrian dynamics to produce stop and go waves. In: Knoop, V.L., Daamen, W. (eds.) Traffic and Granular Flow '15, pp. 161–168. Springer, Cham (2016). https://doi.org/10.1007/978-3-319-33482-0_21

4. Erdmann, J., Krajzewicz, D.: Modelling pedestrian dynamics in sumo. In: SUMO User Conference 2015. Berichte aus dem DLR-Institut für Verkehrssystemtechnik, vol. 28, pp. 103–118. Deutsches Zentrum für Luft- und Raumfahrt e.V. (2015). https://elib.dlr.de/100554/

5. ETSI: TR 103 300-1 v2.1.1, intelligent transport system (its); vulnerable road users (VRU) awareness; part 1: Use cases definition; release 2. Technical report, ETSI (2019)

6. ETSI: TS 103 300-2 v2.2.1, intelligent transport system (its); vulnerable road users (VRU) awareness;part 2: Functional architecture and requirements definition; release 2. Technical report, ETSI (2021). https://www.etsi.org/deliver/etsi_ts/103300_103399/10330002/

7. Helbing, D., Molnár, P.: Social force model for pedestrian dynamics. Phys. Rev. E 51(5), 4282–4286 (1995). https://doi.org/10.1103/PhysRevE.51.4282

8. Helgason, O., Kouyoumdjieva, S.T., Karlsson, G.: Does mobility matter? In: 2010 Seventh International Conference on Wireless On-demand Network Systems and Services (WONS). IEEE (2010). https://doi.org/10.1109/wons.2010.5437138

9. Hess, A., Hummel, K.A., Gansterer, W.N., Haring, G.: Data-driven human mobility modeling. ACM Comput. Surv. 48(3), 1–39 (2015). https://doi.org/10.1145/2840722

10. Hyytä, E., Virtamo, J.: Random waypoint mobility model in cellular networks. Wirel. Netw. 13(2), 177–188 (2007). https://doi.org/10.1007/s11276-006-4600-3

11. Kleinmeier, B., Köster, G., Drury, J.: Agent-based simulation of collective cooperation: from experiment to model. J. R. Soc. Interface 17, 20200396 (2020). https://doi.org/10.1098/rsif.2020.0396

12. Kleinmeier, B., Zönnchen, B., Gödel, M., Köster, G.: Vadere: an open-source simulation framework to promote interdisciplinary understanding. Collective Dynamics 4 (2019). https://doi.org/10.17815/CD.2019.21

13. Krajzewicz, D., Erdmann, J., Härri, J., Spyropoulos, T.: Including pedestrian and bicycle traffic into the traffic simulation sumo. In: 10th ITS European Congress (2014). https://elib.dlr.de/90621/

14. Lara, T., Yáñez, A., Céspedes, S., Hafid, A.S.: Impact of safety message generation rules on the awareness of vulnerable road users. Sensors 21(10), 3375 (2021). https://doi.org/10.3390/s21103375

15. Lopez, P.A., et al.: Microscopic traffic simulation using SUMO. In: 2018 21st International Conference on Intelligent Transportation Systems (ITSC). IEEE (2018). https://doi.org/10.1109/itsc.2018.8569938

16. Luca, M., Barlacchi, G., Lepri, B., Pappalardo, L.: A survey on deep learning for human mobility. ACM Comput. Surv. 55(1), 1–44 (2021). https://doi.org/10.1145/3485125

17. Nardini, G., Stea, G., Virdis, A., Sabella, D.: Simu5g: a system-level simulator for 5G networks. In: Proceedings of the 10th International Conference on Simulation and Modeling Methodologies, Technologies and Applications - SIMULTECH, pp. 68–80. INSTICC, SciTePress. https://doi.org/10.5220/0009826400680080

18. Riebl, R., Gunther, H.J., Facchi, C., Wolf, L.: Artery: extending veins for VANET applications. In: 2015 International Conference on Models and Technologies for Intelligent Transportation Systems (MT-ITS). IEEE (2015). https://doi.org/10.1109/mtits.2015.7223293

19. Schuhbäck, S., Daßler, N., Wischhof, L., Köster, G.: Towards a bidirectional coupling of pedestrian dynamics and mobile communication simulation. In: Proceedings of the OMNeT++ Community Summit 2019 (2019). https://doi.org/10.29007/nnfj

20. Seitz, M.J., Bode, N.W.F., Köster, G.: How cognitive heuristics can explain social interactions in spatial movement. J. R. Soc. Interface **13**(121), 20160439 (2016). https://doi.org/10.1098/rsif.2016.0439

21. Seitz, M.J., Köster, G.: Natural discretization of pedestrian movement in continuous space. Phys. Rev. E **86**(4), 046108 (2012). https://doi.org/10.1103/PhysRevE. 86.046108

22. von Sivers, I.K.M., et al.: Modelling social identification and helping in evacuation simulation. Saf. Sci. **89**, 288–300 (2016). https://doi.org/10.1016/j.ssci.2016.07.001

23. Sommer, C., et al.: Veins: the open source vehicular network simulation framework. In: Virdis, A., Kirsche, M. (eds.) Recent Advances in Network Simulation. EICC, pp. 215–252. Springer, Cham (2019). https://doi.org/10.1007/978-3-030-12842-5_6

24. Vogt, R., Nikolaidis, I., Gburzynski, P.: A realistic outdoor urban pedestrian mobility model. Simul. Model. Pract. Theory **26**, 113–134 (2012). https://doi.org/10. 1016/j.simpat.2012.04.006

25. Vukadinovic, V., Helgason, Ó.R., Karlsson, G.: A mobility model for pedestrian content distribution. In: Proceedings of the Second International ICST Conference on Simulation Tools and Techniques. ICST (2009). https://doi.org/10.4108/icst. simutools2009.5645

26. Wegener, A., Piorkowski, M., Raya, M., Hellbrück, H., Fischer, S., Hubaux, J.P.: TraCI: an interface for coupling road traffic and network simulators. In: Proceedings of the 11th Communications and Networking Simulation Symposium on - CNS 2008, pp. 155–163. ACM Press (2008). https://doi.org/10.1145/1400713.1400740

27. Weidmann, U.: Transporttechnik der Fussgänger, Schriftenreihe des IVT, vol. 90. Institut für Verkehrsplanung, Transporttechnik, Strassen- und Eisenbahnbau (IVT) ETH, Zürich, 2 edn. (1993). https://doi.org/10.3929/ethz-b-000242008

Low Profile CPW Fed Tri-Band Millimeter Wave Antenna Design for Future 5G Application

Golap Kanti Dey[1](✉), Fariha Ali[2], Sarosh Ahmad[3], and Rashid Mirzavand[1]

[1] Department of Electrical and Computer Engineering, University of Alberta, Edmonton, Canada
{golap1,mirzavan}@ualberta.ca

[2] Department of Electrical and Electronic Engineering, Chittagong Independent University, Chittagong, Bangladesh

[3] Department of Signal Theory and Communications, Universidad Carlos III de Madrid, 28911 Leganés, Madrid, Spain
saroshahamad@ieee.org

Abstract. This paper depicts a compact monopole tri-band coplanar antenna with a L shape parasitic element. The monopole antenna consists of a I-shaped resonator connected over a M-shaped resonator, with a circular ground plane, and a coplanar waveguide (CPW) feedline. The overall size proposed design is 9 mm × 9 mm × 0.127 mm on a Rogers RT5880 material with a loss tangent of $\tan\delta = 0.0009$. The reflection coefficient S_{11} remains less than −10 dB for 28 GHz, 38 GHz and 61.5 GHz, with a VSWR < 1.7. The gain of an antenna are 1.365 dB, 3.147 dB and 4.520 dB for 28, 38, and 61 GHz respectively. The proposed design provides a tri-band antenna design with enhanced bandwidth up to 4 GHz, a compact dimension, and a feasible solution for future 5G millimeter-wave communication.

1 Introduction

Millimeter-wave (mm-wave) front end circuits have created enormous attention in high speed, short range 5G wireless applications over the last few years. Researchers are giving substantial efforts for the development as well as for the standardization of active and passive devices at the unlicensed spectrum (60 GHz) ranging from 38 GHz to 66 GHz where an efficient antenna with enhanced bandwidth is a major component of such systems. With the rapid rise of IoT based devices in recent years, the demand for 5G applications has increased. The traditional communication system's spectrum constraints led to research on 5G communication at frequencies of 28, 38, 60, 71–76, and 81–86 GHz. However, mm-wave is not only advantageous for its tremendous amount of bandwidth, it is also great for high speed data transmission, high definition picture quality and video streaming [1, 2]. Conversely, mm-wave has some issues to deal with regarding sensitivity to blockage, directivity and high propagation loss. Therefore, it sets new challenges for architecture and infrastructure for Mm-wave communication [3].

In terms of novel ideas, researchers have offered many strategies to expand the use of the 5G spectrum. For example, T-slotted microstrip patch antenna for 5G WiFi network of 60 GHz frequency is used to improve the WiFi system data transmission rate [4].

© The Author(s), under exclusive license to Springer Nature Switzerland AG 2023
E. Sabir et al. (Eds.): UNet 2022, LNCS 13853, pp. 19–26, 2023.
https://doi.org/10.1007/978-3-031-29419-8_2

The wearable Mm-wave Triband Antenna embedded on a smart watch for wearable IoT applications. Biomedical telemetry antennas are designed to allow doctors to receive data from patients. Moreover, they can be used for tablets endoscopic, pacers, cardioverter-defibrillators, devices for retinal implants and blood glucose [5]. A compact size low-profile ultra-wideband antenna operating at 28 GHz with a bandwidth of 4.47 GHz was reported in [6]. A fully integrated mm-wave multi beam phased array antenna was analyzed in [7]. In [8] the antenna deals with the polarization and beam scanning ability for mm-wave application. The antenna consists of switchable rejection band capabilities designed to reduce interference from other wireless devices working at 3.37 and ends at 27.71 GHz. The alternating state in the resonator was achieved by using two inserted parallel PIN diodes [9]. A complex microstrip phased array antenna operating at 28 GHz was constructed with a capacitive via fences to reduce the size of the element, to improve the beamwidth of the antenna. A U-shaped decoupling structure was introduced between the antenna elements to reduce mutual coupling and to minimize the overall size of the antenna [10]. The array antennas in [11] are co-designed with an aperture transmission line so that the overall antenna element receives RF signals. However, the antenna operates at a licensed 5G mm-wave spectrum of 24.25–27 GHz. A compact coplanar waveguide (CPW) technique is used to enhance the bandwidth of a Multi-Input-Multi-Output (MIMO) antenna. The antenna design is perfect for ultra wideband wireless communication and portable devices [12]. To resolve aerodynamic issues and the connection loss between the IC chip and antenna band in the mm-wave 5G band, was designed in [13]. The fabricated antenna covers 0.84–1.89 GHz, 2.39–5.12 GHz for LTE/Sub-6 GHz 5G bands, 28.2–32.1 GHz and 33.7–34.9 GHz for the mm-wave communication. The gain of 28 GHz is about 10.95dBi. Therefore, the antenna design stands out to be a good candidate for future V2X (vehicle-to-everything) applications. In reference [14] a dual-band, single-feed mmwave antenna with circular polarization is proposed for 5G communication.

In this paper, a compact co-planar waveguide (CPW) fed mm-wave tri-band antenna for future 5G communication is presented. With a bandwidth of 4 GHz, this tri-band antenna is suitable for multiband operation in 5G communication. The proposed antenna has a compact in design, large bandwidth, and has multiband feature. The suggested antenna is composed of low-cost Rogers RT 5880 material and overall size of 9 mm × 9 mm × 0.127 mm.

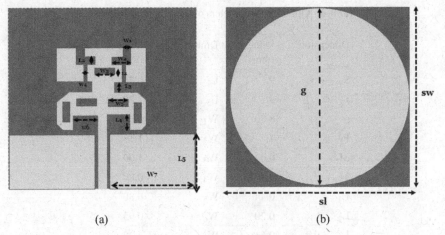

 (a)   (b)

Fig. 1. Front view (a) and rear view (b) of the proposed mm-wave tri-band antenna.

2 Antenna Configuration

A compact CPW fed tri-band monopole antenna has been designed for 5G communication, sized at 9 mm × 9 mm × 0.127 mm which is presented in Fig. 1. The basic antenna consists of a 50Ω CPW feedline, circular ground plane, and a rectangular resonating patch. The width and length of the actual rectangular patch are calculated using Eq. (1) and (2).

$$W_p = \frac{c_o}{2f_o}\sqrt{\frac{2}{1+\varepsilon_r}} W_p = \frac{c_o}{2f_o}\sqrt{\frac{2}{1+\varepsilon_r}} \tag{1}$$

$$L_p = c_o\frac{1}{2f_o\sqrt{\varepsilon_{reff}}}L_p = c_o\frac{1}{2f_o\sqrt{\varepsilon_{reff}}} - 2\Delta L_p\Delta L_p \tag{2}$$

To achieve compact size with multiband as well as to keep the value of reflection coefficient, S_{11} less than -10dB with high gain have become the main focus of our research work. In addition, a coplanar waveguide technique with circular ground plane, rectangular slot and parasitic elements are used to achieve multiband operation. The main radiating element is tapered at the top and at the bottom to shift the radiation towards the desired band for 5G communication as well as to achieve desired frequency bands i.e., 28 GHz and 38 GHz and 61.5 GHz keeping the overall size of the antenna compact. Two L shaped parasitic elements are added to the antenna design to improve overall radiation pattern. The proposed design is made up of three layers: a circular ground plane of height 0.035 mm, a low-cost 0.127 mm-thick (S_h) Rogers RT5880 substrate ($\varepsilon_r = 2.20$ and $\tan\delta = 0.0009$), and a radiating patch of 0.035 mm thickness. The radiating patch is trimmed to a unique form to enable multiband operation. The parasitic element is then truncated from the radiating patch to smooth and enhance the radiation pattern while maintaining a small size for the final design. However, the optimized values of the proposed antenna are summarized in Table 1.

Table 1. Optimized Parameters of the Proposed Design

Dimension	Value (mm)	Dimension	Value (mm)
S_w	9	L_4	0.70
S_l	9	L_5	2.38
g	8.80	W_1	0.63
P_l	4	W_2	1.13
M_t	0.035	W_3	1.00
M_w	0.3945	W_4	0.80
L_1	0.44	W_5	0.80
L_2	0.20	W_6	0.95
L_3	0.60	W_7	4.20

3 Simulated Results and Analysis

The simulated reflection co-efficient (S_{11}) is presented in Fig. 2. Where it is clear that for 28 GHz, 38 GHz and for 61 GHz S_{11} remains at − 17 dB, -11.9 dB and -23.7 dB respectively with a wideband operation at 28 and 61.5 GHz with bandwidth of 4 GHz which are ideal frequency for the 5G communication. Moreover, in all desired frequency range VSWR remain less than 2 depicted in Fig. 3. The gain of the of the designed antenna gradually increasing with increasing the frequency starting from the 1.365 dB, 3.147 dB and 4.520 dB for the 28 GHz, 38 GHz and 61 GHz respectively. Additionally, although for the 28 GHz directivity was 4.355 dBi with the increasing the frequency directivity peaks at 8.026 dBi. The maximum gain over frequency plot and the overall efficiency vs frequency of the proposed antenna have been presented in Fig. 4 and Fig. 5 respectively.

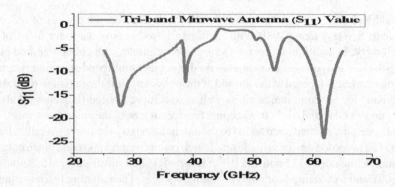

Fig. 2. Simulated result of reflection coefficient, S_{11} of the proposed mm-wave tri-band antenna

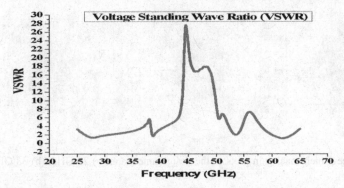

Fig. 3. VSWR reading of the proposed tri-band mm-wave antenna showing the reading below 1.7 for 28 GHz, 38 GHz and 61 GHz.

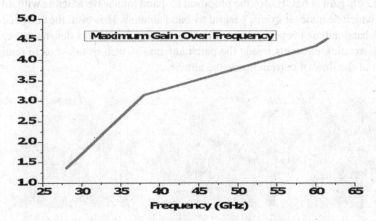

Fig. 4. Maximum gain over frequency for the designed tri-band antenna.

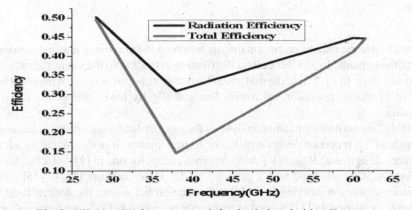

Fig. 5. Efficiency Vs frequency graph for the designed tri-band antenna.

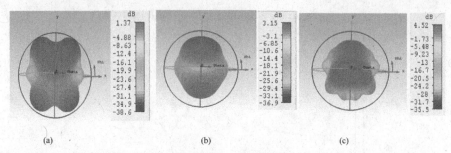

(a)   (b)   (c)

Fig. 6. Three-dimensional gain plots of the design antenna at (a) 28 GHz, (b) 38 GHz and (c) 61 GHz

Three-dimensional gain plots are presented in Fig. 6 where we have achieved maximum 4.52 dB gain at 61 GHz for the proposed tri-band mm-wave antenna with different patterns which degrades it from a general tri-band antenna. However, the current density of the tri-band antenna is presented in Fig. 7. By using the current density, we can find out the resonating elements inside the patch antenna as well as assist us to realize the direction of the flow of current inside the antenna.

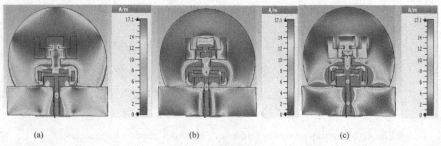

(a)   (b)   (c)

Fig. 7. Surface current distribution of the design antenna at (a) 28 GHz, (b) 38 GHz and (c) 61 GHz.

In 28 GHz the maximum current distribution is on the microstrip line and bottom of the radiating patch. In 38 GHz current distribution extends upto the top of the radiating patch and lastly in 61.5 GHz the maximum current distribution is towards almost whole area of M-shaped resonator, microstrip line and slightly lower part of the I-shaped resonator.

Table 2 shows the comparative analysis of the antenna dimension, material, frequency and gain of the proposed design with the reference antenna. It is shown that the all the reference design used Rogers RT 5880 material except for one in [14] which achieves to work on 5G single band with a gain of 5.32 dB. However, from [15] to [16] all the reference antenna is working in multiband operation but not on the desired band for mmwave frequency. In [17] a good antenna gain is spotted but still not functioning on the desired 5G mmwave band. However, our proposed design is performing in multiband suitable for 5G communication and the overall gain of the antenna gradually increases with the increase in frequency.

Table 2. Comparative Analaysis With Previous Research

Reference	Antenna Dimensions (mm^2)	Substrate Material	Frequency (GHz)	Gain (dB)
[15]	5.5 × 4.35	FR-4	28	5.32
[16]	10 × 10	Rogers RT 5880	26, 35, 50	3.5–7.5
[17]	14 × 12	Rogers RT 5880	28, 38	1.27, 1.83
[18]	7.2 × 5	Rogers RT 5880	37, 54	5.5–6
Proposed design	9 × 9	Rogers RT 5880	28, 38, 61.5	1.37, 3.15, 4.52

4 Conclusion

The design and simulated result of a CPW fed tri-band antenna is presented for future 5G communication. The proposed antenna works as a tri-band antenna at 28 GHz, 38 GHz and 61.5 GHz in the 5G millimeter wave frequency band with enhanced gain and efficiency as the frequency increases. The antenna is compact in size and can be easily fabricated inside 5G devices for wireless communication with a wideband operation at 28 GHz and 61.5 GHz with bandwidth of 4 GHz. Thus, the proposed triband antenna is a perfect candidate for 5G communication.

References

1. Duong, T., Elkashlan, M.: Millimeter-wave communication for 5G: fundamentals. IEEE Common. Mag. **52**(9), 52–54 (2014)
2. Duong, T., Elkashlan, M.: Millimeter-wave communication for 5G - Part 2: application [Guest Editorial]. IEEE Commun. Mag. **53**(1), 166–167 (2015)
3. Seker, C., Güneser, M.T., Ozturk, T.: A review of millimeter wave communication for 5G. In: International Symposium on Multidisciplinary Studies and Innovative Technologies (ISMSIT), pp. 1–5 (2018)
4. Goyal, R.K., Sharma, K.K.: T-slotted microstrip patch antenna for 5G Wi-Fi network. In: International Conference on Advances in Computing, Communications and Informatics, pp. 2684–2687 (2016)
5. Ahmad, S., Ghaffar, A., Li, X.J., Cherif, N.: A millimeter-wave tri-band antenna embedded on smart watch for wearable applications. In: International Symposium on Antennas and Propagation (ISAP), pp. 1–2 (2021)
6. Sandi, E., Rusmono, A.D., Diamah, A., Vinda, K.: Ultra-wideband microstrip array antenna for 5G millimeter-wave applications. J. Commun. **15**(2), 198–204 (2020)
7. Prasad, S., et al.: mmWave multibeam phased array antenna for 5G applications. J. Electromagn. Waves Appl. **35**(13), 1802–1814 (2021)
8. Sun, W., Li, Y., Chang, L., Li, H., Qin, X., Wang, H.: Dual-band dual-polarized microstrip antenna array using double-layer gridded patches for 5G millimeter-wave applications. IEEE Trans. Antennas Propag. **69**(10), 6489–6499 (2021)

 9. Faouri, Y., et al.: Compact super wideband frequency diversity hexagonal shaped monopole antenna with switchable rejection band. IEEE Access **10**, 42321–42333 (2022)
10. Zhao, Z., Zhu, Y., Deng, C.: Microstrip phased array antenna with small element space for 5G millimeter-wave applications. In: IEEE International Conference on Electronic Information and Communication Technology (ICEICT), pp. 620–622 (2020)
11. Khalily, M., Tafazolli, R., Xiao, P., Kishk, A.A.: 'Broadband mm-wave microstrip array antenna with improved radiation characteristics for different 5G applications. IEEE Trans. Antennas Propag. **66**(9), 4641–4647 (2018)
12. Ahmad, S., et al.: A compact CPW-fed ultra-wideband multi-input-multi-output (MIMO) antenna for wireless communication networks. IEEE Access **10**, 25278–25289 (2022)
13. Ko, M., Lee, H., Choi, J.: A planar LTE/sub-6 GHz MIMO antenna integrated with mmWave 5G beamforming phased array antennas. IET Microwaves Antennas Propag. **14**(11), 1283–1295 (2020)
14. Aliakbari, H., et al.: A single feed dual-band circularly polarized millimeter-wave antenna for 5G communication. In: 10th European Conference on Antennas and Propagation, pp. 1–5 (2016)
15. Ghazaoui, Y., et al.: Millimeter wave antenna with enhanced bandwidth for 5G wireless application. J. Instrum. **15**(01), T01003 (2020)
16. Ullah, A., et al.: Coplanar waveguide antenna with defected ground structure for 5G millimeter wave communications. IEEE Middle East North Afr.0 COMMun. Conf. (MENACOMM) **2019**, 1–4 (2019)
17. Hasan, M.N., Bashir, S., Chu, S.: Dual band omnidirectional millimeter wave antenna for 5G communications. J. Electromagn. Waves Appl. **33**(12), 1581–1590 (2019)
18. Lodro, Z., Shah, N., Mahar, E., Tirmizi, S.B., Lodro, M.: mmWave novel multiband microstrip patch antenna design for 5G communication. In: International Conference on Computing, Mathematics and Engineering Technologies (iCoMET), pp. 1–4 (2019)

Trading Off Controlled System Energy and Wireless Communication Energy

Yifei Sun[1($\boxtimes$)], Samson Lasaulce[2], and Michel Kieffer[1]

[1] Université Paris-Saclay - CNRS - CentraleSupélec - L2S,
91192 Gif-sur-Yvette, France
sunyifeifr@gmail.com
[2] CRAN, CNRS-Université de Lorraine, 54000 Nancy, France

Abstract. In contrast with previous cellular systems standard, 5G wireless communications are much more suited to the remote control physical systems (e.g., cars, drones, robots). In this new setting, it becomes relevant to revisit the problem of wireless transmit power control and make it more goal-oriented, the goal being to minimize a given controlled system final performance metric. This work precisely aims at designing the transmit power algorithm so as to find a tradeoff between the system energy and communication energy. This paper focuses on the case of vector linear dynamical systems subject to additive perturbation when communications between the system controllers and the systems to be controlled are subject to packet erasures. Even for the single system case, the corresponding optimization problem is not trivial but turns out to be solvable iteratively. For the multiple system case, we propose a transmit power control algorithm which is generally suboptimal but has the virtue of being distributed and performing better than power control strategies that are usually implemented for controlled systems.

Keywords: Slow power control · Energy-efficiency · Linear systems with perturbations

1 Introduction

The dominant paradigm in system control theory is to assume that information exchanges between the controller(s) and the system(s) to be controlled are perfect. When information exchanges occur over wireless channels, in the case of remote control, this assumption may be questionable and even not realistic at all. This is one of the reasons why there is an active research area at the interface between control theory and wireless communications. Among representative research works of this approach, we can quote the following papers [1,3–6,10,12].

The problem of imperfect communication between the various components of a system is addressed in [6]. In [3], the problem of imperfect feedback is considered when the feedback channel noise is caused by the quantization of transmitted data. In [10], it is shown how a finite communication data rate impacts the controller design. The impact of fast fading wireless channel fluctuations on

E. Sabir et al. (Eds.): UNet 2022, LNCS 13853, pp. 27–40, 2023.
https://doi.org/10.1007/978-3-031-29419-8_3

the control design has been addressed, *e.g.*, in [4,12], and [1]. The coexistence of several controlled systems sharing the same communication channel prone to interference is considered in [5].

In the present paper, in contrast with the existing literature, the main technical focus is not on the system controller but on the control of the wireless transmit power implemented at the system side for reporting its state to the controller through a wireless feedback channel. This scenario may be of interest, *e.g.*, in the remote control of ground or aerial drones, when the control input is evaluated by a remote controller from measurements of the state of the drone that are transmitted over a wireless channel. What characterizes the power approach taken in this paper is as follows. First, the transmit power is adapted to the wireless feedback channel statistics and the system state (which is multidimensional and not merely scalar as [11]). Second, the objective pursued consists of a combination of a system control objective and a communication objective (namely, the wireless transmission energy); managing the wireless transmit power is both relevant in terms of consumed energy and electromagnetic pollution. Third, this adaptation is performed in the presence of an additive perturbation on the (linear) system dynamics and a multiplicative noise for the wireless feedback channel (which corresponds to data packet erasures). Fourth, the case of multiple controlled systems whose communications may interfere is considered (in contrast with [11] where there is only one controlled system). This complete framework has not been addressed yet in the literature.

Good representatives of the closest literature are give by references [2,7,13] where the authors also assume a multiplicative noise model for the communication channel but do not focus on the wireless transmit power control problem by both pursuing a system control objective and a wireless transmission energy objective. Rather, the cited papers focus on a system control-theoretic problem namely system stability.

The present paper is structured as follows. In Sect. 2, the technical problem to be solved is formulated. Determining the best power control policy is shown to amount to solving a non-trivial multilinear problem. To solve it, we resort to an iterative search technique described in Sect. 3. Section 4 addresses of several controlled systems with interfering communication. Then, in Sect. 5, we conduct a numerical performance analysis to illustrate the benefits of controlling properly the wireless transmit power. Conclusions and perspectives are provided in Sect. 6.

2   Problem Formulation

A general distributed multi-controller or multi-agent system is shown in Fig. 1. The signals (output and control signal) are transmitted wirelessly and assume to exploit the same radio resources (same frequency band, same time frame...). The received signals are corrupted by noise coming from the communication channel and by interference coming from the other controller-system or controller-agent pairs.

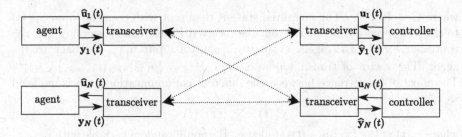

Fig. 1. General remotely controlled distributed multi-agents system

We assume that the communication from a controller to a controlled system or agent is perfect and focus on the communication from the agent to the controller. The architecture of the overall system is shown in Fig. 2.

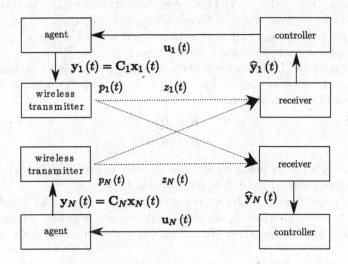

Fig. 2. Communication and control setup

Consider a discrete-time overall system consisting of N agent-controller pairs. We assume that the evolution of the state $\mathbf{x}_i \in \mathbb{R}^{n_x^i}$ of the i-th agent, $i = 1, \ldots, N$, is described by the following discrete-time state equation

$$\mathbf{x}_i(t+1) = \mathbf{A}_i \mathbf{x}_i(t) + \mathbf{B}_i \mathbf{u}_i(t) + \mathbf{d}_i(t), \tag{1}$$

where $t \in \{1, ..., T\}$, $T \geqslant 1$, $\mathbf{A}_i \in \mathbb{R}^{n_x^i \times n_x^i}$, $\mathbf{B}_i \in \mathbb{R}^{n_x^i \times n_u^i}$, and $\mathbf{u}_i(t) \in \mathbb{R}^{n_u^i}$ is the control input, $\mathbf{d}_i(t) \sim \mathcal{N}_{n_x^i}(\mathbf{0}, \mathbf{\Sigma}_{\mathbf{d}_i})$ is the perturbation assumed independent of $\mathbf{x}_i(t)$.

At each discrete time instant t, the i-th agent measures its state via the following measurement equation

$$\mathbf{y}_i(t) = \mathbf{C}_i \mathbf{x}_i(t), \tag{2}$$

where $\mathbf{C}_i \in \mathbb{R}^{n_y^i \times n_x^i}$. The measured state is then sent with transmit power $p_i(t)$ to the i-th remote controller. From the received measurement vector $\widehat{\mathbf{y}}_i(t)$, the controller for the i-th agent evaluates a control input $\widehat{\mathbf{u}}_i(t)$ fed back to the agent. The vector of transmit powers is $p_{1:N}(t) = (p_1(t), p_2(t), \ldots, p_N(t))^T$. The effect of interference between the different communication links is modeled as

$$\widehat{\mathbf{y}}_i(t) = \mathbf{y}_i(t) z_i(t) \tag{3}$$

where $z_i(t) \sim \mathrm{Ber}(\pi_i(p_{1:N}(t)))$ follows a Bernoulli random variable with parameter $\pi_i(p_{1:N}(t))$, denoted by $\pi_i(t)$ in what follows. The parameter

$$\begin{aligned} \pi_i(t) &= \Pr(\mathrm{SINR} \geqslant \gamma_i) \\ &= \Pr[z_i(t) = 1], \end{aligned} \tag{4}$$

determines the success rate of the communication, where γ_i is the signal-to-noise plus interference ratio (SINR) threshold for the i-th decoder. In general, $\pi_i(t)$ depends on $p_j(t), j = 1, \ldots, N$. This accounts for the fact that the transmitted signal has to be received with a sufficiently high SINR to allow error-free decoding, in which case $z_i(t) = 1$. If the received signal is too noisy or subject to too much interference to be decoded correctly then $z_i(t) = 0$.

Assuming that $z_i(t)$ is known at the receiver (*e.g.*, by using a classical cyclic redundancy check procedure), while $z_i(t) = 1$, we consider a static feedback with control input evaluated as

$$\begin{aligned} \mathbf{u}_i(t) &= \mathbf{K}_i \widehat{\mathbf{y}}_i(t) \\ &= \mathbf{K}_i \mathbf{C}_i \mathbf{x}_i(t) z_i(t) \end{aligned} \tag{5}$$

where $\mathbf{K}_i \in \mathbb{R}^{n_u^i \times n_y^i}$. When $z_i(t) = 0$, the receiver cannot decode correctly and the transmitted control input is $\mathbf{u}_i(t) = \mathbf{0}$ as in [8,9].

For each agent $i = 1, \ldots, N$, assuming that $\mathbf{x}_i(1) \sim \mathcal{N}_{n_x^i}(0, \boldsymbol{\Sigma}_{\mathbf{x}_i})$ and considering a finite control horizon T, our aim in what follows is to find, a transmission power policy $p_i^{1:T} = (p_i(1), p_i(2), \ldots, p_i(T))^T$, that minimizes the expected cost

$$\overline{J}_i^{1:T}\left(p_i^{1:T}\right) = \mathbb{E}_{z_i^{1:T}, \mathbf{d}_i^{1:T}}\left[\sum_{t=1}^{T}\left(\mathbf{x}_i^T(t)\mathbf{Q}_i\mathbf{x}_i(t) + \mathbf{u}_i^T(t)\mathbf{R}_i\mathbf{u}_i(t) + p_i(t)\right)\right] \tag{6}$$

under transmission powers bounded by $P_{\max}^i$

$$0 \leqslant p_i(t) \leqslant P_{\max}^i, t = 1, \ldots, T. \tag{7}$$

In (6), $\mathbf{Q}_i$ and $\mathbf{R}_i$ are two symmetric positive definite matrices, and the expectation $\mathbb{E}_{z_i^{1:T}, \mathbf{d}_i^{1:T}}[\cdot]$ is performed with respect to $z_i(1) \ldots z_i(T)$, which depends on the transmission power policies of all agents and with respect to $\mathbf{d}_i(1), \ldots, \mathbf{d}_i(T)$. The cost $\overline{J}_i^{1:T}$ comprises three terms. The two first terms correspond to the system control energy whereas the last term $\mathbb{E}_{z_i^{1:T}, \mathbf{d}_i^{1:T}}\left[\sum_{t=1}^T p_i(t)\right]$ represents the expected communication energy for transmitting T packets to control the dynamical system. This cost only assumes statistical knowledge of the quantities at hand and in particular only the channel distribution information (CDI) is required.

3   Full Analysis of the Point-to-Point Communication

In this section we focus on a single system controller communicating with a given dynamical system. To lighten presentation, the system index i is omitted. In this setting, it is possible to derive the power control policy that implements the best tradeoff between the system control cost and the communication cost. To simplify the optimization problem analysis, we assume a Rayleigh fading communication channel model with average gain $\bar{g}$. When a message is transmitted with transmit power p, the probability of receiving a packet successfully $\pi(p)$ can thus be expressed as:

$$\pi(p) = \Pr[\text{SNR} \geqslant \gamma]$$
$$\Pr\left[\frac{gp}{\sigma^2} \geqslant \gamma\right], \tag{8}$$

where g is the channel gain at time t, σ^2 the variance of some white Gaussian channel noise, and γ the SNR threshold which guarantees a correct reception. Then

$$\pi(p) = \int_{\frac{\gamma\sigma^2}{p}}^{+\infty} \frac{1}{\bar{g}} \exp\left(-\frac{g}{\bar{g}}\right) dg$$
$$= e^{-\frac{\gamma\sigma^2}{p\bar{g}}}. \tag{9}$$

The above relation between π and p represents a change of variable which is very convenient for the analysis of the considered optimization problem.

Using (1), (2), and (5), one can expand $\mathbf{x}(t+1)$, $t \geqslant 1$ as follows

$$
\begin{aligned}
&\mathbf{x}(t+1)\\
&= \mathbf{A}\mathbf{x}(t) + \mathbf{B}\mathbf{u}(t) + \mathbf{d}(t)\\
&= (\mathbf{A} + \mathbf{B}\mathbf{K}\mathbf{C}z(t))\,\mathbf{x}(t) + \mathbf{d}(t)\\
&= \prod_{\ell=1}^{t}(\mathbf{A} + \mathbf{B}\mathbf{K}\mathbf{C}z(\ell))\,\mathbf{x}(1) + \sum_{\ell=1}^{t}\prod_{r=\ell+1}^{t}(\mathbf{A} + \mathbf{B}\mathbf{K}\mathbf{C}z(r))\,\mathbf{d}(\ell)
\end{aligned} \tag{10}
$$

where, by convention $\prod_{r=t+1}^{t}(\mathbf{A} + \mathbf{B}\mathbf{K}\mathbf{C}z(r)) = 1$. Consequently, $\mathbf{x}(t)$ depends on the initial state value $\mathbf{x}(1)$, the indicators of successful communication $z(1), \ldots, z(t-1)$, and the noise realizations $\mathbf{d}(1), \ldots, \mathbf{d}(t-1)$.

One can now reformulate in a convenient manner the problem with (6), (11) and (10) and provide the following results.

Proposition 1. *Denoting* $\pi^{1:T} = (\pi(1), \ldots, \pi(T))^T$, *the problem of minimizing* $\overline{J}^{1:T}(p^{1:T})$ *with respect to* $p^{1:T}$ *under the power constraint (11) can be reformulated as*

$$\min_{\pi^{1:T}} \mathcal{C}\left(\pi^{1:T}\right)$$
$$\text{s.t.} \ -\frac{\gamma\sigma^2}{\bar{g}\ln\pi(t)} - P_{\max} \leqslant 0, \ t = 1 \ldots T. \tag{11}$$

where

$$c\left(\pi^{1:T}\right) = \text{vec}^T\left(\mathbf{\Sigma_x}\right)\text{vec}\left(\mathbf{Q} + \pi\left(1\right)\mathbf{C}^T\mathbf{K}^T\mathbf{R}\mathbf{K}\mathbf{C}\right) +$$

$$\text{vec}^T\left(\mathbf{\Sigma_x}\right)\mathbb{E}_{z^{1:T}}\left[\text{vec}\left(\sum_{t=2}^T\left(\Theta^{1:t-1}\right)^T\left(\mathbf{Q} + z^2\left(t\right)\mathbf{C}^T\mathbf{K}^T\mathbf{R}\mathbf{K}\mathbf{C}\right)\left(\Theta^{1:t-1}\right)\right)\right] +$$

$$\text{vec}^T\left(\mathbf{\Sigma_d}\right)\mathbb{E}_{z^{2:T}}\left[\sum_{t=2}^T\sum_{i=1}^{t-1}\left(\Theta^{i+1:t-1}\right)^T\otimes\left(\Theta^{i+1:t-1}\right)^T\text{vec}\left(\mathbf{Q} + z^2\left(t\right)\mathbf{C}^T\mathbf{K}^T\mathbf{R}\mathbf{K}\mathbf{C}\right)\right]$$

$$-\sum_{t=1}^T\frac{\gamma\sigma^2}{\bar{g}\ln\pi\left(t\right)}$$

is multilinear, $\otimes$ indicates Kronecker product, and

$$\Theta^{t:\ell-1} = \prod_{j=t}^{\ell-1}\left(\mathbf{A} + z\left(j\right)\mathbf{B}\mathbf{K}\mathbf{C}\right).$$

This means that the tradeoff optimization problem (11) is neither convex nor concave, and generally not quasiconvex. Finding $\pi^{1:T}$ is thus not a trivial task. Interestingly, the problem has a recursive structure that can be exploited to determine the best sequence of transmit powers, as explained next.

Indeed, one can decompose (6) as follows.

$$\begin{aligned}\bar{J}^{1:T}\left(p^{1:T}\right) &= \mathbb{E}_{z^{1:T}\mathbf{d}^{1:T}}\left[\sum_{t=1}^T\left(\mathbf{x}^T\left(t\right)\mathbf{Q}\mathbf{x}\left(t\right) + \mathbf{u}^T\left(t\right)\mathbf{R}\mathbf{u}\left(t\right) + p\left(t\right)\right)\right]\\
&= \mathbb{E}_{z^{1:T}\mathbf{d}^{1:T}}\left[\sum_{\ell=1}^{t-1}\left(\mathbf{x}^T\left(\ell\right)\mathbf{Q}\mathbf{x}\left(\ell\right) + \mathbf{u}^T\left(\ell\right)\mathbf{R}\mathbf{u}\left(\ell\right) + p\left(\ell\right)\right)\right.\\
&\qquad\left.\sum_{\ell=t}^T\left(\mathbf{x}^T\left(\ell\right)\mathbf{Q}\mathbf{x}\left(\ell\right) + \mathbf{u}^T\left(\ell\right)\mathbf{R}\mathbf{u}\left(\ell\right) + p\left(\ell\right)\right)\right]\\
&= \bar{J}^{1:t-1}\left(p^{1:t-1}\right) + \bar{J}'^{t:T}\left(p^{1:T}\right),\end{aligned} \quad (12)$$

where

$$\bar{J}^{1:t-1}\left(p^{1:t-1}\right) = \mathbb{E}_{z^{1:t-1}\mathbf{d}^{1:t-1}}\left[\sum_{\ell=1}^{t-1}\left(\mathbf{x}^T\left(\ell\right)\mathbf{Q}\mathbf{x}\left(\ell\right) + \mathbf{u}^T\left(\ell\right)\mathbf{R}\mathbf{u}\left(\ell\right) + p\left(\ell\right)\right)\right]$$

and

$$\bar{J}'^{t:T}\left(p^{1:T}\right) = \mathbb{E}_{z^{1:T}\mathbf{d}^{1:T}}\left[\sum_{\ell=t}^T\left(\mathbf{x}^T\left(\ell\right)\mathbf{Q}\mathbf{x}\left(\ell\right) + \mathbf{u}^T\left(\ell\right)\mathbf{R}\mathbf{u}\left(\ell\right) + p\left(\ell\right)\right)\right].$$

One can observe that $\bar{J}^{1:t-1}\left(p^{1:t-1}\right)$ is independent of $p\left(t\right)$. Proposition 2, in what follows, separates the term containing $p\left(t\right)$ (or $\pi\left(t\right)$) from $\bar{J}'^{t:T}\left(p^{1:T}\right)$.

Proposition 2. $\overline{J}'^{t:T}\left(p^{1:T}\right)$ *can be expressed as*

$$
\overline{J}'^{t:T}\left(p^{1:T}\right) = \mathbb{E}_{z^{1:t-1}\mathbf{d}^{1:t-1}}\left[\mathbf{x}^T\left(t\right) \otimes \mathbf{x}^T\left(t\right)\right]\overline{V}\left(p^{t:T}\right)
$$
$$
+ \mathrm{vec}^T\left(\mathbf{\Sigma_d}\right)\overline{V}_s\left(p^{t+1:T}\right) + \sum_{\ell=t}^T p\left(\ell\right), \tag{13}
$$

where for all $t < T$

$$
\overline{V}\left(p^{t:T}\right) = \mathbb{E}_{z^{t:T}}\left[V\left(p^{t:T}\right)\right]
$$

$$
V\left(p^{t:T}\right) = \mathrm{vec}\Big(\mathbf{Q} + z^2\left(t\right)\mathbf{C}^T\mathbf{K}^T\mathbf{R}\mathbf{K}\mathbf{C} +
$$
$$
\sum_{\ell=t+1}^T \left(\Theta^{t:\ell-1}\right)^T\left(\mathbf{Q} + z^2\left(\ell\right)\mathbf{C}^T\mathbf{K}^T\mathbf{R}\mathbf{K}\mathbf{C}\right)\left(\Theta^{t:\ell-1}\right)\Big),
$$

and for all $t < T - 1$

$$
\overline{V}_s\left(p^{t+1:T}\right) = \mathbb{E}_{z^{t+1:T}}\left[V_s\left(p^{t+1:T}\right)\right]
$$

$$
V_s\left(p^{t+1:T}\right) = \sum_{\ell=t+1}^T \sum_{i=t}^{\ell-1}\left(\Theta^{i+1:\ell-1}\right)^T \otimes
$$
$$
\left(\Theta^{i+1:\ell-1}\right)^T \mathrm{vec}\left(\mathbf{Q} + z^2\left(\ell\right)\mathbf{C}^T\mathbf{K}^T\mathbf{R}\mathbf{K}\mathbf{C}\right)
$$

Furthermore, $\overline{V}\left(p^{t:T}\right)$ and $\overline{V}_s\left(p^{t+1:T}\right)$ can be evaluated by Proposition 3.

Proposition 3. $\overline{V}\left(p^{t:T}\right)$ *and* $\overline{V}_s\left(p^{t+1:T}\right)$ *can be evaluated using the following backward recursions*

$$
\overline{V}\left(p^{t:T}\right) = \mathbb{E}_{z(t)}\left[\mathrm{vec}\left(\mathbf{Q} + z^2\left(t\right)\mathbf{C}^T\mathbf{K}^T\mathbf{R}\mathbf{K}\mathbf{C}\right)\right] +
$$
$$
\mathbb{E}_{z(t)}\left[\left(\mathbf{A} + z\left(t\right)\mathbf{B}\mathbf{K}\mathbf{C}\right)^T \otimes \left(\mathbf{A} + z\left(t\right)\mathbf{B}\mathbf{K}\mathbf{C}\right)^T\right]\overline{V}\left(p^{t+1:T}\right)
$$

for all $t \leqslant T - 1$ *and*

$$
\overline{V}_s\left(p^{t:T}\right) = \overline{V}\left(p^{t:T}\right) + \overline{V}_s\left(p^{t+1:T}\right)
$$

for all $t \leqslant T - 2$.

Considering the transmission power p_T minimizing (6), these backward recursions are initialized by Proposition 4.

Proposition 4. *The transmission power* $p\left(T\right)$ *at time* T *minimizing* (6) *is* $p\left(T\right) = 0$ *and leads to*

$$
\overline{V}\left(p\left(T\right)\right) = \mathrm{vec}\left(\mathbf{Q}\right)
$$

and

$$
\overline{V}_s\left(p\left(T\right)\right) = \mathrm{vec}\left(\mathbf{Q}\right).
$$

We can then determine $\pi(t)$ minimizing (6) when $\pi(t')$ is fixed for all $t' = 1, \ldots, T$, $t \neq t'$. This is shown in Proposition 5.

Proposition 5. *Assume a Rayleigh fading law with mean $\bar{g}$ for g_t. Consider some $t \in \{1, \ldots, T-1\}$ and assume that $\pi(t')$ is fixed for all $t' = 1 \ldots, T$, $t' \neq t$. The value of $\pi(t)$ minimizing (6) with the constraint (11) is either $\pi(t) = 0$ or $\pi(t) = \min\left(e^{-\frac{\gamma\sigma^2}{P_{\max}\bar{g}}}, \pi^0\right)$, where π^0 is such that $e^{-2} < \pi^0$ and*

$$\mathbb{E}_{z^{1:t-1}\mathbf{d}^{1:t-1}}\left[\mathbf{x}^T(t) \otimes \mathbf{x}^T(t)\right] \frac{\partial}{\partial \pi(t)} \overline{V}(p_{t:T}) + \frac{\gamma\sigma^2}{\pi^0 \ln^2 \pi^0 \bar{g}} = 0.$$

Consider a transmission power policy $p^{1:T^{(0)}}$ and its corresponding $\pi^{1:T^{(0)}}$. From Proposition 5, for all $t = 1, \ldots, T$, one can obtain

$$\pi(t)^* = \arg\min_{\pi(t) \in \mathcal{I}} C\left(\pi(1)^{(0)}, \ldots, \pi(t-1)^{(0)}, \pi(t), \pi(t+1)^{(0)}, \ldots, \pi(T)^{(0)}\right)$$

where $\mathcal{I} = \left\{0, \min\left(e^{-\frac{\gamma\sigma^2}{P_{\max}\bar{g}}}, \pi^0\right)\right\}$. The set

$$\mathcal{P} = \left\{\left[\pi(1)^*, \pi(2)^{(0)}, \ldots, \pi(T)^{(0)}\right], \ldots, \left[\pi(1)^{(0)}, \ldots, \pi(T-1)^{(0)}, \pi(T)^*\right]\right\}$$

of associated success vectors is obtained. The vector

$$\pi^{1:T^{(1)}} = \arg\min_{\pi_{1:T} \in \mathcal{P}} C(\pi_{1:T})$$

and the associated transmission power policy $p^{1:T^{(1)}}$ provides a reduced cost. The above process may be repeated. Algorithm 1 summarizes the proposed iterative optimization process. Implementing this algorithm allows one to determine the transmit power control policy that realizes the best tradeoff between system control energy and communication energy.

4   Analysis of Multiple Controller Systems

In this section, we assume the presence of multiple controller-system pairs. The cost function for the controller-system pair $i \in \{1, ..., N\}$ is defined by Equation (6). As explained in the previous section, the relation between the transmit power and the packet success probability allows one to simplify the minimization of the cost function. This is why it is also used in the case of N agents or controllers. When N agents share the same interference channel, for the i-th agent, the success rate is

$$\pi_i(p_1, \ldots, p_N) = \Pr[z_i = 1 \mid p_1, \ldots, p_N]$$
$$= \Pr[\text{SINR}_i \geqslant \gamma_i].$$

Algorithm 1. Transmission power optimization

Input: Time horizon T, $\boldsymbol{\Sigma_x}$, $\mathbf{A}$, $\mathbf{B}$, $\mathbf{K}$, $\mathbf{C}$, $\mathbf{Q}$, $\mathbf{R}$, $\boldsymbol{\Sigma_d}$;

   Initialization: $p\left(1\right)^{(0)} = \ldots p\left(T\right)^{(0)} = 0$, $k = 1$;

Output: Power policy $p^{1:T}$;

   while $k \leqslant k_{\max}$ **do**

      for $t = T : -1 : 1$ **do**

         Using $p\left(1\right)^{(k-1)}, \ldots, p\left(T\right)^{(k-1)}$, (9), and $\overline{V}\left(p_T\right) = \mathrm{vec}\left(\mathbf{Q}\right)$, determine $\overline{V}\left(p^{t:T}\right)$
by backward recursion using Proposition 3;

      end for

      for $t = 1 : T$ **do**

         From $p\left(t-1\right)^{(k-1)}$ and $\mathbb{E}\left[\mathbf{x}^T\left(t-1\right) \otimes \mathbf{x}^T\left(t-1\right)\right]$, evaluate $\mathbb{E}\left[\mathbf{x}^T\left(t\right) \otimes \mathbf{x}^T\left(t\right)\right]$
using (10);

         Determine the minimum of $\frac{\partial J}{\partial \pi\left(t\right)}$ obtained at $\pi\left(t\right) = \min\left(e^{-2}, e^{-\frac{\gamma\sigma^2}{P_{\max}\overline{g}}}\right)$;

         if $\left.\frac{\partial J}{\partial \pi\left(t\right)}\right|_{\pi\left(t\right)} < 0$ **then**

            Determine π^0 and its corresponding power p^0 using (9);

            Determine $\pi(t)^* \in \left\{0, \min\left(\pi^0, e^{-\frac{\gamma\sigma^2}{P_{\max}\overline{g}}}\right)\right\}$ minimizing the cost;

            Determine the power $p\left(t\right)^*$ corresponding to $\pi\left(t\right)^*$ using (9);

         else

            $p\left(t\right)^* = p\left(t\right)^{(k-1)}$;

         end if

      end for

      $\left[p\left(1\right)^{(k)}, \ldots, p\left(T\right)^{(k)}\right]$ is one of the element of $\mathcal{P} = \left\{[p\left(1\right)^*, p\left(2\right)^{(k-1)}, \ldots, p\left(T\right)^{(k-1)}], \ldots, \quad [p\left(1\right)^{(k-1)}, p\left(2\right)^{(k-1)}, \ldots, p\left(T\right)^*]\right\}$
that minimizes the cost (6)

   end while

Considering a Rayleigh-fading interference channel model between the transmitter-receiver pairs, and assuming that agent j transmits with a power p_j, the SINR experienced by the i-th agent is

$$\mathrm{SINR}_i = \frac{p_i g_{ii}}{\sigma_i^2 + \sum_{j \neq i} p_j g_{ji}} \tag{14}$$

where $g_{ji}\left(t\right)$ is the channel gain from controller j to agent i, with mean value $\overline{g}_{ji}$.

In the case of $N = 2$ agents, it is possible to express the probability of success as stated in the next proposition. When $N > 2$, the latter quantity can be evaluated using Monte-Carlo draws, may be learnt or obtained using real measurements.

Proposition 6. *Consider $N = 2$ agents, transmitting at time t at a power p_i and p_j over a Rayleigh-fading interference channel with channel gain with mean value $\overline{g}_{ii}, \overline{g}_{ji}$, and white Gaussian noise with variance σ_i^2. Considering the SINR threshold γ_i for the i-th agent, its success probability is*

$$\pi_i\left(p_i,p_j\right) = \left(1 + \frac{\gamma_i \bar{g}_{ji}}{\bar{g}_{ii}}\frac{p_j}{p_i}\right)^{-1}\exp\left(-\frac{\frac{\gamma_i \sigma_i^2}{\bar{g}_{ii}}}{p_i}\right). \tag{15}$$

As in the single agent case, one can reformulate the problem as

$$\min_{\pi_i^{1:T}} \mathcal{C}_i\left(\pi_i^{1:T}\right) \tag{16}$$
$$\text{s.t. } \pi_i\left(t\right) - \pi_{P_{\max}} \leqslant 0,\; t = 1\ldots T$$

where

$$\pi_{P_{\max}} = \left(1 + \frac{\gamma_i \bar{g}_{ji}}{\bar{g}_{ii}}\frac{p_j}{P_{\max}}\right)^{-1}\exp\left(-\frac{\frac{\gamma_i \sigma_i^2}{\bar{g}_{ii}}}{P_{\max}}\right).$$

As in Sect. 3, one can obtain

$$\bar{J}_i'^{t:T}\left(p_i^{1:T};p_j^{1:T}\right) = \mathbb{E}_{z_i^{1:t-1}\mathbf{d}_i^{1:t-1}}\left[\mathbf{x}_i^T\left(t\right)\otimes \mathbf{x}_i^T\left(t\right)\right]\bar{V}_i\left(p_i^{t:T};p_j^{t:T}\right)$$
$$+ \operatorname{vec}^T\left(\boldsymbol{\Sigma}_{\mathbf{d}_i}\right)\bar{V}_{s_i}\left(p_i^{t+1:T};p_j^{t+1:T}\right) + \sum_{\ell=t}^{T}p_i\left(\ell\right), \tag{17}$$

Furthermore $\bar{V}_i\left(p_i^{t:T};p_j^{t:T}\right)$ and $\bar{V}_{s_i}\left(p_i^{t+1:T};p_j^{t+1:T}\right)$ can be evaluated and initialized as in Sect. 3.

To minimize (6), consider the derivative of $\bar{J}_i^{1:T}\left(p_i^{1:T};p_j^{1:T}\right)$

$$\frac{\partial \bar{J}_i^{1:T}\left(p_i^{1:T};p_j^{1:T}\right)}{\partial p_i\left(t\right)} = \mathbb{E}_{z_i^{1:T}\mathbf{d}_i^{1:T-1}}\left[\mathbf{x}_i^T\left(t\right)\otimes \mathbf{x}_i^T\left(t\right)\right]\frac{\partial}{\partial p_i\left(t\right)}\left(\bar{V}_i\left(p_i^{t:T};p_j^{t:T}\right)\right)$$
$$= \mathbb{E}_{z_i^{1:T}\mathbf{d}_i^{1:T-1}}\left[\mathbf{x}_i^T\left(t\right)\otimes \mathbf{x}_i^T\left(t\right)\right]\times$$
$$\left(\operatorname{vec}\left(\mathbf{C}_i^T\mathbf{K}_i^T\mathbf{R}_i\mathbf{K}_i\mathbf{C}_i\right)+\right. \tag{18}$$
$$\left(\mathbf{A}_i^T\otimes\left(\mathbf{C}_i^T\mathbf{K}_i^T\mathbf{B}_i^T\right)+\left(\mathbf{C}_i^T\mathbf{K}_i^T\mathbf{B}_i^T\right)\otimes\mathbf{A}_i^T+\left(\mathbf{C}_i^T\mathbf{K}_i^T\mathbf{B}_i^T\right)\otimes\left(\mathbf{C}_i^T\mathbf{K}_i^T\mathbf{B}_i^T\right)\right)$$
$$\left.\bar{V}_i\left(p_i^{t+1:T}\right)\right)\times\frac{\partial \pi_i\left(t\right)}{\partial p_i\left(t\right)}-1$$

In the case of multiple agents, the reference is present, leading to a more complicated expression of the success rate whose derivative with respect to p_i is

$$\frac{\partial \pi_i}{\partial p_i} = \frac{\gamma_i \bar{g}_{ii}\bar{g}_{ji}p_j p_i + \gamma_i \sigma_i^2\left(\bar{g}_{ii}p_i + \gamma_i \bar{g}_{ji}p_j\right)}{\left(\bar{g}_{ii}p_i + \gamma_i \bar{g}_{ji}p_j\right)^2 p_i}\exp\left(-\frac{\gamma_i \sigma_i^2}{\bar{g}_{ii}p_i}\right). \tag{19}$$

Searching the minimum value of $\bar{J}_i^{1:T}\left(p_i^{1:T};p_j^{1:T}\right)$ considering the second-order derivative of π_i with respect to p_i is not trivial. A sub-optimal method is proposed in what follows.

The best situation when agent i is sending the measurement signal, corresponds to the no interference case when $p_j = 0$. In that case, Proposition 5 may be used. Searching the minimum value of (6) can then be performed using Algorithm 2, which involves Algorithm 1.

Algorithm 2. Transmission power allocation for the two-agent case

---

Input: Time horizon T, $\mathbf{\Sigma_{x_i}}$, $\mathbf{A}_i$, $\mathbf{B}_i$, $\mathbf{K}_i$, $\mathbf{C}_i$, $\mathbf{Q}_i$, $\mathbf{R}_i$, $\mathbf{\Sigma_{d_i}}$, $i \in \{1, 2\}$;
    Initialization: $p_i(1)^{(0)} = \ldots p_i(T)^{(0)} = 0$, $i \in \{1, 2\}$, $k = 1$;
Output: Power policy $p_i^{1:T}$;
    while $k \leqslant k_{\max}$ **do**
        Evaluate $p_1(1)^{(k)}, \ldots, p_1(T)^{(k)}$ using $p_i(1)^{(k-1)}, \ldots, p_i(T)^{(k-1)}, i \in \{1, 2\}$ and
        Algorithm 1
        Evaluate $p_2(1)^{(k)}, \ldots, p_2(T)^{(k)}$ using $p_1(1)^{(k)}, \ldots, p_1(T)^{(k)}$, $p_2(1)^{(k-1)}, \ldots,$
        $p_2(T)^{(k-1)}$ and Algorithm 1
    end while

---

5 Numerical Analysis

First, the impact of the state perturbation $\mathbf{d}(t)$ is analyzed in the single agent case. For that purpose, consider a dynamical system where $n_x = n_y = n_u = 2$,

$$\mathbf{A} = \begin{pmatrix} 1.1 & 0 \\ 0 & 1.1 \end{pmatrix}, \quad -\mathbf{B} = \mathbf{Q} = \mathbf{R} = \mathbf{\Sigma_x} = \begin{pmatrix} 1 & 0 \\ 0 & 1 \end{pmatrix}, \quad \mathbf{KC} = \begin{pmatrix} 1.8 & 0 \\ 0 & 0.9 \end{pmatrix}, \mathbf{\Sigma_d} =$$

$$\sigma_{\mathbf{d}} * \begin{pmatrix} 1 & 0 \\ 0 & 1 \end{pmatrix} \text{ and } P_{\max} = 3.$$

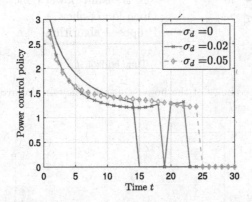

Fig. 3. Obtained transmission power policy for different values of σ_{d} of the state perturbation, when $T = 30$

From Fig. 3, we observe that the need for communication increases as the value of $\sigma_{\mathbf{d}}$ increases. That is due to the fact that a larger value of $\sigma_{\mathbf{d}}$ indicates a stronger perturbation leading to a more perturbed system.

Considering $\sigma_{\mathbf{d}} = 0.05$, Fig. 4 shows the average cost $\overline{J}^{1:T}$ over 10000 realizations with different power control policies: transmission at full power $P_{\max}$ (conventional policy for closed loop systems); send nothing (open loop policy); transmit according to the proposed algorithm. The proposed algorithm has a similar average cost to open loop policy when $T \leqslant 5$. The reason for this is that the system is sufficiently close to dynamical equilibrium within this time horizon, making communication useless. But when $T > 5$, the proposed algorithm yields a better performance compared to other policies.

To analyse the performance of the proposed algorithm for multiple agents, consider two agent-controller pairs with the same parameters as in the single agent case. The result is shown in Fig. 5. The proposed algorithm performs much better than other power policy. As the time horizon increases, the open loop policy becomes less efficient. When $T \leqslant 12$, the average cost of the open loop policy for one agent is larger than the sum of the average costs $\overline{J}_1^{1:T} + \overline{J}_2^{1:T}$ using the proposed algorithm.

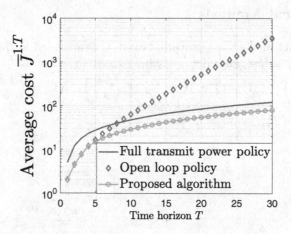

Fig. 4. Impact of the choice of the power control policy on the average cost $\overline{J}^{1:T}$ for different time horizons T

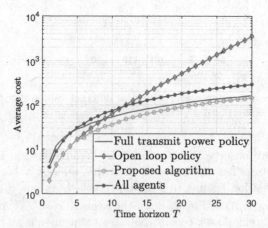

Fig. 5. Impact of the choice of the power control policy: For $T = 30$ using the proposed policy allows the combined cost to be divided by 50.

6   Conclusion

In contrast with the conventional power control literature and the system control literature, the problem of wireless transmit power control consider both the system control energy and the communication energy. The benefits of our approach is shown for controlling vector linear dynamical systems both in the presence of additive dynamical perturbations and communication packet losses. In the case of a single controller-system pair, we show how to determine the best power control policy. For the case of multiple pairs, partial but encouraging results are provided. To provide concrete figures, it is seen that our joint approach may allow the combined cost to be divided by factors as large as 50 for typical simulation settings. The present work would need to be deepened by assuming the distributed nature of the decisions, typically by resorting to game-theoretical tools to come up with fully distributed and reconfigurable transmit power policies.

Acknowledgements. This work was fully supported by the RTE-CentraleSupelec Chair.

References

1. Balaghiinaloo, M., Antunes, D.J., Varma, V.S., Postoyan, R., Heemels, W.M.: LQ-power consistent control: leveraging transmission power selection in control systems. In: 2020 European Control Conference (ECC), pp. 1701–1706 (2020)
2. Besson, O., Vincent, F., Stoica, P., Gershman, A.B.: Approximate maximum likelihood estimators for array processing in multiplicative noise environments. IEEE Trans. Signal Process. **48**(9), 2506–2518 (2000)
3. Delchamps, D.F.: Stabilizing a linear system with quantized state feedback. IEEE Trans. Autom. Control **35**(8), 916–924 (1990)
4. Gatsis, K., Ribeiro, A., Pappas, G.J.: Optimal power management in wireless control systems. IEEE Trans. Autom. Control **59**(6), 1495–1510 (2014)
5. Gatsis, K., Ribeiro, A., Pappas, G.J.: Random access design for wireless control systems. Automatica **91**, 1–9 (2018)
6. Hespanha, J.P., Naghshtabrizi, P., Xu, Y.: A survey of recent results in networked control systems. Proc. IEEE **95**(1), 138–162 (2007)
7. Primbs, J.A., Sung, C.H.: Stochastic receding horizon control of constrained linear systems with state and control multiplicative noise. IEEE Trans. Autom. Control **54**(2), 221–230 (2009)
8. Quevedo, D.E., Gupta, V., Ma, W., Yüksel, S.: Stochastic stability of event-triggered anytime control. IEEE Trans. Autom. Control **59**(12), 3373–3379 (2014)
9. Schenato, L.: To zero or to hold control inputs with lossy links? IEEE Trans. Autom. Control **54**(5), 1093–1099 (2009)
10. Shi, L., Yuan, Y., Chen, J.: Finite horizon LQR control with limited controller-system communication. IEEE Trans. Autom. Control **58**(7), 1835–1841 (2013)
11. Sun, Y., Lasaulce, S., Kieffer, M., Postoyan, R., Nešić, D.: Energy-efficient transmission policies for the linear quadratic control of scalar systems. arXiv preprint arXiv:2205.13867 (2022)

12. Varma, V.S., de Oliveira, A.M., Postoyan, R., Morărescu, I.C., Daafouz, J.: Energy-efficient time-triggered communication policies for wireless networked control systems. IEEE Trans. Autom. Control **65**(10), 4324–4331 (2020)
13. Willems, J.L., Willems, J.C.: Feedback stabilizability for stochastic systems with state and control dependent noise. Automatica **12**(3), 277–283 (1976)

Statistical Moments of the Temporal Spectrum of Electromagnetic Waves in the Equatorial Ionosphere

Giorgi Jandieri[1]([✉]) [iD] and Akira Ishimaru[2]

[1] Georgian Technical University, 0178 Tbilisi, Georgia
`george.jandieri@gtu.ge`
[2] University of Washington, Seattle, WA 98195, USA

Abstract. Second order statistical moments of the temporal spectrum of scattered ordinary and extraordinary electromagnetic waves in the equatorial ionosphere are considered analytically and numerically using geometrical optics approximation and random transport equation. Broadening of this spectrum and shift of its maximum of these waves are analyzed. Investigations are carried out for different distances outside of a plasma slab and different frequencies of electron density pulsations. Statistical moments contain anisotropic coefficient of elongated plasmonic structures, tilt angle of these structures with respect to the external magnetic field, conductivity and velocity of a plasma stream. These factors have an influence on the evaluation of the temporal spectrum varying propagation distances traveling by these waves in the turbulent terrestrial ionosphere. Precursors of scattered extraordinary waves is observed for the extraordinary wave in a plasma slab, a new double-humped effect is revealed. Numerical calculations are carried out using ground-based radar systems and satellites observation data.

Keywords: Ionosphere · Statistical moments · Temporal spectrum

1 Introduction

Theoretical investigations and observations of the statistical characteristics of scattered radio waves in the terrestrial ionosphere is important in many practical applications [1–3]. Fluctuations in signal power and phase often accompany radio wave propagation over earth-space paths as a result of inhomogeneities in the ionospheric electron density. Conductivity has an influence on the statistical moments of radio waves propagating in the ionosphere.

Peculiarities of the spatial spectrum of electromagnetic waves propagating in F-region of the polar ionosphere were considered in [4–9] using the geometrical optics approximation and modify smooth perturbation method. It was shown [10] that anisotropic conductivity has a substantial influence on the statistical characteristics of the temporal spectrum in the polar ionosphere. Spatial-temporal fluctuations of electron density irregularities, anisotropy and the tilt angle of elongated ionospheric plasmonic structures with respect to the geomagnetic lines of forces growth intensity of the frequency

© The Author(s), under exclusive license to Springer Nature Switzerland AG 2023
E. Sabir et al. (Eds.): UNet 2022, LNCS 13853, pp. 41–51, 2023.
https://doi.org/10.1007/978-3-031-29419-8_4

fluctuations of scattered electromagnetic waves. Multiple scattered effects of waves are revealed more strongly when secondary waves with close frequencies propagate in a narrow spatial angle near the direction of an initial wave.

Currently equatorial ionosphere is of great interest. Statistical characteristics of electromagnetic waves scattered in this region were not considered till now. Ionospheric conductivity is one of the important parameters playing a key role in the ionospheric transport mechanism and in dynamics of irregularities having different spatial scales. Harmonic waves scattered on these irregularities become nonharmonic. Spectral lines broaden and the features of the temporal spectrum modify. Spread of the temporal spectrum is connected with quasi-random ionospheric irregularities, and shift of its maximum is associated with the relative motion of the ionospheric plasma.

This paper addresses transformation of the temporal spectrum of both the ordinary (O-wave) and extraordinary (E-wave) electromagnetic waves in the equatorial ionosphere with smoothly-varying ionospheric irregularities. We will use four-dimensional WKB (Wentzel-Kramers-Brillouin) method and stochastic transfer equation for the complex frequency investigating the influence of an absorption and anisotropy on the statistical characteristics of electromagnetic waves in the turbulent collision conductive magnetized plasma. Broadening and shift of the maximum of the temporal spectrum of scattered waves contains anisotropy parameters: geomagnetic field, velocity of a plasma flow, Hall's, Pedersen and longitudinal conductivities, anisotropy coefficient of elongated plasmonic structures and tilt angle of these irregularities with respect to the external magnetic field.

The problem is formulated in Sect. 2, where the second order statistical moments describing the broadening of the temporal spectrum and the displacement of its maximum is derived analytically applying the eikonal equation and the stochastic transport equation for the complex frequency. Numerical calculations are carried out in Sect. 3 applying the experimental data. Conclusions are made in Sect. 4.

2 Statistical Moments of the Temporal Spectrum

Integrated and asymptotic methods are traditional instruments studying propagation and scattering of electromagnetic waves in the turbulent plasma. The geometrical optics method, which is the most developed and proved both theoretically and experimentally, approximately describes wave fields of short (2–40 MHz) radio waves propagation in the Earth ionosphere with smoothly spatial-temporal irregularities [1–3, 11]. This method contains the condition, when the characteristic spatial scale of electron density irregularities exceeds the wavelength of an incident electromagnetic wave, $l >> \lambda$. In this case only forward scattering is important and the WKB solution is valid for the wave propagation. The phase satisfies the eikonal equation for a normal wave $c^2 k^2 = \omega^2 N^2(\omega, k, p_i)$, here $\mathbf{k}(\mathbf{r}, t) = -\nabla \varphi, \omega(\mathbf{r}, t) = \partial \varphi / \partial t$ are the local wave vector and the frequency, respectively, which are slowly-varying functions of position and time; p_i is an arbitrary parameter characterizing turbulent plasma; $N^2(\omega, \mathbf{k})$ is the complex refraction index of a normal wave, c is the speed of light. In general case eikonal equation is nonlinear differential equation for the eikonal $\varphi(\mathbf{r}, t)$. Therefore, it's convenient to consider stochastic transport equation for both the frequency $\omega(\mathbf{r}, t)$ and wave vector [12, 13] are random function of the spatial coordinates and time. Electron concentration contains constant and fluctuating terms which is a random function of position and time $n(\mathbf{r}, t) = n_0 + n_1(\mathbf{r}, t)$, $|n_1| \ll n_0$. Taking into account complexity of refraction index $N(\mathbf{r}, t) = N_0(\mathbf{r}, t) - i N_1(\mathbf{r}, t)$ we can investigate statistical moments of the frequency fluctuations of a scattered electromagnetic wave in the equatorial ionosphere.

In the equatorial ionosphere the external magnetic field is directed along the Y-axis. In this case components of the complex permittivity tensor are: $\tilde{\varepsilon}_{xx} = \tilde{\varepsilon}_{zz} = \varepsilon_\perp - i\,(\tilde{\sigma}_\perp + sg)$, $\tilde{\varepsilon}_{xz} = -s\,æ\,\delta + i\,(\tilde{\sigma}_H + æ)$, $\tilde{\varepsilon}_{yy} = (\varepsilon_\perp + p_0 u) - i\,(\tilde{\sigma}_{||} + s\,v)$, $\tilde{\varepsilon}_{xx} = \tilde{\varepsilon}_{zz}$, $\tilde{\varepsilon}_{zx} = -\tilde{\varepsilon}_{xz}$, $\varepsilon_{xy} = \varepsilon_{yx} = \varepsilon_{yz} = \varepsilon_{zy} = 0$; here: $p_0 = v/(1-u)$, $g = p_0\,(1+u)/(1-u)$, $\delta = 2/(1-u)$, $g_1 = (3-u)/(1-u)$, $æ = p_0\sqrt{u}$. Nondimensional magneto-ionic parameters of the ionosphere plasma $v(\mathbf{r}) = \omega_p^2/\omega^2$ and $u = (e\,H_0/m_e\,c\,\omega)^2$ contains plasma frequency $\omega_p(\mathbf{r}) = \left[4\pi N_e(\mathbf{r})\,e^2/m_e\right]^{1/2}$ and the electron gyro frequency. The normalized conductivity tensor $\tilde{\sigma} = 4\pi\,\hat{\sigma}/k_0 c$ of ionospheric plasma for equatorial latitude [14] contains the Hall's σ_H, Pedersen $\sigma_\perp$ and longitudinal $\sigma_{||}$ conductivities:

$$\sigma_H = e^2 n_e \left(\frac{\omega_e}{m_e\,(v_e^2 + \omega_e^2)} - \frac{\omega_i}{m_i\,(v_{in}^2 + \omega_i^2)} \right),$$

$$\sigma_\perp = e^2 n_e \left(\frac{v_e}{m_e\,(v_e^2 + \omega_e^2)} + \frac{v_i}{m_i\,(v_{in}^2 + \omega_i^2)} \right), \quad \sigma_{||} = e^2 n_e \left(\frac{1}{m_e\,v_e} + \frac{1}{m_m\,v_{in}} \right)$$

here: $k_0 = \omega_0/c$, e and m_e are the charge and mass of an electron, $v_e = v_{en} + v_{in}$ is the effective collision frequency of electrons with other plasma particles; ω_e and ω_i are the electron and ion gyrofrequencies.

Complex refractive index N of the conductive collision ionospheric magnetized plasma in the equatorial region of the terrestrial atmosphere at $s \neq 0$, $\tilde{\sigma}_{ij} \neq 0$ and $s \ll \varepsilon_{ij}$, $\tilde{\sigma}_{ij}$ is as follows:

$$N(n, \omega) = N_0(n_0, \omega) - i\,N_1(n, \omega), \tag{1}$$

here: $N_0 = \sqrt{(r + R_0)/2}$, $N_1 = \sqrt{(r - R_0)/2}$, $R_0 = 1 - 2\,(T_1 T_0 - T_2\,\psi_2)/(T_1^2 + T_2^2)$, $r = \sqrt{R_0^2 + R_1^2}$, $D_1 = \sqrt{(r_1 + B)/2}$, $R_1 = 2\,(T_2 T_0 + T_1\,\psi_2)/(T_1^2 + T_2^2)$, $T_1 = A \pm D_1$, $T_2 = \psi_4 \pm D_2$, $r_1 = \sqrt{B^2 + C^2}$, $D_2 = \sqrt{(r_1 - B)/2}$, $T_0 = p_0\,v(1 - v) + \psi_1$, $B = p_0^2\left[u^2 \sin^4\theta + 4u\,(1-v)^2 \cos^2\theta\right] + (\psi_5 - \psi_7)$, $\Lambda_1 = \tilde{\sigma}_\perp^2 + \tilde{\sigma}_H^2 + 2\,æ\,\tilde{\sigma}_H$, $C = \psi_6 - \psi_8$, $\psi_4 = \Lambda_2 - 2(\tilde{\sigma}_\perp\,\sin^2\theta + \tilde{\sigma}_{||}\,\cos^2\theta)$, $\psi_1 = \Lambda_1(\sin^2\theta - \varepsilon_{||}) + \tilde{\sigma}_{||}\,\tilde{\sigma}_\perp$. $(1 + \cos^2\theta - 2\varepsilon_\perp\,\varepsilon_{||})$, $\psi_2 = \tilde{\sigma}_\perp\,\sin^2\theta + \tilde{\sigma}_{||}\,\cos^2\theta - \Lambda_2 + \tilde{\sigma}_{||}\,(\varepsilon_\perp^2 - æ^2 - \Lambda_1) + 2\,\varepsilon_{||}\,\varepsilon_\perp\,\tilde{\sigma}_\perp$, $\Lambda_2 = 2\,\varepsilon_\perp\,\tilde{\sigma}_\perp\,\sin^2\theta + (\varepsilon_{||}\,\tilde{\sigma}_\perp + \varepsilon_\perp\,\tilde{\sigma}_{||})\,(1 + \cos^2\theta)$, $c = (1 - v)$. $[(1 - v)^2 - u]\,(1-u)^{-1}$, $b = \left[2\,(1-v)^2 - 2u + v\,u\,(1 + \cos^2\theta)\right]\,(1-u)^{-1}$, $A = p_0$.

$[2\,(1-v) - u\,\sin^2\theta] + \psi_3$, $a = 1 - p_0\,(1 - u\,\cos^2\theta)$, $\psi_3 = \Lambda_1\,\sin^2\theta + \tilde{\sigma}_{||}\,\tilde{\sigma}_\perp$. $(1 + \cos^2\theta)$, $\psi_6 = 2\,\Lambda_2\left[\Lambda_1\,\sin^2\theta + \tilde{\sigma}_{||}\,\tilde{\sigma}_\perp\,(1 + \cos^2\theta) - b\right]$, $\psi_5 = \Lambda_1^2\,\sin^4\theta + \tilde{\sigma}_{||}^2\,\tilde{\sigma}_\perp^2\,(1 + \cos^2\theta)^2 + 2\,\Lambda_1\,\tilde{\sigma}_{||}\,\tilde{\sigma}_\perp\,\sin^2\theta\,(1 + \cos^2\theta) - 2b\,\left[\Lambda_1\,\sin^2\theta + \tilde{\sigma}_{||}\,\tilde{\sigma}_\perp\,(1 + \cos^2\theta)\right]$.

$\Lambda_3 = (\tilde{\sigma}_\perp \sin^2 \theta + \tilde{\sigma}_{||} \cos^2 \theta) \left[2\varepsilon_{||} \varepsilon_\perp \tilde{\sigma}_\perp + \tilde{\sigma}_{||} (\varepsilon_\perp^2 - \mathfrak{æ}^2 - \Lambda_1) \right], \psi_7 = 4 \left[\Lambda_3 + a \varepsilon_{||} \right.$
$\left. (\Lambda_1 + 2\varepsilon_\perp \tilde{\sigma}_{||} \tilde{\sigma}_\perp) \right], \psi_8 = a \left[2\varepsilon_{||} \varepsilon_\perp \tilde{\sigma}_\perp + \tilde{\sigma}_{||} (\varepsilon_\perp^2 - \mathfrak{æ}^2 - \Lambda_1) \right] + (\tilde{\sigma}_\perp \sin^2 \theta + \tilde{\sigma}_{||} \cdot$
$\cos^2 \theta) \left[c - \varepsilon_{||} (\Lambda_1 + 2\varepsilon_\perp \tilde{\sigma}_{||} \tilde{\sigma}_\perp) \right]$; upper sign corresponds to the O-wave, lower sign –
to the E-wave; θ is the angle between the $\mathbf{H_0}$ and $\mathbf{k_0}$ vectors. For the collisionless and
nonconductive turbulent plasma we obtain the well-known formula [15].

As is well-known [1–3, 13], at propagation of a radio signal in a randomly nonstationary plasma, the Doppler shift is small compared with the transmitter frequency and
the spectrum broadens. Quantitative estimation of the frequency fluctuations is important
as the broadening of a spectrum limits resolution of a Doppler method studying structure
of the receiving signal. On the other hand, measuring the width of Doppler spectrum,
it is possible to solve the revers tasks receiving the information of statistical properties
of plasma. The ratios connecting changes of frequency with the parameters of moving
plasma irregularities it's necessary application of the statistical methods as the tool of the
solution of direct and reverse problems of radio waves propagation in a non-stationary
plasma.

For an arbitrary spatial-temporal dispersion in the geometrical optics approximation neglecting polarization effects, wave frequency satisfies the stochastic differential
transport equation [12, 13]:

$$\left(\frac{\partial}{\partial t} + (\mathbf{u}_{gr} \nabla) \right) \omega = - \frac{\omega u}{c} \sum \frac{\partial N}{\partial p_i} \frac{\partial p_i}{\partial t}, \tag{2}$$

where: $V_g = (d\omega / d\mathbf{k})_{p_i}$ is the group velocity of the wave.

Correlation function and the variance of the frequency fluctuations are the important
statistical characteristics specifying for a nonstationary plasma. They determine the
broadening of the temporal spectrum in the turbulent plasma and can be measured by
experiment. Applying Eq. (2) in the first order approximation the frequency fluctuation
satisfies the stochastic transport differential equation:

From Eq. (2) follows stochastic differential equation for the frequency fluctuation:

$$\frac{\partial \omega_1}{\partial y} + \frac{1}{V_g} \frac{\partial \omega_1}{\partial t} = - \frac{\omega_0}{V_g \, \partial (N \omega_0 / \partial \omega_0)} \frac{\partial N}{\partial n_0} \frac{\partial n_1}{\partial t}, \tag{3}$$

where: $V_g = c[\partial (N \omega) / \partial \omega]^{-1}$ is the local group velocity of an unperturbed wave
propagating along the Y-axis in a conductive collision absorptive magnetized plasma.
In the anisotropic absorbing plasma of the direction of group speed and a wave vector
cannot coincide. In the absence of the spatial dispersion the energy flux coincides with
the group velocity V_g, it also coincides with the direction of an average Poynting vector.
However, conductivity of plasma can lead to the opposite directions of the Poynting's
vector and a wave vector, and, hence, the group velocity will become negative.

For the solution of Eq. (3) we will apply the Fourier transform

$$\omega_1(\mathbf{r}, t) = \int\limits_{-\infty}^{\infty} d\nu \, \Omega \, (\mathbf{r}, \nu) \, \exp(i\nu t).$$

At the observation point beyond a plasma slab $y > L$ we obtain:

$$\Omega\left(\boldsymbol{\rho}_\perp,\ y,\ v\right) = k_0\, v\,\left(\delta_2 - i\,\delta_1\right)\,\exp\left[\frac{v}{c}\,q_0\left(\delta_0 - i\right)y\right]\int\limits_0^L d\zeta\ n_1\left(\boldsymbol{\rho}_\perp,\ \zeta,\ v\right)$$

$$\exp\left[\frac{v}{c}\,q_0\left(-\delta_0 + i\right)\zeta\right], \tag{4}$$

where: $q_0 = N_0 + \omega_0\,\partial N_0/\partial\omega$, $\delta_1 = \partial N_0/\partial n_0$, $\delta_0 = (N_1 + \omega_0\,\partial\, N_1/\partial\,\omega_0)/q_0$,

$$\delta_2 = \partial N_1/\partial n_0;\ \delta_1 = \frac{1}{4N_0}\left[\left(\frac{R_0}{r_1}+1\right)\frac{\partial R_0}{\partial n_0} + \frac{1}{r_1}\,R_1\,\frac{\partial R_1}{\partial n_0}\right], \delta_2 = \frac{1}{4N_1}\left[\left(\frac{R_0}{r_1}-1\right)\cdots\right.$$

$$\left.\frac{\partial R_0}{\partial n_0} + \frac{1}{r_1}\,R_1\,\frac{\partial R_1}{\partial n_0}\right], \boldsymbol{\rho}_\perp = \{x,\ z\}.$$

$$\mathrm{Re}\ \Sigma_2 = 2\pi\,k_0^2\,L\left(\delta_1^2 - \delta_2^2\right)\int\limits_{-\infty}^\infty dv\ v^2\ W_n\left(\boldsymbol{\rho}_\perp = 0,\ \frac{v}{c}\,q_0,\ v\right), \tag{5}$$

where the asterisk designate complex conjugate, $\mathbf{k}_\perp = (k_x,\ k_z)$, $k_y = v\,q_0/c$. The temporal spectrum can be written as:

$$\Sigma = \Sigma_1 + \Sigma_2. \tag{6}$$

Broadening of the temporal power spectrum $\Sigma \equiv\ <\omega_1^2> /\omega_0^2$ can be easily measured by experiment; $\Sigma_1 \equiv\ <\omega_1\,\omega_1^*> /2\,\omega_0^2$ $\Sigma_2 \equiv \mathrm{Re}\ <\omega_1\,\omega_1> /2\,\omega_0^2$. The fact that violation of coherence of the field in the media with large-scale irregularities is connected generally with the phase fluctuations gives the grounds to consider that dispersion of frequency $<\omega_1^2>$ of a wave keeps the sense and in the presence of diffraction. Diffraction can exert the influence on variance of the frequency fluctuations only in Fraunhofer's zone with respect to the spatial scale of irregularities l at $(y/k_0\,l^2) \gg 1$. Physically this can be explained from the fact that the waves scattered under a big angle attenuate faster along a Y axis.

3 Numerical Calculations

Experimental investigations of Doppler frequency displacement of the ionospheric signal show that index of the power-law spectrum is in the interval $3.8 \le p \le 4.6$. In numerical calculations we use $p \approx 4$ [16]. Ground-based radar systems and remote sensing observations show that plasmonic structures are elongated along the geomagnetic lines of forces; transversal scale of these irregularities varies in the range of 100–500, the magnitude of drift velocity was within the limits $65 - 270$ m/s (the typical velocities of ionospheric motions $V_0 = 60 \div 100$ m/s, velocity 100 m/s is used in numerical calculations. Power-law spectral index is within the limit $p = 1.4 \div 4.8$ applying the "Sura" heating facility working in the frequency band of $4.7 \div 9$ MHz [17].

Measurements at Kingston (Jamaica) show that the irregularities between heights of 153 and 617 km leading to the scintillation are moving along the magnetic lines of forces field lines in the F–region [18]. Inclination angle of the elongated plasmonic structures approximately is 16^0. The anisotropic spectral features in the F–region is defined for the Gaussian and power-law spectra. For F region large scale sizes irregularities (~ 10 km) become unstable, and dissipate their energy by generating small sized irregularities, as is the case in turbulence. In the equatorial region the large-scale irregularities are most likely produced by convective electric field.

An RH-560 rocket flight studying the spread of electron density irregularities in F region show that electron density irregularities were present continuously between 150 and 257 m. Experimental observation show that small-scale electron density irregularities have linear scale in the interval from 20 m up to 200 m corresponding to the anisotropic Gaussian spectrum.

We will use the spatial-temporal spectrum of electron density irregularities [20]:

$$
V_n(\mathbf{k}, \nu) = \frac{\sigma_n^2}{16\pi^2} \frac{l_\parallel^3}{\chi^2 \left\{ 1 + l_\perp^2 [k_x^2 + (\nu q_0/c)^2] + l_\parallel^2 k_z^2 \right\}^2} \exp\left(-\frac{k_x^2 l_\perp^2}{4} - m_0^2 \frac{k_y^2 l_\perp^2}{4} - \right.
$$
$$
\left. - m_1 \frac{k_z l_\parallel}{4} \nu T - m_2 \frac{\nu^2 T^2}{4} \right) \exp\left(-\frac{k_x^2 l_\perp^2}{4} - m_0^2 \frac{k_y^2 l_\parallel^2}{4} - m_1 \frac{k_z l_\parallel}{4} \nu T - m_2 \frac{\nu^2 T^2}{4} \right)
$$

(7)

where: $\zeta = 1 + \tau^2 (l_*/l_\perp)^2$, $p_2 = (\sin^2\alpha + \chi^2 \cos^2\alpha)/\chi^2$, $c_0 = (1/\zeta) + p_2 Q_3^2/Q_0^2$
$m_2 = c_0 + p_2 q_0^2 \tau_0^2/Q_0^2$, $Q_3 = \tau/(\zeta p_2)$, $Q_0 = [1 - \tau/(2\zeta)]^{1/2}$, $Q_1 = (\chi^2 - 1)\tau$
$\sin\alpha \cos\alpha/\chi^2 p_2$, $l_* = l_\perp l_\parallel (l_\perp^2 \sin^2\alpha + l_\parallel^2 \cos^2\alpha)^{-1/2}$, $m_0^2 = a_0 - 1/(p_2 \chi^2)$,
$\tau = V_0 T/l_\parallel$, $b_0 = (Q_1/\zeta) - p_2 Q_2 Q_3/Q_0^2$, $b_0 = (Q_1/\zeta) - p_2 Q_2 Q_3/Q_0^2$,
$Q_2 = (\chi^2 - 1) \sin\alpha \cos\alpha/(\sin^2\alpha + \chi^2 \cos^2\alpha) - (\tau Q_1/\zeta p_2)$, $\tau_0 = l_\parallel/cT$,
$a_0 = (Q_1^2/\zeta) + p_2(Q_2^2/Q_0^2)$.

Elongated electron density irregularities have the anisotropy factor $\chi = l_\parallel/l_\perp$ containing both longitudinal and transversal scales with respect to the geomagnetic lines of forces; α is the inclination angle of these irregularities with respect to the geomagnetic lines of forces. Anisotropy of the shape of irregularities is connected with the diffusion in the field align and field perpendicular directions; $T = l/V$ is the characteristic temporal scale of electron density fluctuations.

Substituting (8) into Eqs. (5) and (6) we obtain the broadening of the temporal spectrum of scattered ordinary and extraordinary waves in the equatorial ionosphere:

$$
\Sigma_1 = \frac{\sigma_n^2}{8\pi} (\delta_1^2 + \delta_2^2) \frac{\xi^2}{\tau_0 q_0 \delta_0 \sqrt{p_1}} \frac{1}{(\omega_0 T)^2} \int_{-\infty}^{\infty} d\eta \frac{\eta}{\left[1 + \left(1 + \frac{4}{\chi^2} \frac{p_2^2}{p_1^2} \right) \tau_0^2 q_0^2 \eta^2 \right]^2}
$$
$$
\exp\left\{ -\frac{\eta^2}{4} \left[1 + 4 q_0^2 \tau_0^2 \left(\frac{p_2}{4} - \frac{p_2^2}{p_1^2} \right) \right] \right\} \left\{ \exp\left[2 q_0 \delta_0 \tau_0 \frac{L}{l_\parallel} \frac{y}{L} \eta \right] - \right.
$$
$$
\left. - \exp\left[2 q_0 \delta_0 \tau_0 \left(\frac{y}{L} - 1 \right) \eta \right] \right\},
$$

(8)

$$
\Sigma_2 = \frac{\sigma_n^2}{4} (\delta_1^2 - \delta_2^2) \frac{\xi^2}{\chi (\omega_0 T)^2 \sqrt{p_1}} \frac{L}{l_\parallel} \int_{-\infty}^{\infty} d\eta \frac{\eta^2}{\left[1 + \left(1 + \frac{4}{\chi^2} \frac{p_2^2}{p_1^2} \right) \tau_0^2 q_0^2 \eta^2 \right]^2}
$$
$$
\exp\left(-\frac{\eta^2}{4} \right)
$$

(9)

These second order statistical moments are valid for both absorbing, and of active media. This effect is connected with the amplification of the frequency along the external geomagnetic field [13], but also amplify. The modulator in our case is a turbulent plasma layer.

Numerical calculations are carried out for an incident wave with frequency 3 MHz. Ionospheric parameters: $u = 0.22$, $v = 0.28$, $k_0 = 6.28 \cdot 10^{-2}\ m^{-1}$.

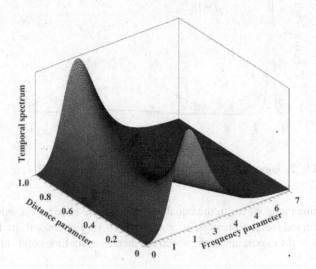

Fig. 1. Three dimensional temporal spectrum

Figure 1 illustrates three-dimensional temporal spectrum vs. dimensionless frequency $((v_0/\omega_0) \sim 10^{-3}$ and distance parameters $(y/L) = 0 \div 1$ in the plasma slab. Frequency of an incident wave on three orders exceeds the frequency of turbulent plasma pulsations. Anisotropy factor of elongated plasmonic structures $\chi = 7$, tilt angle $\alpha = 10^0$, thickness of a slab ten times exceeds longitudinal characteristic spatial scale of electron density fluctuations, $\xi = k_0 l_{\parallel} = 10$.

Curves describing appearance of the precursor in the temporal spectrum for E-wave as a function of dimensionless distance parameter $(y/L) = 0 \div 18$ are plotted on Fig. 2. Anisotropy factor $\chi = 25$, non-dimensional frequency parameter is in the interval $(v_0/\omega_0) = 2.4 \cdot 10^{-4} \div 1 \cdot 10^{-5}$, $(L/l_{\parallel}) = 10$. Precursor arises near the plasma boundary and gradually is disappeared transferring its energy to the main part of the spectrum. Increasing a tilt angle in the interval $5^0 \leq \alpha \leq 15^0$ broadening of the temporal spectrum of E-wave decreases two times and its maximum shifts to the right. For large-scale irregularities $\xi = 890$, at $\alpha = 12^0$, varying anisotropy factor in the interval $8 \leq \chi \leq 15$, all curves have the same maximum at $(y/L) = 10$.

Figure 3 shows evolution of the temporal spectrum for scattered O-wave in the equatorial turbulent plasma for different anisotropy factor χ at $\xi = 890$, $\alpha = 30^0$. Contrary to the previous case, broadening of O-wave precursor is small near the plasma boundary and in the main part of the temporal spectrum it increases in proportion of the anisotropic factor, at $(v_0/\omega_0) = 3 \cdot 10^{-4} \div 1 \cdot 10^{-5}$. Numerical calculations show that at $\chi = 25$ and small tilt angle $\alpha \approx 5^0$ maximum of the temporal spectrum of O-wave displaces to the left. Hence, shift of maximums of the temporal spectrum for the O-

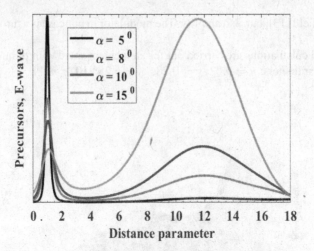

Fig. 2. Formation of precursors in the plasma slab for the E-wave.

and E- electromagnetic waves in the equatorial ionosphere have an opposite direction. For E-wave at fixed inclination angle $\alpha = 4^0$, $\xi = 50$ varying anisotropy factor in the interval $4 \leq \chi \leq 14$ maximum of the spectrum increases six times and shift to the left four times.

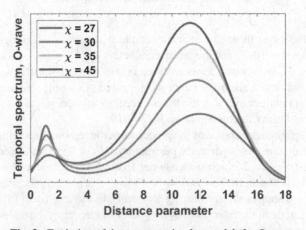

Fig. 3. Evolution of the precursor in plasma slab for O-wave

Figure 4 depicts the broadening of the temporal spectrum and shift of its maximum for scattered O-wave in the equatorial ionosphere as a function of non-dimensional frequency parameter $((\nu_0/\omega_0) \sim 10^{-3}$ at the inclination angle $\alpha = 6^0$ varying anisotropy factor $10 \leq \chi \leq 15$. In this case frequency of turbulent pulsations broadens of the spectrum two times and its maximum displaces to the right two times, while in this case no observed displacement of maximum in E-wave temporal spectrum.

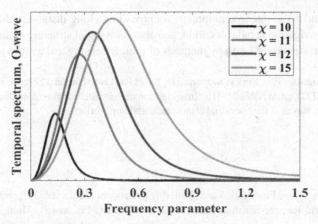

Fig. 4. Broadening of the tmporal spectrum vs. nondimensional frequency parameter for the O-wave

4 Numerical Calculations

Analytical calculation and numerical simulations of the temporal spectrum of scattered electromagnetic waves propagation in the equatorial ionosphere were carried out. Index of refraction for this region of the terrestrial atmosphere has been obtained for the first time. Statistical characteristics of the temporal spectrum (broadening and displacement of its maximum) of scattered ordinary and extraordinary electromagnetic waves propagating in the conductive collision magnetized plasma are investigated in the geometrical optics approximation using the stochastic transport equation for the frequency fluctuation. Experimentally measuring second order statistical moments: correlation function and the variance of the frequency fluctuations characterizing the broadening of the temporal spectrum and shift of its maximum has been obtained for the arbitrary correlation function of electron density fluctuations.

At numerical calculations we use experimental data of the turbulent conductive collision magnetized plasma: plasma flow velocity, anisotropy factor and dip angle of prolate electron density irregularities with respect to the external magnetic field. Investigation show that the anisotropy factor and inclination angle of electron density irregularities have a substantial influence on the broadening of the temporal power spectrum and shift of its maximum of a scattered O- and E- waves in the equatorial ionosphere. New double humped effect has been revealed arises in the temporal spectrum of scattered O-wave in the equatorial region, contrary to the polar ionosphere. Shift of maximums of the temporal spectrum for the O- and E- electromagnetic waves have the opposite directions. Diffraction effects have the greatest influence on the variance of the frequency in the nonstationary plasma at longitudinal propagation, when the absorption is essential.

Investigation of the observing statistical moments by satellite and ground-based radar systems yields the useful information of electron density irregularities in the ionospheric plasma. Relevance of a research is defined by active use of electromagnetic waves of short-wave band in the antenna equipment, for providing a long-distance radio communication, radio navigation, a radar-location, and also studying of structure of an ionosphere - the upper atmosphere of Earth by methods of remote sensing and a radio tomography.

Acknowledgements. This work is supported by Shota Rustaveli National Science Foundation of Georgia (SRNSFG), grant NRG-21-316 "Investigation of the statistical characteristics of scattered electromagnetic waves in the terrestrial atmosphere and application".

References

1. Ishimaru, A.: Wave Propagation and Scattering in Random Media, vol. 2. Turbulence, Rough Surfaces and Remote Sensing, IEEE Press, New Jersey, Piscataway, Multiple Scattering (1997)
2. Gershman, B.N., Erukhimov, L.M., Yashin, Y.Y.: Wave Phenomena in the Ionosphere and Space Plasma, Nauka, Moscow (1984)
3. Rytov, S.M., Kravtsov, Y.A., Tatarskii, V.I.: Principles of Statistical Radiophysics, vol. 4. Waves Propagation Through Random Media, Springer, Berlin, New York (1989). https://link.springer.com/book/9783642726842
4. Jandieri, G., Ishimaru, A., Gavrilenko, V., Kharshiladze, O.: Statistical moments and scintillation level of scattered electromagnetic waves in the magnetized plasma. PIER C **84**, 11–22 (2018)
5. Jandieri, G., Ishimaru, A., Rawat, B.: Peculiarities of the spatial power spectrum of scattered electromagnetic waves in the turbulent collision magnetized plasma. PIER **152**, 137–149 (2015)
6. Jandieri, G., Zhukova, N., Jandieir, I.: Statistical characteristics of scattered radiation in medium with spatial-temporal fluctuations of electron density and external magnetic field. JEMAA **4**, 243–251 (2012)
7. Jandieri, G., Ishimaru, A., Jandieri, V., Khantadze, A., Diasamidze, Z.: Model computations of angular power spectra for anisotropic absorptive turbulent magnetized plasma. PIER **70**, 307–328 (2007)
8. Jandieri, G.: Double-humped effect in the turbulent magnetized plasma. PIER M **48**, 95–102 (2016)
9. Jandieri, G, Diasamidze, Zh., Takidze, I.: Second order statistical moments of the phase fluctuations of scattered radiation in the collision magnetized plasma. In: WORLDCOMP 2016, CSC 2016, pp. 134–138. CSREA Press (2016)
10. Jandieri, G., Ishimaru, A., Rawat, B., Tugushi, N.: Temporal spectrum of scattered electromagnetic waves in the conductive collision turbulent magnetized plasma. Adv. Electromagn. **11**(1), 1–8 (2022)
11. Kravtsov, Y., Orlov, Y.: Geometrical Optics of Inhomogeneous Media. Nauka, Moscow (1980)
12. Kravtsov, Y., Ostrovsky, L.A., Stepanov, N.S.: Geometrical optics of inhomogeneous and nonstationary dispersive media. Proc. IEEE **62**(11), 1492–1510 (1974)
13. Gavrilenko, V.G., Stepanov, N.S.: Statistical characteristics of waves in the chaotically media with spatial-temporal irregularities. Izv. VUZ. Radiophys, **20**, 3–35 (1987)
14. Aydoglu, M., Guzel, E., Yesil, A., Ozcan, O., Canyilmaz, M.: Comparison of the calculated absorption and the measured field strength of HF waves reflected from the ionosphere. Nuovo Chimento **30**(3), 243–253 (2007)
15. Ginzburg, V.L.: Propagation of Electromagnetic Waves in Plasma. Gordon and Beach, New York (1961)

16. Gailit, T.A., Gusev, V.D., Erukhimov, L.M., Shpiro, P.I.: On spectrum of phase fluctuations at ionospheric remote sensing. Izv. VUZ. Radiophys. **26**, 795–800 (1983)
17. Bakhmet'eva, N.V., et al.: Investigation by backscatter radar of artificial irregularities produced in ionospheric plasma heating experiments. J. Atmos. Solar-Terrest. Phys. **59**(18), 2257–2263 (1997). https://doi.org/10.1016/S1364-6826(96)00120-4
18. Chen, A.A., Kent, G.S.: Determination of the orientation of ionospheric irregularities causing scintillation of signals from earth satellites. JATP **34**, 1411–1414 (1972)
19. Raizada, S., Sinha, H.S.: Some new features of electron density irregularities over SHAR during strong spread F. Ann. Geophys. **18**, 141–151 (2000)
20. Jandieri, G., Ishimaru, A., Rawat, B., Diasamidze, Z.: Power spectra of ionospheric scintillations. Adv. Electromagn. **6**, 42–51 (2017)

Resource Allocation in 5G/6G

Towards Facilitating URLLC in UAV-enabled MEC Systems for 6G Networks

Ali Ranjha[✉][iD], Diala Naboulsi[iD], and Mohamed El-Emary

Département de Génie Logiciel et des TI, École de Technologie Supérieure, Montréal, Canada

{ali-nawaz.ranjha.1,mohamed-ibrahim-mahmoud.el-emary.1}@ens.etsmtl.ca, diala.naboulsi@etsmtl.ca

Abstract. This paper jointly studies the fairness and efficient trajectory design problem for facilitating ultra-reliable and low latency communications (URLLC) in unmanned aerial vehicle (UAV)-enabled mobile edge computing (MEC) systems, in the context of sixth-generation (6G) networks. In this regard, a fixed-wing UAV is equipped with an aerial server, and it is programmed to collect critical task allocation data from Internet of things (IoT) devices deployed on the ground. To prolong the operational time of the ground IoT devices, we aim to minimize the maximum energy consumption among the ground IoT devices. Furthermore, due to the non-convexity of the original problem, we use successive convex approximations (SCA) to divide the original problem into two convex sub-problems. To this end, we propose an iterative sub-optimal joint fairness and trajectory design algorithm (JFTDA), which is numerically shown to yield fair data allocation for task offloading and comparable energy consumption among all the ground IoT devices to that of different deployment scenarios. Lastly, the proposed JFTDA also yields a decoding error probability of less than 10^{-5} ensuring URLLC for the UAV-enabled MEC systems.

Keywords: URLLC · UAV-enabled MEC · fairness · trajectory design

1 Introduction

THE sixth-generation (6G) networks are envisioned to provide wireless connectivity to ground Internet of things (IoT) devices, enabling a wide array of mission-critical applications including tactical communications, intelligent transportation systems, factory automation, telemedicine, as well as unmanned aerial vehicles (UAVs) control and non-payload communications (CNPC) [10]. Moreover, these mission-critical applications are facilitated by ultra-reliable and low latency communications (URLLC) services offered by the 6G networks requiring reliability and latency-centric designs instead of throughput-centric designs prevalent in previous mobile generation technologies [1]. Furthermore, subject to

E. Sabir et al. (Eds.): UNet 2022, LNCS 13853, pp. 55–67, 2023.
https://doi.org/10.1007/978-3-031-29419-8_5

the considered mission-critical application, URLLC aims to achieve ultra-high reliability of 10^{-5} and a latency of 1 ms by using short blocklength data packets. In this regard, URLLC uses the short blocklength equation, which is the penalized form of Shannon's capacity equation based on the strong law of large numbers [5,6,8]. This poses a dual challenge for network and system designers as reliability and latency are on two opposite ends of the spectrum, and the short blocklength equation is neither convex nor concave with respect to (wrt) transmit power and the blocklength [9,11,12]. Additionally, IoT devices have limited memory resources and thus, cannot execute computationally intensive tasks such as required by frequent mission-critical updates, functional status of factory apparatus, essential vitals of a soldier in a warzone, or a critical patient under medical observation. Resultantly, mobile edge computing (MEC) systems have emerged to remedy these issues. Due to the critical nature of the aforementioned applications, traditional fixed edge servers installed at the terrestrial base stations (BSs) are undesirable, and a new paradigm is needed. Consequently, UAV-enabled MEC has gained traction owing to flexible mobility and favorable line-of-sight (LoS) communication links compared to terrestrial BSs [2].

Recently, the research community has made a valiant effort to study the intricated problems of resource allocation, trajectory design, and task scheduling in UAV-enabled MEC systems. In [3], the authors studied task offloading, intending to minimize the energy consumption on the UAV side. The authors jointly optimized user transmit power, task load allocation, and the UAV trajectory to achieve this goal. To this end, the authors proposed the so-called Dinkelbach algorithm to tackle the formulated non-convex problem. Similarly, in [4], the authors proposed a reflective intelligent surface (RIS)-assisted UAV for MEC to address the blockage caused by ground obstacles leading to poor quality-of-service (QoS) in terms of higher latency. In this regard, the authors addressed the problem using successive convex approximations (SCA). Comparably, in [7], the authors investigated multi-UAV-assisted multiaccess MEC systems. Moreover, the authors jointly optimized user transmit power, bandwidth allocation, UAVs trajectories, and data allocation. Nonetheless, in these works, the authors did not consider a joint resource allocation, i.e., fairness in data allocation and trajectory design framework for facilitating URLLC systems utilizing short blocklength data packets, essential for fully exploiting the benefits of UAV-enabled MEC, especially for 6G networks. To this end, in this paper, we study the problem of minimizing the maximum energy consumption by jointly designing fair data allocation among IoT devices and efficient trajectory design for the UAV hovering above them in the service area. Furthermore, we utilize successive convex approximations (SCA) to decompose the original non-convex problem into two convex sub-problems. Additionally, we utilize successive convex approximations (SCA) to decompose the original non-convex problem into two convex sub-problems. In this regard, we propose an iterative sub-optimal joint fairness and trajectory design algorithm (JFTDA) to tackle the original non-convex problem. Finally, we show that our proposed JFTDA optimizes trajectory, ensures fair data allocation, yields comparable results to distinct deployment scenarios as well as gives a decoding error probability of less than 10^{-5}, which establishes URLLC for the UAV-enabled MEC systems.

2 System Model and Problem Formulation

As illustrated in Fig. 1, we assume an aerial MEC system primarily composed of a fixed-wing UAV, which is equipped with an on board aerial computing server as well as a total of K IoT devices, which are denoted by $\mathcal{K} = \{1, 2, \ldots, K\}$ deployed on the ground. During a time horizon T of finite duration, each IoT device denoted by k performs partial task offloading, such that the task data in bits is independent and the computing server executes it at the UAV side. Without loss of generality, we assume that the location of IoT devices on the ground is fixed within the time horizon T. Moreover, we divide T into N time slots, such that the size of each time slot is denoted by $\delta = T/N$, where δ is infinitesimal such that the UAV location is fixed during each δ. Furthermore, each k is allocated equal bandwidth B and it uses orthogonal frequency division multiple access (OFDMA) to offload the task data represented by $\mathcal{A}_{kn} \triangleq (\mathcal{D}_{kn}, \mathcal{X}_{kn})$ to the UAV. Additionally, each IoT device k in the n-th time slot has input-data represented by $\mathcal{D}_{kn}$ (bits) as well as the required amount of task data of IoT device k is $\mathcal{D}_k^{\text{req}}$ (bits). Similarly, the computing intensity required by each IoT device k in the n-th time slot is given as $\mathcal{X}_{kn}$ (CPU cycles per bit). Now, we assume that each IoT device k on the ground is located at $\mathbf{w}_k = [w_{k1}, w_{k2}, 0]^T$, $\forall k \in \mathcal{K}$ in a three-dimensional (3D) cartesian coordinate system, whereas the UAV is located at $\mathbf{q}_n = [q_{n1}, q_{n2}, H]^T$, $\forall n \in \mathcal{N}$ in the n-th time slot, where H is fixed. Likewise, each IoT device k in the n-th time slot transmits with a fixed power given as p_{kn}, whereas the velocity of the UAV in the n-th time slot is represented by $\mathbf{v}_n$. In this regard, we set up UAV mobility constraints to bound the UAV in the service area, which are as follows

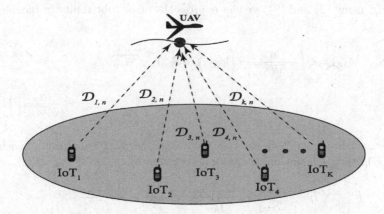

Fig. 1. Illustration of facilitating URLLC in UAV-enabled MEC system

$$\mathcal{C}_1 : \begin{cases} \mathbf{q}_1 = \mathbf{q}_i, \\ \mathbf{q}_{N+1} = \mathbf{q}_f, \\ \mathbf{v}_n = \dfrac{\mathbf{q}_{n+1} - \mathbf{q}_n}{\delta}, \ \forall n \in \mathcal{N}, \end{cases} \tag{1}$$

where $\mathbf{q}_i$ and $\mathbf{q}_f$ denote the initial as well as the final locations of UAV, respectively. Moreover, we assume that a line-of-sight link dominates the ground-to-UAV channels. Furthermore, according to [6], the short blocklength transmission rate of the IoT device k in the n-th slot is given by

$$\mathcal{R}_{kn} = B \log_2 (1 + \mathcal{S}_{kn}) - \frac{B}{\ln 2} \sqrt{\frac{\mathcal{V}(\mathcal{S}_{kn})}{\mathcal{M}_{kn}}} \cdot P(\varepsilon_{kn}),$$

$$\mathcal{V}(\mathcal{S}_{kn}) = 1 - \frac{1}{(1 + \mathcal{S}_{kn})^2}, \qquad g_{kn} = \frac{\beta_0}{\|\mathbf{q}_n - \mathbf{w}_k\|_2^2}, \tag{2}$$

$$\mathcal{S}_{kn} = \frac{p_{kn} g_{kn}}{\sigma^2} = \frac{p_{kn} \beta_0}{\sigma^2 \|\mathbf{q}_n - \mathbf{w}_k\|_2^2} = \frac{\gamma_{kn}}{\|\mathbf{q}_n - \mathbf{w}_k\|_2^2},$$

$$P(Q(x)) \equiv x, \qquad Q(x) = \frac{1}{\sqrt{2\pi}} \int\limits_x^\infty e^{-\frac{t^2}{2}} \, dt,$$

Here, the term $\mathcal{S}_{kn}$ means signal-to-noise ratio (SNR), σ^2 is the noise power, and β_0 represents channel power gain at a reference distance of 1 m. Moreover, the terms $\varepsilon_{kn} \leqslant \varepsilon_{\max}$ and $\mathcal{M}_{kn} \leqslant \mathcal{M}_{\max}$, and g_{kn} represent decoding error probability, blocklength, and the channel gain between the UAV and the IoT device k in the n-th slot. Furthermore, the function $\mathcal{V}(\mathcal{S}_{kn})$ represents channel dispersion and $P(\varepsilon_{kn})$ is a composite Gaussian Q-function. Additionally, by following the work of [2], we can write the short blocklength transmission rate as

$$\mathcal{R}_{kn} = B \cdot \frac{\mathcal{D}_{kn}}{\mathcal{M}_{kn}}, \tag{3}$$

Similarly, using (2) and (3), we can express the error probability in blocklength as

$$\varepsilon_{kn}(\mathcal{S}_{kn}, \mathcal{M}_{kn}) = Q\left(\frac{\ln 2}{\sqrt{\mathcal{V}(\mathcal{S}_{kn})}} \cdot \left[\log_2 (1 + \mathcal{S}_{kn}) \cdot \sqrt{\mathcal{M}_{kn}} \right. \right.$$

$$\left. \left. - \frac{\mathcal{D}_{kn}}{\sqrt{\mathcal{M}_{kn}}} \right] \right). \tag{4}$$

Likewise, according to [2–4], the task delay and energy consumption of each IoT device k in the n-th slot on the ground are given by

$$\mathcal{T}_{kn} = \frac{\mathcal{D}_{kn}}{\mathcal{R}_{kn}} + \frac{\mathcal{X}_{kn} \mathcal{D}_{kn}}{f_{kn}} = \frac{\mathcal{M}_{kn}}{B} + \frac{\mathcal{X}_{kn} \mathcal{D}_{kn}}{f_{kn}},$$

$$E_{kn} = p_{kn} \frac{\mathcal{D}_{kn}}{\mathcal{R}_{kn}} = p_{kn} \frac{\mathcal{M}_{kn}}{B}, \tag{5}$$

where f_{kn} (CPU cycles per second) denotes the computing rate of each IoT device k in the n-th slot. Additionally, we assume that the delay at the computing server is negligible. In order to guarantee min-max fairness among all the IoT devices deployed on the ground, we seek to minimize the maximum energy consumption of all the deployed IoT devices on the ground by jointly tackling the optimization of the fairness of the data allocation and the UAV's trajectory. Therefore, the formulated optimization problem is given as

$$\textbf{P1}: \min_{\mathcal{D}_{kn},\mathcal{M}_{kn},\mathbf{q}_n} \max_k \left\{ \sum_{n=1}^{N} E_{kn} \right\} \tag{6a}$$

$$\text{s.t.} \qquad \mathcal{C}_1. \tag{6b}$$

$$T_{kn} \leqslant \delta, \quad \forall k \in \mathcal{K}, \quad \forall n \in \mathcal{N}, \tag{6c}$$

$$\|\mathbf{v}_n\|_2 \leqslant V_{\max}, \quad \forall n \in \mathcal{N}, \tag{6d}$$

$$\|\mathbf{v}_n\|_2 \geqslant V_{\min}, \quad \forall n \in \mathcal{N}, \tag{6e}$$

$$\sum_{n=1}^{N} \mathcal{D}_{kn} = \mathcal{D}_k^{\text{req}}, \quad \forall k \in \mathcal{K}, \tag{6f}$$

$$\varepsilon_{kn}(\mathcal{S}_{kn}, \mathcal{M}_{kn}) \leqslant \varepsilon_{max}, \; \forall k \in \mathcal{K}, \forall n \in \mathcal{N}. \tag{6g}$$

where $V_{\max}$ and $V_{\min}$ as the name suggests, denote the maximum and minimum velocity of the UAV. Here, constraint (6b) represents the UAV's mobility constraints given in (1), constraint (6c) guarantees that task delays for all IoT devices in each of the time slots do not exceed the size of each slot denoted by δ, constraints (6d) and (6e) ensures that the UAV's velocity should be greater than the minimum, while less than maximum velocity during its flight operation. Similarly, constraint (6f) represents the constraint of data allocation for each task, and constraint (6g) guarantees high reliability. It is worth mentioning that **P1** is challenging to solve since (6c), (6e), and (6g) are non-convex. Now, we aim to divide **P1** into two convex sub-problems by performing successive convex approximations (SCA). Consequently, we expand **P1** by expanding the objective function (6a) and the constraints (6c) and (6g) as follows

$$\textbf{P2}: \min_{\mathcal{D}_{kn},\mathcal{M}_{kn},\mathbf{q}_{[n]}} \max_k \frac{1}{B} \sum_{n=1}^{N} p_{kn} \mathcal{M}_{kn}, \tag{7a}$$

$$\text{s.t.} \qquad \mathcal{C}_1. \tag{7b}$$

$$\frac{\mathcal{M}_{kn}}{B} + \frac{\mathcal{X}_{kn}\mathcal{D}_{kn}}{f_{kn}} \leqslant \delta, \quad \forall k \in \mathcal{K}, \forall n \in \mathcal{N}, \tag{7c}$$

$$\|\mathbf{v}_n\|_2 \leqslant V_{\max}, \quad \forall n \in \mathcal{N}, \tag{7d}$$

$$\|\mathbf{v}_n\|_2 \geqslant V_{\min}, \quad \forall n \in \mathcal{N}, \tag{7e}$$

$$\sum_{n=1}^{N} \mathcal{D}_{kn} = \mathcal{D}_k^{\text{req}}, \quad \forall k \in \mathcal{K}, \tag{7f}$$

$$Q\left(\frac{\ln 2 \cdot \alpha_{kn}}{\sqrt{\mathcal{V}(\mathcal{S}_{kn})}} \right) \leqslant \varepsilon_{max}, \; \forall k \in \mathcal{K}, \forall n \in \mathcal{N}. \tag{7g}$$

where $\alpha_{kn} = \left[\log_2 \left(1 + \mathcal{S}_{kn} \right) \cdot \sqrt{\mathcal{M}_{kn}} - \dfrac{\mathcal{D}_{kn}}{\sqrt{\mathcal{M}_{kn}}} \right]$. Moreover, since $Q(x)$ is a monotonically decreasing function, hence the same holds true for the inverse function $P(y)$. Therefore, the following inequalities hold

$$Q(x) \leqslant y, \qquad x \geqslant P(y). \tag{8}$$

Therefore, in terms of (7g)

$$\frac{\ln 2}{\sqrt{\mathcal{V}(\mathcal{S}_{kn})}} \cdot \left[\log_2 \left(1 + \mathcal{S}_{kn} \right) \cdot \sqrt{\mathcal{M}_{kn}} - \frac{\mathcal{D}_{kn}}{\sqrt{\mathcal{M}_{kn}}} \right] \geqslant P \left(\varepsilon_{\max} \right),$$

$$\forall k \in \mathcal{K}, \quad \forall n \in \mathcal{N}, \tag{9}$$

Since, H is a large value[1] thus, the inequality $\mathcal{S}_{kn} \leqslant \frac{\gamma_{kn}}{H^2}$ can be considered small. Resultantly, we can use the following approximations

$$\ln \left(1 + \mathcal{S}_{kn} \right) \approx \mathcal{S}_{kn},$$
$$\mathcal{V} \left(\mathcal{S}_{kn} \right) = 1 - \left(1 - \mathcal{S}_{kn} + \mathcal{S}_{kn}^2 - \dots \right)^2,$$
$$\approx 1 - \left(1 - 2\mathcal{S}_{kn} \right), \tag{10}$$
$$= 2\mathcal{S}_{kn},$$

Now, we rewrite the inequality in (9) as follows

$$\frac{\ln 2}{\sqrt{2\mathcal{S}_{kn}}} \cdot \left[\frac{\mathcal{S}_{kn}}{\ln 2} \cdot \sqrt{\mathcal{M}_{kn}} - \frac{\mathcal{D}_{kn}}{\sqrt{\mathcal{M}_{kn}}} \right] \geqslant P \left(\varepsilon_{\max} \right),$$

$$\frac{1}{\sqrt{2\mathcal{S}_{kn}\mathcal{M}_{kn}}} \cdot \left[\mathcal{S}_{kn}\mathcal{M}_{kn} - \ln 2 \cdot \mathcal{D}_{kn} \right] \geqslant P \left(\varepsilon_{\max} \right), \tag{11}$$

$$\mathcal{S}_{kn}\mathcal{M}_{kn} - \ln 2 \cdot \mathcal{D}_{kn} \geqslant P \left(\varepsilon_{\max} \right) \cdot \sqrt{2\mathcal{S}_{kn}\mathcal{M}_{kn}},$$

$$\mathcal{S}_{kn}\mathcal{M}_{kn} - \sqrt{2}P \left(\varepsilon_{\max} \right) \cdot \sqrt{\mathcal{S}_{kn}\mathcal{M}_{kn}} - \ln 2 \cdot \mathcal{D}_{kn} \geqslant 0.$$

Thereafter, we focus of the left side of the inequality in (11). Moreover, we assume that

$$x = \sqrt{\mathcal{S}_{kn}\mathcal{M}_{kn}}, \tag{12}$$

Then, we have

$$x^2 - \sqrt{2}P \left(\varepsilon_{\max} \right) \cdot x - \ln 2 \cdot \mathcal{D}_{kn} = 0, \tag{13}$$

which has two roots represented by

$$x = \frac{\sqrt{2}P \left(\varepsilon_{\max} \right) \pm \sqrt{2P^2 \left(\varepsilon_{\max} \right) + 4 \ln 2 \cdot \mathcal{D}_{kn}}}{2}, \tag{14}$$

Since, $\mathcal{D}_{kn} \geqslant 0$, then only positive root is considered for further analysis. Consequently, the minimal positive solution of inequality $x^2 - \sqrt{2}P \left(\varepsilon_{\max} \right) \cdot x - \ln 2 \cdot$

---

[1] According to 3GPP release 15, UAV height is set to be reasonably large such that it is flying at a height of at least 80 m, where there is a 100% probability of achieving LoS.

$D_{kn} \geqslant 0$ is the positive root given in (14). Furthermore, the blocklength $\mathcal{M}_{kn}$ in (12) takes the form

$$
\begin{aligned}
M_{kn} &= \frac{x^2}{S_{kn}} \\
&= \frac{\|\mathbf{q}_n - \mathbf{w}_k\|^2}{\gamma_{kn}} \cdot \frac{\left(\sqrt{2}P(\varepsilon_{\max}) + \sqrt{2P^2(\varepsilon_{\max}) + 4\ln 2 \cdot D_{kn}}\right)^2}{4}, \\
&= \frac{\|\mathbf{q}_n - \mathbf{w}_k\|^2}{\gamma_{kn}} \cdot \left[\rho_{kn} + \zeta_{kn}\right],
\end{aligned}
\tag{15}
$$

where $\rho_{kn} = P^2(\varepsilon_{\max}) + \ln 2 \cdot D_{kn}$ and $\zeta_{kn} = P(\varepsilon_{\max})\sqrt{P^2(\varepsilon_{\max}) + 2\ln 2 \cdot D_{kn}}$. It is worth mentioning that (15) is optimal and a feasible solution exists, as we aim to minimize all $\mathcal{M}_{kn}$ in **P2**. Here, objective function (7a) can be rewritten as

$$
\mathcal{O}_1 = \min_{\mathcal{D}_{kn}, \mathbf{q}_{[n]}} \max_k \frac{1}{B} \sum_{n=1}^{N} p_{kn} \frac{\|\mathbf{q}_n - \mathbf{w}_k\|^2}{\gamma_{kn}} \cdot \left[\rho_{kn} + \zeta_{kn}\right], \tag{16}
$$

Furthermore, by combining (7c) and (15), we have

$$
\frac{\|\mathbf{q}_n - \mathbf{w}_k\|^2}{B\gamma_{kn}} \cdot (P^2(\varepsilon_{\max}) + \ln 2 \cdot \mathcal{D}_{kn} + P(\varepsilon_{\max})
$$
$$
\sqrt{P^2(\varepsilon_{\max}) + 2\ln 2 \cdot \mathcal{D}_{kn}})) + \frac{\mathcal{X}_{kn}\mathcal{D}_{kn}}{f_{kn}} \leqslant \delta, \tag{17}
$$

Additionally, after a few mathematical manipulations, we get

$$
\left(\frac{\|\mathbf{q}_n - \mathbf{w}_k\|^2}{B\gamma_{kn}} \cdot \ln 2 + \frac{\mathcal{X}_{kn}}{f_{kn}}\right) \cdot D_{kn} + \frac{\|\mathbf{q}_n - \mathbf{w}_k\|^2}{B\gamma_{kn}} \cdot P(\varepsilon_{\max})
$$
$$
\sqrt{P^2(\varepsilon_{\max}) + 2\ln 2 \cdot \mathcal{D}_{kn}} \leqslant \delta - \frac{\|\mathbf{q}_n - \mathbf{w}_k\|^2}{B\gamma_{kn}} \cdot P^2(\varepsilon_{\max}). \tag{18}
$$

It is noteworthy that (18) is non-convex with respect to $\mathcal{D}_{kn}$. As such, to solve this problem, we use the constant local value $\mathcal{D}_{kn}^{\text{local}}$ instead of $\mathcal{D}_{kn}$. Hence, we have

$$
\mathcal{C}_2 = \left(\frac{\|\mathbf{q}_n - \mathbf{w}_k\|^2}{B\gamma_{kn}} \cdot \ln 2 + \frac{\mathcal{X}_{kn}}{f_{kn}}\right) \cdot \mathcal{D}_{kn} \leqslant \delta - \frac{\|\mathbf{q}_n - \mathbf{w}_k\|^2}{B\gamma_{kn}}
$$
$$
\cdot \left(P^2(\varepsilon_{\max}) + P(\varepsilon_{\max})\sqrt{P^2(\varepsilon_{\max}) + 2\ln 2 \cdot \mathcal{D}_{kn}^{\text{local}}}\right). \tag{19}
$$

Similarly, we convert (6e) to the convex form. As such, it could be represented as

$$
\|\mathbf{v}_{[n]}\|_2^2 \geqslant V_{\min}^2, \tag{20}
$$

For any given local point $\mathbf{v}_{[n]}^{\text{local}}$ in the feasible domain, $\frac{d^2 \left\| \mathbf{v}_{[n]} \right\|_2^2}{d\mathbf{v}_{[n]}^2} > 0$, hence it is convex. Resultantly, we take the inequality based on the first-order Taylor expansion as follows

$$\left\| \mathbf{v}_{[n]} \right\|_2^2 \geq \left\| \mathbf{v}_{[n]}^{\text{local}} \right\|_2^2 + 2 \left(\mathbf{v}_{[n]}^{\text{local}} \right)^T \cdot \left(\mathbf{v}_{[n]} - \mathbf{v}_{[n]}^{\text{local}} \right),$$
$$\mathcal{C}_4 = \left\| \mathbf{v}_{[n]}^{\text{local}} \right\|_2^2 + 2 \left(\mathbf{v}_{[n]}^{\text{local}} \right)^T \cdot \left(\mathbf{v}_{[n]} - \mathbf{v}_{[n]}^{\text{local}} \right) \geq V_{\min}, \quad \forall n \in \mathcal{N}, \tag{21}$$

Thus, the problem **P2** can be reformulated as

$$\mathbf{P3}: \quad \mathcal{O}_1, \tag{22a}$$
$$\text{s.t.} \quad \mathcal{C}_1, \tag{22b}$$
$$\mathcal{C}_2, \tag{22c}$$
$$\left\| \mathbf{v}_{[n]} \right\|_2 \leq V_{\max}, \quad \forall n \in \mathcal{N}, \tag{22d}$$
$$\mathcal{C}_4, \tag{22e}$$
$$\sum_{n=1}^{N} \mathcal{D}_{kn} = \mathcal{D}_k^{\text{req}}, \quad \forall k \in \mathcal{K}, \tag{22f}$$

Still, **P3** is difficult to solve since objective function (22a) as well as (22c) are non-convex wrt $\mathcal{D}_{kn}$ and $\mathbf{q}_n$ simultaneously. Consequently, we aim to replace **P3** problem by dividing it into two sub-problems. As such, the two convex objective functions can be written as

$$\mathcal{O}_2 = \min_{\mathcal{D}_{kn}} \max_{k} \frac{1}{B} \sum_{n=1}^{N} p_{kn} \frac{\left\| \mathbf{q}_n - \mathbf{w}_k \right\|^2}{\gamma_{kn}} \cdot \left[\rho_{kn} + \zeta_{kn} \right], \tag{23}$$

$$\mathcal{O}_3 = \min_{\mathbf{q}_{[n]}} \max_{k} \frac{1}{B} \sum_{n=1}^{N} p_{kn} \frac{\left\| \mathbf{q}_n - \mathbf{w}_k \right\|^2}{\gamma_{kn}} \cdot \left[\rho_{kn} + \zeta_{kn} \right], \tag{24}$$

Resultantly, the two sub-problems can now be written as

$$\mathbf{P3.1}: \quad \mathcal{O}_2, \tag{25a}$$
$$\text{s.t.} \quad \mathcal{C}_2, \tag{25b}$$
$$\sum_{n=1}^{N} \mathcal{D}_{kn} = \mathcal{D}_k^{\text{req}}, \quad \forall k \in \mathcal{K}, \tag{25c}$$

$$\mathbf{P3.2}: \quad \mathcal{O}_3, \tag{26a}$$
$$\text{s.t.} \quad \mathcal{C}_1, \tag{26b}$$
$$\left\| \mathbf{v}_{[n]} \right\|_2 \leq V_{\max}, \quad \forall n \in \mathcal{N}, \tag{26c}$$
$$\mathcal{C}_4, \tag{26d}$$

Finally, we obtained **P3.1** and **P3.2**, which are two convex optimization problems. In this regard, **P3.1** solves the fairness in data allocation problem and **P3.2** solves the trajectory design problem.

3   Proposed Approach

As discussed earlier, **P1** is difficult to solve due to the non-convexity of its constraints, and thus it is difficult to obtain a globally optimal solution. Therefore,
based on our analysis, we rigorously transform **P1** into two convex sub-problems
of **P3.1** and **P3.2**. After that, we propose a sub-optimal joint fairness and trajectory design algorithm (JFTDA) to tackle the aforementioned sub-problems.

Algorithm 1: Joint fairness and trajectory design Algorithm (JFTDA) to
facilitate URLLC in UAV-enabled MEC

---

1 Initialize $\{\mathbf{q}_n, \mathcal{D}_{kn}, \text{MaxEnergy}\}^0$.

2 Set $j = 1$, $\mathbf{v}_n^{\text{local}} = \mathbf{v}_n^0$, and a tolerance $\epsilon = 10^{-4}$. **while**
$|\text{MaxEnergy}^j - \text{MaxEnergy}^{j-1}| \leqslant \epsilon$ **do**

3   Solve **P3.1** with given $\mathbf{q}_n^j$, $\text{MaxEnergy}^j = \text{MaxEnergy}^*$ and obtain the
     optimal solutions denoted by $\mathcal{D}_{kn}^*$ and MaxEnergy^*

4   Solve **P3.2** with given $\mathcal{D}_{kn}^l$ and obtain the optimal solutions denoted by $\mathbf{q}_n^*$,
     MaxEnergy^*

5   **Set** $j = j + 1$, and $\{\mathbf{q}_n, \mathcal{D}_{kn}\}^j = \{\mathbf{q}_n^*, \mathcal{D}_{kn}^*\}$

6 end

7 Return an optimized solution

It is worth mentioning that **P3.1** has a higher computational complexity than
P3.2. In this regard, **P3.1** contains $K+KN$ linear constraints and KN variables.
Resultantly, the complexity of **P3.1** is $O\left(K^3 N^3\right)$, which is the complexity of
Algorithm 1.

4   Simulation Results and Discussion

In this section, we set the parameters as $K = 8$ IoT devices, $N = 80$, $T = 16$ s,
$\delta = T/N = 1/5$, $B = 400$ MHz, $H = 100$ m, $V_{\min} = 3$ m/s, $V_{\max} = 50$ m/s,
$\beta_0 = 140$ dB, $f_{kn} = 1.2$ Gcps, $\mathcal{D}_k^{\text{req}} = 2$ MBits, and $p_{kn} = 15$ dBm, $\forall k \in \mathcal{K}$;
$\forall n \in \mathcal{N}$, $\varepsilon_{max} = 10^{-5}$, and $\sigma^2 = 5$ dBm^2. To verify the efficacy of our proposed
JFTDA, we use two different trajectory cases, i.e., Case I and Case II. In this
regard, the initial positions of Case I and Case II are both the same, which
is $(-50; 0; 100)$. In contrast, the final positions of Case I and Case II are different, which are $(50; 100; 100)$ and $(-50; 0; 100)$, respectively. Additionally, the
proposed algorithm for the aforementioned UAV trajectory cases is compared
with different deployment scenarios based on random placement of IoT devices
in the service area and an algorithm based on the lower bound of the maximal
energy consumption. Figure 2(a) shows that for Case I, the UAV has a uniform
trajectory for all the IoT devices placed in the service area. Initially, the UAV

---

[2] All simulations are performed on the MATLAB R2018a.

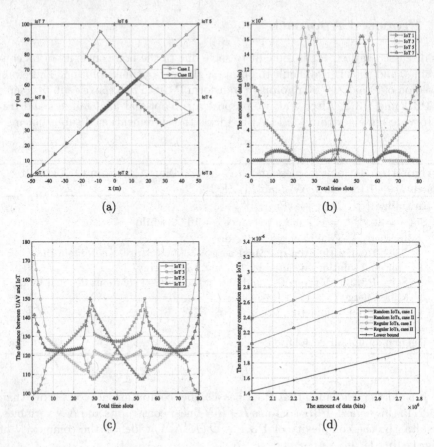

Fig. 2. (a) UAV trajectories (b) Data allocation versus total time slots (c) UAV distance versus total time slots (d) Comparison of algorithm with different deployment scenarios.

is moving steadily but it slows down its speed during the middle part of the trajectory. The reason behind this phenomenon is that during the middle trajectory there exists a minimal distance between the UAV and all the IoT devices compared to the start or the end of the trajectory specifically for Case I. Consequently, the IoT devices energy consumption can be reduced. Comparably, Case II forms a butterfly shaped UAV trajectory that is also uniform in nature same as the Case I. Thus, the two optimized trajectories for both cases account for fair data allocation among the IoT devices in the service area. Moreover, taking the advantage of uniform trajectory, Fig. 2(b) only shows odd numbered IoT devices as the even numbered IoT devices will have similar results. By simultaneously viewing both Fig. 2(b) and Fig. 2(c) it can be observed that the task data allocation is not inversely proportional to the distance existing between the UAV and the odd numbered IoT device. This happens to guarantee fairness among IoT devices as transmitted data becomes greater or smaller so does the

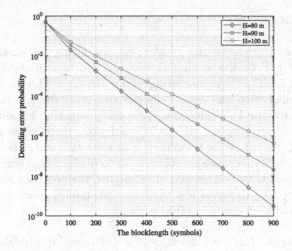

Fig. 3. Decoding error probability versus the blocklength.

distance in a few time slots. As mentioned before, to illustrate the execution of our proposed algorithm, we make its relevant comparisons with other deployment scenarios. In this regard, "Random IoTs" deployment scenario as the name suggests considers IoT devices that are deployed randomly inside the rectangle, whereas "Regular IoTs" represents the proposed algorithm considering uniform placement of IoT devices over each side of the rectangle, as seen in Fig. 2(d). Furthermore, we change the distance between the UAV and the IoT device to its minimal reachable value H. For this case we obtain lower bound of the maximal energy consumption, which can be mathematically represented as

$$\frac{\sigma^2}{\beta_0 B} \sum_{n=1}^{N} \mathcal{D}_{kn} \cdot H^2 = \frac{\sigma^2 H^2}{\beta_0 B} \cdot \mathcal{D}_k^{\text{req}} \leqslant \frac{\sigma^2 H^2}{\beta_0 B} \cdot \max_k \mathcal{D}_k^{\text{req}}. \qquad (27)$$

It is observed that the proposed algorithm denoted by "Regular IoTs" consume less energy than "Random IoTs" for each of the two considered UAV trajectories. In contrast, the proposed algorithm i.e., Regular IoTs, consumes more energy when compared to lower bound of the maximal energy consumption which represents the lowest possible values of energy for a given amount of transmitted data, which intuitively makes sense. Finally, Fig. 3 shows decoding error probability versus the blocklength graph by varying the UAV height from 80 m to 100 m. Generally, it is observed that when UAV is flying at 80 m the decoding error is smaller compared to when UAV flies at 100 m. Additionally, for larger blocklenghts, the three considered heights yield a decoding error of less than 10^{-5} thus, guaranteeing URLLC for the given UAV-enabled MEC system.

5   Conclusions

In this paper, we introduced the problem of minimizing the maximum energy consumption of IoT devices communicating critical task allocation data with a UAV-enabled MEC system operating under URLLC. The goal was to perform fair data allocation and ensure efficient trajectory design. To achieve this goal, we optimized the UAV mobility, data allocation, and decoding error constraints based on our proposed JFTDA. Simulation results show that our proposed algorithm optimizes the trajectory, guarantees fair data allocation among the IoT devices and yields comparable results to distinct deployment scenarios. Lastly, for different UAV heights and blocklengths, the proposed algorithm gives a decoding error probability of less than 10^{-5} therefore, guaranteeing URLLC for the considered UAV-enabled MEC system.

Acknowledgement. This work was supported by Mitacs/Ultra Intelligence & Communications through project IT25839 and the National Natural Sciences and Engineering Research Council of Canada (NSERC) through research grant RGPIN-2020-06050.

References

1. Bennis, M., Debbah, M., Poor, H.V.: Ultrareliable and low-latency wireless communication: tail, risk, and scale. Proc. IEEE **106**(10), 1834–1853 (2018)
2. Diao, X., Zheng, J., Cai, Y., Wu, Y., Anpalagan, A.: Fair data allocation and trajectory optimization for UAV-assisted mobile edge computing. IEEE Commun. Lett. **23**(12), 2357–2361 (2019)
3. Li, M., Cheng, N., Gao, J., Wang, Y., Zhao, L., Shen, X.: Energy-efficient UAV-assisted mobile edge computing: resource allocation and trajectory optimization. IEEE Trans. Veh. Technol. **69**(3), 3424–3438 (2020)
4. Mei, H., Yang, K., Shen, J., Liu, Q.: Joint trajectory-task-cache optimization with phase-shift design of RIS-assisted UAV for MEC. IEEE Wireless Commun. Lett. **10**(7), 1586–1590 (2021)
5. Narsani, H.K., Ranjha, A., Dev, K., Memon, F.H., Qureshi, N.M.F.: Leveraging UAV-assisted communications to improve secrecy for URLLC in 6G systems. Digital Commun. Netw. (2022)
6. Polyanskiy, Y., Poor, H.V., Verdú, S.: Channel coding rate in the finite blocklength regime. IEEE Trans. Inf. Theory **56**(5), 2307–2359 (2010)
7. Qin, X., Song, Z., Hao, Y., Sun, X.: Joint resource allocation and trajectory optimization for multi-UAV-assisted multi-access mobile edge computing. IEEE Wireless Commun. Lett. **10**(7), 1400–1404 (2021)
8. Ranjha, A., Kaddoum, G.: Quasi-optimization of distance and blocklength in URLLC aided multi-hop UAV relay links. IEEE Wireless Commun. Lett. **9**(3), 306–310 (2019)
9. Ranjha, A., Kaddoum, G.: Quasi-optimization of uplink power for enabling green URLLC in mobile UAV-assisted IoT networks: a perturbation-based approach. IEEE Internet Things J. **8**(3), 1674–1686 (2020)
10. Ranjha, A., Kaddoum, G.: URLLC-enabled by laser powered UAV relay: a quasi-optimal design of resource allocation, trajectory planning and energy harvesting. IEEE Trans. Veh. Technol. **71**(1), 753–765 (2021)

11. Ranjha, A., Kaddoum, G., Dev, K.: Facilitating URLLC in UAV-assisted relay systems with multiple-mobile robots for 6G networks: a prospective of agriculture 4.0. IEEE Trans. Ind. Inf. **18**(7), 4954–4965 (2021)
12. Ranjha, A., Kaddoum, G., Rahim, M., Dev, K.: URLLC in UAV-enabled multicasting systems: a dual time and energy minimization problem using UAV speed, altitude and beamwidth. Computer Commun. **187**, 125–133 (2022)

Resource Allocation and Power Control for Heterogeneous Cellular Network and D2D Communications

Ramiro Agila[1]([✉]) [iD], Rebeca Estrada[1] [iD], and Katty Rohoden[2] [iD]

[1] Escuela Superior Politécnica del Litoral (ESPOL), Guayaquil, Ecuador
{ragila,restrada}@espol.edu.ec
[2] Universidad Técnica Particular de Loja (UTPL), Loja, Ecuador
karohoden@utpl.edu.ec

Abstract. Improving network capacity and reliability while decreasing delay and providing acceptable QoS in 5G wireless networks are one of the most challenging drawbacks to solve nowadays. In this paper, we propose a joint algorithm for resource allocation and power control based on a Stackelberg game considering a heterogeneous network (HetNet) with several small base stations deployed in the coverage area of one macrocell coexisting with multiple device-to-device communications. Small BS and D2D are introduced in mobile communications to improve spectral efficiency and avoid or reduce the interference caused between layers.

Hybrid Access small cells grant access to public users in order to offload traffic from the macrocell. Furthermore, D2D allows direct connection between two devices without connection to the macro base station, releasing resources in the macrocell. To estimate the power that must be transmitted by mutual agreement such as that interference is minimized, we propose to use a game that is solved in a Stackelberg equilibrium and that also ensures that the D2D communication continues with an optimal transmission power. Simulation results show that the proposed model reduces interference in the HetNets while increasing the network throughput.

Keywords: 5G · HetNets · Hybrid access smallcells · D2D · Stackelberg game

1 Introduction

With 5G technology, the number of mobile users and the demand for resources are expected to increase rapidly. Accordingly, Heterogeneous Networks (HetNets) and Device-to-Device (D2D) communications are one of the promising technologies to cope with these issues. Three-tier heterogeneous networks consisting of small base stations (SBS) deployment and D2D communications help to offload traffic from macro base stations (MBS). We identify the advantages and disadvantages of integrating D2D communications into HetNets and propose possible

E. Sabir et al. (Eds.): UNet 2022, LNCS 13853, pp. 68–81, 2023.
https://doi.org/10.1007/978-3-031-29419-8_6

solutions. If the gains from such integration are to be maximized, interference avoidance is a motivating factor in this research through radio resource management. Thus, it is important to properly allocate resources to ensure reliability, increase data rate and capacity in heterogeneous cellular networks.

The vast majority of previous resources allocation approaches consider the HetNet either with only SBSs or only D2D communications. In our research, we consider a three-tier network, which means the interaction of MBSs with SBSs and the great contribution of D2D communications and propose a resource allocation model using Stackelberg game. Previous studies using this game considered the configuration of leader, leader, follower for MBS, SBS and D2D, respectively, which limits the performance of the HetNet. In addition, the distances of D2D pairs are fixed and the access mode for femto BSs are only closed or open. Unlike previous related work, we propose to use the configuration as leader, follower, follower for MBS, SBS and D2D, respectively.

Unlike prior research works, we perform the pairing of D2D users based on the distance that initially exists between macrocell user equipments (MUES). In addition, we consider the hybrid access smallcells mode where MUES can be granted service from them whenever they are within the coverage area of the SBS. Given all these considerations and due to the number of iterations performed by the computer, we have considered implementing a heuristic algorithm in order to reduce the computational cost. We also take into account the interference caused by a D2D user equipment DTx, MUEs and a femo user equipment (SUE) in heterogeneous uplink networks, as well as co-tier and cross-tier interference in order to improve the performance of D2D communications. Hence, our solution consists of three components. First, D2D pairing is performed by comparing minor distances. Secondly, we propose an approach to formulate the resource allocation problem through utility function optimization while guaranteeing the Quality of Service (QoS) for different type of users. Third, a power control algorithm based on a Stackelberg game with a leader-follower-follower scheme is proposed to maximize the utility of the macro BS, the small BSs and the D2D links.

The main contributions of this work are: i) an iterative algorithm for the allocation of power to D2D transmitters, SUEs and HMUEs and ii) a Stackelberg game with a leader-follower-follower scheme to improve the throughput in a three-tier network.

The remaining of the paper is organized as follow: Sect. 2 presents the related work while Sect. 3 describes the system model and problem formulation. Section 4 presents the components of the resource allocation and power control approach. The simulation scenario and numerical results are presented in Sect. 5. Finally, Sect. 6 concludes the research work.

2   Related Work

This section presents a brief summary of the related research work focused on resource allocation in heterogeneous networks taking into account different optimization approaches. HetNets are attractive because they can increase mobile network capacity and reduce the communication problems considering several available access technology. A heterogeneous network consists of multiple radio access technologies, architectures, transmission solutions, and several base stations with different transmission power or coverage area. In particular, we review the resource allocation approaches proposed for Hetnet such as two-tier networks (i.e. macro-small cell networks) with D2D communications.

2.1   Resource Allocation for Macro-Small Cell Networks

The problem of resource allocation has been addressed in several previous works. For example, the authors addressed the resource optimization problem using Linear Programming to solve the BS selection together with the resource allocation taking into account the spectrum partitioning and spectrum sharing respectively in [3,6]. Other alternative optimization tools that use Genetic Algorithm and Particle Swarm Optimization are presented in [5,12] respectively. These prior works showed that these two optimization techniques find a satisfying near-to-optimal solution with reduced running time than the optimal resource allocation model. In [4], a clustering technique was proposed to keep the traffic load balanced among the established clusters together with the distributed Weighted Water Filling based resource allocation algorithm. In addition, it was shown that the load balanced clustering outperforms the clustering based on the interference levels. Considering the cluster formation, several algorithms from game theory were investigated to solve the resource allocation problem between the macrocell and smallcell (SC) clusters in [15–17] to reduce the inter-cluster interference while guaranteeing the stability of the clusters. To reduce the interference, an approach based on stackelberg game was proposed in [2] where the macro BS is the leader and the SCs are the followers. In this case, the leader issues the price of interference charged to the followers to maximize its own profit and the followers choose the strategies to maximize their payoffs (e.g. difference between the capacity and the cost of the interference paid to the leader). In [20], the authors proposed a prediction model for the interference such as this prediction value can be used to improve the resource allocation. In [11], a pricing incentive mechanism is proposed to encourage SBSs to adopt a hybrid access strategy while receiving profits from the MBS in order to maximize downlink transmission rates for users between two-tier smallcell networks and macrocells.

2.2   Resource Allocation for D2D Communication

The resource allocation problem for D2D-enabled networks has been previously investigated by the research community [21]. Due to the large computational complexity to allocated resources in a D2D-enabled cellular network, the vast majority of the related work investigates a single-cell scenario for the theoretical analysis with several assumptions such as an advanced interference mitigation schemes on top of the per-cell allocation algorithms [19]. For instance, the authors of [1] propose a centralized resource allocation scheme to minimize the total power consumption. In [8], it was proposed a heuristic proportional fair scheduling, with at most one cellular and one D2D communication per channel. In [7], a suboptimal model for multi-cell D2D underlaid cellular networks was proposed, adopting exclusion regions around the BSs to mitigate cochannel interference. In [13], the problem of wireless resource virtualization with D2D communication underlaying the LTE network was formulated. Their results showed that wireless resource virtualization increased the system throughput. Also, D2D communication helped mitigate the effect of worsening channel conditions. Moreover, the heuristic algorithm achieved close to optimal performance while having a much lower computational complexity.

2.3 Resource Allocation Considering a Macro-Small Cell Network Together with D2D Communications

In [9], a Stackelberg game framework was presented for power allocation of D2D communication and SBSs in a heterogeneous network. The authors of [10] proposed a Stackelberg game framework for joint power control, channel allocation and scheduling of D2D communication in heterogeneous macrocell-small cell network system (leader, follower, follower). In [14], a dynamic two leader-multiple follower Stackelberg game was proposed for resource allocation in heterogeneous three-tier D2D networks. The authors of [18] investigated resource allocation for D2D communications sharing uplink resources in a fully loaded cellular network in order to maximize the overall throughput while ensuring the QoS requirements of both celullar users and D2D users.

3 System Model

We consider the uplink communications of a Macro cell/Small cell/D2D system in a single cell with one MBS in the center and N orthogonal MUEs evenly located in the cell, where the uplink signal links are indicated by solid arrows while the interference signal links are denoted by dotted arrows, as shown in Fig. 1. In addition, several small cells and D2D pairs are located in the same cell, each of the D2D pairs consist of a transmitter $D2DTx$ and a receiver $D2DRx$. The small cells are assumed to be round with one SBS in the center and several SUEs and hybrid user equipments (HMUEs) evenly located within it in order to simulate a dense heterogeneous network. There are four types of users UEs: MUEs, SUEs, D2Ds, and HMUEs. Each SBS serves at least one SUE and one HMUE in its coverage area when provisioned with the hybrid access strategy. The MUE that is served by the SBS is called HMUE. SUE and HMUE in SBS_i ($i \in 1, 2, \ldots, N$) are expressed as SUE_i and $HMUE_i$, respectively. The MBS and SBS can be operated within regions of radius R_m and R_f, respectively. No active user is assumed to be in the overlap region between any two SBSs, and only one channel is assumed to be allocated to users. Hence, N SUEs share the same channel.

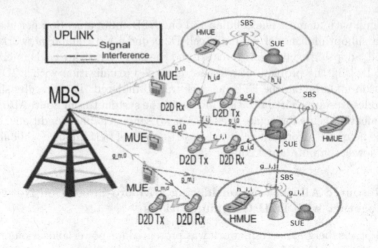

Fig. 1. Heterogeneous network.

3.1 Problem Formulation

In order to perform the power allocation, the average channel gain for each user has to be determined. Therefore, the average channel gain between $D2DTx_i$ and $D2DRx_j$ is given by

$$\overline{f}_{i,j} = \begin{cases} K_{fi}min(D_{i,j}^{-\alpha_{f_0}},1), & i=j, i,j>0 \\ K_{f0}min(D1_{i,j}^{-\alpha_{f_0}},1), & i \neq j, i,j>0 \end{cases} \tag{1}$$

The average channel gain between SUE_i and SBS_j, $i,j \in I = (1,2,...,N)$ can be estimated using Eq. 2

$$\overline{g}_{i,j} = \begin{cases} K_{fi}R_f^{-\beta}, & i=j>0 \\ K_{f0}W^2min(D_{i,j}^{-\alpha_{f_0}},1), & i \neq j, i,j>0 \end{cases} \tag{2}$$

while the average channel gain between $HMUE_i$ and SBS_j is given by

$$\overline{h}_{i,j} = \begin{cases} K_{fi}R_f^{-\beta}, & i=j>0 \\ K_{f0}W^2min(D1_{i,j}^{-\alpha_{f_0}},1), & i \neq j, i,j>0 \end{cases} \tag{3}$$

where K_{fi} is the fixed loss between either SUE_i or $HMUE_i$ to its own base station, K_{f0} is the fixed loss between a SBS or MBS and other user, and f is the carrier frequency. β, α_0, and α_{f_0} are path loss exponents for indoor, outdoor, and indoor-to-outdoor, respectively, and W is a specific value to simulate the loss during indoor-outdoor propagation. The distances between a BS and a user are defined by $D_{i,j}$ as shown in the Table 1.

It should be noticed that the subscripts i, j refer to receiver i and transmitter j, respectively, where $i = j$ indicates that the transmitter, i.e. SBS, and the receiver including SUE and HMUE, are in the same small cell otherwise $i \neq j$.

Table 1. Notation of the distances between a BS and a user.

Name	Description
$D1_{i,j}$	Distance between SBS_j and $HMUE_i$
$D_{i,0}$	Distance between the MBS and SUE_i
$D1_{i,0}$	Distance between the MBS and $HMUE_i$
$D2_{i,0}$	Distance between the MBS and $D2D_i$
$D_{i,d}$	Distance between the $D2D_i$ and $HMUE_i$
$D1j, m$	Distance between SBS_j and $D2D_i$
$D2j, m$	Distance between SBS_j and MUE_m
$D2_{0,m}$	Distance between MBS and MUE_m

If the MUE is served by the MBS, then, the channel gain is defined by Eq. 4, while Eq. 5 represents the average channel gain between $HMUE_i$ and $D2DRx_j$.

$$\overline{h}_{i,0} = K_{f0}Wmin(D_{i,0}^{-\alpha_{f0}}, 1), j = 0, i > 0 \tag{4}$$

$$\overline{h}_{i,d} = K_{f0}Wmin(D_{i,d}^{-\alpha_{f0}}, 1), j = 0, i > 0 \tag{5}$$

$\overline{g}_{i,0}$ denotes the average channel gain between the SUE_i and MBS while $\overline{g}_{i,d}$ denotes the average channel gain between the SUE_i, $D2DRx_j$, which are represented by Eqs. 6 and 7, respectively.

$$\overline{g}_{i,0} = K_{f0}Wmin(D_{i,0}^{-\alpha_{f0}}, 1), j = 0, i > 0 \tag{6}$$

$$g_{i,d} = K_{f0}Wmin(D2_{0,m}^{-\alpha_{f0}}, 1), j = 0 \tag{7}$$

The average channel gain between the $D2DTx_i$ and the MBS, $\overline{g}_{d,0}$, and between the $D2DTx_d$ and the FBS_j, $\overline{g}_{d,j}$, are denoted by Eqs. 8 and 9, respectively.

$$\overline{g}_{d,0} = K_{f0}min(D2_{i,0}^{-\alpha_{f0}}, 1), j = 0, i > 0 \tag{8}$$

$$\overline{g}_{d,j} = K_{f0}Wmin(D1_{j,m}^{-\alpha_{f0}}, 1), j > 0 \tag{9}$$

On the other hand, $\overline{g}_{m,j}$ denotes the average channel between the MUE_m and the SBS_j (Eq. 10), $\overline{g}_{m,d}$ defines the average channel between the MUE_m and the $D2DRx_d$ (Eq. 11), and $\overline{g}_{m,0}$ represents the average channel between the MUE_m and MBS (Eq. 12).

$$\overline{g}_{m,j} = K_{f0}Wmin(D2_{j,m}^{-\alpha_{f0}}, 1), j > 0 \tag{10}$$

$$\overline{g}_{m,d} = K_{f0}min(D_{i,0}^{-\alpha_{f0}}, 1), j = 0, i > 0 \tag{11}$$

$$\overline{g}_{m,0} = K_0min(D2_{0,m}^{-\alpha_0}, 1), j = 0 \tag{12}$$

The fixed decibel propagation loss between the MUE and the MBS is given as $K_0 = 30 \log 10(f)$ - 71 dB. When the current communication environment is considered, the signal link is susceptible to the influence of the environment. In this paper, we consider that the uncertainties of the signal links, and the signal link gains are defined as $f_{i,i} = G1\overline{f_{i,i}}$, $g_{i,i} = G2\overline{g_{i,i}}$, $h_{i,i} = G3\overline{h_{i,i}}$, and $g_{0,m} = G4\overline{g_{m,0}}$, where G1, G2, G3, and G4 are assumed to be exponentially distributed by a unit-mean Rayleigh fading model.

The received SINR at D2D pair using the same channel is expressed as:

$$\gamma_{d,d} = \frac{p_d G1\overline{f_{i,i}}}{p_h \overline{h}_{i,d} + p_s \overline{g}_{i,d} + \sum_{j=1,j\neq i}^{N} p_d \overline{f}_{ij} + \sigma^2} \tag{13}$$

p_d is the transmission power of the D2D and σ^2 denotes the background noise power. In this paper, the background noise power σ^2 received at every user is assumed to be the same.

Since the SBS_i provides services to SUEs and HMUEs, the SINR for these users are given by Eqs. 14 and 15, respectively.

$$\gamma_{s,i} = \frac{p_s G2\overline{g_{i,i}}}{\sum_{j=1,j\neq i}^{N} p_s \overline{g}_{i,j} + \sigma^2 + p_d \overline{g}_{d,j} + p_m \overline{g}_{m,j} + p_h \overline{h}_{i,i}} \tag{14}$$

$$\gamma_{h,i} = \frac{p_h G3\overline{h_{i,i}}}{\sum_{j=1,j\neq i}^{N} p_h \overline{h}_{i,j} + \sigma^2 + p_d \overline{g}_{d,j} + p_m \overline{g}_{m,j} + p_s \overline{g}_{i,i}} \tag{15}$$

where p_s is the transmission power of SUE_i, p_m is the transmission power of the MUE_i, and p_h is the transmission power of the $HMUE_i$. Similarly, the SINR between MUE m and the MBS is defined as

$$\gamma_M^m = \frac{p_m G4\overline{g_{m,0}}}{p_h \overline{h}_{i,0} + p_s \overline{g}_{i,0} + p_d \overline{g}_{d,0} + \sigma^2} \tag{16}$$

3.2   Utility Function

The channel rate r_i for user i can be estimated using its respective SINR (e.g. γ):

$$r_i = \begin{cases} log_2(1 + \gamma_{d,d}), & for\ D2D\ user\ i \\ log_2(1 + \gamma_m^M), & for\ MUE\ i \\ log_2(1 + \gamma_{s,i}), & for\ SUE\ i \\ log_2(1 + \gamma_{h,i}), & for\ HMUE\ i \end{cases} \tag{17}$$

As D2D communication and small cell communication take place underlaying the primary cellular network, the goal of this work is on the power control and scheduling of the D2D, SUEs and HMUEs users, while the transmit power and channel of MUEs are assumed to be fixed. The interference from D2D/Small cell system to the cellular system should be limited. Thus, the transmit power of the D2D, SUEs and HMUEs users should be properly controlled. This section focuses on the behavior of a one-leader-three followers. First, the power allocation problem using Stackelberg game based scheme formulation, then the optimal transmit power of D2D Tx, SUE and HMUE is obtained, and the optimal price for MUEs. Leader and followers share the same channel resource, the leader owns the channel resource and it can charge the followers some fees for using the channel. In order to maximize its own profit, the leader establishes a set of prices for the followers in order to limit the interference caused by the followers on the same band to protect itself. Thus the leader has an incentive to share the channel with the followers if it is profitable. Given the charging price, the followers can choose the optimal transmit power to maximize their payoffs.

For the followers, the utility is its throughput performance minus the cost it pays for using the channel. The utility functions of the three followers are described in Eqs. 18, 19 and 20.

$$U_{d2d_i} = r_i - m_1 p_d \times \overline{g}_{m,d} \tag{18}$$

$$U_{SUE_i} = r_i - m_2 p_s \times \overline{g}_{m,j} \tag{19}$$

$$U_{HMUE_i} = r_i - m_3 p_h \times \overline{g}_{m,j} \tag{20}$$

where m_1, m_2, and m_3 are the charging prices of the D2DTx, SUE, and HMUE, respectively. The utility of the leader can be defined as its own throughput performance plus the revenue it earns from the followers, see Eq. 21.

$$U_{MUE_i} = r_i + m_1 p_d \beta_1 \overline{g}_{m,d} + m_2 p_s \beta_2 \overline{g}_{m,j} + m_3 p_h \beta_3 \overline{g}_{m,j} \tag{21}$$

where β_1, β_2 are β_3 are scale factors to denote the ratio of the leaders gain and the followers payment ($\beta_1 > 0$, $\beta_2 > 0$, $\beta_3 > 0$).

3.3 Optimization Problem

A Stackelberg game is used to formulate the power control and nonuniform price bargaining problem in three-tier macro-small cell networks and D2D communications. In the Stackelberg game, one player is chosen as the leader, while the remaining players participate as followers. The leader first declares and implements his strategy, and then the followers respond accordingly. The optimization problem of the followers-level are to set proper transmit power to maximize its utility:

$$\begin{aligned} &\max U_{d2d_i}, U_{SUE_i}, U_{HMUE_i} \\ &\text{s.t.} \quad pd_{min} < pd < pd_{max} \\ &\qquad ps_{min} < ps < ps_{max} \\ &\qquad ph_{min} < ph < ph_{max} \end{aligned} \tag{22}$$

The optimization problem of the leader-level game is to establish a set of charging prices that maximize its utility:

$$\begin{aligned} &\max U_{MUE_i} \\ &\text{s.t.} \quad pm_{min} < pm < pm_{max} \end{aligned} \tag{23}$$

where pd_{min}, ps_{min}, ph_{min}, pm_{min}, are the minimum transmit power of D2D Tx, SUE, HMUE, and MUE, respectively, which must guarantee the QoS of users.

3.4   Game Analysis

The best response of the followers are derived by solving Eq. 24:

$$\frac{\partial U_{d2d}}{\partial p_d} = 0, \frac{\partial U_{SUE}}{\partial p_s} = 0, \frac{\partial U_{HMUE}}{\partial p_h} = 0 \tag{24}$$

The best transmit power of the followers are defined by Eqs. 25, 26 and 27:

$$p_d^* = \frac{1}{ln2\, m_1\, \overline{g}_{m,d}} - \frac{\overline{h}_{i,d} + \overline{g}_{i,d} + \overline{f}_{i,j} + \sigma^2}{\overline{f}_{i,i}} \tag{25}$$

$$p_s^* = \frac{1}{ln2\, m_2\, \overline{g}_{m,j}} - \frac{\overline{g}_{i,j} + \overline{g}_{d,j} + \overline{h}_{i.i} + \sigma^2}{\overline{g}_{i,i}} \tag{26}$$

$$p_h^* = \frac{1}{ln2\, m_3\, \overline{g}_{m,j}} - \frac{\overline{h}_{i,j} + \overline{g}_{i,j} + \overline{g}_{i,i} + \sigma^2}{\overline{h}_{i,i}} \tag{27}$$

Substituting the follower's strategy into the leader's utility function:

$$U_{MUE_i} = r_M^m + m_1 p_d^* \beta_1 g_{m,d} + m_2 p_s^* \beta_2 g_{m,j} + m_3 p_h^* \beta_3 g_{m,j} \tag{28}$$

The best price is derived by solving:

$$\frac{\partial U_{MUE}}{\partial m_1} = 0, \frac{\partial U_{MUE}}{\partial m_2} = 0, \frac{\partial U_{MUE}}{\partial m_3} = 0 \tag{29}$$

Then:

$$\frac{\partial^2 U_{MUE}}{\partial m_1{}^2}, \frac{\partial^2 U_{MUE}}{\partial m_2{}^2}, \frac{\partial^2 U_{MUE}}{\partial m_3{}^2} \tag{30}$$

The solution is:

$$m_1^* = \frac{\overline{f}_{i,i}}{\overline{g}_{m,d}\beta_1 ln2(\overline{h}_{i,d} + \overline{g}_{i,d} + \overline{f}_{i,j} + \sigma^2)} - \frac{1}{p_m \overline{g}_{m,0} ln2} \tag{31}$$

$$m_2^* = \frac{\overline{g}_{i,i}}{\overline{g}_{m,j}\beta_2 ln2(\overline{g}_{i,j} + \overline{g}_{d,j} + \overline{h}_{i,j} + \sigma^2)} - \frac{1}{p_s \overline{g}_{i,j} ln2} \tag{32}$$

$$m_3^* = \frac{\overline{h}_{i,i}}{\overline{g}_{m,j}\beta_3 ln2(\overline{h}_{i,j} + \overline{g}_{i,j} + \overline{g}_{i,i} + \sigma^2)} - \frac{1}{p_h \overline{h}_{i,j} ln2} \tag{33}$$

4   Joint Resource Allocation and Power Control

When optimal m_1^* is calculated the MBS should know the instantaneous information about m_2 and m_3. Similarly, in order to calculate the optimal m_2^*, the MBS should know the instantaneous information about m_1 and m_3. Finally, the m_3^* is calculated and the MBS should know the instantaneous information about m_1 and m_2. The updating of the MBS's price can be described by a vector equality of the form:

$$m = H_x(m) \qquad (34)$$

where $x = $ 1-d2d, 2-SUE, 3-HMUE, $m = m_1, m_2, m_3$. The leader would obtain the optimal price for the followers, which will maximize its utility.

$$m(t+1) = H(m(t)) \qquad (35)$$

The Iterative Power Allocation Algorithm (IPAA) is presented in Algorithm 1. The strategies adopted by the leader and his followers come to an agreement for the balance of the Stackelberg game. This equilibrium is obtained through a self-optimization that ensures that none of the players deviate from achieving an optimal point.

Algorithm 1. IPAA

1: Given CSI, TTI t.
2: Initialize the transmit powers p and the prices m.
3: Given the scale factor β_1, β_2, β_3.
4: Calculate the optimal prices m_1^*, m_2^*, m_3^*.
5: Calculate the optimal transmit powers p_d^*, p_s^*, p_h^*.

---

5 Simulation Results

In this section, the performance of the proposed model is shown in terms of users transmitted power and data rate, interference levels, network throughput, and running times of the algorithm. In addition, the results were compared with two benchmark models described in Sect. 3. The simulations were carried out using MATLAB by adopting a realistic LTE on an Intel(R) Core(TM) i7-5500U CPU@2.40 GHz with 8 GB RAM. The system parameters are summarized in Table 2.

5.1 Simulation Scenario

The simulated scenario consists of several MUE, SUE, and HMUE users. Furthermore, 50 small cells were deployed in an area of one macrocell, as shown in Fig. 2. The available spectrum is split between the macro-tier and the femto-tier to avoid the cross-tier interference.

5.2 Numerical Results

In this section, we present and analyze the results obtained with the Matlab simulations. Figures 3a and 3b present the convergence of transmit powers for D2DTx, SUE and HMUE users. It can be observed that the proposed scheme has fast convergence since it takes less than 3 iterations. Figure 4a shows the CDF

Table 2. System parameters

Parameter	Value	Units
R_m	500	m
R_f	25	m
D2D distance	0–10	m
Maximum transmit power of the followers	2	W
Transmit power of the leader	2	W
Noise spectral density	−174	dBm/Hz
Bandwidth	200	KHz
$\beta_1, \beta_2, \beta_3$	1, 3, 5	–

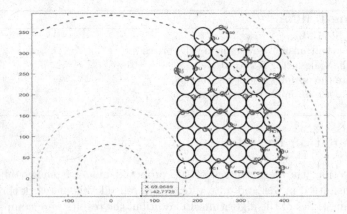

Fig. 2. Simulation scenario

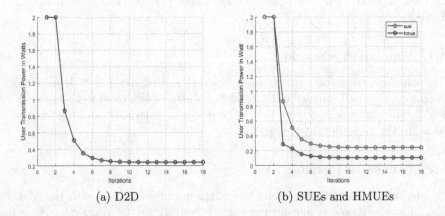

(a) D2D   (b) SUEs and HMUEs

Fig. 3. Transmit power vs iterations

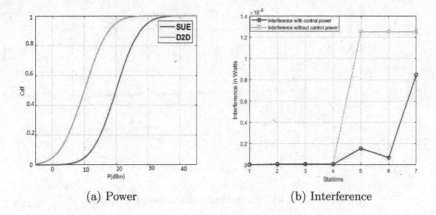

(a) Power   (b) Interference

Fig. 4. Power and Interference for small cell users and D2D users

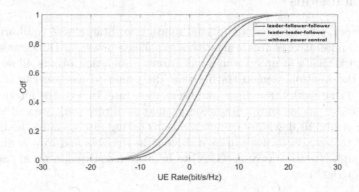

Fig. 5. Rate distribution

of SUE and D2DTx transmit power and Fig. 4b show the interferences with and without IPAA. The follower will use higher transmit power, besides, it can be observed that the transmit power of D2DTx is smaller than SUE.

The performance of the IPAA algorithm is presented in Fig. 6, which works with leader, follower, follower. In can be seen that this algorithm improves with respect to the algorithm that is implemented as leader, leader, follower. Furthermore, it is observed that the proposed algorithm improves the data rate to the results obtained if no power optimization is implemented (Fig. 5).

Figure 6 shows the network throughput for the proposed model with or without IPAA. It can be noticed that the throughput is enhanced when using IPAA. In this case, throughput stability is also achieved thanks to the power control that is implementing enabling the reduction of interference levels. The running times for an heuristic algorithm and a BIP (Binary Integer Programming) algorithm were estimated as 0.011 s and 0.047 s, respectively, which represents a reduction of 76.6% for the heuristic algorithm.

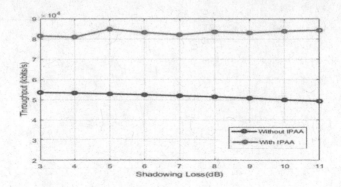

Fig. 6. Network throughput comparison for models

6 Conclusions

In this paper, we presented an optimal solution for Stackelberg equilibrium and proposed an iterative heuristic algorithm to allocate power for D2D transmitters, SUEs and HMUEs in uplink communications. Simulation results allowed us to validate the solution, demonstrating that the proposed method can effectively improve the network throughput and users' data rate. In fact, the interference is also reduced by means of the Stackelberg game. As future work, we will carry out a similar study for downlink communications taking into account the incentive mechanisms for SBS to work in hybrid mode in HetNets and to investigate the use of Graph Neural Networks (GNN) to improve resource allocation and power control for HetNets.

References

1. Belleschi, M., Fodor, G., Abrardo, A.: Performance analysis of a distributed resource allocation scheme for d2d communications. In: IEEE GLOBECOM Workshops (GC Wkshps), pp. 358–362 (2011)
2. Duong, N.D., Madhukumar, A.S., Niyato, D.: Stackelberg bayesian game for power allocation in two-tier networks. IEEE Trans. Veh. Technol. **65**(4), 2341–2354 (2016)
3. Estrada, R., Jarray, A., Otrok, H., Dziong, Z., Barada, H.: Energy-efficient resource-allocation model for ofdma macrocell/femtocell networks. IEEE Trans. Vehicular Technol. **62**(7), 3429–3437 (2013)
4. Estrada, R., Otrok, H., Dziong, Z.: Clustering and dynamic resource allocation for macro-femtocell networks. In: 16th International Telecommunications Network Strategy and Planning Symposium, pp. 1–6 (2014)
5. Estrada, R., Otrok, H., Dziong, Z.: Resource allocation model based on particle swarm optimization for ofdma macro-femtocell networks. In: IEEE International Conference on Advanced Networks and Telecommuncations Systems, pp. 1–6 (2013)
6. Estrada, R., Jarray, A., Otrok, H., Dziong, Z.: Base station selection and resource allocation in macro-femtocell networks under noisy scenario. Wireless Networks, pp. 1–17. Springer (2013)

7. Feng, H., Wang, H., Xu, X., Xing, C.: A tractable model for device-to-device communication underlaying multi-cell cellular networks. In: 2014 IEEE International Conference on Communications Workshops (ICC), pp. 587–591 (2014)

8. Gu, J., Bae, S.J., Hasan, S.F., Chung, M.Y.: Heuristic algorithm for proportional fair scheduling in d2d-cellular systems. IEEE Trans. Wireless Commun. **15**(1), 769–780 (2016)

9. Han, Y., Tao, X., Zhang, X.: Power allocation for device-to-device underlay communication with femtocell using stackelberg game. In: 2018 IEEE Wireless Communications and Networking Conference (WCNC), pp. 1–6. IEEE (2018)

10. He, Y., Wang, F., Wu, J.: Resource management for device-to-device communications in heterogeneous networks using stackelberg game. Int. J. Antennas Propagation (2014)

11. Liu, Z., Wang, W., Chan, K.Y., Ma, K., Guan, X.: Rate maximization for hybrid access femtocell networks with outage constraints based on pricing incentive mechanism. IEEE Trans. Veh. Technol. **69**(6), 6699–6708 (2020)

12. Marshoud, H., Otrok, H., Barada, H., Estrada, R., Jarray, A., Dziong, Z.: Resource allocation in macrocell-femtocell network using genetic algorithm. In: IEEE International Conference on Wireless and Mobile Computing, Networking and Communications, pp. 474–479 (2012)

13. Moubayed, A., Shami, A., Lutfiyya, H.: Wireless resource virtualization with device-to-device communication underlaying lte network. IEEE Trans. Broadcast. **61**(4), 734–740 (2015)

14. Rathi, R., et al.: Stackelberg game approach for resource allocation in device-to-device communication with heterogeneous networks. Robotics and Autonomous Systems, p. 104222 (2022)

15. Rohoden, K., Estrada, R., Otrok, H., Dziong, Z.: Game theoretical framework for clustering and resource allocation in macro-femtocell networks. Comput. Netw. **138**, 164–176 (2018)

16. Rohoden, K., Estrada, R., Otrok, H., Dziong, Z.: Stable femtocells cluster formation and resource allocation based on cooperative game theory. Comput. Commun. **134**, 30–41 (2019)

17. Rohoden, K., Estrada, R., Otrok, H., Dziong, Z.: Evolutionary game theoretical model for stable femtocells' clusters formation in hetnets. Comput. Commun. **161**, 266–278 (2020)

18. Saied, A., Okaf, A., Qiu, D.: An efficient resource allocation for d2d communications underlaying in hetnets. In: International Symposium on Networks, Computers and Communications (ISNCC), pp. 1–6. IEEE (2021)

19. Wang, J., Zhu, D., Zhao, C., Li, J.C.F., Lei, M.: Resource sharing of underlaying device-to-device and uplink cellular communications. IEEE Commun. Lett. **17**(6), 1148–1151 (2013)

20. Yanez, J., Estrada, R.: Interference model for macro-femtocell networks. In: 2021 IEEE Latin-American Conference on Communications (LATINCOM), pp. 1–6 (2021)

21. Zulhasnine, M., Huang, C., Srinivasan, A.: Efficient resource allocation for device-to-device communication underlaying lte network. In: IEEE 6th International Conference on Wireless and Mobile Computing, Networking and Communications, pp. 368–375 (2010)

Optimized Network Coding
with Real-Time Loss Prediction
for Hybrid 5G Networks

Ramesh Srinivasan[✉][iD] and J. J. Garcia-Luna-Aceves[iD]

University of California, Santa Cruz, CA 95064, USA
rameshs@soe.ucsc.edu

Abstract. Two novel mechanisms are introduced to take advantage
of network coding in TCP (Transmission Control Protocol), namely:
TCP with Network-Coded Window Transformation (TCP-NWT) and
TCP-NWT augmented with dynamic loss prediction, called Predictive-
Network-Coding (TCP-PNC). TCP-NWT uses network coding to handle
packet losses without retransmissions. TCP-PNC predicts the expected
loss-ratio on an ongoing basis during the course of a TCP-NWT session, which in turn changes the number of network coded packets that
are transmitted. These mechanisms result in a more efficient use of
network-coded packet transmissions in TCP. Simulation results indicate
a throughput increase of more than 22% compared to TCP in scenarios
involving dynamic changes in loss ratios in the midst of a TCP session.

Keywords: TCP · Real-time · Network-Coding

1 Introduction

Many of the current network-coding enhancements used in TCP use a predetermined loss-ratio for computing the amount of redundancy to be introduced
with additional network-coded packets, which is fixed for the duration of a TCP
session. This is a significant limitation, because of two key reasons. First, the
proliferation of different types of mobile end devices and ubiquitous wireless
last-mile access has resulted in dynamic transient fluctuations of packet-loss
ratios in the midst of an ongoing TCP session that need not reflect any real
network congestion. This renders the use of a predetermined loss-ratio throughout a TCP session ineffective. Second, end user applications require continuous
availability of services, service providers need to attain the most efficient use of
the available bandwidth over wired or wireless links, and more and more end
users are mobile. Some applications need real-time reliable data delivery with
predictable upper-bounds on data delivery. Hence, the static loss-ratio approach
used in prior enhancements of TCP based on network coding must be revisited
to account for the fact that a given TCP session may have varying loss-ratios
during the course of its session. Section 2 provides a survey of related work that

E. Sabir et al. (Eds.): UNet 2022, LNCS 13853, pp. 82–97, 2023.
https://doi.org/10.1007/978-3-031-29419-8_7

reveals that prior TCP variants based on network coding have relied on a static loss-ratio. The closest approach to our work is the Vegas Loss Predictor [10], which is implemented at the Network Coding layer (between Layer 4 and Layer 3) [13] to know when the network experiences congestion; however, the RTT (round trip time) values used do not factor in the additional time incurred due to potential link-layer retransmissions in last-mile wireless-links, which we try to incorporate in our work.

This paper introduces a new approach to detect the network health in a network-coding enabled TCP session and then predicts the expected loss-ratio and adapts to it by generating network-coded data to proactively compensate for the expected data loss. The proposed approach is particularly attractive for deployments of 5G networks and beyond, because it easily accommodates the use of heterogeneous transmission media, mobile end-nodes and comes very close to guaranteed data delivery in real-time with most optimal usage of network resources.

Section 3 describes TCP with Network-Coded Window Transformation (TCP-NWT) and Sect. 4 describes TCP-NWT with Predictive-Loss-Ratio, namely Predictive Network Coding (TCP-PNC). TCP-NWT proactively addresses packet losses without re-transmissions, while ensuring that all TCP session metrics are suitably transformed and passed back to the original TCP stack. This is accomplished by transforming the original TCP sliding window into another sliding window comprising of Network Coded data segments. TCP-PNC improves on TCP-NWT by dynamically predicting the expected loss-ratio on an ongoing basis during the course of a TCP session. This ensures that the optimal amount of network coded packets are transmitted.

Section 5 describes the results of simulations conducted with TCP-NWT and with other deployed TCP versions including TCP-Cubic and Sect. 6 outlines and compares the results observed. Section 7 concludes the paper.

2   Related Work

The use of network coding (NC) in TCP has been an area of active research. A comparative study of the actual approaches can be found in [8]. We only outline some of the most salient aspects and issues with these approaches.

TCP/NC [13] uses a new interpretation of acknowledgments (ACK), the sink acknowledges every linear combination of packets that reveals one unit of new information, even if it does not reveal an original packet immediately. This scheme has the property that packet losses are essentially masked from the congestion control algorithm. Therefore, this algorithm reacts to packet drops in a smooth manner, resulting in an effective approach for congestion control over networks involving lossy links. However, packet losses due to congestion are also masked in this approach and therefore effective flow-control is inhibited.

A redundancy adaptation scheme for network coding in TCP Vegas [10] uses loss predictor to decide whether the network is congested based on rate estimators [2,7,14]. The Vegas Loss Predictor is implemented at the Network Coding layer, between the network and transport layers, to know when the network experiences congestion and to adjust accordingly as in [2]. However, the RTT values used do not factor in the additional time incurred due to potential link-layer retransmissions in last-mile wireless-links. The effectiveness of NC has been analyzed by multiple authors [1,5,13]. The results indicate that NC does not provide big performance gains if it used below the transport layer in conjunction with a standard TCP implementation, as messages need to be delayed in a buffer to be able to encode them. The RTT is increased at each hop, and TCP interprets the RTT increases as a sign of congestion and reduces the transmission rate, which prevents the effective use of the transmission medium.

In summary, TCP has been augmented with a modular NC sub-layer to facilitate quick and easy adoption. However, that has resulted in many of the core intrinsic TCP session parameters and metrics like RTT and packet throughput not being accurately captured to reflect the exact status of the network along with introduction of additional delays. In this work, we ensure these metrics are accurately captured and relayed back to the transport layer and also optimal amount of network coded segments are generated with minimal additional introduction of delays.

3   TCP-NWT

TCP-NWT is a TCP congestion window transformation protocol which transforms the original TCP sliding congestion window with data segments into a new TCP congestion window comprising of network coded data segments. On the receiver side, on detecting the receipt of a TCP-NWT network coded segment, TCP-NWT window transformation protocol transforms the TCP-NWT receiver window into the corresponding original TCP receiver window comprising of the original TCP data segments generated by decoding the received group of coded TCP segments. Additionally, we propose a novel mechanism for processing of the acknowledgment packets so that the path metrics like RTT measurements by the TCP-NWT network coded segments are accurately relayed back to the original TCP. The design of TCP-NWT assumes a fixed loss-ratio and its specification consists of: (a) The TCP packet header augmentation needed to support network coding, (b) the available choice of coefficients values supported by our design and (c) the enumeration of the permitted group sizes.

We have taken an example to illustrate how TCP-NWT transformation works on group size of 1, which provides sufficient insight and clarity as to how it would work on larger group sizes. Encoding, decoding as well as processing of acknowledgments including relaying of the observed network health through RTT back to original TCP window are elaborated in great detail. A key consideration in our approach has been to keep the computation overhead of generating the network coded segments for transmission at the sender side as well as the subsequent decoding at the receiver side to bare minimal, as we are targeting mobile end-nodes which have significant computing, memory and in many cases power constraints.

We augment the TCP header with a new Boolean field indicating if its a header of an TCP-NWT segment. The group-number corresponding to this coded segment as well as the RLC coefficients used to generate this, namely CE1, CE2 and so on, also need to be included in the header. Figure 1 illustrates the new proposed TCP-NWT packet header. The first 20 bytes of the TCP header are always used in TCP-NWT. The options field is of variable size and it starts from the 6th row and can go up to 40 bytes. We use the TCP Option Kind number 25 [6,11]. The newly introduced TCP options field entries to support NWT are: (a) kind equal to 25 (8 bits); (b) length in bytes (8 bits); (c) network_coded_:1 (8 bits); (d) group_size equal to 1, 2, 4 or 8 (8 bits); (e) group_id: Grp Seq Num (32 bits); and (f) CEi equal to 1, 2, 4, 8, 16 /or 32 with $i = 1$ to 32 (6 unique values can be represented by 3 bits, however we have allocated 4 bits for each CE).

The group sizes permitted are 1 or 2 or 4 or 8. The permitted coefficients are one of six values namely 1, 2, 4, 8, 16 or 32, which ensures that multiplication with these coefficients is simply a bit-shifting operation and thus incurs minimal computation overhead. The group size indicates the number of segments, from the original non-coded data segments, which are combined (added) together after being multiplied by one of the random linear coefficients listed below, to generate the required number of coded segments. In the example below in Fig. 2, a fixed loss-ratio is assumed and the entire set of segments 4 in the initial group from Original TCP sliding window are coded using random coefficients to generate 5 coded segments for the 15% loss-ratio scenario. These are placed in the new TCP-NWT window.

Table 1. Definitions

Abbreviations	Definitions
RLC	Random linear coefficients
Orig-Grp-size	Number of segments in a group in Original TCP Window
grp_sz	Number of segments in current group in Original TCP Window
group_id	ID corresponding to an entire group used to generate coded segments
Grp Seq Num	The group_id from where coded segment got generated
RLC grp packets	Random Linear Coded Pkts of a group
Coded-Grp-size	Number of coded segments generated from the group in Original TCP Window
WLR	Worst Case Loss Ratio
D_i	$Datagram_i$ in Original TCP window
CD_i	$Coded_D atagram_i$ in TCP-NWT window
CE1, CE2..CE16	Random Linear Coefficient (RLC)1, RLC2... RLC16
SRTT	Smoothed Round Trip Time
RTTVAR	Round Trip Time Variation
$SRTT_{8.1}$	Smoothed Round Trip Time for $CD_{8.1}$ in TCP-NWT
$RTTVAR_{8.1}$	Round Trip Time Variation for $CD_{8.1}$ in TCP-NWT
$SRTT_8$	Smoothed Round Trip Time for Group 8 in original TCP window
$RTTVAR_8$	Round Trip Time Variation for Group 8 in original TCP window
RTO	Round Trip Timeout
R	Initial Round Trip Time Measurement
R'	Next Round Trip Time Measurement

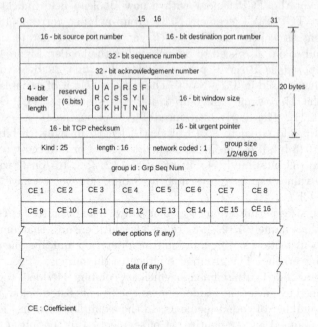

Fig. 1. TCP-NWT Packet header

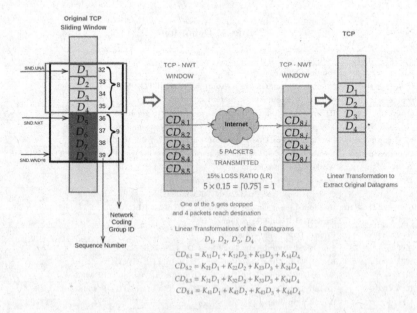

Fig. 2. Network coding

TCP-NWT Protocol Description

Each generated RLC segment has the following additional fields:

1. Orig-Grp-size: (≤ 16) permitted values in our design: 1 or 2 or 4 or 8.
2. List of RLC coeffcents: the number of these coefficients is exactly equal to the Orig-Grp-size, listed above.
3. Unique Group ID: Group Sequence number for each group (similar to the sequence number for individual packets) and is common for all members of a group. The random linear codes used for generating each of the new coded packets are always a unique tuple of dimension Orig-Grp-size (max possible is 8)
4. Coded-Grp-size = Orig-Grp-size/(1 - WLR)

Group Size 1. Figure 3 depicts the scenario where a group contains just a single TCP segment.

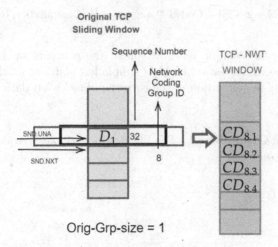

Fig. 3. Group Size 1

Sending Side. When there is a single segment in the sliding window and there are no other data/segments queuing in from higher layers for this TCP session, then group size (Orig-Grp-size) is set to 1. Depending on the loss-ratio, the number of coded segments generated could range from 2 to possibly 4. In the above example, the network coding group-id is 8 and the number of coded segments generated has been chosen to 4.

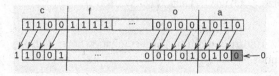

Kind : 25	length : 16	network coded : 1	group size 1
group id : 8			
2			

Fig. 4. Group Size 1: Coded Datagram 8.1's TCP Header

The relevant portions of the modified TCP header for network coded segment using a coefficient of 2 is depictedin Fig. 5.

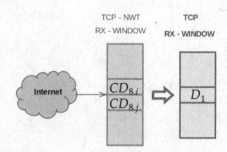

Fig. 5. Group Size 2: CE1-2 Coded Datagram 8.1's Computation by bit shifting

As can be seen a simple left shift of all the contents by 1 bit results in generation of the coded data. Similarly simple left shifts of all the contents by 2/3/4 bits results in generation of the corresponding coded data for coefficients of 4/8/16.

Receiving Side Group Size 1. The Fig. 6 depicts the receive mechanism when there is a single segment.

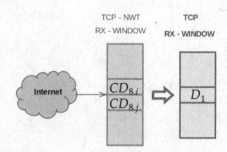

Fig. 6. Group Size 1 RX

Receipt of any one coded segment suffices to recompute the original segment, by a simple bit shift operation to the right according the value of the CE1. If CE1 = 2, right shift by 1 bit, if CE1 = 4, right shift by 2 bits, if CE1 = 8, right shift by 3 bits and if CE1 = 16, right shift by 4 bits to generate original Segment D1.

Acknowledgement for Group Size 1. The receipt of an ACK for any one coded segment in a group of size of one confirms receipt of the data for that group. One of the contributions of this work is ensuring that the health of the network is captured accurately and relayed back as-is to the higher layer by the combined TCP stack. To compute the current RTO, a TCP sender maintains two state variables, SRTT and RTTVAR. We compute the RTO at the end of receipt of acknowledgement for each of the four coded segments transmitted using the exact method outlined in RFC-2988 [9]. When the first RTT measurement R is made, the host updates SRRT, SRRT and RTO as follows:

SRTT $\leftarrow$ R; RTTVAR $\leftarrow$ R/2

RTO $\leftarrow$ SRTT + max (G, K*RTTVAR); where K = 4

For each subsequent RTT measurement R' in a given NC group, the sender updates RTTVAR and SRTT for TCP-NWT window, as follows till measurements for all coded segments are completed.

$RTTVAR_{8.1} \leftarrow (1\text{-beta})*RTTVAR_8 + beta* \mid SRTT - R_{8.1}' \mid$

$SRTT_{8.1} \leftarrow (1 - alpha) * SRTT_8 + alpha * R_{8.1}'$

$RTTVAR_{8.2} \leftarrow (1 - beta)*RTTVAR_{8.1} +$
$\qquad\qquad beta * \mid SRTT_{8.1} - R_{8.2}' \mid$

$SRTT_{8.2} \leftarrow (1 - alpha) * SRTT_{8.1} + alpha * R_{8.2}'$

$RTTVAR_{8.3} \leftarrow (1 - beta) * RTTVAR_{8.2} + beta * \mid SRTT_{8.2} - R_{8.3}' \mid$

$SRTT_{8.3} \leftarrow (1 - alpha) * SRTT_{8.2} + alpha * R_{8.3}'$

$RTTVAR_{8.4} \leftarrow (1 - beta) * RTTVAR_{8.3} + beta * \mid SRTT_{8.3} - R_{8.4}' \mid$

$SRTT_{8.4} \leftarrow (1 - alpha) * SRTT_{8.3} + alpha * R_{8.4}'$

$RTTVAR_9 \leftarrow RTTVAR_{8.4}$

$SRTT_9 \leftarrow SRTT_{8.4}$

The RTTVAR and SRRT corresponding to $CD_{8.4}$ from TCP-NWT window are then assigned to the updated RTTVAR and SRRT corresponding to completion of successful transmission of D1 and receipt of ACK. The computation mechanism for other group sizes on both sending and receiving side are similar to that for group size 1.

Algorithm - TCP-NWT. We state the algorithm for encoding a group of segments and the algorithm for decoding a group of segments below. Once the receiver has received sufficient number of coded segments for a group, equal to the size of the group, the decoding steps are initiated. We use the Gaussian-elimination [4] procedure for solving a system of linear equations to decode and arrive at the original data sent.

Algorithm 1. encode(group)

1: Determine the group (group_id) of the set of packets to be encoded.
2: Size of the group, grp_sz;
3: Initialize the group_seq_num for each individual packet within the group to the group_id of this group.
4: Based on LR (Loss_Ratio), determine the number of encoded packets to be generated: numEncoded
5: **for** i = 1; i ≤ numEncoded; i ++ **do**
6:     Determine the unique set of NC Coefficients Tuples: CE[1], CE[2], ⋯, CE[numEncoded]
       /* (based on the group_id_ and group_seq_num for each encoded packet to be generated.) */
7:     Clear RLC_PAC[i];
8:     Compute the contents of the coded packet.
9:     **for** j =1 ; j ≤ grp_sz; j++ **do**
10:        RLC_PAC[i] = RLC_PAC[i] + CE[i][j] × PAC[j]
11:    **end for**
12:    Populate the packet hdr of RLC_PAC[i] with the the NC Coefficients used to generate it;
13:    Upload RLC_PAC[i] the newly generated coded packet into new TCP_NWT window.
14: **end for**

Algorithm 2. decode(group)

1: **while** TCP Session is still active **do**
2:     Wait for the receipt of a packet. if times out waiting, quit;
3:     Determine the group (group_id_) of the received segment.
4:     Determine the group Size of the group, grp_sz;
5:     Determine if there is already a sink created to gather all segments of this group.
6:     if not, create a new sink for this group and initialize grp_rcv_cnt, group receive count to 1;
7:     Check if grp_sz for this group equals grp_rcv_cnt for this sink
8:     if yes pass the set of packets to the GaussianElimination function, which will return the original segments of this group.
9: **end while**

---

4 TCP-PNC

Based on the current dynamically estimated loss-ratio of the network at a given point in time and using a new enhanced approach based off [15], the number of network coded data packets (n) to be generated from an initial dataset (m) of data packets is computed. We evaluate the dynamic loss ratio as indicated below:

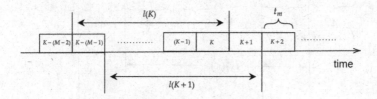

Fig. 7. Dynamic loss-ratio prediction

Loss-Ratio for different range of the time periods "M" starting from 2 to about 32 is computed in every measurement period tm. Let $l_M(k)$ be the packet loss ratio of the k-th measurement, which is calculated as the number of dropped packets over the total number of packets arrived during the latest M periods (see Eq. 1); where $N_d(k)$ is the number of packets dropped in the k-th measurement period, and $N_a(k)$ is the number of packets arrived in the k-th measurement period.

$$l_M(k) = \frac{\left(\sum_{i=0}^{M-1} N_d(k-i)\right)}{\left(\sum_{i=0}^{M-1} N_a(k-i)\right)}, \quad M = 2, 3, 4, \cdots, 32 \tag{1}$$

In real scenario M can be any value ≥ 0:

$$M = 0, \; LR(k) = l_0(k) \tag{2}$$

$$M = 1, \; LR(k) = \frac{l_0(k) + 2^{-1}l_1(k)}{2^0 + 2^{-1}} \tag{3}$$

$$M = 2, \; LR(k) = \frac{l_0(k) + 2^{-1}l_1(k) + 2^{-2}l_2(k)}{2^0 + 2^{-1} + 2^{-2}} \tag{4}$$

$$LR(k) = \frac{2^0 \times l_0(k) + 2^{-1} \times l_1(k) + 2^{-2} \times l_2(k) + \cdots + 2^{-n} \times l_n(k)}{2^0 + 2^{-1} + 2^{-2} + \cdots + 2^{-n}} \tag{5}$$

4.1 TCP-PNC Predictive Network Coding - Protocol Description by Example

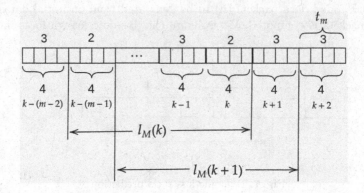

Fig. 8. An example of dynamic loss-ratio prediction

We are taking an actual example in order to succinctly illustrate our proposed mechanism for dynamically arriving at the predicted loss at the next upcoming time interval. Value of M determines the number of time periods over which the loss ratio is computed. We are proposing here of assigning a weight of 1 for loss ratio $l_0(k)$, 2^{-1} for $l_1(k)$, 2^{-2} for $l_2(k)$ and so on, to ensure the data comprising just the immediate past is given a higher importance compared to the data corresponding to a slightly larger duration from the past. In the above example, we have taken the actual data which indicates that in the k-th measurement, out of 4 packets sent, 2 are successfully received and acknowledged. In the (k+1)th measurement, out of 4 packets sent, 3 are successfully received and acknowledged.

$$M = 0; \quad l_0(k-1) = \frac{3}{4} = 0.75; \quad LR(k-1) = \frac{1 * l_0(k-1)}{1} = 0.75 \qquad (6)$$

$$M = 0; \quad l_0(k) = \frac{2}{4} = 0.5 \qquad (7)$$

$$M = 1; \quad l_1(k) = \frac{3+2}{4+4} = \frac{5}{8} = 0.625 \qquad (8)$$

$$LR(k) = \frac{1 * l_0(k) + (1/2) * l_1(k)}{1 + 1/2} = 0.54 \qquad (9)$$

$$M = 0; \quad l_0(k+1) = \frac{3}{4} = 0.75 \qquad (10)$$

$$M = 1; \quad l_1(k+1) = \frac{3+2}{4+4} = \frac{5}{8} = 0.625 \tag{11}$$

$$M = 2; \quad l_2(k+1) = \frac{3+2+3}{4+4+4} = \frac{8}{12} = 0.67 \tag{12}$$

$$LR(k+1) = \frac{1 * l_0(k+1) + (1/2) * l_1(k+1) + (1/4) * l_2(k+1)}{1 + 1/2 + 1/4} = 0.70 \tag{13}$$

Expected Dynamic Loss Ratio: Using $LR(k-1)$,LR(k), and $LR(k+1)$ we try to predict the PLR Predicted loss Ratio at the next three time intervals PLR(k+2), PLR(K+3), PLR(k+4) using following simple mechanisms. We do a linear extrapolation of the Observed loss ratio values at (k) and (k+1) to arrive at PLR(k+2). LR(K) is 0.54 and LR(K+1) is 0.70 and therefore initial estimate for PLR(k+2) is 0.90. However since in our example we are sending 4 segments in a timeslot, the actual possible values for $l_0(k+2)$ are 0, 0.25, 0.5, 0.75 and 1. Since our initial estimate of 0.90 is between 0.75 and 1, we would take the lower of the two namely 0.75 as the PLR(k+2). Similarly taking the values of OLR(K+1) and PLR(k+2) and doing a similar linear extrapolation we estimate PLR(K+3), which in our example turns out to be 0.75. Similarly taking PLR(k+2) and PLR(K+3) we estimate PLR(k+4), which also turns out to be 0.75. Next we try to predict the Worst case loss-ratio by taking the minimum of the observed loss ratio in the last two measurement periods and the predicted loss ratio in the upcoming two measurement periods:

MIN($LR(k), LR(k+1), PLR(k = 2)PLR(K = 3)PLR(k = 4)$), namely MIN(0.54, 0.70, 0.75, 0.75, 0.75), which is 0.54. This is closest to 0.5, which would be the worst case loss-ratio in the above example. For a given session, at every 2 secs interval the Observed Loss Ratio (OLR) is computed and saved in a LossRatioTable for last hour (array size is $3600/2 = 1800$). Using the past saved values of the observed loss ratio - along with currently observed loss ratio extrapolation of the gradient/trend and prediction of the PLR (Predicted Loss Ratio) values for the next 3 time periods is done. Based on this trend, the MIN (OLR(t0-4), OLR(t0-2), PLR(t0), PLR(t0+2), PLR(t0+4)) is chosen as the WLR(t0) potential Worst-case Loss Ratio scenario to be addressed while deriving the number of RLC (Random Linear Coded) TCP datagrams. Coded_Grp_size = Orig_Grp_size/(WLR).

5 Testing and Simulation

We evaluated the performance of TCP-WSC using discrete-event simulation. The NS-2 simulator [12] was used. NS-2 [12] provides substantial support for simulation of TCP, Routing, and Multicast Protocols over wired and wireless (local and satellite) networks. The TCP implementation was modified to support the new proposed protocols.

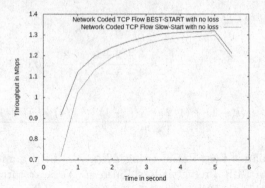

Fig. 9. TCP-NWT with No-Loss

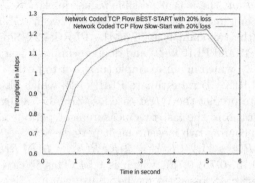

Fig. 10. TCP-NWT with 20%Loss

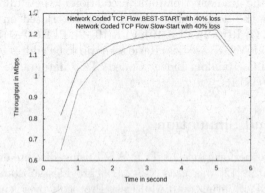

Fig. 11. TCP-NWT with 40%Loss

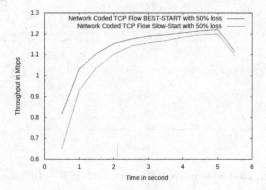

Fig. 12. TCP-NWT with 50%Loss

Numerous scenarios and options were tried out to truly validate the gains and benefits of the proposed approach here.

As very succinctly evident in the results of the simulation, the performance has been maintained at the same level despite varying levels of errors, all the way from 20% loss in Fig. 10, 40% loss in Fig. 11 and finally even with 50% loss as seen in the Fig. 12. Comparing these with the loss-less scenario in Fig. 9, clearly shows we can guarantee performance and throughput despite level of errors/losses with one big CAVEAT to remember, namely: these errors are ONLY due to wireless link-layer errors and NOT due to a true congestion per-se in the network. The above results were with TCP-NWT Only, without the predictive dynamic Loss-ratio incorporated.

The Simulation Scenario with TCP-PNC, which comprises TCP-NWT and additionally incorporates the Predictive loss Ratio.

This section describes simulations from 4 scenarios - 2 each with

a. standard TCP ns-2 [12] new Reno
   (i) Using a wireless topology with an almost lossless wireless link
   (ii) Using the same wireless topology with a substantial lossy wireless link at both the wireless end-nodes
b. standard TCP ns-2 [12] new Reno implementation modified with our proposed enhancements for networks with wireless end-nodes.
   (a) Using the same wireless topology with an almost lossless wireless link
   (b) Using the same wireless topology with a substantial lossy wireless link (10% and subsequently 20%)

6   Results

There was an improvement in overall throughput observed with the new implementation - especially as transmission errors (link-layer losses) increase. Comparative results with TCP Cubic as well as TCP newReno [3] show that our

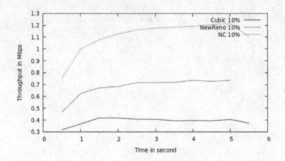

Fig. 13. Cubic vs New Reno vs TCP-PNC - 10% loss

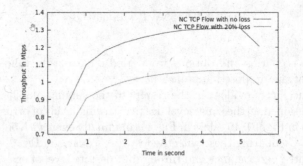

Fig. 14. TCP-PNC - Throughput Comparison with no loss vs 20% loss

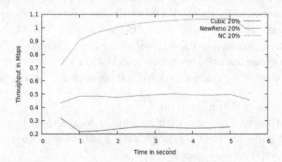

Fig. 15. Cubic vs New Reno vs TCP-PNC- 20% loss

Predictive Network Coding TCP-PNC provides a significantly higher through-put of about 22%. The results clearly demonstrate that dynamic adjustment of amount of additional network coded segments being generated based on accu-rate prediction of the loss-ratio results in a much more optimal effective usage of the network resources as well as ensuring minimizing retransmission for lost segments, thus significantly improving throughput.

7 Conclusion and Future Work

The prediction of the loss ratio proposed in this paper constitutes a solution based on rudimentary machine learning. This is a nascent area with the potential for much more innovations based on proactive response based on machine-learning techniques, and there could be many more ways to predict the loss-ratio more accurately. Saving past TCP sessions metrics and parameters is another promising way to predict the current expected network behaviour for the same destinations.

References

1. Alferaidi, K., Piechocki, R.: TCP-MAC cross layer integration for Xor network coding. In: Arai, K., Kapoor, S., Bhatia, R. (eds.) SAI 2018. AISC, vol. 857, pp. 860–875. Springer, Cham (2019). https://doi.org/10.1007/978-3-030-01177-2_64
2. Brakmo, L.S., Peterson, L.L.: TCP VEGAS: end to end congestion avoidance on a global internet. IEEE J. Sel. Areas Commun. **13**(8), 1465–1480 (1995)
3. Floyd, S., Henderson, T., Gurtov, A.: Rfc3782: The newreno modification to tcp's fast recovery algorithm (2004)
4. Gauss, C.F.: Gaussian elimination method solving matrix equations (1850). https://mathworld.wolfram.com/GaussianElimination.html
5. Huang, Y., Ghaderi, M., Towsley, D., Gong, W.: TCP performance in coded wireless mesh networks. In: 2008 5th Annual IEEE Communications Society Conference on Sensor, Mesh and Ad Hoc Communications and Networks, pp. 179–187. IEEE (2008)
6. IANA: 5g network deployment scenarios (2020). https://www.iana.org/assignments/tcp-parameters/tcp-parameters.xhtml (2022)
7. Martignon, F., Fratta, L.: Loss differentiation schemes for TCP over wireless networks. In: Ajmone Marsan, M., Bianchi, G., Listanti, M., Meo, M. (eds.) QoS-IP 2004. LNCS, vol. 3375, pp. 586–599. Springer, Heidelberg (2005). https://doi.org/10.1007/978-3-540-30573-6_46
8. Matsuda, T., Noguchi, T., Takine, T.: Survey of network coding and its applications. IEICE Trans. Commun. **94**(3), 698–717 (2011)
9. Paxson, V., Allman, M.: RFC 2988: Computing TCP's retransmission timer (2000)
10. Ruiz, H.M., Kieffer, M., Pesquet-Popescu, B.: Redundancy adaptation scheme for network coding with TCP. In: 2012 International Symposium on Network Coding (NetCod), pp. 49–54. IEEE (2012)
11. S. Bradner, V.P.: RFC 2780: IANA allocation guidelines for values in the internet protocol and related headers (2000)
12. S. McCanne, S.F., Fall, K.: Network simulator. Public domain software (1995)
13. Sundararajan, J.K., Shah, D., Médard, M., Mitzenmacher, M., Barros, J.: Network coding meets TCP. In: IEEE INFOCOM 2009, pp. 280–288. IEEE (2009)
14. Tian, Y., Xu, K., Ansari, N.: TCP in wireless environments: problems and solutions. IEEE Commun. Mag. **43**(3), S27–S32 (2005)
15. Wang, C., Liu, J., Li, B., Sohraby, K., Hou, Y.T.: LRED: a robust and responsive AQM algorithm using packet loss ratio measurement. IEEE Trans. Parallel Distrib. Syst. **18**(1), 29–43 (2006)

TCP-RTA: Real-time Topology Adaptive Congestion Control Strategy in TCP

Ramesh Srinivasan$^{(\boxtimes)}$ (ID) and J. J. Garcia-Luna-Aceves (ID)

University of California, Santa Cruz, CA 95064, USA
rameshs@soe.ucsc.edu

Abstract. The congestion-control mechanisms currently implemented in different variants of the Transmission Control Protocol (TCP) do not account for the possibility that an inherent topology change is the cause of changes in the perceived end-to-end round-trip time (RTT) in a TCP session, rather than network congestion. This results in low throughput and inefficient use of the available bandwidth. We introduce TCP-RTA (TCP Real-time Topology Adaptiveness), a TCP variant that dynamically detects a topology change and in real-time adapts to an appropriate congestion-control strategy in order to maximize the effective use of the total available bandwidth. Simulation results indicate a throughput increase of more than 35% in scenarios involving dynamic topology changes in the midst of a TCP session.

Keywords: TCP · Real-time · Congestion-Control

1 Introduction

The congestion-control mechanisms that are used in the Transmission Control Protocol (TCP) today are not able to detect changes in the underlying topology that lead to drastic changes in the round-trip time (RTT) experienced in a TCP session. Instead, TCP senders interpret such changes as the presence of congestion. Furthermore, current TCP implementations reply on a specific congestion-control strategy that is fixed for the duration of a TCP session. This is rapidly becoming a major limitation of TCP in today's Internet, because of two key factors. First, the proliferation of very different types of transmission media that have disparate bandwidth-delay products and reliability renders the use of a single congestion-control strategy that is unaware of the impact of the underlying topology on the delays of TCP sessions highly ineffective. Second, end user applications and deployment scenarios including Anglova [15] require continuous availability of services, service providers need to attain the most efficient use of the available bandwidth over wired or wireless links, and more and more end users are mobile. Hence, the original approach used in TCP of interpreting increases in delay as the ensuing of congestion must be revisited to account for the fact that a given TCP session may use different types of transmission media as end users move and different transmission media are used as a result.

© The Author(s), under exclusive license to Springer Nature Switzerland AG 2023
E. Sabir et al. (Eds.): UNet 2022, LNCS 13853, pp. 98–112, 2023.
https://doi.org/10.1007/978-3-031-29419-8_8

The key contribution of this paper is the introduction of a new approach to congestion-control in TCP that chooses an apt congestion-control algorithm depending on the perceived use of different underlying transmission media resulting from changes in the measured RTT within ongoing TCP sessions. The approach uses a congestion-control algorithm that is best suited for a given range of RTT values and switches among different algorithms as needed. This is particularly relevant for the support of TCP sessions involving end-devices that are mobile during the midst of an ongoing TCP session. In addition, the proposed approach to congestion control in TCP is particularly attractive for future deployments of 5G networks and beyond, because it easily accommodates the use of heterogeneous transmission media.

Section 2 discusses related work. As our survey of prior variants of TCP reveals, TCP variants in the past have relied on a single congestion-control algorithm. The closest approach to our work is D-TCP (Dynamic TCP) [22], wherein the bandwidth-delay product is dynamically computed and a congestion metric derived off this computation. This is then used to determine the response of the congestion control algorithm to increase/decrease the congestion window during the RTT update and loss detection. However, this is done within a single algorithm and it is not very robust.

Section 3 presents the approach and architecture of TCP-RTA (TCP with Real-Time Topology Adaptiveness). TCP-RTA is a new TCP variant with a comprehensive set of enhancements, specific for dynamically detecting topology changes and according adapting to an appropriate congestion control strategy.

Based on various studies of observed RTT for various underlying network topologies [29], we categorize the initial starting topology of a new TCP session being initiated based on the observed RTT values during the initial three-way handshake. Thereafter the RTT values are monitored and anytime three consecutive RTTs change and in the range of a different underlying topology, TCP-RTA dynamically enables a change to the corresponding specific congestion-control strategy for the newly perceived topology. This ensures that the ongoing TCP session has the best congestion-control strategy in place. TCP-RTA explicitly invokes separate congestion-congestion control algorithms for each of the specific topologies perceived through the RTT measurements.

Section 4 describes the results of simulations conducted with TCP-RTA and with other deployed TCP versions including TCP Cubic and Sect. 5 outlines and compares the results observed. Section 6 concludes the paper.

2   Related Work

Outlined below is a survey of the various current deployed versions of TCP and the way they handle the introduction of wireless links.

A comparative study of the actual approaches used in the different TCP implementations can be found in the paper titled "A Comparative Analysis of TCP Tahoe, Reno, New-Reno, SACK and Vegas" [11]. There are several

TCP implementations including [26] Tahoe [20], Reno [19], New-Reno [13], TCP-SACK [24], TCP-Vegas [6], TCP-Jersey [31], TCP-DCR [5], TCP Santa Cruz [25] which address various short-comings in TCP implementations.

For high-speed network requirements, the following TCP variants have been proposed including FAST [16], HSTCP [12], STCP [23] TCPNewReno [13], CUBIC [17], SQRT TCP [18], TCP-Westwood [10], BIC TCP [32] Binary Increase Congestion control, CUBIC [17], TCP-Illinois [21], TCP-Hybla [8], YeAH-TCP [1], Compound TCP (CTCP) [30], BBR [9].

Mobile end-devices may undergo underlying topology changes during the course of an ongoing TCP session, simply due to their physical movement. The resultant changes observed in end-end packet Round-Trip-Time would get misinterpreted as a congestion in the network by existing TCP implementations.

For completeness, would like to mention that RFC1185 and RFC1123 were among the initiatives to enable TCP extensions for high speed networks providing for scaled windows and timestamps.

The approaches proposed to improve TCP performance over networks with wireless links can be divided into two major categories, namely: those that work at the transport level, and others that work at the link level.

Transport level proposals include Explicit Bad State Notification (EBSN) [3], Freeze-TCP [14], Indirect-TCP (I- TCP) [2], Snoop [4], fast-retransmission [7].

Snoop [4] is a well-known link level proposal. In this scheme, the base station sniffs the link interface for any TCP segments destined for the mobile host, and buffers them if buffer space is available. Segments are forwarded to the mobile host only if the base station deems it necessary.

In WTCP [28] the base station is involved in the TCP connection. WTCP [28] requires no modification to the TCP code that runs in the mobile host or the fixed host. Based on duplicate acknowledgment or timeout, the base station locally retransmits lost segments. In case of timeout, by quickly reducing the transmission window, potentially wasteful wireless transmission is avoided and the interference with other channels is reduced. Also WTCP [28] hides the wireless link errors from the source by effectively subtracting the residence time of the segment at the WTCP [28] buffer from the RTT value computed at the source, thus the RTT computation excludes wireless link layer retransmission delays.

Prior work related to our specific proposal here, includes D-TCP Dynamic TCP [22] Congestion Control Algorithm for Next Generation Mobile Networks, wherein Bandwidth-Delay product is dynamically computed and a congestion metric derived off this computation, which is used to determine the response of the congestion control algorithm to increase/decrease the CWND during the RTT update and loss detection. Thus only a single parameter is being dynamically modified and the underlying Congestion Control algorithm is the same for all scenarios and through the life-cycle of the current session and thereafter till the TCP stack is changed.

In this work, we are proposing TCP-RTA, which dynamically recognizing potential underlying topology change in the end-end path of the current TCP session and transitioning and thus adapting in real-time, to the apt congestion control algorithm applicable for this updated new topology, experienced by the TCP Session.

3   TCP-RTA Approach and Architecture

In this section, we elaborate on TCP-RTA (TCP with Real-time Topology Adaptiveness), which comprises numerous enhancements to maximize the throughput of TCP sessions, particularly in hybrid 5G networks with wireless interfaces, which experience a topology change in the midst of an ongoing TCP session.

3.1   TCP-RTA Approach

There are proven very well performing and optimized congestion-control custom strategies for specific environments as exemplified by some of the TCP variants including, for example, TCP Hybla [8] for satellite links, HSTCP [12] for networks with a large bandwidth-delay product along with low-latency, as well as some generic TCP variants like TCP NewReno [13], among others. We are proposing a new mechanism, wherein we leverage apriori categorized values of some of the ranges of TCP parameters (example RTT), as corresponding to a particular underlying nature of the environment (Topology). We use the above information to help identify the actual environment encountered by a TCP Session at any given point during the course of the given session. On detection of a significant consistent change in our TCP session parameters of interest (RTT in our scenario), which definitively point to a topology/environment change we transition over completely to the custom congestion control strategy, which is apt for the transitioned environment/topology. An example would be a significant consistent increase in RTT would imply a change of the environment to a "satellite - very low speed link" from a regular environment. Our mechanism would respond as follows: Starting with default TCP NewReno [13], on detection of the significant consistent RTT increase pointing to a transition to a path involving a satellite, we initiate a switch over of the congestion-control algorithm from that of TCP NewReno's [13] congestion-control algorithm to that of TCP-Hybla's [8] congestion control algorithm.

3.2   TCP-RTA Architecture

TCP-RTA uses the following high-level approach to effect the transition across congestion control algorithms. We dynamically adapt the congestion control strategy as enumerated below.

For any TCP session, it starts with a default configuration including a congestion control strategy, which we have chosen as that of TCP NewReno for our study and simulation. To clarify, this default TCP configuration can be any variant of TCP which is apt for the environment of the TCP session, as it is established. One of the proposed enhancements that is envisaged in future is the inclusion of negotiation and convergence on the apt initial default configuration in TCP's initial 3-way handshake protocol. Comparing the observed RTT during the initial 3-way handshake, with the corresponding default RTT thresholds for each environment, we arrive at the nature of the underlying topology and accordingly configure the default initial configuration of the TCP session. For our default TCP NewReno configuration, the RTT-threshold is accordingly initialized to 300 ms. In our dynamic TCP-RTA algorithm, we keep track of the last three observed RTT at any point in time: RTT-Current, RTT-Prev and RTT-Prev-Prev.

Table 1. Definitions

Variable	Definition
RTT	Round Trip Time (implies end-end)
RTT-Current	RTT for the most recent segment
RTT-Prev	RTT for the segment prior to the last segment (prior segment)
RTT-Prev-Prev	RTT for the segment prior to the prior segment

The salient steps in our proposed approach are:

1. The above 3 variables are initialized at the start of a session to the default-RTT-threshold (300ms in our environment).
2. After receipt of every acknowledgement and the corresponding immediate computation of the observed RTT (RTT-new), we update the value of
   i RTT-Prev-Prev with RTT-Prev
   ii RTT-Prev with RTT-Current
   iii RTT-Current with RTT-new
3. if the three observed values of RTT are all above 800 ms, we infer that there must have been an underlying topology change and based on some of the observed RTT times for TCP sessions going over a satellite link [8], we infer that a topology change has happened and the path now involves a satellite link. Hence we initiate a change in the congestion control strategy which is more apt for the newly observed dynamically changed environment, wherein the TCP session now includes a path through a significantly larger delay (typically attributed to a satellite link), namely TCP Hybla [8].
4. If only one or two of the observed values are above the 800 ms threshold and subsequently the RTT comes back to prior regular values, then these transients are ignored and the congestion control strategy is left unchanged.
5. The above steps are repeated till the end of the TCP session, with an additional check happening after every update to the observed RTT. If we find that the last three observed RTT values are all below RTT-threshold for a non-satellite link, which we have chosen as 300 ms based on reported observations in [8], we revert back the congestion control strategy to that of TCP NewReno.

The high level algorithm below clearly depicts the control flow of the newly proposed dynamic TCP-RTA and its congestion control strategy.

Algorithm 1. TCP-RTA-Overview

1: Def_RTT_TCP_NEWRENO = 500
2: Def_RTT_TCP_HYBLA = 800
3: m_adaptiveAlgProg = TCP_NEWRENO
4: RTT-Current = Def_RTT_TCP_NEWRENO
5: RTT-Prev = Def_RTT_TCP_NEWRENO
6: RTT-Prev-Prev = Def_RTT_TCP_NEWRENO
   do
7: **if** (m_adaptiveAlg == TCP_NEWRENO) **then**
8:   **if** ((RTT-Current > Def_RTT_TCP_HYBLA) &&
     (RTT-Prev > Def_RTT_TCP_HYBLA) &&
     (RTT-Prev-Prev > Def_RTT_TCP_HYBLA)) **then**
9:      m_adaptiveAlg = TCP_HYBLA;
10: **end if**
11: **else if** (m_adaptiveAlg == TCP_HYBLA) **then**
12:   **if** ((RTT-Current < Def_RTT_TCP_NEWRENO) &&
     (RTT-Prev > Def_RTT_TCP_NEWRENO) &&
     (RTT-Prev-Prev > Def_RTT_TCP_NEWRENO)) **then**
13:      m_adaptiveAlg = TCP_NEWRENO;
14:   **end if**
15: **end if**
16: wait till next ACK recd;
17: RTT-new = ComputeNewRTT();
18: RTT-Prev-Prev = RTT-Prev;
19: RTT-Prev = RTT-Current;
20: RTT-Current = RTT-new;
   while (TCP Session is still active)

The main underlying premise is that if there is a distinct change suddenly observed in the RTT and that change is consistently maintained for at least 3 consecutive segments back to back without any packet loss, then we predict the cause of such a change should be an underlying topology change rather than a sporadic congestion in the network.

Since TCP does not know whether a delayed ACK is caused by a congestion experienced by a segment or possibly a topology change, it waits for a small number of additional ACKs to be received. It is assumed that if there is just a temporary increase in RTT, there will be typically one or two delayed ACKs at most, before either the RTT returns to prior normal values or it increases more and possibly ending in a timeout and a packet drop. The underlying premise is that any network congestion scenario is not a stable condition and thus a transitory state, which would quickly either return to normalcy or become worse.

So, if there are 3 or more ACKs consistently delayed by similar value and received in a row, then we presume it is a strong indication that the segments are most probably using a new stable path(topology) with a new different (increased or decreased) RTT.

We ensure the hand-off happens seamlessly across from the current congestion control strategy to the appropriate target congestion control strategy for the newly identified topology to which the network has transition to. This is particularly very relevant for mobile end-nodes which are ubiquitous with the proliferation of the 5G technology.

As part of our proposed TCP-RTA approach, we also ensure that our adaptive congestion control strategy does not respond to any sporadic one-off drastic different behaviour in the TCP parameters in any significant manner. Another significant aspect of our proposed approach is that one-off sporadic changes are not even passed onto TCP congestion control mechanism, so effectively it acts like a low-pass filter preventing these exceptions from impacting the parameters impacting the throughput and performance of the TCP session.

Detailed algorithm outlined below spell out the steps. We did experiment with having same threshold for transition across different Congestion Control Strategies as well as having a common gray area, whose thresholds had to be crossed clearly by the parameter (RTT) used to identify topology change.

Algorithm 2. TCP-RTA::SlowStart

1: **input** Ptr_SocketState, segmentsAcked
2: **if** (segmentsAcked $\geq$ 1 && m_adaptiveAlg == TCP_NEWRENO) **then**
3:     sndCwnd = tcb$\rightarrow$ m_cWnd;
4:     tcb$\rightarrow$m_cWnd   =   min((sndCwnd+(segmentsAcked*tcb $\rightarrow$m_segmentSize)),tcb $\rightarrow$m_ssThresh);
5:     **return**   segmentsAcked-((tcb $\rightarrow$m_cWnd-sndCwnd)/tcb $\rightarrow$m_segmentSize);
6: **else if** (segmentsAcked $\geq$ 1 && m_adaptiveAlg == TCP_HYBLA) **then**
7:     /* slow start
8:     INC = 2^ρ - 1 */
9:     increment = pow(2, m_ρ) - 1.0;
10:    incr = increment*tcb$\rightarrow$m_segmentSize;
11:    tcb$\rightarrow$m_cWnd = min (tcb$\rightarrow$m_cWnd + incr, tcb$\rightarrow$m_ssThresh);
12:    **return** segmentsAcked - 1;
13: **end if**
14: **return** 0;

TCP-RTA incorporates the following additional list of enhancements:

1. **Slow Start Enhancement** in TCP NewReno, cwnd is increased by one segment per acknowledgment. In TCP-RTA, cwnd is changed to SegAcked * Segment size. (similar to Cubic [17])

Algorithm 3. TCP-RTA::CongestionAvoidance

1: **input** Ptr_SocketState, segmentsAcked
2: **if** (segmentsAcked > 0 && m_adaptiveAlg == TCP_HYBLA) **then**
3:     INC = ρ^2/W
4:     segCwnd = tcb $\rightarrow$ GetCwndInSegments ();
5:     increment = std::pow (m_ρ, 2)/static_cast<double> (segCwnd);
6:     m_cWndCnt += increment;
7:     segmentsAcked -= 1;
8: **end if**
9: **if** (segmentsAcked > 0 && m_adaptiveAlg == TCP_NEWRENO) **then**
10:     **if** (m_adaptiveAlgProg $\neq$ ALOG_INPROGRESS) **then**
11:         w = tcb $\rightarrow$ m_cWnd/tcb $\rightarrow$ m_segmentSize;
12:         **if** (w == 0) **then**
13:             w = 1;
14:         **end if**
15:         **if** (m_cWndCnt $\geq$ w) **then**
16:             m_cWndCnt = 0;
17:             tcb $\rightarrow$ m_cWnd += tcb $\rightarrow$ m_segmentSize;
18:         **end if**
19:         m_cWndCnt += segmentsAcked;
20:         **if** (m_cWndCnt $\geq$ w) **then**
21:             delta = m_cWndCnt/w;
22:             m_cWndCnt -= delta * w;
23:             tcb $\rightarrow$ m_cWnd += delta * tcb $\rightarrow$ m_segmentSize;
24:         **end if**
25:     **end if**
26:     **else**
27:         m_adaptiveAlgProgCnt–;
28:         tcb $\rightarrow$ m_cWnd = m_bd/tcb $\rightarrow$ m_segmentSize;
29: **end if**
30: **if** (m_cWndCnt $\geq$ 1.0 && m_adaptiveAlg == TCP_HYBLA) **then**
31:     inc = m_cWndCnt;
32:     m_cWndCnt -= inc;
33:     **if** (m_adaptiveAlgProg $\neq$ ALOG_INPROGRESS) **then**
34:         tcb $\rightarrow$ m_cWnd += inc * tcb $\rightarrow$ m_segmentSize;
35:     **end if**
36:     **else**
37:         tcb $\rightarrow$ m_cWnd = m_bd/tcb $\rightarrow$ m_segmentSize;
38: **end if**

---

2. **Congestion Avoidance Enhancement** In TCP NewReno, cwnd is increased by (1/cwnd). In TCP-RTA, the following changes are introduced: In congestion avoidance phase, the number of bytes that have been ACKed at the TCP sender side are stored in a 'bytes_acked' variable in the TCP control block. When 'bytes_acked' becomes greater than or equal to the value of the cwnd, 'bytes_acked' is reduced by the value of cwnd. Next, cwnd is incremented by a full-sized segment (SMSS). (Similar to Linux Reno [19] implementation)

3. On Fast restransmit, we update ssthresh to half of current cwnd: ssthresh = bytesinflight/2; In order to recover faster, it is enhanced as follows: sstresh = (bytesInFlight * 2) /3.

4. Default boost of a factor of 10 (constant) of the Bandwidth*Delay product while switching from LAN to Satellite and vice versa.

We have not impacted or changed any of the fairness with respect to other TCP co-existing as the underlying congestion control strategy adopted by us is that of TCP-Hybla, when the topology change is detected through a consistent increase in RTT. The fairness of TCP-Hybla and earlier that of TCP NewReno has been already established and proven and thus its applicable here as well. Even in the transition from congestion control strategies from TCP-Hybla to TCP NewReno, the only change is our non-responsiveness to transients and that too for only 3 segments. Thus fairness is guaranteed.

4   Testing and Simulation

We evaluated the performance of TCP-RTA using NS-3 discrete-event simulator. NS-3 provides substantial support for simulation of TCP, Routing, and Multicast Protocols over wired and wireless (local and satellite) networks. The TCP implementation was modified to support the new proposed protocol including several of the enhancements listed earlier.

Numerous scenarios and options were tried out to truly validate the gains and benefits of the proposed approach here. After close analysis of the various findings, decided to use TCP NewReno and TCP-Hybla to simulate and study the behaviour for the quite significantly impactful change of a topology going through a local LAN in a home office or a corporate network to a data path involving a satellite for wireless inducing a very highly significant additional delay in the observed RTT. We observed the behaviour during the initial slow-start phase of the TCP-session as well as subsequently in the congestion avoidance phase as well. The throughput was observed across the above phases and during the transition of the "underlying topology". Consistently we have seen that TCP-RTA outperforms the others significantly in every one of the phases and across all topology transitions.

As the results below succinctly indicate we do see a very clear increase in the CWND size on transition to satellite environment. We have used NS3 for our simulation and have injected a significant delay from time t = 5 secs to time t = 15 secs to simulate a transition to a satellite back-haul and a subsequent transition back from it.

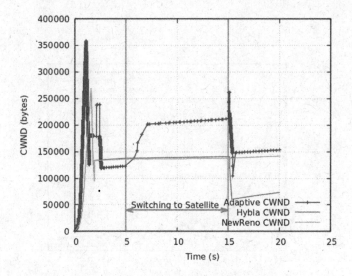

Fig. 1. CWND - TCP-RTA vs TCP Hybla vs TCP NewReno

5   Results

For our simulation studies here, we have earmarked RTT values, consistently observed in the range upwards of 800 ms to denote an environment/topology with a satellite backhaul. Similarly we have earmarked RTT values, consistently observed in the range downwards of 800 ms for one set of experiments and for others used a lower value 500 ms, to denote a environment/topology without a satellite backhaul. Later various other RTT ranges could be added as needed to correspond to specific topology/environments, for which we have an specific apt TCP variant with its own congestion control algorithm, which provides the best optimal bandwidth usage and performance for that environment. It can be observed from the results that there is a significant boost in the Congestion window size when the transition to a satellite link happens, with its corresponding increase in the Bandwidth X Delay product as can be seen in the Fig. 4. Similarly it can be observed in the optimal efficient usage of the network bandwidth close to 33% increase on the average across many simulation scenarios. However for the very specific transitory phase to a satellite link as seen in Fig. 6 the throughput increase is almost double that of TCP Hybla as well as TCP NewReno. This work can be further extrapolated and we do not have to restrict ourselves to the specific topologies depicted here and the transitions between them.

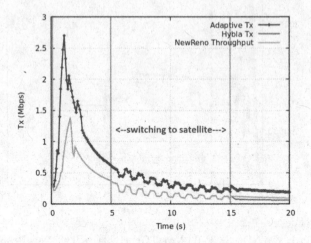

Fig. 2. TX - TCP-RTA vs TCP Hybla vs TCP NewReno

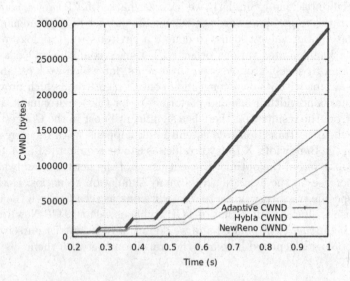

Fig. 3. CWND before transition to satellite - TCP-RTA vs TCP Hybla vs TCP NewReno

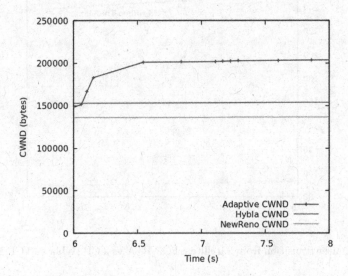

Fig. 4. CWND after transition to Satellite - TCP-RTA vs TCP Hybla vs TCP NewReno

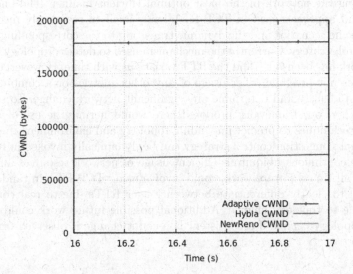

Fig. 5. CWND after transition from Satellite - TCP-RTA vs TCP Hybla vs TCP NewReno

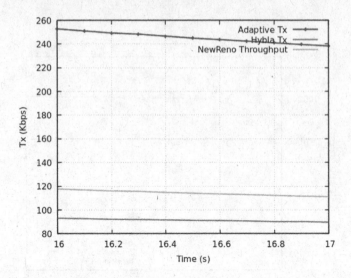

Fig. 6. TX after transition from Satellite - TCP-RTA vs TCP Hybla vs TCP NewReno

6   Conclusion and Future Work

TCP-RTA provides a framework and mechanism to leverage the "apt" congestion control strategy for a given dynamic scenario, thus ensuring we are at all
times using the network in the most optimal efficient manner. The underlying
design and approach used in TCP-RTA lends itself to seamlessly incorporate
other specific scenarios and the dynamic transition to the corresponding congestion control strategy. Currently the mechanism used to detect "topology change"
in our work has been RTT and the RTT variations with time. However, our approach does not preclude other usage of any other metrics or a combination of
metrics to identify and determine any significant network change. To scale our
work further, our framework proposed here would permit the use of machine
learning techniques to predict impending topology and environment changes, so
that an apt congestion control strategy can be dynamically invoked in real-time
to ensure continuous ubiquitous efficient usage of network resources and bandwidth at all times. Future work, could involve using TCP-RTA in tandem with
ECN [27] to clearly differentiate between longer RTTs due to real congestion
versus due to topology change. Additional possible future work could be vali-
dating topology change if a consistent hop-count change is observed from prior
values.

References

1. Baiocchi, A., Castellani, A.P., Vacirca, F.: Yeah-TCP: yet another highspeed TCP.
   In: Proceedings of PFLDnet, vol. 7, pp. 37–42 (2007)

2. Bakre, A.V., Badrinath, B.: Handoff and systems support for indirect TCP/IP. In: Symposium on Mobile and Location-Independent Computing, pp. 11–24 (1995)
3. Bakshi, B.S., Krishna, P., Vaidya, N.H., Pradhan, D.K.: Improving performance of TCP over wireless networks. In: Proceedings of 17th International Conference on Distributed Computing Systems, pp. 365–373. IEEE (1997)
4. Balakrishnan, H., Seshan, S., Katz, R.H.: Improving reliable transport and handoff performance in cellular wireless networks. Wireless Netw. **1**(4), 469–481 (1995)
5. Bhandarkar, S., Sadry, N.E., Reddy, A.N., Vaidya, N.H.: TCP-DCR: a novel protocol for tolerating wireless channel errors. IEEE Trans. Mob. Comput. **4**(5), 517–529 (2005)
6. Brakmo, L.S., O'Malley, S.W., Peterson, L.L.: TCP vegas: new techniques for congestion detection and avoidance. In: Proceedings of the Conference on Communications Architectures, Protocols and Applications, pp. 24–35 (1994)
7. Caceres, R., Iftode, L.: Improving the performance of reliable transport protocols in mobile computing environments. IEEE J. Sel. Areas Commun. **13**(5), 850–857 (1995)
8. Caini, C., Firrincieli, R.: TCP HYBLA: a TCP enhancement for heterogeneous networks. Int. J. Satell. Commun. Netw. **22**(5), 547–566 (2004)
9. Cardwell, N., Cheng, Y., Gunn, C.S., Yeganeh, S.H., Jacobson, V.: BBR: congestion-based congestion control. Commun. ACM **60**(2), 58–66 (2017)
10. Casetti, C., Gerla, M., Mascolo, S., Sanadidi, M.Y., Wang, R.: TCP Westwood: end-to-end congestion control for wired/wireless networks. Wireless Netw. **8**(5), 467–479 (2002)
11. Fall, K., Floyd, S.: Simulation-based comparisons of tahoe, reno and sack TCP. ACM SIGCOMM Comput. Commun. Rev. **26**(3), 5–21 (1996)
12. Floyd, S.: Rfc3649: Highspeed TCP for large congestion windows (2003)
13. Floyd, S., Henderson, T., Gurtov, A.: Rfc3782: The newreno modification to TCP's fast recovery algorithm (2004)
14. Goff, T., Moronski, J., Phatak, D.S., Gupta, V.: Freeze-TCP: a true end-to-end TCP enhancement mechanism for mobile environments. In: Proceedings IEEE INFOCOM 2000. Conference on Computer Communications. Nineteenth Annual Joint Conference of the IEEE Computer and Communications Societies (Cat. No. 00CH37064), vol. 3, pp. 1537–1545. IEEE (2000)
15. Group, N.I.R.T.: 5g network deployment scenarios (2022). https://anglova.net/
16. Jin, C., et al.: Caltech FAST TCP: from theory to experiments, Low Eng. Appl.. Sci. (2005)
17. Ha, S., Rhee, I., Xu, L.: Cubic: a new TCP-friendly high-speed TCP variant. ACM SIGOPS Oper. Syst. Rev. **42**(5), 64–74 (2008)
18. Hatano, T., Fukuhara, M., Shigeno, H., Okada, K.I.: TCP-friendly sqrt TCP for high speed networks. In: Proceedings of APSITT (November 2003), pp. 455–460 (2003)
19. Jacobson, V.: Modified TCP congestion avoidance algorithm. Technical Report (1990)
20. Jacobson, V.: Congestion avoidance and control. ACM SIGCOMM comput. Commun. Rev. **18**(4), 314–329 (1988)
21. Jacobson, V., Braden, R., Borman, D.: TCP extensions for high performance. Tech. rep., RFc 1323, May (1992)
22. Kanagarathinam, M.R., Singh, S., Sandeep, I., Roy, A., Saxena, N.: D-TCP: Dynamic TCP congestion control algorithm for next generation mobile networks. In: 2018 15th IEEE Annual Consumer Communications Networking Conference (CCNC), pp. 1–6 (2018). https://doi.org/10.1109/CCNC.2018.8319185

23. Kelly, T.: Scalable TCP: Improving performance in highspeed wide area networks. ACM SIGCOMM Comput. Communi. Rev. **33**(2), 83–91 (2003)

24. M. Mathis, J. Mahdavi, S., Romanow., A.: TCP selective acknowledgment options. RFc 2018, October (1996)

25. Parsa, C., Garcia-Luna-Aceves, J.J.: Improving TCP congestion control over internets with heterogeneous transmission media. In: Proceedings. Seventh International Conference on Network Protocols, pp. 213–221. IEEE (1999)

26. Polese, M., Chiariotti, F., Bonetto, E., Rigotto, F., Zanella, A., Zorzi, M.: A survey on recent advances in transport layer protocols. IEEE Commun .Surv. Tutor. **21**(4), 3584–3608 (2019). https://doi.org/10.1109/COMST.2019.2932905

27. Ramakrishnan, K.K., Floyd, S., Black, D.L.: The addition of explicit congestion notification (ECN) to IP. RFC 3168, pp. 1–63 (2001)

28. Ratnam, K., Matta, I.: WTCP: an efficient mechanism for improving TCP performance over wireless links. In: Proceedings Third IEEE Symposium on Computers and Communications. ISCC'1998. (Cat. No. 98EX166), pp. 74–78. IEEE (1998)

29. Sessini, P., Mahanti, A.: Observations on round-trip times of TCP connections (January 2006)

30. Tan, K., Song, J., Zhang, Q., Sridharan, M.: A compound TCP approach for highspeed and long distance networks. In: Proceedings-IEEE INFOCOM (2006)

31. Xu, K., Tian, Y., Ansari, N.: TCP-jersey for wireless IP communications. IEEE J. Sel. Areas Commun. **22**(4), 747–756 (2004)

32. Xu, L., Harfoush, K., Rhee, I.: Binary increase congestion control (BIC) for fast long-distance networks. In: IEEE INFOCOM 2004, vol. 4, pp. 2514–2524. IEEE (2004)

Rio_DSA: Redirecting I/O Scheme for Dynamic Storage Allocation on Docker Container

Sehoon Kwon[1], Jaechun No[1(✉)], and Sung-soon Park[2]

[1] College of Electronics and Information Engineering, Sejong University, 209 Neungdong-Ro, Gwangjin-Gu, Seoul, Korea
jano@sejong.ac.kr
[2] Deptartment of Computer Engineering, Anyang University and Gluesys Co. LTD, Anyang 5-Dong, Manan-Go, Korea
sspark@gluesys.com

Abstract. In this paper, we present a dynamic storage extension scheme for docker containers. In the current implementation of docker containers, in the case that the default storage of a container runs out of space in the middle of application executions, those applications would abruptly stop to execute, leading to either application restart or data loss. Our proposed scheme can prevent such a harmful situation from taking place, by providing I/O redirection to *rio_DSA* extended storage in the overlay filesystem. We evaluated the performance of *rio_DSA* by using IOzone and FIO benchmarks, and showed that our scheme performed well without causing any malicious effect in I/O performance. Moreover, we can observe that the performance potential due to leveraging high-speed I/O devices, such as NVMe SSD, can be preserved as it is in the existing docker container implementation.

Keywords: *Rio_DSA* · Docker container · I/O redirection · Overlay filesystem · Storage extension

1 Introduction

Container-based virtualization [1–5] is becoming popular in the cloud computing environment because of its strong advantage of the lightweight deployment compared to hypervisor-based virtualization [6, 7]. The capability of virtualizing all host resources, such as network port or host's backing filesystem, by sharing the host kernel with small overhead makes it possible for containers to be an alternative to hypervisor-based virtualization [8, 9].

However, with docker, a representative container-based virtualization, computing resources assigned to containers are provided by user specification at creation time. Such a resource allocation method can incur a critical problem, in the case that applications running on top of docker containers generate a large-scale data enough to exceed the storage capacity allocated at docker creation time.

In the existing implementation of docker containers, if applications executing on a container generate a large-scale data exceeding the storage capacity given at container

E. Sabir et al. (Eds.): UNet 2022, LNCS 13853, pp. 113–125, 2023.
https://doi.org/10.1007/978-3-031-29419-8_9

creation time, the application execution would abruptly stop, leading to either application restart or data loss. In this case, it is not possible to increase the storage capacity of running containers unless otherwise stopped application executions. As a result, user should terminate application executions on the problematic container and increase the disk capacity size based on the inaccurate user prediction about future storage usage.

In this paper, we present a dynamic storage extension scheme for docker containers, called *rio_DSA* (*R*edirecting *IO for D*ynamic *S*torage *A*llocation on Docker Container). In our scheme, the initial storage capacity of docker container can dynamically be extended, by monitoring the storage usage in real-time. Once the initial storage capacity of a docker runs out of space, switching to *rio_DSA* extended storage can be done without causing any execution stop or data loss.

The rest of this paper is organized as follows. In Sect. 2, we discuss related works and in Sect. 3, we present the design and implementation of *rio_DSA*. Section 4 discusses the performance evaluation of *rio_DSA*, by using two benchmarks, IOzone and FIO, and Sect. 5 concludes.

2 Related Works

Achieving multi-tenancy via virtualization is an essential aspect in recent data centers. Traditionally, hypervisor-based virtualization [6] has commonly been used by emulating a virtual computer equipped with virtual peripheral devices. Although such a virtualization provides a desirable, isolated application executions while effectively managing resources [7], it could suffer from heavy overhead due to multiple s/w layers between guest operating system, hypervisor and host operating system. Because of such drawbacks, a relatively new scheme of container-based virtualization is receiving strong attention in IT community.

The container-based virtualization, such as Linux containers (LXC) or docker, shares most of software and hardware components with host operating system, while isolating application executions by utilizing host operating system features, such as cgroups and namespaces. Especially, docker is a cross-platform container scheme whose main components are composed of containers, images and registries [14].

In the docker container, overlay filesystem [15, 16] is used for effectively sharing files through the copy-on-write mechanism [12, 13]. The overlay provides two directories, lower (read-only) and upper (writable), and merges those two to transparently export files to users on top of containers. Also, the storage capacity per container is statically be determined at creation time, not being able to change during the container running period. Since such a static storage allocation per container can run out of space with a large-scale data being generated in application executions, there should a way of avoiding such a lack of storage capacity per container. In this paper, we address this issue by proposing an efficient way of dynamically extending the storage capacity per container.

As docker containers are becoming popularized, several researches have been done to analyze the strengths by contrasting to hypervisor [10, 11]. They showed that the major features impacting performance difference between containers and VMs are I/O and OS interaction while consuming extra cycles for each I/O. [11] showed that the performance interference of containers is higher than that of VMs because hypervisors support more robust isolated virtualization even though such an effectiveness in disk I/O is mitigated due to the shared I/O path among VMs.

For the fast container startup, [2] implemented a docker storage driver, called slacker, to delay pulling per-container image data until actually needed, by providing all container image data on NFS server to be shared by all daemons. [13] proposed a prefetching method that brings up the image files to the upper layer in advance to reduce the copy-up cost.

3 Implementation Details

3.1 System Architecture

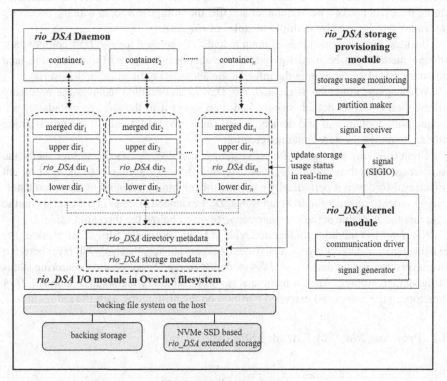

Fig. 1. *rio_DSA* structure.

The objective of *rio_DSA* is to dynamically extend the storage capacity of docker container so that the abrupt execution stop due to the lack of the available storage space would not take place. In this paper, the initial storage size of a container given at creation time is referred as the default container storage and the additional storage size assigned by our scheme is referred as the *rio_DSA* extended storage.

The data movement between the default container storage and *rio_DSA* extended storage is transparently performed to users without causing any changes in applications.

Moreover, we attempt to leverage the performance potential of NVMe SSD by utilizing it as *rio_DSA* extended storage.

Figure 1 illustrates an overall structure of *rio_DSA*. The structure is composed of four components. The daemon process responsible for collecting the container states, such as execution or creation states and disk quota allocated at the creation time. The *rio_DSA* kernel module plays an intermediate role between background daemon and storage provisioning process executing on the user address space, while transmitting signals implying the existence of a new container between the daemon process and the storage provisioning process.

The storage provisioning module takes care of mapping *rio_DSA* layer of I/O module in the overlay filesystem to the associated partition of *rio_DSA* extended storage. Also, it provides the monitoring statuses of both storages to appropriately redirect data movement, according to the available storage capacity. Finally, it receives the signal indicating the existence of a new container and fills the storage metadata with the necessary information to be used by multiple modules of *rio_DSA*.

Besides, there are two kinds of main metadata to be used for *rio_DSA* components: storage metadata to be used for the storage monitoring and partition mapping, and directory metadata containing the information about I/O redirection in the overlay.

When a new container is created, *rio_DSA* kernel module receives the necessary information about its default storage and then stores it to the storage metadata, such as quota-id, container id and device. It also sends *rio_DSA* signal to the provisioning module to notify the new container creation.

Upon receiving the signal, the provisioning module accesses the storage metadata, to leverage them to partition *rio_DSA* extended storage and map it to the host mount directory. Moreover, it periodically monitors the remaining capacity of the default storage, in order to redirect the I/O path to *rio_DSA* extended storage in the overlay, in the case that the available default storage capacity drops below the threshold value.

Rio_DSA I/O module is integrated with I/O path of overlay filesystem. Besides the existing upper and lower layers, it provides one more layer, called *rio_DSA* layer between two layers, to forward data to *rio_DSA* extended storage based on the monitoring status of the default storage. Also, it maintains *rio_DSA* directory metadata to map *rio_DSA* directory to the associated extended partition on the host, along with I/O redirection.

3.2 Providing *Rio_DSA* Extended Storage

Table 1. *rio_DSA* storage metadata.

Type	Value	Description
unsigned int	id	quota ID
char	con_path	container path
char	special	backingFSBlockDev

Table 1 shows *rio_DSA* storage metadata to be received from the daemon upon the new container creation. The *rio_DSA* kernel module makes it possible that both daemon and provisioning processes can communicate the necessary information in real-time via system calls, to monitor the corresponding container storage states. Further, it sends a creation signal to the provisioning process to make it access the storage metadata.

There are two main roles for the provisioning module. Before creating containers at host, it first divides the NVMe SSD-based *rio_DSA* storage into the desirable number of partitions, and maps it to the host mount directory. In the case that more partitions are needed as the number of containers increases, *rio_DSA* checks the available storage space in *rio_DSA* extended storage and then allocates more partitions to deal with such a situation. Also, it defines the signal call function being executed on the creation signal receipt from the kernel module.

Second, the provisioning module accesses the storage metadata via system calls to leverage them for periodically checking the default storage status of the associated container. When the storage usage exceeds 85% of the total capacity, it instructs *rio_DSA* I/O module to redirect I/O path to *rio_DSA* extended storage in overlay file system.

3.3 *Rio_DSA* I/O Module in Overlay Filesystem

Analyzing Overlay Filesystem for rio_DSA Integration
The I/O module of *rio_DSA* has been implemented in the overlay filesystem, to move I/O path of a container where the application executes to the corresponding *rio_DSA* partition, if necessary. We briefly take a look at the overlay structure, before going into the details of *rio_DSA* I/O module.

When user creates a new container, the docker daemon issues a mount command on the overlay filesystem, such as *mount -t overlay overlay -o lowerdisk = lower/, upperdir = upper/, workdir = work/ merged*. In the overlay filesystem, multiple functions, including *ovl_parse_opt, ovl_get_upper, ovl_get_workdir* and *ovl_get_lowerstack*, are executed to separate the directory path of upper and lower directories and to bring the real dentries of both directories from the backing filesystem on the host, leading to map them to the associated inodes of the overlay filesystem.

Two major directories are associated to a container in the overlay filesystem: the lower directory is the read-only and the upper directory is the writable. Both directories are merged in the merged directory to be exported to users on the container.

In the case of write operations, the file of interest in the lower directory is copied to the upper directory, called copy-up operation, and the duplicated file in the upper directory is overwritten. In the case of creating a new file, the overlay can create the new one in the upper directory since the lower directory is the read-only and cannot be modified.

Figure 2 represents the steps for organizing upper and lower directories at the container start time. When the container starts to execute, the files residing in the upper and lower directories are traced while mapping their fake inodes to the corresponding dentries of the host upper and lower directories. This is because the file operations taking place in the overlay filesystem can easily map to the real dentries of the backing filesystem via their fake inodes in the overlay.

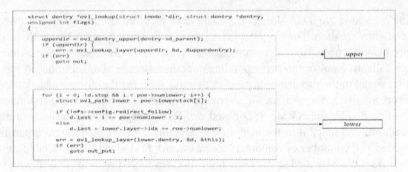

```
struct dentry *ovl_lookup(struct inode *dir, struct dentry *dentry,
unsigned int flags)
{

    upperdir = ovl_dentry_upper(dentry->d_parent);
    if (upperdir) {
        err = ovl_lookup_layer(upperdir, &d, &upperdentry);
    if (err)
        goto out;



    for (i = 0; !d.stop && i < poe->numlower; i++) {
        struct ovl_path lower = poe->lowerstack[i];

        if (lofs->config.redirect_follow)
            d.last = i == poe->numlower - 1;
        else
            d.last = lower.layer->idx == poe->numlower;

        err = ovl_lookup_layer(lower.dentry, &d, &this);
        if (err)
            goto out_put;
```

Fig. 2. Steps for organizing upper and lower directories in the overlay filesystem

In the case that a file write operation issues on the container, the file data is stored in the upper layer mapped to the upper directory of the host. To keep the existing directory hierarchy, overlay first searches for the parent directory of the new file in the lower directory. If the parent exists in the lower directory, the overlay performs the copy-up operation to duplicate the same directory hierarchy to the upper layer, and then creates the new file below the parent.

For each file and directory of the overlay filesystem, there exists the fake dentry and real dentry information. In the file write, the overlay first accesses the fake dentry of the new file to bring the real dentry of the parent and searches for the real dentry of the new file by referring to the real parent dentry, dentry of the new file and its length. This information is transferred to the backing filesystem on host where the real file write operation takes place.

Implementing rio_DSA I/O Module

When a new container is created, *rio_DSA* makes an additional entry in the directory metadata, pointing to *rio_DSA* directory mapped to the corresponding extended storage in the host. Figure 3 shows an example of *rio_DSA* directory metadata for two containers, whose IDs are *7cfe...33f3* and *1007...75a2*, and their directories mapped at host are /root/.../rio_DSA_1 and /root/.../rio_DSA_2, respectively.

The check flag of the directory metadata is modified by the provisioning process, according to the available capacity of the container default storage. If the remaining storage size of the container drops below the threshold, the check flag of the directory metadata is switched to the redirection value, leading to switching I/O path in the overlay from the default directory to *rio_DSA* directory, while reflecting the modification to the entity on the associated overlay inode.

In Fig. 3, the I/O path of the second container is currently redirected to *rio_DSA* extended storage, but that of the first container keeps the default container storage. The change is also reflected on the overlay inode. At container start time, it checks if the container is already existed. If so, the information about the current I/O path resided in the directory metadata is accessed and added in the overlay inode:

For the directory traversal to write a file, *rio_DSA* first checks to see if the desirable directory resides in the upper directory and if so, the associated dentry is stored in memory (page cache). If it does not exist, the search goes to the next *rio_DSA* layer. In

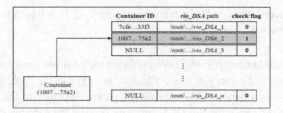

Fig. 3. *Rio_DSA* directory metadata

```
struct ovl_inode {
    union {
        struct ovl_dir_cache *cache; /* directory */
        struct inode *lowerdata; /* regular file */
    };

    const char *redirect;
    u64 version;
    unsigned long flags;
    struct inode vfs_inode;
    struct dentry *__upperdentry;

    struct dentry *rio_DSA_dentry;

    struct inode *lower;
    /* synchronize copy up and more */
    struct mutex lock;
};
```

Fig. 4. Inode Modification for *rio_DSA*

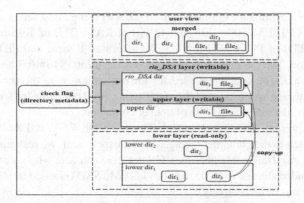

Fig. 5. File write operation in *rio_DSA*

case of the default container implementation, only upper and lower layers are examined to find the directory of interest. In *rio_DSA*, however, one more layer between upper and lower layers exists to support I/O path redirection (Fig. 4).

The steps for the traversal as follows: Let *D* be the directory of interest.

1. Check the upper layer to see if *D* exists. If so, save its dentry,../*upper/D*, in page cache
2. Otherwise, check *rio_DSA* layer for *D* existence. If so, save its dentry,../*rio_DSA/D*, in page cache

3. Check the lower layer for D if not found in step 2. If D is found in this layer, save its dentry,../lower/D, in page cache

If D is not found until step 3, rio_DSA performs the creation function, as can be seen in Fig. 5. If the parent directory of a new file does not exist in the upper directory, it first performs the copy-up operation to duplicate the parent directory of the lower directory to the upper directory and the rio_DSA directory, unlike the existing operation where the directory is coped from lower layer to upper layer only.

In Fig. 5, the parent directory, dir3, of two new files, file1 and file2, is copied from lower layer to both upper layer and rio_DSA layer. Since at the time of writing file2, I/O redirection is instructed due to the lack of the available default storage capacity, file2 is created at rio_DSA layer, but in case of writing file1, the default upper layer is used for writing the file. Also, the actual file data is stored in either the container's default storage or rio_DSA extended storage, according to the redirection path.

It is noted that no matter in which layer those files are written, the directory hierarchy of those files is exposed under the same parent, dir3, at user side, indicating that I/O redirection is transparently performed to users.

4   Performance Evaluation

We executed the performance evaluation of rio_DSA by using a host server equipped with Intel® Xeon® CPU E5-2609 1.70 GHz, 16 GB of RAM, 2TB of Toshiba HDWD120 and Samsung 1TB of PCI-e NVMe SSD. We also used IOzone and FIO benchmarks for the evaluation. The OS installed on the server was CentOS Linux 7 and the backing filesystem was xfs. The containers used for the evaluation share the server resources. We tested the storage space extensibility facilitating rio_DSA extended storage, in case of the lack of the default storage size of docker containers.

Figure 6 represents I/O throughput of IOzone, while 4 GB and 8 GB of files are repeatedly written to the container storage. In this experiment, we restricted the default storage size of rio_DSA containers to 1 GB for convenience, while varying the disk type of its extended storage to HDD, SSD and NVMe SSD (labelled as HDD, SSD and NVMe SSD in Fig. 6, respectively).

Since the default storage size is constrained to 1 GB, writing 4 GB and 8 GB of files repeatedly facilitates rio_DSA extended storage after the default storage size exceeds the threshold. We compared the performance of rio_DSA with the original container (labelled as Original HDD in Fig. 6) where the large storage size is assigned to the original container enough to store those files without causing storage space shortage.

As can be seen the figure, the read performance of either Read or Random Read does not reveal much difference between original container and rio_DSA container. However, in the write performance, we can observe much difference between both containers. Since NVMe SSD reveals the highest I/O throughput, we recommend leveraging NVMe SSD as rio_DSA extended storage.

Moreover, as can be seen in Fig. 6, utilizing rio_DSA has little performance effect compared to the original case equipped with the same type of disk (HDD and Original

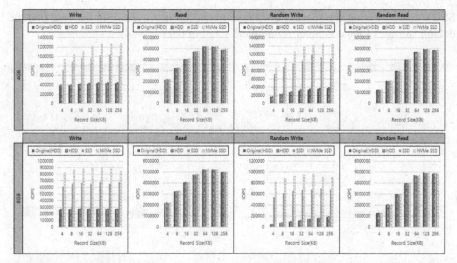

Fig. 6. I/O performance comparison using IOzone. The original (HDD) denotes the case that sufficient default storage space is given to the container. The remaining three cases (HDD, SSD, NVMeSSD) are I/O performances of *rio_DSA* where the three devices mentioned imply the disk type of its extended storage.

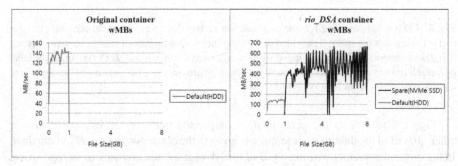

Fig. 7. Comparison based on the disk space availability between original case and *rio_DSA*

HDD), but rather guarantees to keep up with almost the same I/O performance when sufficient default storage space is given to the container.

Figure 7 represents the comparison of storage availability between the original container where the default storage space is not enough to accommodate application data being generated on the container and *rio_DSA* container where *rio_DSA* extended storage is installed, besides the same size of the default storage space as in the original container. In both cases, we constrained the default storage size to 1 GB for convenience.

As can be seen in Fig. 7, in the original container, if the data to be written to storage becomes larger than 1 GB, the I/O performance rapidly drops due to the lack of storage space. However, in *rio_DSA* container, even in the case of continuously writing 1 GB of file data, *rio_DSA* shows little performance degradation (or even higher with NVMe

SSD), demonstrating the successful storage extension in *rio_DSA*, in the case that the default storage of the container is completely full of data.

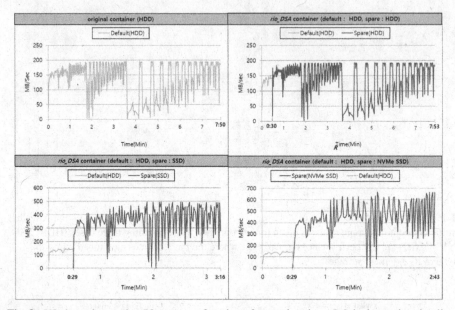

Fig. 8. I/O throughput using IOzone as a function of execution time. Original container implies that sufficient storage space is provided to the container so that no lack of storage capacity occurs. *Rio_DSA* container is the one equipped with the extended storage. In *rio_DSA* container, the label of Default implies the default storage and the one of Spare does *rio_DSA* extended storage where its disk type varies from HDD to NVMe SSD.

Figure 8 represents the performance comparison between the original container where 10 GB of the default storage space is given to the container and *rio_DSA* container. In the original container, writing 8 GB of files does not cause any lack of storage space. The other three graphs show I/O performances of *rio_DSA* where the extended storage of *rio_DSA* varies between HDD, SSD and NVMe SSD. Since the default storage size of *rio_DSA* container is restricted to 1 GB, continuously writing 8 GB of data causes I/O redirection to *rio_DSA* extended storage to safely store file data.

In the performance, the performance behavior of between the original container and the *rio_DSA* whose extended storage uses the same HDD shows almost the same I/O performance, implying that successful switching of data reservoir to *rio_DSA* extended storage has been taken place. If NVMe SSD is utilized as its extended storage, higher I/O performance can be obtained due to its performance potential.

Figure 9 represents I/O throughput of FIO benchmark while varying *rio_DSA* extended storage between HDD, SSD and NVMe SSD. In this experiment, we executed FIO for 6 h. In the meantime, because of the lack of the default storage space, the switching to *rio_DSA* extended storage has been occurred.

As can be seen in the figure, if the disk type of the default storage and the one of *rio_DSA* extended storage are the same, little performance turbulence due to the storage

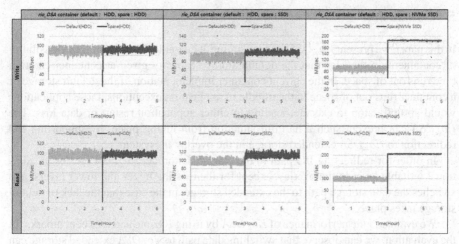

Fig. 9. I/O throughput of *rio_DSA* using FIO as a function of execution time.

switching takes place, like observed in IOzone. On the contrary, leveraging SSD and NVMe SSD as *rio_DSA* extended storage shows higher performance than writing to the default storage because of their performance superiority.

According to the experiment, we can conclude that switching the data reservoir to *rio_DSA* extended storage because of the need for extending the container storage does not exacerbate I/O performance. Rather, utilizing *rio_DSA* extended storage guarantees the disk availability even in the case that the default storage of a container runs out of space. Also, the performance advantage to be obtained by accommodating either SSD or NVMe as its extended storage remains the same.

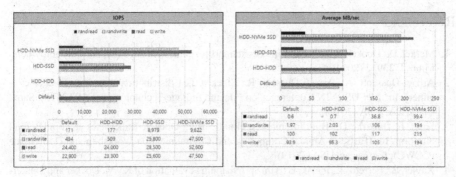

Fig. 10. IOPS of *rio_DSA* using FIO while varying the extended storage type

Figure 10 shows IOPS of *rio_DSA* with FIO, while changing the disk type of *rio_DSA* extended storage. We can observe the same performance behavior to Fig. 9, producing little performance fluctuation with the same disk type between the default storage and *rio_DSA* extended one. Moreover, the performance potential with SSD and NVMe SSD can be preserved with little overhead in *rio_DSA* storage switching.

5 Conclusion

In this paper, we present *rio_DSA* scheme aiming at guaranteeing the storage extensibility of containers, in the case that the default storage capacity given at container creation time runs out of space. In the current container implementation, if the default storage of a container runs out of space in the middle of application executions, those applications would abruptly stop to execute, leading to either application restart or data loss. The *rio_DSA* can prevent such a harmful situation from taking place, by supporting I/O redirection to *rio_DSA* extended storage in the overlay filesystem.

In order for redirecting I/O path to the extended storage, *rio_DSA* creates an additional writable layer in the overlay, except for the existing upper and lower layers, and switches the data storage path to the extended storage, in the case that the lack of default storage takes place.

We evaluated the performance of *rio_DSA* by using IOzone and FIO benchmarks. In the evaluation, we can observe that switching data path to *rio_DSA* extended storage can be performed without causing any malicious effect in I/O performance. Furthermore, the performance potential to be obtained by leveraging high-speed I/O devices, such as NVMe SSD, is also observed in *rio_DSA* as it is in the existing (original) container implementation. We will evaluate *rio_DSA* with more applications and benchmarks to verify its effectiveness.

Acknowledgements. This work was supported by the National Research Foundation of Korea (NRF) grant funded by the Korea Government (MSIT)(No. 2022R1A2C1004156). Also, this work was supported by Institute of Information & communications Technology Planning & Evaluation (IITP) grant funded by the Korea government (MSIT)(No. 2021–0-00219, Exascale Data Storage and High Performance Computing Technology).

References

1. Merkel, D.: Docker: lightweight Linux containers for consistent development and deployment. Linux J. **239**, 2 (2014)
2. Arpaci-Dusseau, A., Arpaci-Dussear, R.: Slacker: fast distribution with lazy Docker containers. In: 14th USENIX Conference on File and Storage Technologies (FAST2016), Santa Clara, CA, USA (2016)
3. Shah, J., Dubaria, D.: Building modern clouds: using Docker, Kubernetes & google cloud platform. In: IEEE 9th Annual Computing and Communication Workshop and Conference (CCWC), Las Vegas, USA (2019)
4. Xavier, B., Ferreto, T., Jersak, L.: Time provisioning evaluation of KVM, Docker and Unikernels in a cloud platform. In: 16th IEEE/ACM International Symposium on Cluster, and Grid Computing, Cartagena, Colombia (2016)
5. Manco, F., et al.: My VM is lighter (and Safer) than your container. In: ACM SIGOPS 26th Symposium on Operating Systems Principles (SOSP2017), Shanghai, China (2017)
6. Dong, Y., Yang, X., Li, J., Liao, G., Tian, K., Guan, H.: High performance network virtualization with SR-IOV. J. Parallel Distrib. Comput. **72**, 1471–1480 (2012)
7. Har'El, N., Gordon, A., Landau, A.: Efficient and scalable Paravirtual I/O System. In: 2013 USENIX Annual Technical Conference, pp. 231–242, San Jose, USA (2013)

8. Zhu, J., Jiang, Z., Xiao, Z.: Twinkle: a fast resource provisioning mechanism for internet services. In: 2011 Proceedings IEEE INFOCOM (2011)

9. Razavi, K., Kielmann, T.: Scalable virtual machine deployment using VM image cache. In: SC'13 on High Performance Computing, Networking, Storage and Analysis, Denver, USA (2013)

10. Ferreira, A., Rajamony, R., Rubio, J.: An updated performance comparison of virtual machines and Linux containers. In: IEEE International Symposium on Performance Analysis of Systems and Software (ISPASS), Philadelphia, PA, USA (2015)

11. Chaufournier, L., Sharma, P., Shenoy, P.: Containers and virtual machines at scale: a comparative study. In: 17th International Middleware Conference, Trento, Italy (2016)

12. Wu, X., Wang, W., Jiang, S.: TotalCOW: unleash the power of copy-on-write for thin-provisioned containers. In: 6th Asia-Pacific Workshop on Systems, Tokyo, Japan (2015)

13. Jiang, Y., Liu, W., Shi, X., Qiang, W.: Optimizing the copy-on-write mechanism of Docker by dynamic prefetching. Tsinghua Sci. Technol. **26**, 266–274 (2021)

14. Anwar, A., et al.: Improving Docker registry design based on production workload analysis. Oakland, CA, USA (2018)

15. Mizusawa, N., Kon, J., Seki, Y., Tao, J., Yamaguchi, S.: Performance improvement of file operations on OverlayFS for containers. In: IEEE International Conference on Smart Computing (SMARTCOMP), Taormina, Sicily, Italy (2018)

16. Lu, L., Zhang, Y., Do, T., Al-Kiswany, S., Arpaci-Dusseau, A., Arpaci-Dusseau, R.: Physical disentanglement in a container-based file system, Broomfield, CO, USA (2014)

Internet of Things and Vehicular Communications

VANET-Based Traffic Light Management for an Emergency Vehicle

Adel Izadi[✉], Ashkan Gholamhosseinian[iD], and Jochen Seitz[iD]

Technische Universität Ilmenau, Communication Networks Group, Ilmenau, Germany
{adel.izadi,ashkan.gholamhosseinian,jochen.seitz}@tu-ilmenau.de

Abstract. Wireless communications have affected our lifestyle in the last decades. It is helpful to improve quality of life for communities. Communications among vehicles usually take place in vehicular ad-hoc networks (VANETs). Vehicle-to-vehicle (V2V) and vehicle-to-infrastructure (V2I) communications are aspects of communications in the transportation which are growing rapidly. They can play a pivotal role in the transportation field. Management of traffic lights (TLs) is crucial to control traffic flow especially at an intersection. The goal of this paper is to manage the TLs at an intersection when an emergency vehicle (EV) is approaching. First, we simulate an intersection which includes TLs via simulation of urban mobility (SUMO). Later, we simulate VANETs communication to manage the TLs at the intersection when the EV is coming with the help of objective modular network testbed in C++ (OMNeT++) and vehicles in network simulation (Veins). Finally, the impact of V2I communication on delivery efficiency of the emergency service is investigated. Simulation results show an improvement in delivery efficiency of the emergency service.

Keywords: VANETs · SUMO · OMNeT++ · Veins · IEEE 802.11p · vehicle-to-infrastructure communications (v2i) · emergency vehicle (ev) · traffic lights (tls) · vehicle-to-vehicle communications (v2v)

1 Introduction

Increasing number of vehicles has caused more traffic jams especially at crossroads during the recent years. Traffic jams at the intersection may cause many problems and increase response time specifically for EVs such as ambulance, rescue truck, etc. To control the intersection, the advent of TLs has really helped to increase the traffic performance. Management of the traffic flow at an intersection can increase delivery efficiency of the emergency services. It has been demonstrated that human errors have a pivotal role in road accidents by 75% [1,2]. It is obvious that an EV should arrive at the location immediately.

Testing new technologies in a real world is expensive and not safe. Besides, it is difficult to repeat the experiment and control the conditions in the real world for repetition, so simulation would have some benefits in this regard. Typical

© The Author(s), under exclusive license to Springer Nature Switzerland AG 2023
E. Sabir et al. (Eds.): UNet 2022, LNCS 13853, pp. 129–137, 2023.
https://doi.org/10.1007/978-3-031-29419-8_10

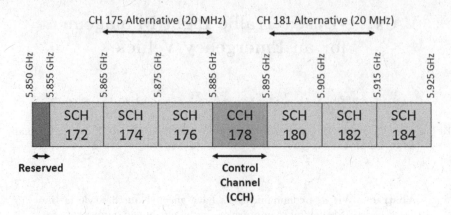

Fig. 1. DSRC channel spectrum in the U.S.

application of VANETs-based communications are EV warning or accident alert [2,3]. VANETs-based communications have been regulated in the IEEE-802.11p standard [1].

Dedicated short range communication (DSRC) was developed to add wireless access in vehicular environment and support vehicle-to-everything (V2X) communications. DSRC works using a 75 MHz spectrum in 5.9 GHz frequency band in the United States while in Europe and Japan it performs on a 30 MHz spectrum in the 5.8 GHz band. It can prepare services to both V2V and V2I up to 1 km and supports data rate of up to 27 Mbps [4,5]. The spectrum of DSRC is divided into seven 10 MHz channels with a 5 MHz guard band at the low part. Pairs of 10 MHz channels can also be combined to a 20 MHz channel. The United States federal communication commission (FCC) has nominated each channel as either service channel (SCH) or as control channel (CCH). The CCH notion labels one channel (channel number 178) in the U.S. as a "rendezvous" channel. The U.S. FCC has nominated channel 172 specially for V2V safety communications and accident avoidance, mitigation, safety of life and property applications [6]. DSRC band plan is illustrated in Fig. 1. DSRC stack depicts standards for layers: physical (PHY), data link (including MAC layer), network/transport and application layers. At the PHY and MAC layers, DSRC exploits IEEE 802.11p. In the middle, a suite of standards defined by 1609 working group are applied. At the top, the SAE J2735 defines a set of message formats that support a diversity of vehicle-based applications. The most prominent of all is the basic safety message (BSM) which transfers vehicle state information. BSM messages contain position, sender speed and channel number (CCH 178) [6].

One of the goals of this research is to decrease the response time which is one of the crucial issues for an EV especially in large cities with heavy traffic jams. The EV must travel through the intersection without any problem and delay. One of the solutions involves the construction of new infrastructure. This solution is very costly and requires huge investments. However, new technologies such as V2I and VANETs are cost-effective solutions to control traffic flow and manage TLs at the intersections [7,8].

The remainder of the paper is organized as follows. Section 2 is about the current state of the art. Section 3 deals with the frameworks that have been used for the simulation and our implementation. Results are evaluated in Sect. 4, where the impact of TLs on travel time of an EV by VANETs is assessed. Finally, a conclusion and future work are provided in the last section.

2   State of the Art

Jayaraj et al. [9] proposed an automatic green light during traffic flow for an EV in a specific route using SUMO and NS-2. It showed a traffic scenario where there was signalling transmission between the EV and other vehicles or TLs. When the TL received the message from the EV, it needed to alter from red to green. The green signal was maintained for that lane or road till that particular vehicle passed. The idea served to improve the network efficiency where there was minimum loss of data packets and minimum end-to-end delay. Authors in [10] discussed about the system design of an EV warning system called SafeSmart using V2I communications. A primary model of the system was tested and simulated including EVs and TLs. System performance was examined to compare the travel times for EVs in normal traffic with the time when the system is in use. System results provided EVs with a faster and safer path from one point to another, mostly in traffic jam scenarios where other drivers might not have enough space to clear the path for the EV.

Furthermore, Padmapriya et al. [11] adopted an EV transit approach (EVTA) associated with the road side unit (RSU) and traffic management center (TMC) for transport of EVs. Accurate location of the EVs were offered by both GPS and Kalman Algorithm (KA) to the EVTA. The proposed approach aimed to minimize the travel time of the EVs to reach the hospital with the concerted effort of the RSU and TMC. Simulation results confirmed that geographical parameters prepared by GPS are continuous. However, mentioned parameters provided by KA are 5% more authentic than GPS method. In a research project by Noori et al. [2], conducted for Cologne city in Germany, 20 EVs were involved in the simulation. In the experiments, authors aimed to analyze the response time and delay of the waiting vehicles at red light when TL status changed to green for an EV 50 m, 300 m and 5 km away from the crossroad. In case of 50 m, response time showed the highest value, but the waiting time for the other vehicles remained minimum in the junction. However, 5 km distance from the intersection experienced the lowest response time and the highest waiting time for other vehicles.

Moreover, Obrusnik et al. [12] utilized a new method for EV preemption at a signalized intersection. Simulation was conducted for a part of Brno City in Czech Republic. V2I communications were used to estimate the number of vehicles in the queue and a mathematical model was used to clear the queue of vehicles. There existed three simulations in different modes as follows. First, EV had no preference on the TLs. Second, EV was broadcasting preemption request after crossing a specific distance from the intersection. Third, EV was propagating its location and the TL controller decides about starting time of the preference based on actual traffic situation. Varga et al. [13] devised a feasible architecture for V2X communication centric TL controller. Their solution employed regulated C-ITS messaging techniques and helped vehicles to base their junction crossing measures on actual information coming from the infrastructure. A controller was also involved to make its decision on applicable information coming from vehicles. To implement the introduced V2X communication-centric controller system, five elements were designed, i.e. a Java-based STLM module, Commsignia RSU, Raspberry PI 2, NETIO equipment and TLs.

3   Simulation

We have benefited from SUMO as an open source traffic simulator [14], OMNeT++ and Veins [15] to simulate VANET-based TLs management. SUMO simulates traffic flow, vehicles and TLs while OMNeT++ handles wireless communications between nodes such as EV and the RSU. Veins bidirectionally connects SUMO and OMNet++ via a TCP socket. Traffic simulation starts in SUMO and OMNeT++ acts as a network simulator. Then, OMNeT++ considers all vehicles as nodes and simulates the scenario. When a change happens in OMNeT++, Veins is able to apply that in SUMO accordingly [16,17]. For instance, when EV sends its message to the RSU and asks for changing the state of the TL, transferring this request to SUMO to change the state of the TL is carried out by Veins. A disadvantage of Veins is that it only recognizes vehicles in OMNeT++. Therefore, TL also is considered as a node.

Forty conventional vehicles are inserted in a four-leg intersection and start traveling on four 400 m road length as depicted in Fig. 2. There are no communications between vehicles and the RSU. On the other hand, a connected EV is inserted on the perpendicular road and travels downward broadcasting a BSM once per second to the RSU. When it arrives at 300 m distance from the intersection and the BSM is received by the RSU, then TLs change their state to green for the EV and red for the other road. Ten seconds after EV has crossed the intersection, status of the TLs return to the previous status. Basically, state of the TLs change every 15 s from red to green and vice versa, also there is three seconds yellow state in between. Signal propagation conditions inherit from free space model. Main parameters of the simulation are shown in the Table 1. Algorithms 1 and 2 feature the behavior of EV and the RSU in sending and receiving the BSM respectively.

Algorithm 1. EV in sending state

1: **Input:** State of the vehicle
2: **Output:** BSM
3: Broadcast BSM every 1 s

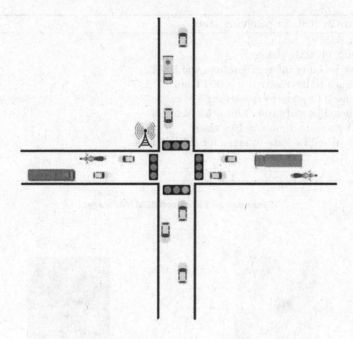

Fig. 2. Intersection layout

Table 1. Simulation parameters

Parameters	Values
Tx Power	20 mW
Bit Rate	6 Mbps
RSU Beacon Interval	1 s
Channel Number	178
Road Length	4 × 400 m
TLs green phase duration	15 s
Vehicle speed	70 km/h

4   Evaluation of Results

4.1   BSM Message

BSM is one of the message types for V2X communications that we have used in this simulation. It is transmitted over DSRC and it is suitable for low latency and localized broadcast which is required in V2X safety applications. Connected V2X safety applications are generated around SAE J2735 BSM [18]. Number of sent and received BSM messages are derived from OMNeT++. Totally, 21 BSM messages were disseminated by EV and 20 BSM messages were received

Algorithm 2. RSU in receiving state

1: **Input:** BSM
2: **Output:** TL state change
3: Retrieve mobility information from the BSM
4: **if** Distance to intersection == 300 **then**
5:    Change TLs state to green for EV
6:    Change TLs state to red for other vehicles
7:    **if** EV crossing time == 10 s **then**
8:       Change TLs state to green for other vehicles
9:    **end if**
10: **end if**

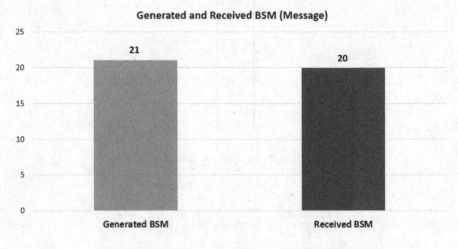

Fig. 3. Number of sent and received BSM messages

by the RSU. Success ratio of packet delivery exhibited 95.2%. Number of sent and received BSM messages are shown in Fig. 3.

4.2 Travel Time

Travel time of EV is a crucial factor in saving human lives. Figure 4 shows the comparison of average travel time for EV and some vehicles traveling ahead of the EV in traditional and connected intersections. Average travel time of EV and cars demonstrated 34 and 35 s in a traditional intersection respectively. However, their travel time improved to 21 and 22 s in the intersection where EV was connected to the TLs. Figure 4 manifested lower EV travel time at a connected intersection compared to the traditional one. This implies that in the connected intersection, EV could constantly pass through the intersection while in the other scenario EV along with other leading vehicles had to stop behind the TLs for some time. Furthermore, connected intersection hugely enhanced the average travel time of the vehicles ahead of the EV. This occurred due to the EV

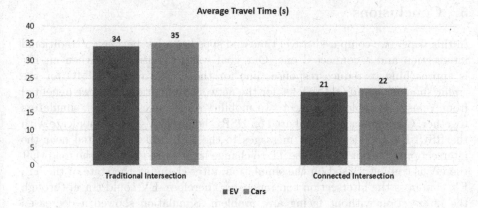

Fig. 4. Travel time of the vehicles (s)

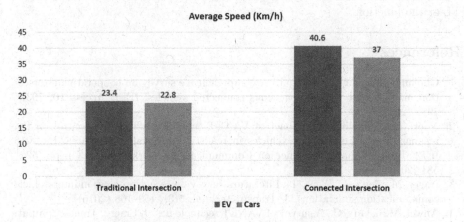

Fig. 5. Speed comparison of vehicles (km/h)

that altered the TLs state to green in advance such that they could continuously travel through the intersection together with the EV.

4.3 Vehicles Speed

Speed comparison of the EV and some other vehicles are in traditional and connected intersections are illustrated in Fig. 5. As mentioned before, EV and leading vehicles cross the intersection continuously in a connected intersection that results in higher average speed. On the other hand, in a traditional intersection, EV is blocked by some cars which greatly decreases its average speed. Besides, vehicles traveling in front of the EV also experienced lower average speed as they stopped at the intersection entrance due to the red TLs.

5   Conclusions

In this paper, we compared travel time and speed of a EV between a traditional intersection and a connected one. Our goal was to control TLs when an EV is approaching to reduce response time for the EV. We used SUMO for the traffic simulation and OMNeT++ for the network simulation. Also, we benefited from Veins to be able to connect two mobility and wireless network simulators together. Communication was based on DSRC helping EVs to communicate with the RSU. EV broadcast BSM messages to the RSU which is located near the intersection. Later, it signals the TL to change its state to green for the road that the EV is coming. Based on the simulation, after changing the state of the TL, EV can cross the intersection continuously. Therefore, EV could travel through the intersection without facing any problem. Simulation showed a decreased response time and an improved delivery efficiency of the EV as well as the leading vehicles. Future work includes a simulation of a train and controlling a TL at the junction.

References

1. Gholamhosseinian, A., Seitz, J.: A comprehensive survey on cooperative intersection management for heterogeneous connected vehicles. IEEE Access **10**, 7937–7972 (2022)
2. Noori, H.: Modeling the impact of VANET-enabled traffic lights control on the response time of emergency vehicles in realistic large-scale urban area. In: 2013 IEEE International Conference on Communications Workshops (ICC), pp. 526–531 (2013)
3. Hager, M., Seitz, J., Waas, T.: Literature survey on recent progress in inter-vehicle communication simulations. J. Transp. Technol. **5**(3), 159–168 (2015)
4. Anwer, M.S., Guy, C.: A survey of VANET technologies. J. Emerg. Trends Comput. Inf. Sci. **5**(9), 661–671 (2014)
5. Arena, F., Pau, G., Severino, A.: A review on IEEE 802.11p for intelligent transportation systems. J. Sens. Actuat. Netw. **9**(2) (2020)
6. Kenney, J.B.: Dedicated short-range communications (DSRC) standards in the united states. Proc. IEEE **99**(7), 1162–1182 (2011)
7. Noori, H.: Realistic urban traffic simulation as vehicular ad-hoc network (VANET) via veins framework. In: 2012 12th Conference of Open Innovations Association (FRUCT), pp. 1–7 (2012)
8. Noori, H., Valkama, M.: Impact of VANET-based V2X communication using IEEE 802.11p on reducing vehicles traveling time in realistic large scale urban area. In: 2013 International Conference on Connected Vehicles and Expo (ICCVE), pp. 654–661 (2013)
9. Jayaraj. V., Hemanth. C.: Emergency vehicle signalling using VANETS. In: 2015 IEEE 17th International Conference on High Performance Computing and Communications, IEEE 7th International Symposium on Cyberspace Safety and Security, and 2015 IEEE 12th International Conference on Embedded Software and Systems (2015)
10. da Costa, L., et al.: Poster: safesmart-a VANET system for efficient communication for emergency vehicles. In: IFIP Networking Conference (Networking) (2020)

11. Padmapriya, V., Ashok, A.K., Sujatha, D.N., Venugopal, K.R,: Road side unit assisted emergency vehicle transit approach for urban roads using VANET. In: IEEE International Conference on Electrical, Computer and Communication Technologies (ICECCT) (2019)
12. Obrusník, V., Herman, I., Hurák, Z.: Queue discharge-based emergency vehicle traffic signal preemption. IFAC-PapersOnLine **53**(2), 14 997–15 002 (2020)
13. Varga, N., Bokor, I., Takács, A., Kovács, J., Virág, L.: An architecture proposal for V2X communication-centric traffic light controller systems. In: 2017 15th International Conference on ITS Telecommunications (ITST), pp. 1–7 (2017)
14. SUMO. [Online]. https://www.eclipse.org/sumo/
15. Veins. [Online]. https://veins.car2x.org/
16. OMNeT++ Network Simulation Framework. [Online]. http://www.omnetpp.org/
17. Izadi, A., Gholamhosseinian, A., Seitz, J.: Modeling and evaluation of the impact of motorcycles mobility on vehicular traffic. J. Transp. Technol. **11**(3), 426–435 (2021)
18. Cronin, B.:Vehicle based data and availability. United States Department of Transportation ITS Program Advisory Committee, 2012. [Online]. https://documents.pub/document/vehicle-based-data-and-availability-intelligent-based-data-and-availability-brian.html

Deep Reinforcement Learning to Improve Vehicle-to-Vulnerable Road User Communications in C-V2X

Andy Triwinarko[1,2]($\boxtimes$), Zoubeir Mlika[1], Soumaya Cherkaoui[3], and Iyad Dayoub[4]

[1] Université de Sherbrooke, Sherbrooke, QC J1K2R1, Canada
[2] Politeknik Negeri Batam, Batam 29641, Indonesia
andy@polibatam.ac.id
[3] Polytechnique Montréal, Montréal, QC, Canada
soumaya.cherkaoui@polymtl.ca
[4] University Polytechnique Hauts-de-France, 59313 Valenciennes, France
iyad.dayoub@uphf.fr

Abstract. In this paper, we study the problem of optimizing the performance of vehicle-to-everything (V2X) using deep reinforcement learning techniques while sharing the spectrum between vehicle-to-infrastructure (V2I) links and vehicle-to-vulnerable road users (V2VRU) links in Cellular V2X (C-V2X). The objective is to protect VRU by improving the performance of V2VRU communications while maximizing the performance of V2I communications. Specifically, we formulate a spectrum sharing optimization problem with a two-objective function where the first objective is to improve the packet reception ratio (PRR) of VRU, whereas the second objective is to maximize the data rate of V2I communication links. To solve this challenging problem, we propose a deep reinforcement learning algorithm. A single agent controlling the vehicular network observes the environment and takes decisions accordingly by appropriately selecting the spectrum sub-bands and the transmission power levels. The simulation results show that the proposed scheme attains high performance compared to baseline solutions and solves the trade-off between maximizing the data rates of the vehicle users (V2I links) and improving the PRR of the V2VRU links.

Keywords: Vehicular communications · vulnerable road users · Deep Reinforcement · spectrum sharing · optimization

1 Introduction

Vehicular-to-everything (V2X) communication is considered one of the key pillars of future generations of wireless networks. It offers diverse services ranging from infotainment services to safety services, such as road safety, ubiquitous Internet access, traffic efficiency, etc. The 3rd Generation Partnership Project (3GPP) organization and other industries have already started working to provide V2X communication and improve its services [1–4].

E. Sabir et al. (Eds.): UNet 2022, LNCS 13853, pp. 138–150, 2023.
https://doi.org/10.1007/978-3-031-29419-8_11

In this paper, we design a spectrum sharing strategy for vehicular networks that includes vulnerable road users (VRU) and non-VRU that supports different connectivity such as vehicle-to-VRU (V2VRU) and vehicle-to-infrastructure (V2I) connectivity [5]. The V2VRU communication concerns the links among vehicles and VRU, whereas the V2I communication concerns the links between vehicles and infrastructures such as roadside units (RSU). As discussed in 3GPP for V2V [2], the V2VRU communication is established on a side-link radio interface (called PC5), but the V2I communication is established on a cellular radio interface (called Uu).

The use case proposed in this paper consists of supporting two different services: (1) application or infotainment services for high data rate V2X communication and (2) advanced driving for high-reliability V2X communication. Our supported use case aims to serve two types of vehicular users: non-VRU (or simply vehicle users) and VRU, such as pedestrians, cyclists, etc. VRUs are particularly important to protect since pedestrians account for over 21% of road fatalities and motorcycles, bicycles and scooters over 26% [5,6]. VRUs are generally unpredictable in their movements and are not always visible in a line of sight manner to other non-VRU, which makes the propagation characteristics of V2VRU communication different from classical V2V or V2I communication. To support this use case, we aim (1) to maximize the data rate of non-VRU (V2I communications) and at the same time (2) to improve the packet reception ratio (PRR) of VRU while allocating the shared spectrum between both types of road users. This paper chooses pedestrians as our VRU, so we use vehicle-to-pedestrians (V2P) as our V2VRU communication.

1.1   Related Works

Although many research efforts have been made to solve the resource allocation problem in V2V communication [7–12], only few papers discussed V2VRU communication to protect VRU, even though the number of road fatalities for VRU is high. The authors in [13] investigate the performance radio access technology (RAT) standards IEEE 802.11p, 802.11bd, 4G LTE-V2X and 5G NR-V2X for V2VRU communication. Each RAT complies with the safety applications requirements, with 20–100 ms latency and 0.5–700 Mbps throughput. We want to improve the performance of the V2VRU communication links; hence it can also improve the protection of VRU.

The authors in [14] proposed resource sharing as a multi-agent reinforcement learning problem, where multiple V2V links reuse the frequency spectrum occupied with the V2I links. Several vehicles connected with V2V links act as an agent that observes the environment and learns to improve the spectrum and power allocation. We were inspired by this approach for our V2VRU communications, where we need to consider that the VRU channel model is different from the V2V and V2I channel models.

In [15] the authors studied the problem of network slicing to optimize the resource allocation problem in V2X communication while optimizing the coverage area of vehicles, transmission power, and RB allocation. The objective of the problem is to maximize the number of two types of packets: infotainment packets and safety packets. The authors proposed a multi-agent deep reinforcement learning approach to solve the problem. The difference between this work and ours is that we consider spectrum sharing as well as V2VRU communication.

The authors in [16] proposed the channel model for vehicle-to-pedestrians (V2P) communication in three main scenarios, i.e., 1) the vehicle to static pedestrian, 2) vehicle to moving pedestrian, and 3) vehicle to pedestrians with crowd shadowing scenarios. We used the findings of this paper to model the V2P channel in our work.

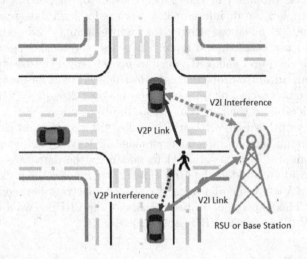

Fig. 1. An illustrative system of V2X networks consists of V2I and V2P links and its interference signal. The V2I links are preoccupied the spectrum bands and the V2P links will have a spectrum sharing with the V2I link.

2   System Model

We consider a vehicular network composed of a set of vehicles (non-VRU) and a pedestrian as our VRU. The vehicular network operates in a geographical zone covered by a cellular network (e.g., LTE or 5 G), where a RSU is present to serve the road users. We consider two kinds of communications where vehicles communicate with the RSU (also known as V2I communication) and non-VRU that communicate with pedestrian (also known as V2VRU communication). We assume that there are m V2I links as well as n V2VRU links. The illustration of V2X communication using spectrum sharing between V2I and V2VRU (or V2P) links can be seen in Fig. 1.

The Mode 4 defined in cellular V2X communication is considered where all the vehicular users (VRU and non-VRU) share a pool of radio resources of V2I communication from which they must select appropriate resources to communicate between each other for the V2VRU communication. The overlap between

V2I resources and V2VRU resources can help in improving the spectral efficiency provided that the resources are optimally allocated. That is, interference caused by V2VRU should be carefully managed to improve the performance of both V2I and V2VRU communications.

As done in [14], we assume that the resources allocated to the V2I communication are assumed to be orthogonal among each other so that the interference is neglected in the V2I communication. In other words, V2I link $i = 1, \cdots, m$ is assumed to communicate over the spectrum sub-band i. The main challenge is thus how to share the spectrum sub-band $i = 1, \cdots, m$ between the V2I communication and the V2VRU so that the data rate of the V2I communication and the packet reception rate (PRR) of the V2VRU communication are maximized.

Note that each sub-band is defined simply as a set of consecutive sub-carriers that are grouped together. Here, orthogonal frequency division multiplexing (OFDM) is used as in [14] to transform the frequency selective channels into a set of parallel flat channels over multiple sub-carriers. It is further assumed that the channel fading is constant over the same sub-band but varies independently from one sub-band to another.

Once a V2VRU link j is allocated sub-band $i = 1, \cdots, m$, its channel power gain is given by:

$$g_{j,j}^i = \mathrm{PL}_{j,j} j h_{j,j}^i, \tag{1}$$

where $\mathrm{PL}_{j,j}$ is the large-scale fading that includes path-loss and shadowing propagation effects. It mainly depends on the distance of the V2VRU link j. The small-scale fading is denoted by $h_{j,j}^i$, which is frequency-dependent and generally assumed to follow an exponential distribution. However, in this work, the propagation characteristics of V2VRU link j is modeled differently to capture the effect of VRU.

The channel power gain over the V2I link i is denoted as $g_{i,0}^i$ (between the transmitter of link i and the RSU denoted by 0), which includes small-scale and large-scale fading as in (1). (The superscript i denotes the sub-band i allocated to V2P link i.)

There are three types of interference in our system model.

- V2I-to-V2VRU interference: The interference caused by V2I link i on the V2VRU link j (after allocating sub-band i to link j) is denoted by $I_{0,j}^i = p_i g_{0,j}^i$. Here, $g_{0,j}^i$ denotes the channel power gain between the transmitter of the V2I link i and the receiver of the V2VRU link j over sub-band i.
- V2VRU-to-V2VRU interference: The interference caused by other V2VRU link j' on V2VRU j when both links are allocated sub-band i is denoted by $I_{j',j}^i = p_{j'}^i g_{j',j}^i$. Here, $g_{j',j}^i$ denotes the channel power gain between the transmitter of the V2VRU link j' and the receiver of the V2VRU link j over sub-band i.
- V2VRU-to-V2I interference: The interference caused by V2VRU link j on the RSU when the V2VRU link j is allocated sub-band i is denoted by $I_{j,0}^i = p_j^i g_{j,0}^i$. Here, $g_{j,0}^i$ denotes the channel power gain between the transmitter of the V2VRU link j and the receiver of the V2I link i over sub-band i.

All channel power interference discussed previously are assumed to be defined similarly to (1). The model of our wireless channel of the V2I and the V2VRU are given respectively in [2] and [16].

On the one hand, the data rate of the V2I link i (over sub-band i) is given as:

$$R_i = B \lg(1 + \text{SINR}_i), \tag{2}$$

where B is the bandwidth of each sub-band and SINR_i is given in the following equation:

$$\text{SINR}_i = \frac{p_i g_{i,0}^i}{\sigma^2 + \sum_j x_j^i I_{j,0}^i}, \tag{3}$$

where the denominator in (3) contains the noise over sub-band i and the interference coming from all other V2VRU links j that are transmitting over sub-band i as well. The variables x_j^i are used to denote whether sub-band i is allocated to the V2VRU link j or not. The transmission power of the transmitter in the V2I link i is denoted as p_i (constant) and the transmission power of the transmitter in the V2VRU link j over sub-band i is denoted as p_j^i (variables).

On the other hand, the data rate of the V2VRU link j (over sub-band i, i.e., $x_j^i = 1$) is given as:

$$R_j^i = B \lg(1 + \text{SINR}_j^i), \tag{4}$$

where SINR_j^i is given in the following equation:

$$\text{SINR}_j^i = \frac{p_j^i g_{j,j}^i}{\sigma^2 + I_{0,j}^i + \sum_{j' \neq j} x_{j'}^i I_{j',j}^i}, \tag{5}$$

where the denominator in (5) contains the noise over sub-band i and the interference coming from all other V2VRU links j' that are transmitting over sub-band i as well as from the transmitter of the V2I link i. To protect VRU from accident and other fatalities, we have to guarantee a reliable communication for the safety-critical message exchanged over the V2VRU links. For this reason, we use the performance metric called packet reception rate (PRR) [14] which mainly measure how much safety packets are delivered during a defined time window. Mathematically, the PRR is defined as [14]:

$$\Pr\left[\sum_{t=1}^{T} \sum_{i=1}^{m} x_j^i R_j^i(t) \geq \gamma_j / \delta_T\right], \forall \text{ V2VRU link } j, \tag{6}$$

where T denotes a defined period of time during which the packet of the V2VRU link j should be transmitted and γ_j is the size of the safety packet of the V2VRU link j. The variable δ_T denotes the channel coherence time. We added the time index t to the notation of the data rate of the V2VRU link j over sub-band i, $R_j^i(t)$, to denote the data rate at each time instant t (each coherence time-slot). We used $\Pr[\cdot]$ to denote the probability function.

3   Problem Formulation

In this paper, the objective is to maximize the data rate of the V2I links as well as the packet reception rate of the V2VRU links. This problem is formulated as follows:

Problem 1.

$$\text{maximize}_{\mathbf{x},\mathbf{p}} \quad \alpha \sum_i R_i + \beta \sum_{j=1}^n \Pr\Big[\sum_{t=1}^T \sum_{i=1}^m x_j^i R_j^i(t) \geq \gamma_j/\delta_T\Big] \quad (7)$$

$$\text{subject to} \quad x_j^i \in \{0,1\}, p_j^i \geq 0 \forall i, j, \quad (8)$$

$$\sum_{i=1}^m x_j^i \leq 1, \forall j, \quad (9)$$

$$\sum_{i=1}^m p_j^i \leq \bar{p}_j, \forall j. \quad (10)$$

The variable $\mathbf{x}$ is a matrix notation for the binary variables x_j^i for the sub-band allocation whereas the variable $\mathbf{p}$ is a matrix notation for the real variables p_j^i for the power allocation. Constraints (9) guarantee that each V2VRU link is allocated at most one sub-band i. Constraints (10) guarantee that each V2VRU link j is allocated a maximum transmission power $\bar{p}_j$ over all its allocated sub-bands. The parameters α and β are used to weigh the two-objective function to make it unit-less.

Problem (1) is challenging to solve due to the non-convexity of the objective function. To efficiently solve it, we propose a machine learning approach based on single-agent deep reinforcement learning (SARL).

4   Proposed Solution

In this section, we describe our proposed SARL approach. First, we describe the agent, the action and the state spaces, and the transition probability function. Then, we describe the algorithm.

The DRL agent is implemented in the RSU. This means that it is a centralized agent that observes the initially unknown vehicular environment and collects information to take actions accordingly. The agent exchanges information between non-VRU and VRU using dedicated wireless channels without excessive overheads.

The state space is roughly the vehicular network. More precisely, at each coherence time instant t, a state s_t is observed. The state s_t is generally unknown and includes channel conditions of all vehicles, vehicle movements, radio access information such as transmission power and spectrum allocation, etc. The DRL agent can extract useful information from this unknown state s_t through an observation function that maps each unknown state s_t into a well-defined and known observation variable o_t. The observation o_t includes the channel power gains g_j^i, $g_{i,0}$ as well as the interference $I_{j,0}^i$, $I_{j',j}^i$, and $I_{0,j}^i$. It also includes the sum of interference illustrated in the SINR formulas in (3) and (5). Finally, we add to the observation o_t the variables γ_j^r and $T^r = T - t$ which denote the remaining number of bits of V2VRU's j packet and the remaining time interval. Note that, we can, for simplicity, exchange the s_t and the o_t notations.

The action space includes the sub-band spectrum allocation as well as the transmission power levels. We assume a set of P transmission power levels from which each V2VRU link can choose. Thus an action at time instant t is given by $\mathbf{a}_t = [(p_1(t), x_1(t)), \cdots, (p_j(t), x_j(t)), \cdots, (p_n(t), x_n(t))]^\top$ which is a vector of length n—the number of V2VRU links. Each element of the vector $\mathbf{a}_t$ at time instant t is a pair $(p_j(t), x_j(t))$ of transmission power levels $p_j(t) \in \{1, 2, \cdots, P\} \cup \{0\}$ and of sub-band allocation $x_j(t) \in \{1, 2, \cdots, m\}$. The power level 0 indicates no transmission and $x_j(t) = i$ indicates that the V2VRU link j is allocated the sub-band i at time instant t.

The reward of the DRL agent is chosen to reflect the objective function in problem (1). That is, given the current state s_t, the reward of the DRL agent is given as $\eta_1 > 0$ or $0 < \eta_2 \ll \eta_1$. The value of η_1 (resp. η_2) denotes the number of V2VRU links that terminated transmitting (still transmitting) their safety packets. In this way, we encourage the DRL agent to accumulate as large reward as possible by serving V2VRU links and finishing successfully their safety packet transmissions.

The transition from one state to another is given by a probability distribution that gives how to transition from state s_t to state s_{t+1}, given action a_t, i.e. $\Pr[s_{t+1}, r_{t+1}|s_t, a_t]$ is the probability of moving to state s_{t+1} from state s_t and obtaining the reward r_{t+1} when taking action a_t. This probability distribution depends on the dynamical vehicular environment including the channel conditions and the vehicle mobility and it is generally hard to compute explicitly due to the complex nature of the vehicular environment.

The proposed algorithm is based on deep-Q-learning (DQL). DQL combines the well-known Q-learning method and deep neural networks. Q-learning creates a table of state-action pairs called the Q-table and finds the best action given a certain state using a greedy exploration approach, called ϵ-greedy, In ϵ-greedy, an action is chosen at random with probability ϵ and the action that gives the best reward is chosen otherwise. The drawback of Q-learning appears when the state and action spaces become large. Also, once the size of the table grows very large, many states will be very rarely visited, which deteriorates the learning strategy.

The key success of deep-Q-networks (DQN) is the use of experience replay memory technique where the tuple of state, action, reward, and next state are stored in a replay buffer. Next, the DRL agent samples from this replay buffer to perform learning. DQL is a promising approach that can be used to solve the curse of dimensionality in RL [15] by approximating the Q-table. We combine DQN with independent Q-learning.

Initially, the experience replay memory and all parameters are initialized. Then, the proposed algorithm SARL operates over a set of episodes. In each episode, the DRL agent explores the action space using the ϵ-greedy policy.

Table 1. Log-Distance Path Loss Parameters in V2I and V2P Based on Reference [14, 16]

V2X Types	Parameters	Values
V2I Link	Path loss	128.1 dB
	Path loss exponent	3.76
	Shadowing standard deviation	8 dB
	Break-point distance	50 m
V2P scenario 1 (static pedestrian)	Path loss	46.77 dB
	Path loss exponent	2.03
	Shadowing standard deviation	3.20 dB
V2P scenario 2 (moving pedestrian)	Path loss	40 dB
	Path loss exponent	2.44
	Shadowing standard deviation	5.47 dB
V2P scenario 3 (crowded pedestrian)	Path loss	67 dB
	Path loss exponent	1.26
	Shadowing standard deviation	3.35 dB

Each episode e covers a time horizon of T time-slots. At the beginning of the first time-slot, the starting state of the vehicular environment (initial positions of the vehicles, of the pedestrians, etc.) is revealed to the DRL agent. For subsequent time-slot t, the DRL agent chooses an action $\mathbf{a}_t$ for each V2VRU link, according to the ϵ-greedy approach. In other words, the DRL agent chooses a transmission power level and a sub-band for each V2VRU link $j = 1, 2, \cdots, n$. Once all V2VRU links have been allocated a transmission power level and a sub-band, the DRL agent evaluates the reward function r_{t+1} based on the expression of (2) and (4). Next, each V2VRU link (each vehicle and pedestrian) moves, according to its mobility model, and the next state is revealed to the DRL agent. The resulting tuple $(s_t, \mathbf{a}_t, r_{t+1}, s_{t+1})$ is collected and is stored in the prioritized experience replay memory of the DRL agent. This experience replay memory is associated some positive priority weight. After a few episodes, a mini-batch is sampled according to their priorities from the prioritized experience replay memory. This mini-batch is used to update the DQN weight parameters using a variant of the stochastic gradient descent algorithm to minimize the loss function. The loss function is given by the mean square error as follows:

$$\sum_{(s_t, \mathbf{a}_t, r_{t+1}, s_{t+1})} \left(r_{t+1} + \gamma \max_a \left(Q(s_{t+1}, a; \mathbf{w}^-) \right) - Q(s_t, \mathbf{a}_t; \mathbf{w}) \right)^2, \quad (11)$$

where the DQN is represented mathematically by the Q-function $Q(s_t, \mathbf{a}_t; \mathbf{w})$ (the function that the DQL tries to approximate) and $\mathbf{w}^-$ is the weight parameter of a duplicate copy of the original DQN (called the target DQN) that is created in order to update the original DQN from occasionally. The creation of a target DQN is suggested by the quasi-static target network method [17] to set the targets of the Q values.

5   Simulation Results

In this section, we present the simulation results of V2X spectrum sharing for V2I links and V2VRU links using the proposed SARL. We built our simulation using Python and TensorFlow software. For the evaluation methodology, we used the urban crossing environment described by 3GPP, which gives the vehicle mobility models, vehicle densities etc. [2]. We used previously reported channel characterization to implement the V2VRU communications [16]. We used the Rayleigh fast fading channel model and log-distance path loss model with log-normal shadowing distribution. The budget time constraint T used for V2VRU data packet transmissions is 100 ms, the time for path loss and shadowing update is 100 ms, and the time for fast fading update is 1 ms. The simulation parameters are listed in Table 1, which describes the channel models characterization for both V2I and V2VRU links. Table 2 describes the major simulation parameters, which are similar to those in [14]. For the V2VRU communication, where VRU

Table 2. Simulation Parameters Based on Reference [14]

Parameters	Values
Number of vehicles	4
Carrier Frequency	5.9 GHz
Bandwidth	10 MHz
RSU or BS height	25 m
RSU or BS antenna gain	8 dBi
RSU or BS receiver noise figure	5 dB
Vehicle or VRU antenna height	1.5 m
Vehicle or VRU antenna gain	3 dBi
Vehicle or VRU receiver noise figure	9 dBm
Vehicle speed	10 m/s
V2I transmit power	23 dBm
V2P transmit power	[23, 10, 5, −100] dBm
Noise power	−114 dB
V2P Packet size	[1..6] x 1 KB
Time constraint for V2P packet transmission	100 ms
Path loss and shadowing update	Every 100 ms
Fast fading model	Rayleigh fading
Fast fading update	Every 1 ms

is a pedestrian, we used three scenarios based on [16]: (1) vehicle-to-static-VRU, (2) vehicle-to-moving-VRU, and (3) vehicle-to-VRU-with-crowd-shadowing.

The proposed DQN consists of 3 connected hidden layers with 500, 250, and 120 neurons. The DQN training lasts 3000 episodes. The packet size of VRU is 2 KB in the training phase, and it varies from 1 to 6 KB in the testing phase to verify the robustness of the proposed SARL algorithm.

We compared the proposed SARL for V2I and V2VRU spectrum sharing against the baseline of random resource allocation. The random baseline chooses the spectrum sub-band and transmission power in a random fashion at each time instant. We simulate 4 vehicles that are using 4 sub-bands where each sub-band has a bandwidth of 1 MHz. The transmission power for the V2VRU links is predetermined using the value of $[23, 15, 5, -100]$ dBm, while the transmission power for V2I is fixed at 23 dBm. The value of -100 dBm is equivalent to 0 transmission power. We also compared the proposed solution against another baseline that used a fixed maximum transmission power for the V2P communication (23 dBm).

From Fig. 2, both the data rate and PRR decrease when the packet size increases due to the time budget constraint. The larger packet size will need a higher transmission power to improve the reception probability in the receiver side, hence leading to a higher interference. As we can see from Fig. 2, our proposed solution gave the best performance compared to the other baselines as it gave higher data rates for V2I communication. It also gave around the same performance for PRR of the Maximized V2P transmission power. However this maximized V2P transmission power gives a higher value of interference, hence reducing the data rate of V2I communication. In terms of performance metrics, the proposed SARL algorithm gives better performance compared to the random baseline. With a trained model using the packet size of 2 KB, we obtained 13% improvement in the data rate and a4% improvement in PRR. Furthermore, the proposed SARL shows a consistently better performance with different packet

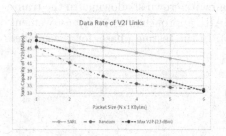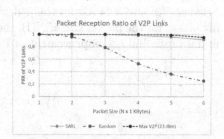

Fig. 2. The performance of SARL, random baseline and maximum transmission power for V2P (23 dBm) baseline in scenario 1 (Static Pedestrian).

sizes. For the packet size of 1 KB, the data rate improved by 6% even if the PRR did not improve significantly, while for the packet size of 6 KB, the data rate improvement was 20% and the PRR performance improved by around 67%.

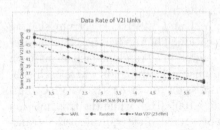
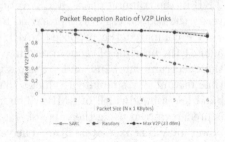

Fig. 3. The performance of SARL, random baseline and maximum transmission power for V2P (23 dBm) baseline in scenario 2 (moving pedestrian).

From Fig. 3, we can see that the proposed SARL offers a better performance for the scenario 2 which is spectrum sharing between V2I and V2VRU for the moving pedestrian. In the training phase, for the packet size of 2 KB, the SARL approach gives 12% improvement in data rate and 6% in PRR. For the smaller packet size of 1 KB, the performance of PRR is almost the same, and the performance of the data rate is improved by 5%; while for the larger packet size of 6 KB, the PRR improvement is 16% and the PRR performance is improved by 58%. The performance of the scenario 2 has the same results as in scenario 1, where the maximized transmission power of 23 dBm for the V2P communication gave around the same performance for the PRR of the proposed SARL solution. However, it reduced the data rate performance of the V2I communication due to the higher value of the interference.

Figure 4 shows the results for the scenario 3 which is the spectrum sharing between V2I and V2VRU for the pedestrian with crowd shadowing. In the training phase, for the packet size of 2 KB, the SARL approach gives 16% improvement in data rate and 6% improvement of PRR. In the testing phase, for the smaller

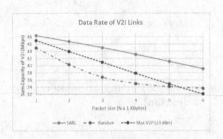
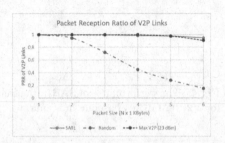

Fig. 4. The performance of SARL, random baseline and maximum transmission power for V2P (23 dBm) baseline in scenario 3 (crowded pedestrian).

packet size of 1 KB, the data rate improved by 8% while the performance of the PRR remained unchanged. While for the larger packet size of 6 KB, the data rate improvement was 16% and the PRR performance was improved by 80%. The data rate and PRR performances of the scenario 3 also gave the similar results to scenarios 1 and 2, where the proposed SARL solution gave the best performance and the maximized transmission power of the V2P communication gave around the same performance for the PRR of the V2P communication, but gave a reduced data rate for V2I communication due to high interference.

6   Conclusions

In this paper, we addressed the problem of optimizing the spectrum sharing of the V2X communication by improving the PRR of V2VRU links, and maximizing the data rate of V2I links. We proposed a DRL approach for spectrum sharing between V2I and V2VRU. A single-vehicle selects the spectrum sub-bands and the transmission power based on the trained DQN using acquired information from the environment. We compared our proposed model with a random baseline that randomly chooses the spectrum and power transmission. We also compared it with another baseline that uses the maximized transmission power of V2VRU communication (23 dBm). Our simulation result showed a significant improvement in the V2I data rate and V2VRU PRR for different VRU communication scenarios. The improvement of PRR implies more reliable V2VRU communication, which int turn improves the reliability of safety applications intended for VRU protection on the road. At the same time, the proposed SARL gave better data rates for V2I communications, thus enabling better performance for higher-data rate V2I-applications.

References

1. 3rd Generation Partnership Project (3GPP): Technical Specification Group Radio Access Network; Study on enhancement of 3GPP Support for 5G V2X Services; (Release 15). Technical Report (TR), Version 15.1.0, (2017)
2. 3rd Generation Partnership Project (3GPP): Technical Specification Group Radio Access Network; Study on LTE-based V2X Services; (Release 14). Technical Report (TR), Version 14.0.0, (2016)
3. Molina-Masegosa, R., Gozalvez, J.: LTE-V for Sidelink 5G V2X vehicular communications: a new 5G technology for short-range vehicle-to-everything communications. IEEE Veh. Technol. Mag. **12**(4), 30–39 (2017). https://doi.org/10.1109/MVT.2017.2752798
4. Alalewi, A., Dayoub, I., Cherkaoui, S.: On 5G-V2X use cases and enabling technologies: a comprehensive survey. IEEE Access **9**, 107710–107737 (2021). https://doi.org/10.1109/ACCESS.2021.3100472
5. Linget, T.: Vulnerable road user protection. 5GAA White Paper (2020)
6. Abid, M.A., Chakroun, O., Cherkaoui, S.: Pedestrian collision avoidance in vehicular networks. In: IEEE International Conference on Communications (ICC 2013), pp. 2928–2932. IEEE, Budapest (2013). https://doi.org/10.1109/ICC.2013.6654987

7. Rezgui, J., et al.: Deterministic access for DSRC/802.11p vehicular safety communication. In: 7th International Wireless Communications and Mobile Computing Conference, pp. 595–600. IEEE, Istanbul (2011). https://doi.org/10.1109/IWCMC.2011.5982600
8. Azizian, M., et al.: An optimized flow allocation in vehicular cloud. IEEE Access **4**, 6766–6779 (2016). https://doi.org/10.1109/ACCESS.2016.2615323
9. Chakroun, O., et al.:Overhead-free congestion control and data dissemination for 802.11p VANETs. Veh. Commun. **1**(3), 123–133 (2014). https://doi.org/10.1016/j.vehcom.2014.05.003
10. Rezgui, J., et al.: About deterministic and non-deterministic vehicular communications over DSRC/802.11p. Wireless Commun. Mobile Comput. **14**(15), 1435–1449 (2014). https://doi.org/10.1002/wcm.2270
11. Azizian, M., et al.: Improved multi-channel operation for safety messages dissemination in vehicular networks. In: Proceedings of the fourth ACM International Symposium on Development and Analysis of Intelligent Vehicular Networks and Applications (DIVANet 2014), pp. 81–85. Association for Computing Machinery, New York (2014). https://doi.org/10.1145/2656346.2656410
12. Azizian, M., et al.: A distributed D-hop cluster formation for VANET. In: IEEE Wireless Communications and Networking Conference, pp. 1–6. IEEE, Doha (2016). https://doi.org/10.1109/WCNC.2016.7564925
13. Triwinarko, A., Cherkaoui, S., Dayoub, I.: Performance of radio access technologies for next generation V2VRU networks. In: IEEE International Conference on Communications (ICC 2022), pp. 1524–1529. IEEE, Seoul (2022). https://doi.org/10.1109/ICC45855.2022.9838580
14. Liang, L., Ye, H., Li, G.Y.: Spectrum sharing in vehicular networks based on multi-agent reinforcement learning. IEEE J. Sel. Areas Commun. **37**(10), 2282–2292 (2019). https://doi.org/10.1109/JSAC.2019.2933962
15. Mlika, Z., Cherkaoui, S.: Network slicing for vehicular communications: a multi-agent deep reinforcement learning approach. Ann. Telecommun. **76**(9), 665–683 (2021). https://doi.org/10.1109/JSAC.2019.2933962
16. Rashdan, I., de Ponte Muller, F., Wang, W., Schmidhammer, M., Sand, S.: Vehicle-to-Pedestrian channel characterization: wideband measurement campaign and first results. In: 12th European Conference on Antennas and Propagation (EuCAP 2018), 340 (5 pp.)-340 (5 pp.). Institution of Engineering and Technology (2018)
17. Mnih, V., et al.: Human-level control through deep reinforcement learning. Nature **518**(7540), 529–533 (2015)

Pervasive Computing for Efficient Intra-UAV Connectivity: Based on Context-Awareness

Biruk E. Tegicho[✉] [iD], Tadilo E. Bogale, and Corey Graves

North Carolina A&T State University, Greensboro, NC, USA
btegicho@aggies.ncat.edu, {tebogale,cag}@ncat.edu

Abstract. Swarms of unmanned aerial vehicles are increasingly being utilized for a variety of operations. However, extremely variable environmental circumstances alter their intra-UAV minimum safe distance, resulting in collision, and those near swarm's edge become increasingly vulnerable to connectivity loss. Context-awareness as a strategy for developing pervasive computing in UAVs is gaining popularity to tackle these difficulties. A context awareness-based pervasive computing system model is proposed in this research to improve the safety and connectivity of individual UAVs in a swarm with their neighboring UAVs. To acquire the contexts of different environments the following systems were utilized: For physical, light intensity from real-time picture taken using camera; for human, facial recognition algorithm; for UAV local ICT, the UAV's built-in CPU utilization percentage; for network ICT, wireless network signal strength using received signal strength analysis. Following simulation, we evaluated the accuracy, reaction time, and significant limits that must be considered. Most situations were recognized with great accuracy, ranging from 84.85% to 100%. On a machine with 16 GB of RAM and a 64-bit operating system, the total system performance had an average reaction time of 2.15 s in a scenario where all contexts were used in a prioritized manner. The environments under consideration, as well as the kind of UAV and its internal hardware system processing capacity, were determined to be key limits on the system's performance. Analyzing the proposed system's application, a UAV swarm can complete tasks without colliding while retaining intra-UAV connectivity by transmitting information across a reliable communication network.

Keywords: Context-awareness · Unmanned Aerial Vehicles (UAV) · Swarm · Pervasive computing

1 Introduction

The fast development of unmanned aerial vehicles (UAVs) and its application areas has piqued the interest of both academics and industry [7,10,12,14,15,17, 22,23]. Swarms of Unmanned Aerial Vehicles (UAVs) have been investigated for a range of uses in recent years. The application areas include aerial photography,

E. Sabir et al. (Eds.): UNet 2022, LNCS 13853, pp. 151–163, 2023.
https://doi.org/10.1007/978-3-031-29419-8_12

delivering goods, traffic management, serving as communication platform, military missions, surveillance, monitoring, surveying, target tracking, search and rescue missions, and entertainment. Soon, swarms of UAVs flying over national airspace will play a key role in the deployment of increasingly sophisticated applications and services [7]. To efficiently perform the assigned operations, a stable flight environment is required. In addition, increased autonomy of a UAV swarm in its operation will contribute to a faster response in its decision-making. However, the amount of autonomy in most of the real life demonstrations of a UAV swarm has been minimal [22,23,26].

Pervasive computing(ubiquitous computing), which is a developing trend of embedding computational capacity into common items to make them efficiently interact and execute valuable activities in a way that reduces human involvement, substantially benefits these aims of stability and enhanced autonomy [6]. UAVs with pervasive computing capabilities are continually accessible and networked. Delivering consistent adaptive behaviors and context-aware systems in a vast volume of sensor data for services that need to enhance accuracy, precision, and dynamism is the core challenge of ubiquitous computing. This research is particularly interested in the use of context awareness as a method for the development of ubiquitous computing in a UAV swarm application scenario.

Current UAV swarm demonstrations use one of two types of swarm communication architecture. Infrastructure-based swarm architecture and ad-hoc network-based architecture are the two types. In Infrastructure based swarm communication architecture, a ground control station takes data from all UAVs and coordinates the swarm by controlling each UAV independently [8]. On the contrary, ad-hoc network-based architecture coordinates communication amongst UAVs in a single network without the use of existing infrastructure [18]. All UAVs in this type of ad-hoc network are connected in real time via a communication network built between them. Because there is no need for an infrastructure-based decision engine, direct communication between UAVs drives decentralised decision-making [19]. For an effective decision making in these kinds of ad-hoc networks, pervasive computing plays an important role. As pervasive computing is a new paradigm in the realm of communication and computing, large number of intelligent devices participate in acquiring data, exchanging data, and making collaborative decisions.

This paper proposes, designs, and analyzes a MATLAB-based pervasive computing system for acquiring and transmitting various types of context awareness information between individual UAVs in a swarm in order to mitigate the effects of sudden environmental changes the swarm may face during its mission. For example, when a sudden turbulence occurs, an individual UAV detects its current state and sends information to its neighbors about objects near collision, its wireless connectivity being affected, its CPU usage level by other control systems in it trying to stay in flight, etc. This research's contribution is aimed at achieving the stated sensing and communication, and also the full realization and enhancement of intra-UAV connectivity and safety of a UAV swarm by use of context awareness. Furthermore, it aids the development of autonomy in UAV swarm decision-making under unknown environmental conditions.

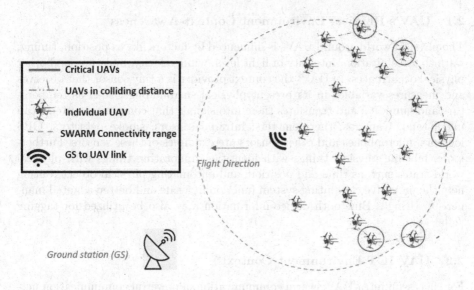

Fig. 1. UAV swarm system architecture [22]

The remainder of the paper is laid out as follows. A background about context awareness and its different types is presented in Sect. 2. In Sect. 3, we describe the main objective of the paper and associated system model. In relation to the system model, Sect. 4 discusses the context acquiring, processing and transmission processes. The findings and additional discussions of the proposed technology are discussed in Sect. 5. Conclusions and recommendations for further study are presented in Sect. 6.

2 Background

In human reasoning, context has an intuitive meaning [16]. The purpose of this reasoning is to provide the system more flexibility and effective decision-making. By supplying fresh information about UAVs or users and their surroundings, context contributes to our understanding of "where, what, and who." According to [1], context is also defined as the interrelated conditions in which something exists or occurs. The idea of contexts has been studied in several publications [5,11,25]. Context-aware computing enables each UAV's computing system flexibility, agility, and autonomy. There are several types of context-awareness with respect to intra-UAV communication: physical environment context, UAV ICT environment context, human environment context, and so on. The primary forms of context-awareness that are used in this study are given in the following subsections.

2.1   UAV's Physical Environment Context-Awareness

The physical world around UAVs is influenced by factors like as position, timing, warmth, precipitation, intensity of light level, wind velocity, moisture, and other physical occurrences. In UAVs the context provider is a tiny sensor that observes and measures variables in its present physical surroundings, such as temperature and humidity, and translates them into signals that computing systems can understand. Cameras, thermometers, infrared sensors, smoke detectors, GPS locators, microphones and other sensors are examples of these sensors. Furthermore, labeling physical things with identities, annotating things with physical world states such as time and position, and automating physical object routing help the pervasive computing system function in a safe and better-adapted manner [9]. Using a Bluetooth device information may also be utilized for tagging [24].

2.2   UAV ICT Environment Context

For successful intra-UAV swarm communication, a powerful communication network and high-performance capability of UAV's local ICT system is required. Pervasive computing in UAVs consists of several ICT components, including as the central processor unit (CPU), memory, power supply, wireless network, and internet connection, whose performance has an influence on the entire computer system [13]. It might, for example, comprise CPU load, memory utilization, wireless network data rate, and so on.

2.3   Human Environment Context-Awareness

Human identity, social milieu, activity levels, prior knowledge of an environmental scenario, and other human related activities are among the contexts in this type of context-awareness. Sensors such as accelerometers, physiological sensors, and cameras are now becoming a rich source of these data in a variety of interactions that may be gathered by measuring normal operations, calendar entries, and so on. Human face recognition is employed in this research.

3   Objective and System Model

3.1   Objective

One of the main reasons why one or more UAVs in a swarm of UAVs lose connectivity and safety is because of changes in highly variable environmental parameters like wind. In a windy environment, UAVs in a swarm may collide, and some near the swarm's perimeter may lose communication, compromising the overall goal of the swarm. As a result, those UAVs that are affected are in a critical or abnormal conditions. Individual UAVs can be equipped with a system that alerts them to nearby impediments, wireless network status, and the condition of their local ICT system, among other things, to avoid the effects of the being in a critical condition. The main objective of this research paper is to provide a context awareness based pervasive computing system model that provides individual UAVs with knowledge about their environment and increases the effectiveness of the swarm's decision making. The swarm as a whole can make better decisions in avoiding the effects of environmental changes like wind turbulence while maintaining safety and connectivity by using the information obtained from each UAV's pervasive system. This research also aims to demonstrate how the proposed model works, as well as its applicability, accuracy, and response rate. This is accomplished through the development and demonstration of a MATLAB application.

3.2   System Model Formulation

Consider a UAV swarm sent to examine a densely populated metropolitan region that encountered a dramatic change in wind speeds and turbulence. Individual UAVs may collide with each other, nearby objects, or fall out of the swarm in this situation, resulting in communication failure. However, if each UAV is equipped with a system that is aware of its surroundings and communicates its status to neighboring UAVs, collective action to prevent UAV loss and connectivity might be undertaken.

Here, a system architecture of UAV swarm flying at lower altitudes, shown in Fig. 1, where each UAV acquires context awareness data from different sensors and communicates with each other for an effective decision making is considered. Algorithm 1 gives a level-0 depiction of the proposed system. In the considered system architecture, there are UAVs near collision and some to be out of the connectivity range. These cases can be considered as physical environment context and ICT environment context. By detecting nearby UAVs in the physical/human environment context awareness, a UAV can take measures to avoid collision. Similarly, by understanding the communication network strength that an individual UAV is receiving the swarm as a whole and the individual UAV can make changes to the swarm formation, speed, and flight direction to keep the individual UAV from loosing connectivity. To capture these environment contexts, different approaches together with sensors are utilized.

The light intensity of the environment where the UAVs are flying is taken into account to accurately depict the physical environment context surrounding them. Because the image is already a measure of light intensity in the scene, the light intensity could well be measured from a real-time image. The overall light intensity of the UAV swarms flight path and immediate surroundings is determined by taking the mean intensity of the image captured each step. The light intensity data helps the UAVs avoid night time flights where vision through the cameras is low or else gives a signal to deploy a headlight(or similar light source) to get clear view of the surrounding, based upon the swarm mission.

Algorithm 1: Context awareness based pervasive computing algorithm for safe swarm operations

---

Result: Safe UAV Swarm
while *Still flying* **do**
    $i \leftarrow mean(light\_intensity\_realtime\_image)^\bullet$;
    $j \leftarrow Boolean(objects\_detected\_by\_camera?)$;
    $k \leftarrow Percentage(CPU\_memory\_usage)$;
    $l \leftarrow Percentage(Network\_signal\_quality)$;
    if $i < i_{min}$ **then**
        Broadcast information to neighbor UAVs;
        Abort mission due to low visibility;
    else if $j = True$ **then**
        Broadcast information to neighbor UAVs;
        Adjust UAV Speed based on relative location;
        Move in the X or Y direction to avoid collision based on ;
    else if $k < k_{min} \cup l < l_{min}$ **then**
        Broadcast information to neighbor UAVs;
        Adjust UAV Speed based towards strong signal;
        Drop tasks with less priority;
    else
        Keep current flight path and speed ;
    end
end

The ICT context was addressed in two ways. First is the UAV local ICT system environment context which is presented measuring the CPU usage level of the UAV. This information helps the neighboring UAV's to share group level tasks in case the UAV under consideration is in a higher busy state. The critical condition in a local ICT context is therefore defined us high CPU usage. To get the usage information, we needed to tell MATLAB to instantiate a *System.Diagnostics.PerformanceCounter* object. This .net object neatly calculates the CPU usage [4].

The next ICT environment context awareness is detecting the communication network environment, which is implemented with the measurement of the network signal strength. This information tells the UAV's in the swarm if their neighboring UAV is loosing communication or is in a weak signal spot relative in the swarm. As shown in [20], the received signal strength indicator (RSSI) indicates the energy measured from signal transmission. By using the formulas shown in [20], the signal strength is calculated and its value is shown in percentage. The path loss model is as follows, which is measured at the real distance d(m).

$$P(d) = P(d_0) - 10 * n * log(\frac{d}{d_0}) - X_\sigma \qquad (1)$$

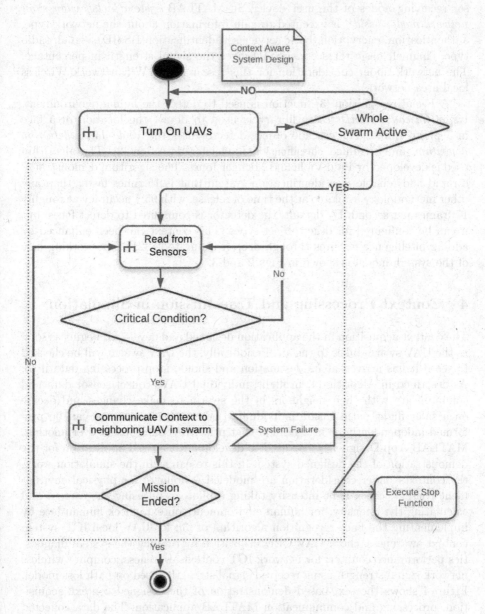

Fig. 2. The designed system's process flow

Here, $P(d)$ indicates received signal strength when the measured real distance is $d(m)$ while $P(d_0)$ indicates received signal strength when the reference distance is d_0, while $X_\sigma \sim N(0, \sigma^2)$ is a cover factor. In a specific environment, n indicates the path loss index. Receiver signal strength indicator (RSSI) is read from the register RSSI_VAI in the data packets which are received from sensor receiving nodes of the user device. In MATLAB $system('netsh\ wlan\ show\ network\ mode=bssid')$ is executed to gain information about the network type, authentication, encryption, basic service set identification(BSSID), signal, radio type, channel, basic rates etc. BSSID gives the signal strength in percentage. The network under consideration for this research is a Wifi network(Wireless local area network).

A Facial recognition [3] function is used to detect the human environment. *vision.CascadeObjectDetector* library is used to detect the location of a face in a photo frame. The cascade object detector uses the *Viola-Jones detection algorithm* and a trained classification model for detection [2]. The algorithm used is developed by Paul Viola and Michael Jones. The algorithm demonstrated a rapid and reliable face identification system that is 15 times faster than any other methodology available at the time of release, with 95% accuracy at roughly 17 frames per second. By default, the detector is configured to detect faces, but it can be configured for other object types. This context can been enhanced by adding intelligence features through deep learning tools [21]. The working flow of the system model is shown in Figs. 2 and 3.

4   Context Processing and Transmission in Simulation

The context acquisition in the application designed and developed begins as soon as the UAV swarm takes to the air. Periodically, the UAV swarm will be checked to see if it has arrived at its destination and should stop processing data if so. As described in Algorithm 1, in flight, individual UAVs collect sensor data and communicate with their neighbors in the swarm to make changes and decide on a safer flight path. Inside individual UAVs context-awareness can be performed independently or in a fashion that prioritizes one context over another. MATLAB App Designer is also used to develop a text-based application for the demonstration of the designed system in this research. In the simulation work, the contexts under consideration are modeled as follows: for physical environment context, check light intensity taking a photograph using the camera and calculating the intensity; for human environment context, check human face by implementing the Face recognition algorithm of [3]; for UAV local ICT system context awareness, check UAV CPU utilization by running the system diagnostics performance counter; for network ICT context awareness, compute wireless network signal strength using received signal strength based on path loss model. Figure 4 shows the text-based demonstration of the designed context acquisition, processing and communication MATLAB application. The data collected from the sensors and communicated between individual UAVs in a swarm are represented with the text messages displayed on the app.

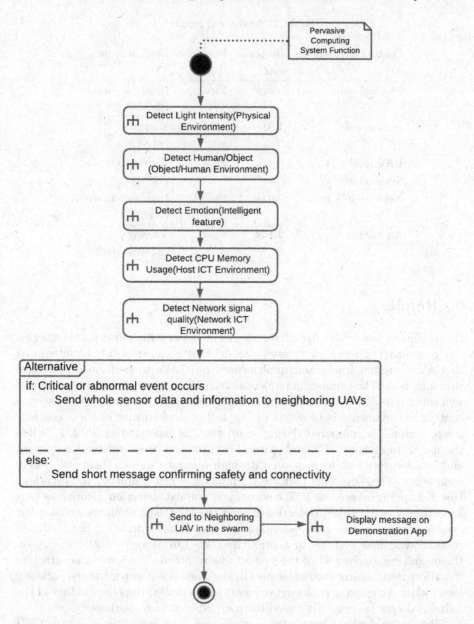

Fig. 3. Interrupt routine of the designed system with context implementation that is prioritized.

Table 1. Analysis of results

Context environment	Response rate	Response speed	Level of accuracy
Physical only	0.96 s	Fast	Highly accurate (98%)
Human only	1.03 s	Moderate	Moderate (84.85%)
UAV local ICT System only	0.8 s	Fast	Highly accurate (100%)
Network ICT only	0.92 s	Fast	Highly accurate (100%)
All prioritized	2.15 s	Slow	Varying (84.85%–100%)

5 Results

By combining the knowledge about swarm of UAVs with context-aware pervasive computing systems, we created a model that is can smoothly be integrated to UAV's internal frame and implemented on UAVs to perform an effective thorough task. The simulation implementation of the system was successful and well coordinated. A MATLAB application simulating and demonstrating several context environments is provided in Fig. 4. The performance of these context-aware systems is compared during simulation, as indicated in Table 1. When simulated stand-alone, ICT and physical environment context detection systems and sensors were fast to respond with high accuracy due to their low system complexity. These systems performed Similarly, when compared to the others based on performance, all ICT environment context detection algorithms performed best, with object detection having the least best accuracy and longest delay compared to the other individual systems. When simulating the combined context awareness systems in a prioritized way, an average of 2.15 s delay on the overall responsiveness of the system was recorded. The level of accuracy in the prioritized context awareness gave us the same result in percentage accuracy levels when considering each environment, which proved the repeatability of the individual systems even if we used them in different combinations.

The device used to analyze this performance is an Intel Core i5-7200U CPU with 16 GB RAM and a 64-bit operating system, which has different applications running on the background. The response time readings for a demonstrative simulation is also provided in Table 1. The values of the response time and accuracy measures are an average value taken from 100 runs of the same system in different environmental settings.

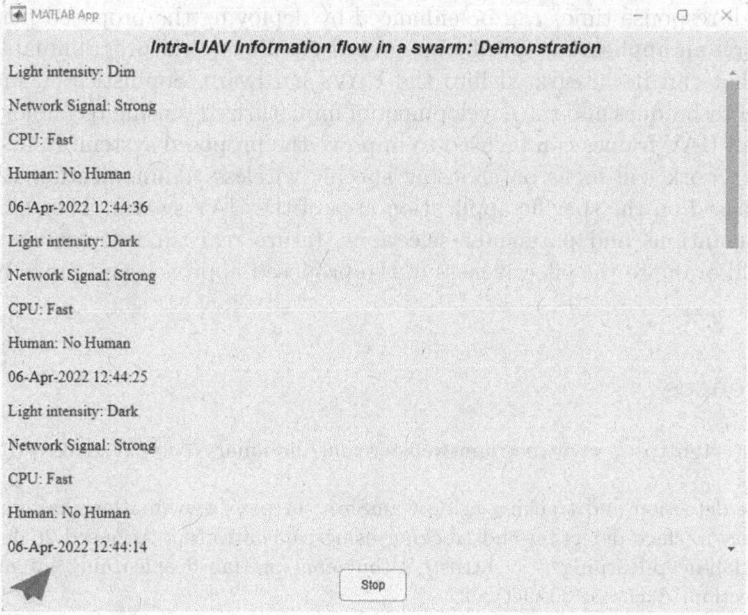

Fig. 4. Text based MATLAB App demonstration of the proposed pervasive computing system.

6   Conclusion and Future Directions

Pervasive computing is increasingly being used in different application areas and is one of the main technologies that will continue in the future. One of those application areas is in computing systems of UAVs. The design and simulation of a MATLAB-based solution for effective context awareness in intra-UAV swarm communication are described in this research study. The physical environment, human environment, and ICT environment are all taken into account for demonstration purposes. Even though the considered sensing systems and their applications have been implemented individually in different projects and researches, the suggested ubiquitous computing system's integrated and prioritized implementation offers a promising benefit for intra-UAV safety in a swarm. This work provides a way of implementation of pervasive computing in a UAV swarm setting and can be used as a very effective way to enhance safety and connectivity in a swarm.

6.1   Future Works

Future works will focus on real implementation and testing on two or more UAVs in a distributed swarm computing environment. This incorporates designing a printed circuit board that will accept all the inputs from different sensors and execute possible actions, while its size should fit into the UAV frame space.

The high response times can be enhanced by deploying the proposed pervasive system on an application specific integrated circuit or field-programmable gate array that can be integrated into the UAVs hardware. Sophisticated machine learning techniques and the development of miniaturized sensing technology that fits small-UAV frames can be used to improve the proposed system. In addition, our next work will focus on choosing specific wireless communication network choice based on the specific application area of the UAV swarm. Through these implementations and parameter selections, future real time deployments and tests will evaluate the effectiveness of the proposed approach and prove its correctness.

References

1. Context. https://www.merriam-webster.com/dictionary/context. Accessed 20 Mar 2022
2. Face detection and tracking using CamShift. https://www.mathworks.com/help/vision/ug/face-detection-and-tracking-using-camshift.html. Accessed 26 Jan 2022
3. Matlab-deep-learning.   https://github.com/matlab-deeplearning/mtcnn-face-detection. Accessed 20 Oct 2022
4. Show CPU cores utilization in Matlab. https://stackoverflow.com/questions/25950727/show-cpu-coresutilization-in-matlab. Accessed 22 Jan 2022
5. Abdelfattah, A.S., Abdelkader, T., EI-Horbaty, E.S.M.: Reliable web service consumption through mobile cloud computing. In: Mobile Computing-Technology and Applications. IntechOpen (2018)
6. Al-Muhtadi, J., Saleem, K., Al-Rabiaah, S., Imran, M., Gawanmeh, A., Rodrigues, J.J.: A lightweight cyber security framework with context-awareness for pervasive computing environments. Sustain. Urban Areas 66, 102610 (2021)
7. Argrow, B., et al.: The NCAR/EOL community workshop on unmanned aircraft systems for atmospheric research. Ph.D. thesis, National Center for Atmospheric Research (2017)
8. Bekmezci, I., Sahingoz, O.K., Temel, Ş: Flying ad-hoc networks (FANETs): a survey. Ad Hoc Netw. 11(3), 1254–1270 (2013)
9. Daud, M., Khan, Q., Saleem, Y.: A study of key technologies for IoT and associated security challenges. In: 2017 International Symposium on Wireless Systems and Networks (ISWSN), pp. 1–6 (2017). https://doi.org/10.1109/ISWSN.2017.8250042
10. Han, Y., Liu, L., Duan, L., Zhang, R.: Towards reliable UAV swarm communication in d2d-enhanced cellular networks. IEEE Trans. Wirel. Commun. 20(3), 1567–1581 (2021). https://doi.org/10.1109/TWC.2020.3034457
11. Henricksen, K., Indulska, J.: A software engineering framework for context-aware pervasive computing. In: Proceedings of the Second IEEE Annual Conference on Pervasive Computing and Communications, 2004, pp. 77–86 (2004). https://doi.org/10.1109/PERCOM.2004.1276847
12. Hosseini, N., Jamal, H., Haque, J., Magesacher, T., Matolak, D.W.: UAV command and control, navigation and surveillance: a review of potential 5g and satellite systems. In: 2019 IEEE Aerospace Conference, pp. 1–10 (2019). https://doi.org/10.1109/AERO.2019.8741719
13. Lin, H., Yan, Z., Fu, Y.: Adaptive security-related data collection with context awareness. J. Netw. Comput. Appl. 126, 88–103 (2019)

14. Mahama, E., et al.: Testing and evaluating the impact of illumination levels on UAV-assisted bridge inspection. In: 2022 IEEE Aerospace Conference (AERO), pp. 1–8 (2022). https://doi.org/10.1109/AERO53065.2022.9843209
15. Mahama, E., et al.: Testing and evaluation of radio frequency immunity of unmanned aerial vehicles for bridge inspection. In: 2021 IEEE Aerospace Conference (50100), pp. 1–8 (2021). https://doi.org/10.1109/AERO50100.2021.9438457
16. Mostefaoui, G., Pasquier-Rocha, J., Brezillon, P.: Context-aware computing: a guide for the pervasive computing community. In: The IEEE/ACS International Conference on Pervasive Services, 2004. ICPS 2004. Proceedings, pp. 39–48 (2004). https://doi.org/10.1109/PERSER.2004.1356763
17. Mozaffari, M., Saad, W., Bennis, M., Nam, Y.H., Debbah, M.: A tutorial on UAVs for wireless networks: applications, challenges, and open problems. IEEE Commun. Surv. Tutor. **21**(3), 2334–2360 (2019). https://doi.org/10.1109/COMST.2019.2902862
18. Plathottam, S.J., Ranganathan, P.: Next generation distributed and networked autonomous vehicles: review. In: 2018 10th International Conference on Communication Systems Networks (COMSNETS), pp. 577–582 (2018). https://doi.org/10.1109/COMSNETS.2018.8328277
19. Sahingoz, O.K.: Networking models in flying ad-hoc networks (FANETs): concepts and challenges. J. Intell. Robot. Syst. **74**(1), 513–527 (2014)
20. Shang, F., Su, W., Wang, Q., Gao, H., Fu, Q.: A location estimation algorithm based on RSSI vector similarity degree. Int. J. Distrib. Sens. Netw. **10**(8), 371350 (2014)
21. Silva, C., Sobral, A., Vieira, R.T.: An automatic facial expression recognition system evaluated by different classifiers. In: X Workshop de Visão Computacional, at Uberlândia, Minas Gerais, Brazil, pp. 208–212 (2014)
22. Tegicho, B.E., Bogale, T.E., Eroglu, A., Edmonson, W.: Connectivity and safety analysis of large scale UAV swarms: based on flight scheduling. In: 2021 IEEE 26th International Workshop on Computer Aided Modeling and Design of Communication Links and Networks (CAMAD), pp. 1–6 (2021). https://doi.org/10.1109/CAMAD52502.2021.9617780
23. Tegicho, B.E., Geleta, T.N., Bogale, T.E., Eroglu, A., Edmonson, W., Bitsuamlak, G.: Effect of wind on the connectivity and safety of large scale UAV swarms. In: 2021 IEEE International Black Sea Conference on Communications and Networking (BlackSeaCom), pp. 1–6 (2021). https://doi.org/10.1109/BlackSeaCom52164.2021.9527821
24. Tegicho, B.E., Graves, C.: Automatic emoji insertion based on environment context signals for the demonstration of pervasive computing features. In: SoutheastCon 2021, pp. 1–6 (2021). https://doi.org/10.1109/SoutheastCon45413.2021.9401878
25. Yılmaz, Ö., Erdur, R.C.: IConAwa-an intelligent context-aware system. Expert Syst. Appl. **39**(3), 2907–2918 (2012)
26. Zeng, T., Semiari, O., Mozaffari, M., Chen, M., Saad, W., Bennis, M.: Federated learning in the sky: joint power allocation and scheduling with uav swarms. In: ICC 2020–2020 IEEE International Conference on Communications (ICC), pp. 1–6 (2020). https://doi.org/10.1109/ICC40277.2020.9148776

Road Accident Analysis of Dhaka City Using Counter Propagation Network

Nazmus Sakib, Sohel Bashar(✉), and Ashikur Rahman(✉)

Department of CSE, BUET, Dhaka, Bangladesh
1605081@ugrad.cse.buet.ac.bd, sohelbashar11@gmail.com,
ashikur@cse.buet.ac.bd

Abstract. In this world of motorization, road accident is one of the vital cause behind the death of many people. The impact of this hazard is more evident in Bangladesh, especially in the capital city Dhaka. This paper aspire to identify the most accident prone regions of Dhaka city using Counter Propagation Network and portrays a comparative analysis between Counter Propagation Network and K-means clustering. The data for predictions has been provided by Accident Research Institute (ARI) at Bangladesh University of Engineering and Technology (BUET). For identification of most accident prone regions, K-means clustering and Counter Propagation Network have been used.

Keywords: Clustering · Neural Networks · Artificial Intelligence

1 Introduction

Road accident is perhaps one of the most frequent and agitating situation in Bangladesh. It can be defined as the collision of a vehicle with another vehicle, human being, animal or stationary objects. According to Bangladesh police, in the first eight months of 2021, a total of 3,502 people were killed and 3,479 sustained injuries in 3,701 road accidents [1]. Dhaka, being the capital of Bangladesh is an overpopulated city with high density which makes the scenario even worse in the city due to sheer number of vehicles and people on the streets.

Although accident related researches have been conducted in other developed countries, it is not that familiar in Bangladesh. Lately, some initiatives have begun to conduct research works on road accident related events in Bangladesh in order to tackle the issue. In our analysis, we have implemented and utilized Counter Propagation Network, which is a neural network, to identify the most accident-prone regions of Dhaka city and also provided a comparative analysis of our model with K-means clustering to validate the accuracy of the neural network. At last, a cluster map of Dhaka city identifying accident-prone regions has been rendered.

The identification of these accident-prone regions is significant because the government can design and develop an efficient system to monitor these regions to reduce the number of accidents and also the general mass can be made aware of these regions and can be provided with a safer route to travel to avoid these highly accident prone regions.

E. Sabir et al. (Eds.): UNet 2022, LNCS 13853, pp. 164–179, 2023.
https://doi.org/10.1007/978-3-031-29419-8_13

2 Background

Since road accident is ubiquitous, the goal of our analysis is to determine the most-accident prone regions of Dhaka city. To achieve this goal, at first we accumulate the data and present it to the clustering models to segregate the clustered regions. Then, based on the data, cluster with the most-accident prone regions is recognized and points underlying the cluster can be acknowledged as our coveted result. In our analysis, we have utilized some state-of-the-art validity indices for the selection of hyper parameters and to validate the quality of clustering algorithms. The indices are described below:

Silhouette Analysis: In Silhouette analysis [8], silhouette coefficient is measured for each point, which connotes how much close a point is to its assigned cluster compared to other clusters. An average of all the silhouette coefficients yield silhouette score for that value of k. The value of silhouette coefficient varies between [-1,1]. It signifies how well the data point fits into the cluster, so a high value manifest that it fits into the cluster satisfactorily and lower value depicts the opposite. Silhouette coefficient for data point $i \in C_I$ (data point i in the cluster C_I) are:

(a) Compute $a(i)$: Average distance of the point from the other points of the same cluster.
(b) Compute $b(i)$: Average distance of the point from all the points of the nearest cluster (i.e., in any cluster of which i is not a member).
(c) Compute silhouette coefficient: It is calculated using the formula provided below—

$$s(i) = \frac{b(i) - a(i)}{\max(b(i), a(i))} \qquad (1)$$

Calinski-Harabasz Index: This index [5] is an approximation of the estimation of how close a data point is to it's centroid in comparison with the global centroid. Here, two parameters are measured namely *cohesion* and *separation*. Cohesion refers to the estimation of nearness of a data point to it's centroid and the calculation of separation is based on distance between the global centroid and the cluster's centroid. The mathematical formula can be depicted as follows: For a dataset E of size N which has been clustered into k clusters, the Calinski-Harabasz score s is:

$$s = \frac{tr(B_k)}{tr(W_k)} * \frac{N - k}{k - 1} \qquad (2)$$

where $tr(B_k)$ is the trace of the between group dispersion matrix and $tr(W_k)$ is the trace of the within-cluster dispersion matrix that can be defined by:

$$W_k = \sum_{q=1}^{k} \sum_{x \in C_q} (x - c_q)(x - c_q)^T \qquad (3)$$

$$B_k = \sum_{q=1}^{k} n_q(c_q - c_E)(c_q - c_E)^T \qquad (4)$$

where C_q is the set of points in cluster q, c_q is the center of cluster q, c_E is the center of E and n_q is the number of points in cluster q.

Davies-Bouldin Index: Davies-Bouldin index is another popular method for evaluating how good the clustering has been, based on features inherent to the dataset. For n dimensional points, if C_i be cluster of data points and X_j be an n-dimensional feature vector assigned to C_i,

$$S_i = \left(\frac{1}{T_i} * \sum_{j=1}^{T_i} \|X_j - A_j\|_p^q \right)^{1/q} \tag{5}$$

Here, T_i is size of the cluster i and A_j is the centroid of C_i. If q=1, then, S_i is the average distance between feature vectors in cluster i and the centroid of the cluster. For q=2, it becomes a Euclidean distance function. If D_{i_j} is the within cluster distance ratio for i^{th} and j^{th} cluster,

$$D_{i_j} = \frac{d_i + d_j}{d_{i_j}} \tag{6}$$

where, d_i and d_j is the distance between every data points in the clusters i and j. And, d_{i_j} is the Euclidean distance between centroids of two clusters. The Davies-Bouldin Index [2], DB will be:-

$$DB = \frac{1}{N} * \sum_{j=1}^{k} \max_{j \neq i} D_{i_j} \tag{7}$$

3   Related Works

Some promising works on road accidents have been conducted recently. Labuib et al. [6] performed road accident analysis and predicted accident severity using Decision Tree, K-Nearest Neighbors (KNN), Naïve Bayes and AdaBoost. They classified the severity of accidents into four categories namely Fatal, Grievous, Simple Injury and Motor collision where the best performance was achieved by AdaBoost method. In another work [4], a deep learning model was trained on historical crash data, road maps, satellite imagery and GPS to enable high-resolution crash maps that could lead to safer roads. Siddiq et al. [9] use four models such as Decision Tree, K-Nearest Neighbors (KNN), Naïve Bayes and Logistic Regression to predict the death of road accidents in Bangladesh based on the road crash data derived from the *Prothom Alo* newspaper.

4   Methodology

4.1   Data Characterization

In order to correctly identify the most accident prone regions, accident related data of different regions of Dhaka is a prerequisite. For this purpose, the data has been collected in comma separated values format from Accident Research Institute at Bangladesh University of Engineering and Technology. In this dataset, Dhaka city is partitioned into 60 regions and accident related data for this 60 regions are available. There are about ten features in this dataset including X and Y coordinates of the accident point and type of intersection of those regions. But the irrelevant and the redundant features are ignored and only four main features are considered for our analysis. The attribute considered for incorporating into the model for each region includes:

Total Accidents: This attribute designate total number of accidents in that region.

Fatal Accidents: This attribute denotes total number of accidents which caused serious injury to one or more person.

Pedestrian Accidents: The number of accidents where pedestrian were involved.

Pedestrian Fatal Accidents: This attribute denotes total number of accidents where pedestrian had fatal injuries.

4.2   Model Depiction

In an effort to determine the most accident prone regions, two clustering methods have been applied. The two methods are illustrated below:

4.2.1   K-means Clustering

K-means clustering is one of the most popular and simplest unsupervised algorithm. This algorithm aspire to group the similar data points without perception of the label and fathom the underlying patterns. To simply characterize, it is the aggregation of similar data points. Given a target number k, it distributes the points into k aggregates. The algorithm can be explained briefly as follows:

- Commencing from a random selection of centroids, iterate until a stable value of centroids have been acquired.
- In each iteration, assign each data point to the nearest cluster or centroid and calculate the new value of centroids averaging the values of the data points affiliated to each centroid.

The initial selection of the values of the centroids are very crucial in pace of the convergence of the values of the centroids. To this end, Forgy method [3] is used here, which means the clusters are randomly assigned from the records, a random cluster is designated to a record. Now, an important part of k-means clustering is determining the value of k, what value of k will fit the data appropriately. For it's determination, various methods and indices have been utilised. One such method is the so-called *Elbow method* which is described as follows:

In **Elbow method** [10], value of k is varied within a particular range, here 1–15 and the value of sum of squared distance between each point and centroid of a cluster is estimated for each value of k. If we map k vs sum of squared distance (Fig. 1a), then an elbow shape graph is witnessed. An analysis of the graph portrays that, initially the value reduces rapidly with the increase of value of k and after certain point, it becomes parallel to the X-axis. That certain point correspond to the optimal value of k. Beside using elbow method, various other validity indices has been used which are described in the following sections.

4.2.2   Counter Propagation Network

Counter Propagation Network is a neural network. A neural network is a system under artificial intelligence which is meant to replicate and act like human brain. A neural network consists of a number of layers of interconnected nodes which are known as neurons. The first layer is the input layer, the last layer is the output layer and there are some hidden layers of neurons. The network is trained on some input, so that it can predict similar inputs correctly later as output. There are some edges connecting neurons of one layer to the neurons of the next layer. The edges have some values associated with them called weights based on which computation are done in middle layers which helps to predict the output in the final layer. First, the inputs are preprocessed and fed to the input layer. Then, value at each neuron of next layer is computed by taking sum of product of weight of incoming edges and value associated with neuron from the previous layer corresponding to those edges. This value is added with a value associated with each neuron called the bias and that value is then passed through a function called activation function. The value of the activation function determines if the neuron will be activated or not. The activated neurons transmits information to the next neuron. This process continues throughout the hidden layers til the output layer. In output layer, the values determines probability of each of the possible output and the neuron with highest value determines the output. This process is called forward propagation. Then the output of the last layer is matched against actual output to determine error or how off the output result is from actual output. This information is then fed in backward direction and based on that, weights are adjusted. This process is backward propagation. In this way by feeding a lot of inputs and continuous process of backward and forward propagation repetitively for many times, the neural network is trained until it can predict outputs against input properly.

For clustering here, we used Counter Propagation Network which has a strong power of generalization. The number of neurons in the input layer equals the number of features of the data, while number of neurons in the Kohonen layer equals number of clusters we allow. We set the number of clusters equal to the number of clusters for which we got best result using K-means clustering. For our intended purpose, we only need first two layers that would help us to classify the data points into clusters.

Each of the neurons in the middle layer has a connecting edge for each of the neuron of the first layer. Each of the edges has a weight associated with them, which influences the outcome of the clustering. The weights are set at random

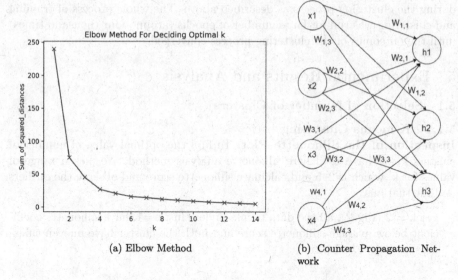

(a) Elbow Method

(b) Counter Propagation Network

Fig. 1. Elbow method for K-means clustering and counter propagation network

initially and then they are trained in unsupervised learning method using real life data.

Let's say we have five features from our dataset. For a data point, x_1, x_2, x_3, x_4, x_5 be their values which are applied to the corresponding neurons in the input layer. For a particular neuron (say S_i,) of the second layer, the weights of the edges connecting it with the five neurons of the input layer be w_{1j}, w_{2j}, w_{3j}, w_{4j}, w_{5j} respectively. The output of that neuron R_j will be calculated as:

$$R_j = \sum_{i=1}^{\infty} w_{i,j} * x_i \tag{8}$$

The neuron with highest associated output value, calculated in this fashion, will be the "winner neuron" for the particular data point.

Next, the weight of edges between "winner neuron" and the neurons in the first layer has to be updated by using the following formula:

$$w_{i,j} = w_{i,j}(old) + \beta * (x_i - w_{i,j}(old))^2 \tag{9}$$

where, x_i is the ith neuron in input layer and β is the learning rate.

We continued this process until the outcomes of the clustering converge [7].

While implementing it in code, the values of the features from the input for all data points were scaled up. Otherwise, during the process of calculation, difference between the data points with the centroids of the clusters becomes very close to each other and the data points falls under one or two specific clusters. The weights of the edges between the layers were set to same value. The weights of the edges later adjusted according to the internal calculations during the clustering process as described above. The whole process of training and clustering was run for large number of epochs (around four thousand times) until the outcomes of the clustering process converged.

5   Experimental Results and Analysis

5.1   Selection of Number of Clusters

5.1.1   K-means Clustering
Inspection of the Silhouette Plot: To find the optimal value of number of clusters k, we have used here silhouette analysis method. We pick a range of values for k, which is 2–5 and calculate silhouette score and observe the outliers and fluctuations.

- For k = 2 (Fig. 2), all the data points under cluster=1, have silhouette coefficient below average silhouette score and both the cluster have uneven thickness, so it is a bad pick.

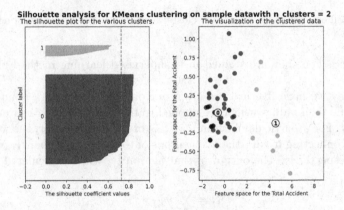

Fig. 2. Silhouette method analysis for K-means for k=2

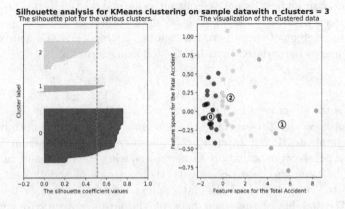

Fig. 3. Silhouette method analysis for K-means for k=3

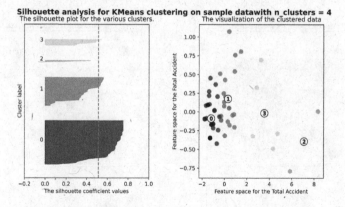

Fig. 4. Silhouette method analysis for K-means for k=4

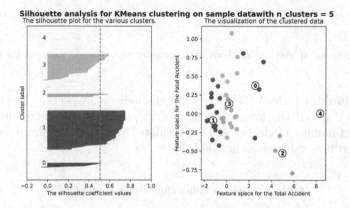

Fig. 5. Silhouette method analysis for K-means for k=5

- For k = 3 (Fig. 3), all the clusters have data points having silhouette coefficient above average silhouette score and unevenness is somewhat less than that for k=2.
- The silhouette plot for k = 4 (Fig. 4) shows that it is also a bad pick since all points under cluster 2 lies below average silhouette score.
- The silhouette plot for k = 5 (Fig. 5) portrays that, cluster 4 has absolutely zero points. Therefore, it is also considered a bad pick since higher number of k is redundant.

Calinski-Harabasz Index: In our analysis, we computed the score of calinski-harabasz index for value of k from 2 to 6 and higher value of this index connotes the more optimal value of number of clusters. This is a representation of how well the clusters are concentrated around the centroid and well detached the clusters are. A table depicting the value of the score for cluster 2–6 is given in (Table 1):

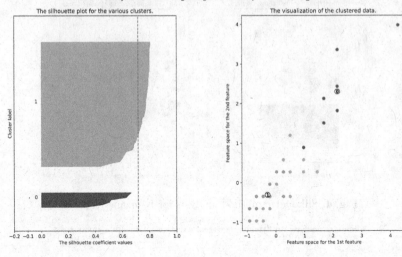

Fig. 6. Silhouette method analysis using counter propagation network for k = 2

Davies-Bouldin Index: The Davis-Bouldin index score is calculated for value of k from 2–6 and the lower the value of the score is, the more optimal the selection of number of cluster is. The calculated value of the score for each k is represented by a table given in (Table 1):

Table 1. Value of indices for K-means and CPN

Cluster	K-means		CPN	
	Calinski Harabasz score	Davies Bouldin score	Calinski Harabasz score	Davies Bouldin score
2	126.75	0.488	172.95	0.42
3	122.96	0.66	160.72	0.61
4	148.21	0.68	90.98	0.96
5	146.1	0.56	110.72	0.95
6	152.2	0.72	90.02	1.14

5.1.2   Counter-Propagation Network
Inspection of the Silhouette Plot:

- For k = 2 (Fig. 6), all the data points under cluster=2, have silhouette coefficient below average silhouette score and both the cluster have uneven thickness, so it is a bad pick
- For k = 3 (Fig. 7), all the clusters have data points having silhouette coefficient above average silhouette score

- The silhouette plot for k = 4 (Fig. 8), shows that it is also a bad pick since all points under cluster 2 lies below average silhouette score.
- The silhouette plot for k = 5 (Fig. 9),portrays that, cluster 1 has all data points below average silhouette score.

Calinski-Harabasz Index: As already described, the higher value of calinski-harabasz index denotes the more optimal value of number of clusters, which represents how well the clusters are concentrated around the centroid and well detached the clusters are. A table depicting the value of the score for cluster 2–6 is given in (Table 1):

Davies-Bouldin Index: As it was said above, for Davies-Bouldin Index, the lower the value of the score is, the more optimal the selection of number of cluster is. The calculated value of the score for each k from 2–6 is represented by the table given in (Table 1):

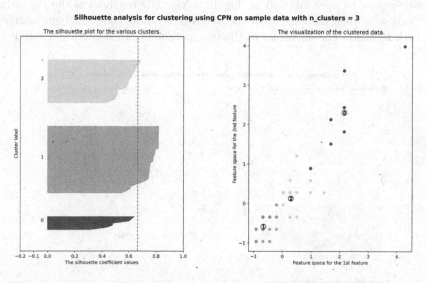

Fig. 7. Silhouette method analysis using counter propagation network for k = 3

Table 2. Comparison of validity index of K-means clustering and Counter Propagation Network

Validity index	Validity for K-means	Validity for CPN
Silhouette_Score	0.51	0.534
Calinski_Harabasz_Score	122.96	160.717
Davies_Bouldin_Score	0.66	0.611

5.2   Comparative Analysis Between K-means Clustering and Counter Propagation Network

The absence of target variable in unsupervised learning makes it challenging to predict the accuracy of the clustering algorithm and perform comparative analysis between two or more clustering algorithms. To compare both the methods depicted here, we have used some validity indices which can also be defined as the measurement of similarity. The comparison is given in Table 2:

Based on all the indices and scores, 3 is nominated as the best choice for selection of number of clusters for both the methods and here, we can easily comprehend that, the value of the three scores are better for Counter Propagation Network method than that of K-means clustering.

To validate and compare the accuracy of two methods, we attached labels to the dataset. The data points with total accident value from 0 to 4 were labelled with 'low risky', the data points with total accident value ranging from 5 to 9 were labelled with 'moderately risky' and those with total accident value equal or larger than 10 were labelled as 'highly risky'. The outcome of the clustering methods were then matched with the labels to see how many of them matched for each method. The outcomes of the two methods is illustrated in Table 3:

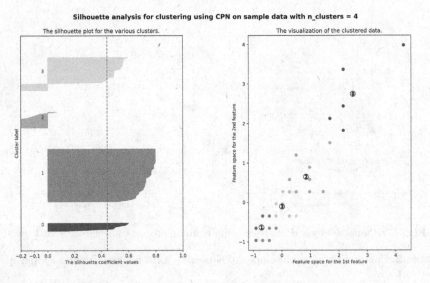

Fig. 8. Silhouette method analysis using counter propagation network for k = 4

Table 3. Accuracy of K-means clustering and counter propagation network

Method	Correctly classified	Accuracy
K-means	53	88.33
Counter propagation network	56	93.33

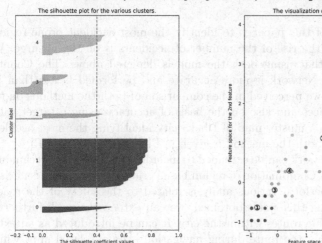

Fig. 9. Silhouette method analysis using counter propagation network for k = 5

Table 4. Number of data points in each cluster for K-means and CPN

Cluster region	K-means		CPN	
	Number of points	Percentage	Number of points	Percentage
Low	37	61.67	33	55
Mid	18	30	21	35
High	5	8.33	6	10

5.3 Analysis of Data Points of K-means Clustering and Counter Propagation Network

The total number of data points that fell in each cluster for both methods are given below:

In K-means clustering (Table 4), a large number of regions falls in the low accident prone region, which is about 61.67% and in mid about 30% and about 8.33% falls in high accident prone region which is our main concern.

In case of Counter Propagation Network (Table 4), the percentage of high accident prone region is more than that of K-means which is 10% and in the low and mid accident prone regions about 55% and 35%.

6   Conclusion

The main purpose of this paper is to identify the most accident prone regions of Dhaka city since the rise of the number of accidents is on the upsurge. We have accomplished that using both the models depicted above. The Counter Propagation Neural Network is more accurate and performed better than K-Means clustering as we perceived in the comparison of both the methods on the basis of validity indices and also on the basis of accuracy using a target value based on consensus. A cluster map of Dhaka city identifying the most accident prone regions using both the method is given in Figs. 10, 11, 12, and 13.

To conclude, this work can be extended to include other clustering techniques and neural networks. Combination of region based crime-data with accident data can be utilized to perform various analysis related to the safety of the roads. For example, utilizing this result obtained, we can extend the work further to find the safest possible routes within the city. It can be introduced as an extra feature in determining the route during navigation in map-related apps which will provide safety. Besides, the idea of a smart city is inconceivable without the assurance of travel safety and for that purpose, identification of the most and least prone regions of a city plays an indispensable role. On the other hand, a smart city paradigm provides for copious information thus assisting in more accurate prediction of the most accident prone regions.

Fig. 10. Cluster map of Dhaka city using K-means (Part-1)

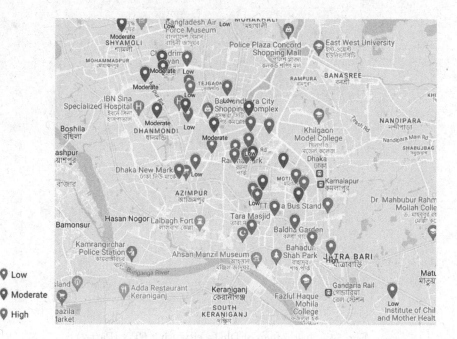

Fig. 11. Cluster map of Dhaka city using K-means (Part-2)

Fig. 12. Cluster map of Dhaka city using CPN (Part-1)

Fig. 13. Cluster map of Dhaka city using CPN (Part-2)

Acknowledgement. The author acknowledges Bangladesh University of Engineering and Technology (BUET) for its generous support to make this work publishable by providing *Basic Research Grant.*

References

1. Road Accident Analysis by the business standard. https://www.tbsnews.net/bangladesh/bangladesh-106th-among-183-countries-having-most-road-accidents-report-335299
2. Davies, D.L., Bouldin, D.W.: A cluster separation measure. IEEE Trans. Pattern Anal. Mach. Intell. PAMI. **1**(2), 224–227 (1979)
3. Hamerly, G., Elkan, C.: Alternatives to the k-means algorithm that find better clusterings. In: Proceedings of the Eleventh International Conference on Information and Knowledge Management, pp. 600–607 (2002)
4. He, S., Sadeghi, M.A., Chawla, S., Alizadeh, M., Balakrishnan, H., Madden, S.: Inferring high-resolution traffic accident risk maps based on satellite imagery and GPS trajectories. In: Proceedings of the IEEE/CVF International Conference on Computer Vision, pp. 11977–11985 (2021)
5. Kozak, M.: A dendrite method for cluster analysis by Calinski and Harabasz: a classical work that is far too often incorrectly cited. Commun. Statist. Theory Methods. **41**, 2279–2280 (2011)
6. Farhan Labib, Md., Sady Rifat, A., Mosabbir Hossain, Md., Kumar Das, A., Nawrine, F.: Road accident analysis and prediction of accident severity by using machine learning in Bangladesh. In: 2019 7th International Conference on Smart Computing and Communications (ICSCC), pp. 1–5 (2019)

7. Rahman, A., Rahman, C.M.: A new approach for compressing color images using neural network. In: CIMCA (2003)
8. Rousseeuw, P.J.: Silhouettes: a graphical aid to the interpretation and validation of cluster analysis. J. Comput. Appl. Math. **20**, 53–65 (1987)
9. Siddik, M.A.B., Arman, M.S., Hasan, A., Jahan, M.R., Islam, M., Biplob, K.B.B.: Predicting the death of road accidents in Bangladesh using machine learning algorithms. In: Singh, M., Tyagi, V., Gupta, P.K., Flusser, J., Ören, T., Sonawane, V.R. (eds.) ICACDS 2021. CCIS, vol. 1441, pp. 160–171. Springer, Cham (2021). https://doi.org/10.1007/978-3-030-88244-0_16
10. Syakur, M.A., Khotimah, B.K., Rochman, E.M.S., Satoto, B.D.: Integration k-means clustering method and elbow method for identification of the best customer profile cluster. IOP Conf. Ser. Mater. Sci. Eng. **336**, 012017 (2018)

Artificial Intelligence-Driven Communications

Reinforcement Learning for Protocol Synthesis in Resource-Constrained Wireless Sensor and IoT Networks

Hrishikesh Dutta[✉], Amit Kumar Bhuyan, and Subir Biswas

Michigan State University, East Lansing, USA
{duttahr1,bhuyanam}@msu.edu, sbiswas@egr.msu.edu

Abstract. This article explores the concepts of online protocol synthesis using Reinforcement Learning (RL). The study is performed in the context of sensor and IoT networks with ultra-low-complexity wireless transceivers. The paper introduces the use of RL and Multi Arm Bandit (MAB), a specific type of RL, for Medium Access Control (MAC) under different network and traffic conditions. It then introduces a novel learning-based protocol synthesis framework that addresses specific difficulties and limitations in medium access for both random access and time-slotted networks. The mechanism does not rely on carrier-sensing, network time-synchronization, collision detection, and other low-level complex operations, thus making it ideal for ultra-simple transceiver hardware used in resource-constrained sensor and IoT networks. Additionally, the ability of independent protocol learning by the nodes makes the system robust and adaptive to the changes in network and traffic conditions. It is shown that the nodes can be trained to learn to avoid collisions, and to achieve network throughputs that are comparable to ALOHA-based access protocols in sensor and IoT networks with simplest transceiver hardware. It is also shown that using RL, it is feasible to synthesize access protocols that can sustain network throughput at high traffic loads, which is not feasible in the ALOHA-based systems. The system's ability to provide throughput fairness under network and traffic heterogeneities are also experimentally demonstrated.

Index Terms: Reinforcement Learning · Multi-Armed Bandits · Sensor Network · IoT · Medium Access Control · Resource Constrained Networks

1 Introduction

Traditionally, wireless network protocols are designed based on heuristics and past experience of human designers. Most of the well-known wireless access protocols such as ALOHA, CSMA, and their derivatives including Bluetooth, Zigbee, and WiFi are products of such design processes [1, 2]. The choice of a network protocol is often steered by the availability of transceiver level hardware support for carrier sensing, collision detection, communication energy constraints, etc. In spite of their general success, these approaches do underperform under certain topology and traffic load heterogeneities, and specialized prioritization requirements. For instance, in case of the well-known ALOHA and SLOTTED-ALOHA MAC logics, a surge in network traffic can lead to a complete throughput collapse caused by collision avalanches. Such phenomena are particularly harmful for IoT and Sensor networks in which energy and other resource wastage can be operationally detrimental. Such effects are aggravated for heterogeneous traffic and topological diversities. Furthermore, topologically disadvantageous nodes in an arbitrary mesh network may not receive a fair share of bandwidth due to its disproportionate collision experience. All these effects point to a need for alternative protocol design approaches beyond the existing empirical designs.

To that end, Reinforcement Learning (RL) has been applied in the literature [3–14] for protocol synthesis via online learning. A protocol constitutes inter-node transmission logic, which is modeled as a Multi-Agent Markov Decision Process (MA-MDP) problem. Such MA-MDPs are then solved using an online temporal difference solution approach, namely RL. The online learning ability of RL makes the nodes learn and adapt to the best transmission logic (i.e., protocol) on the fly without *a priori* training. Additionally, the multi-agent approach enables independent learning for the node, thus making the solutions more robust and adaptive.

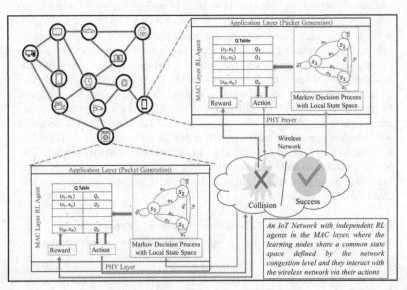

Fig. 1. System Level Architecture of an IoT Network with Embedded Learning Components

Such learning can be explored in two broad areas of MAC logics, namely, random access and scheduled with time-slotting. While the first category including ALOHA, CSMA, and their higher order derivatives can be synthesized using traditional RL [15], for scheduled access such as TDMA would need a special class of RL without state abstraction, known as Multi-Armed Bandits (MAB).

The existing work in this area has the following limitations. First, most of the RL solutions are centralized [5, 6] in which a single learning entity maintains current network-level information and learns transmission policies for all the network nodes. This entails frequent node-to-learner information and learner-to-node policy transfers, requiring additional control plane bandwidth. Moreover, the learner requires to maintain a network-scale learning table which adds to its storage and computation expenses. These bandwidth, storage, and single point of computation overheads make centralized learning non-scalable and vulnerable to single point of failure. The second major limitation is that network and traffic heterogeneities and traffic prioritization are neglected in the existing techniques [9]. This makes some of these approaches unsuitable in application-specific networks with specialized network configurations and performance needs. Additionally, many of the existing RL solutions assume non-sensor and IoT friendly complex transceiver capabilities including carrier-sensing, collision detection in few cases, and network time-synchronization for the MAB-based transmission scheduling.

This paper attempts to avoid those limitations using a novel RL and MAB-based learning approach for synthesizing MAC logic. The key approach here is to leverage interactive individual learning, where each node learns transmission policies independently by observing the impacts of their RL/MAB transmission actions on collisions experienced by all other nodes in the neighborhood. This is done without carrier-sensing, collision detection, and time-synchronization, thus making it suitable for low-complexity and resource-constrained networks. Specifically, the developed framework caters to two broad classes of medium access schemes, viz, random access and scheduling-based. It makes the nodes learn independently in order to attain and maintain the maximum achievable throughput for random access, and to obtain a collision-free slot allocation in scheduling-based approaches. Figure 1 shows a generalized system architecture of the IoT network with the embedded learning components, where each IoT node acts as a learning agent. With the long-term goal of developing a generalized learning framework for protocol synthesis, this paper specifically demonstrates the concept of protocol synthesis in resource-constrained networks with low-complex transceivers not relying on aforementioned complex hardware requirements.

Specific contributions of this work are as follows. First, an online learning-based framework is developed for minimizing packet collisions in resource-constrained networks with random access and scheduling-based Medium Access schemes. Second, a novel slot-defragmentation mechanism is proposed for handling the trade-off between learning convergence time and spectral usage efficiency in transmission scheduling in networks without time synchronization. Third, the developed framework is decentralized such that each node learns its own transmission schedule independently relying only on localized neighborhood information. Finally, the developed learning framework is functionally validated, and performance is evaluated under heterogeneous network and traffic conditions with extensive simulation experiments.

2 Related Works

Many Reinforcement Learning (RL) based approaches were proposed in the literature for wireless MAC protocol synthesis. The paper in [3] uses RL for wireless sensor network MAC to minimize energy expenditure while maximizing throughput. It works with slotted time and uses stateless Q-learning for nodes to find collision-free transmission slots. Q-learning-based protocols for resource allocation are also proposed in [5, 10]. These mechanisms can learn and adapt with new and departing nodes while maximizing throughput. Using carrier-sensing, the nodes learn to transmit/wait [10] or to increase/decrease access contention window [5] to reduce collisions. The mechanism in [4] uses RL for solving a Partially Observable Markov Decision Process (POMDP) in order to minimize the interference amongst primary and secondary users in a cognitive network.

Researchers have also used RL and its variants for slot scheduling in TDMA-based MAC systems. An RL-based MAC protocol is proposed in [7], which improves network throughput by reducing collisions in a time-synchronous slotted network. Using stateless Q-learning nodes learn to transmit in collision-free slots. The mechanism in [8] allows nodes to learn radio schedules based on instantaneous packet traffic load in their immediate neighborhoods. The mechanism in [9] minimizes MAC layer energy expenditure via RL-based learning. Such learned low-energy protocols with sleep/active scheduling are claimed to be useful for high-density communication in wireless sensor networks. A learning-based slot allocation scheme is developed in [12] for optimizing energy and packet delay in large networks with high traffic loading. Another RL-based congestion control scheme for satellite IoT networks is proposed in [13], where the aim is to allocate channels efficiently in a TSCH network. The proposed mechanism relies on centralized arbitration at a satellite. The framework presented in [14] uses Multi-Armed Bandits (MAB) to learn an optimal back-off period in a contention-based time-slotted underwater network. The objective is to simultaneously minimize collisions and energy with the assistance of a centralized arbitration. Apart from the scalability issues of centralized RL approaches [16–18], the proposed policies require individual end nodes to download learnt policies, thus requiring additional bandwidth/channel for such control information sharing.

All these RL-based MAC frameworks rely on various combinations of underlying hardware features such as time-slotting, time-synchronization, and carrier-sensing, which can often be infeasible for ultra-resource-constrained sensor and IoT nodes. In this paper, the main focus is to explore online learning using RL and its variants for networks without such complex and energy-expensive features. The paper first demonstrates the feasibility of these learning frameworks to maximize performance in networks using random access schemes without time-slotting ability. It is shown how the maximum network throughput can be achieved and maintained using RL with fair bandwidth share for the nodes. Next, it shows how a stateless variant of RL can be used for collision-free transmission slot scheduling without network time synchronization. This is done using a slot defragmentation operation embedded with MAB components to reduce bandwidth redundancy arising from slot allocation in the absence of network time synchronization. To be noted, the framework proposed in this work is decentralized in the sense that all nodes learn the transmission schedule independently using localized network information.

3   Network and Traffic Model

The network models considered in this paper are generalized multi-point to point with arbitrary mesh topologies (Fig. 1) and traffic patterns. In order to understand and analyze the impacts of network information availability, both fully and partially connected topologies are considered. For fully connected, each node can possess complete network-wide information including congestion, throughput etc. For partially connected, a node can possess only localized information within its neighborhood.

As for packet generation, constant packet rate and Poisson distributed packets have been used. The MAC layer traffic load model is created such that a packet generated from a node is sent to one of its uniformly randomly chosen 1-hop neighbors. This is done on a packet-by-packet basis.

Networks without and with time slotting are investigated. In both cases, no network time synchronization is assumed. As described later in Section V, the network model includes the ability of piggybacking very low data-rate control information using parts of the data packets. Such control information is used for local information sharing needed by the RL learning.

4   Reinforcement Learning and Multi-armed Bandit

Reinforcement Learning (RL) is a model-free approach used to solve a Markov Decision Process (MDP) [15]. One of the commonly used RL techniques is a value-based tabular update method known as Q-Learning. Each entry in the table $Q(s, a)$ is a Q-value representing the importance of taking an action a when the system is in state s. This table is updated by taking repeated actions stochastically with a bias towards the action with the highest Q-value, which is updated based on the acquired reward. For a received reward, the Q-value for a state-action pair is updated using the Bellman's temporal difference equation [15]. A special class of RL problems for non-associative settings are known as Multi-Armed Bandits (MAB), where there is no state abstraction and the agent's goal is to determine the best set of actions that would maximize its expected reward [15].

A variant of Q-table updates, used in multi-agent RL environments, known as Hysteretic Updates [15], is used in this work. Without knowing the actions taken by the rest of the agents, each agent learns to achieve a coherent joint behavior by observing the effects of its own actions on the system. The key challenge is that an agent's cumulative reward not only depends on its own actions, but also those of the others. Even if an agent takes a good action, it may still receive a penalty because of other agents' poor actions. Hysteretic Learning addresses this by assigning less importance to penalties as compared to the rewards by using two different learning rates. The higher learning rate is used if an agent's action produces desired beneficial effects. Otherwise, the lower learning rate is used so that lesser importance is given to actions that are deemed suitable by the agent but did not produce beneficial results probably due to unfavorable actions taken by the other agents in the environment. This prevents the Q-values of good actions to go down, thus accelerating learning convergence. A detailed description of RL, MAB and Hysteretic Learning can be found in [15] and [19].

5 Reinforcement Learning for Random Access MAC

5.1 Modeling Network Protocol Synthesis as MDP

Each network node acts as an independent RL agent and the wireless network acts as the environment through which the agents interact via their actions. In what follows, it is shown as to how node transmission behavior can be modeled as a Markov Decision Process (MDP), and when the MDP is solved using RL, it can give rise to probabilistic transmission strategies that represent a MAC protocol. The details of different RL components are as follows.

Actions: An RL agent's (i.e., a node) actions are represented by transmission probabilities in the range [0, 1]. Meaning, the action defined by the probability p represents a packet transmission with that probability. The probabilities are discretized at equal intervals in order to keep the action space discrete. The interval size determines the action space size, and the resulting RL performance and convergence properties. In this work, the interval size of 0.05 is chosen empirically based on the performance and convergence speed tradeoffs. The learning error, represented as the difference between the throughput obtained via RL and that of a known benchmark, as described in the next subsection goes down, and convergence time goes up with increase in the size of the action space. The actions are selected following an ϵ-greedy exploration policy, where the agents explore all the possible actions randomly with a probability ϵ, and take the action based on the maximum Q-value with probability $1 - \epsilon$.

States: The state experienced by an agent/node is represented by the congestion level it encounters. A node estimates its state during a learning epoch from the number of packet collisions it experiences during the epoch. It is encoded as the collision probability computed as the ratio of number of collided to transmitted packets. As done for the action space, collision probabilities are also discretized into a fixed interval size (in range [0, 1]), which determines the state space size. There exists a tradeoff between learning performance and convergence time for different state space sizes. A state space size of 5 has been chosen empirically for all presented results in this paper.

Reward: Since learning is node-independent and the nodes do not possess network-wide information, the reward is decided based on a node's localized information collected in-band using piggybacking over the MAC layer PDUs.

Let s_i be the current throughput of node i and $s_{i \to j}$ be the portion of node i's throughput for which j (one-hop neighbor of i) is the intended receiver. Node j periodically piggybacks $s_{i \to j}$ in its outgoing MAC layer PDUs. Node i then calculates its own throughput $s_i = \sum_{\forall 1-\text{hopneighbor}j} s_{i \to j}$, which it periodically piggybacks along with its one-hop neighbors' throughput s_j in its outgoing PDUs.

Now, given that a node i knows its own throughput as well as its two-hop neighbors' throughput (i.e., s_i, s_j), it calculates its localized neighborhood throughput as $S_i = s_i + \sum_{\forall j} s_j$. The packet transmissions from nodes that are within a 2-hop locality can lead to collisions at the receiver. Thus, throughput of a node is affected by its all 2-hop neighborhood transmission policies and hence, 2-hop neighborhood throughput is considered for reward formulation. Using this information, a reward function is formulated with the aim of maximizing network throughput while minimizing the deviation of throughputs of each individual node. Thus, an action is rewarded if both the throughput and fairness gradients as defined by $\Delta S_i = S_i(t) - S_i(t-1)$ and $\Delta f_i = f_i(t) - f_i(t-1)$ respectively are positive. Here, f_i is the fairness coefficient computed as:

$f_i(t) = -\sum_{\forall k \neq i} |s_i(t) - s_k(t)|$, $k \epsilon$ onehop neighborhood of i.

Thus, a temporal gradient-based reward is formulated as follows.

$$R_i(t) = \begin{cases} +50, & \Delta S_i - \varepsilon_s > 0, \ \Delta f_i - \varepsilon_f > 0 \\ -50, & otherwise \end{cases} \tag{1}$$

Here, coefficients ϵ_s and ϵ_f are used so that the agents don't get stuck in a near optimal solution. Experimentally chosen learning hyper-parameters are set to: Hysteretic Learning rates of 0.9 and 0.1, and a discount factor of 0.95. Using this reward arrangement, each node independently learns a probabilistic transmission strategy such that the network wide throughput is maximized while attempting to maintain node-level fair bandwidth distribution. This behavior gives rise to the proposed RL-based Random Access MAC (RRA-MAC) Protocol. Note that although each node independently learns transmission policies, their learning process is mutually affected by the collisions caused by their individual actions. A learning convergence in such situation is when all nodes are able to choose the correct transmissions probabilities for given collisions in its up to 2-hop neighborhood.

5.2 Results and Analysis

In this section we present the performance of RRA-MAC framework that uses RL to solve network protocol modeled as a Markov Decision Process (MDP). In Fig. 2, the performance of RRA-MAC is compared with the simplest known sensor/IoT random access, namely ALOHA, that does not rely on complex hardware features including carrier sensing and time-slotting. The figure shows performance for a 5-nodes partially-connected topology in which nodes 1, 2, 3 and 4 form a square and node 5 is connected only to node 4. The first observation is that unlike for ALOHA, RRA-MAC is able to provide a fair bandwidth distribution for all five nodes. Since nodes 1, 3 and 5 are topologically disadvantageous in that they experience higher collision rates compared to nodes 2 and 4, with ALOHA those three nodes experience lower overall throughputs. Such unfair access performance aggravates as traffic loading increases. The RL-based RRA-MAC circumvents that by using a fairness-aware reward structure. This allows the proposed learning-based mechanism to handle topological heterogeneity in a fair manner.

The second notable observation is that unlike the ALOHA family of protocols, the learning-based access can sustain high throughput at high loading conditions. With ALOHA, excessive collisions bring sustainable throughput down beyond a critical loading point. With RRA-MAC, this is avoided by the RL agents via learning to reduce transmission probabilities (i.e., actions) in states that indicate increasing collisions in the neighborhood. This causes the RRA-MAC throughput to be sustained at higher loads, while maintaining node level throughput fairness.

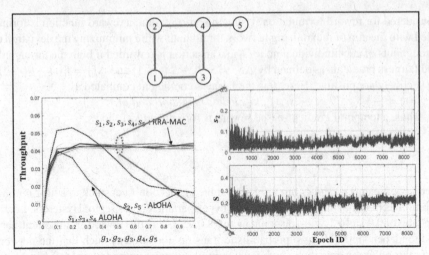

Fig. 2. RRA-MAC in a 5-node partially-connected topology and the learning convergence behavior

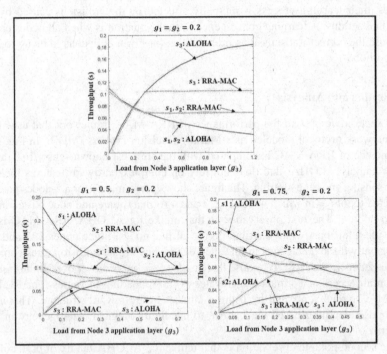

Fig. 3. Performance of RRA-MAC for heterogeneous loading conditions

Figure 2 also shows the learning convergence behavior for both network-wide and individual throughputs for individual node load $g_i = 0.5, 1 \leq i \leq 5$. Here, g_i is the application layer load (Erlangs) in node i. Post convergence, the nodes learn to take actions so that network throughput (S) is maximized while maintaining fairness in available bandwidth distribution.

Performance of RRA-MAC in a 3-nodes fully-connected topology for heterogeneous traffic is shown in Fig. 3. With ALOHA access, there is a high variation of throughputs among the three nodes for heterogeneous load distribution. In contrast, with RRA-MAC, the differences in throughputs of individual nodes are significantly smaller. In each of the three plots in Fig. 3, the loads from node-1 (g_1) and node-2 (g_2) are kept fixed at different values, and the node-level throughput variations are observed for varying load from node-3 (g_3). These represent the scenarios: $g_1 \leq \hat{g}, g_2 \leq \hat{g}, g_1 \leq \hat{g}, g_2 > \hat{g} or g_1 > \hat{g}, g_2 \leq \hat{g}$, and $g_1 > \hat{g}, g_2 > \hat{g}$. It can be observed that with DRLI-MAC, the RL agents in nodes learn to adjust the transmit probability such that the available wireless bandwidth is fairly distributed. Also notable is the fact that the RRA-MAC logic can hold the maximum fair throughput for higher network loads, even under heterogeneous loading conditions.

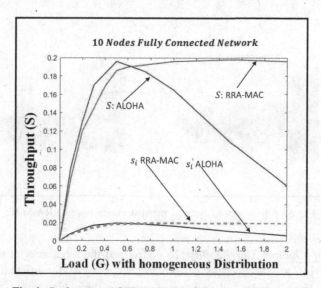

Fig. 4. Performance of RRA-MAC in fully-connected topology

The ability of the proposed mechanism to maximize and sustain network throughput in a fair manner for fully-connected topologies is shown in Fig. 4. Throughput attained using RRA-MAC increases, reaches a maximum and then sustains with increase in network load. Figure 5 shows the ability of the RL-based protocol to adjust to dynamic network conditions. The ability to adapt to time-varying network traffic is shown for a 12-node partially connected topology in Fig. 5 (a). It can be observed that learning adjustment to a change in network load is faster as compared to the initial convergence. It is because, once a Q-table is learnt, the updated table maintains some information regarding which actions are better at a particular state representing a certain collision probability. Hence, the learning agent already has certain level of intelligence regarding the best sets of possible actions which helps it to converge quicker as compared to the case of fresh random initialization of Q-values. This effect can be further investigated on a dynamic node failure/node addition scenario as shown in Figs. 5 (b) and (c). While for the node failure scenario, convergence is faster than that of fresh start due to the reasons explained above, convergence does not speed up as much for the node additions. This is because, on addition of a node, it has to start its learning from the scratch with random initialization of Q-table, thus delaying the convergence.

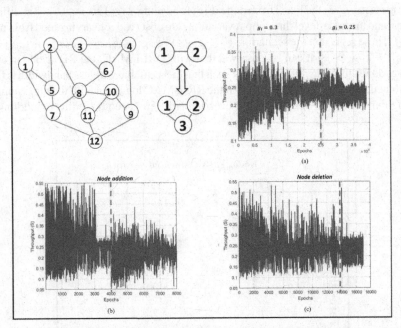

Fig. 5. Adjustment to dynamic network conditions by RRA-MAC

__Effects of Channel Unreliability__: To understand the robustness of the learning-based RRA-MAC to channel errors, performance was analyzed for different packet error probabilities. For a 3-nodes fully connected topology, throughput ratio ($\frac{S_{RRA-MAC}}{S_{ALOHA}}$) and convergence time were observed to be 1.83, 1.86, 1.82 and 6.5, 6.8 and 7.1 ($\times 10^3$ epochs) for packet error probability values of 0%, 5% and 10% respectively. With increase in packet error probability, a greater number of packets gets dropped. This makes each node to require more learning epochs to get an estimate of the correct neighborhood throughput to compute rewards and to update the Q-table values. Although the convergence slows with more channel errors in general, the slowdown is acceptable for the practical range of packet error probabilities (0 − 10%). Similarly, the post-convergence throughput ratio remains in the same ballpark value for different values of packet error probabilities up to 10%. This indicates that the impacts of channel errors on RRA-MAC are no worse than those on the ALOHA protocol logic.

To summarize, Reinforcement Learning for medium access in wireless network can make nodes learn transmission policies in a cooperative manner in order to maximize throughput and fairness. This is achieved in a resource constrained system in the absence of complex hardware support such as time-slotting, carrier-sensing, time-synchronization, and collision detection, thus making it suitable for low-complexity IoT and sensor nodes.

6 MAB for Time-Asynchronous TDMA MAC

In the presence of time slotting, MAC packet collisions can be largely avoided by TDMA-based packet transmission scheduling. This section presents a learning mechanism towards that goal, specifically when network time-synchronization is not available. High resolution and accurate time-synchronization over wireless can be expensive, especially in low-cost sensor and IoT nodes with limited processing and communication resources. Moreover, performance of TDMA MAC protocols that rely on network time-synchronization can be very sensitive to time-synchronization drifts. This section shows how MAC layer packet scheduling can be learned in the absence of time-synchronization using Multi-arm Bandit (MAB) techniques.

Since time is not synchronized, the scope of a node's TDMA frame is strictly local. It decides the start time of its own frame, and the end time is decided based on a predefined frame duration, which is denoted by T_{frame}. The node does not know about the start times of the other nodes' frames. Within a frame, a node can schedule a packet transmission only in certain discrete time instances away from its frame start time. The intervals between those time instances are referred to as mini-slots, the duration of which is an integer submultiple of the fixed size packet duration, and is equal at all nodes.

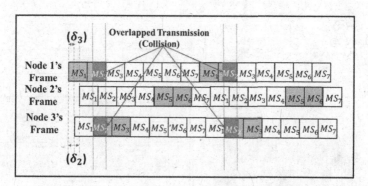

Fig. 6. Asynchronous frames in a 3-nodes fully-connected network

This arrangement of mini-slot-based asynchronous TDMA is shown for a 3-node fully connected network in Fig. 6. Frames of nodes 2 and 3 lag from that of 1 by δ_2 and δ_3 durations. Here, the frame size equals 7 mini-slots and a mini-slot is half of packet duration. A node can select any of these 7 mini-slots within its frame as the starting point of its packet transmission. The figure depicts a situation where for packet transmissions, nodes 1, 2 and 3 select mini-slots 1, 5 and 2 respectively in their own frames and periodically transmit in those mini-slots in subsequent frames. Packets from nodes 1 and 3 collide because of their time-overlapped transmissions (indicated by red), whereas packets from 2 are successfully transmitted.

The transmission scheduling problem in this context boils down for each node to be able to choose a start-transmission mini-slot within its own frame, and that is without colliding with other nodes. Such collision-free mini-slots should be selected locally at each node in a fully independent manner without the help of any centralized allocation coordinators and network time-synchronization. This is achieved by the framework comprising of two distinct components: MAB-learning-based slot (mini-slot) scheduling and slot-defragmentation operation to minimize any bandwidth redundancy resulting from the time-asynchronous scheduling by MAB. The entire flow is captured in Fig. 7.

This slot allocation problem can be modeled as a multi-Agent MAB. Each node in this scenario acts as an independent 'f-armed bandit', where f is the frame size in number of mini-slots. In other words, the action of an agent is to select a start-transmission mini-slot in the frame. The MAB environment is the wireless network itself through which the bandits interact via the selection of the arms (i.e., start-transmission mini-slots). The reward is designed such that the bandit receives a reward of $+1$ if the packet transmission in the selected mini-slot is successful. Else, a penalty of -1 is assigned.

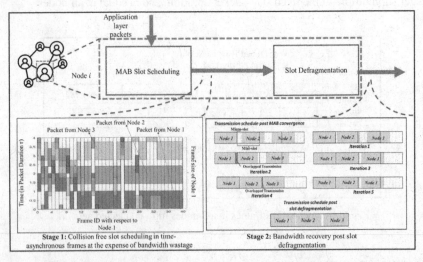

Fig. 7. MAC slot scheduling in time-asynchronous networks using Multi-arm Bandit learning

Using this MAB model, all nodes individually learn collision-free transmission schedules in an independent manner. Figure 7 (Stage 1) shows the learning convergence in a 3-node fully-connected network for a constant data rate $\lambda = 1$ packet per frame per node, and the number of arms $f = 4$. Packet transmission dynamics by all nodes are plotted in the figure with node 1's frame as the frame of reference. Frames of nodes 2 and 3 lag that of node 1 by 0.4τ and 0.75τ respectively, where τ represents the packet duration. Note that while there are collisions initially, after learning convergence, the nodes learn to select collision-free start-transmission mini-slots. Such learning takes place without network time-synchronization.

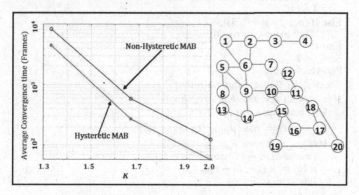

Fig. 8. Convergence time variation with K

Since this framework requires each node to perform its own iterative search for a collision free start-transmission mini-slot independently, short-term collisions and scheduling deadlocks can occur. This can be mitigated by making frame size f larger than the absolute needed minimum f_{min} in the presence of time-synchronization. This leads to certain amount of bandwidth redundancy and is represented by a factor K, defined as $K = \frac{f}{f_{min}}$.

1: **Initialize:** $\mu_{shift_i} = 0, c_i = 0$ // μ_{shift_i}: Number of micro-slot that node i has shifted; c_i:
Status of the micro-slot search (1, *if search is complete, else*, 0)
2: **If** (! Tx in the beginning of frame), do:
3:     Shift to previous micro-slot
4:     μ_{shift_i} + +
5:     Check Collision
6:     **If** (Collision ==TRUE):
7:         Check action in the previous frame $a(t-1)$
8:         **If** $(\mu_i(t) > \mu_i(t-1))$:
9:             Shift to next micro-slot
10:            Check Collision
11:            **If** (Collision ==TRUE):
12:                Shift to previous micro-slot
13:            **End If**
14:        **Else If** $(\mu\_i(t) < \mu\_i(t-1))$:
15:            Shift to next micro-slot
16:    **End If**
17:    Set $c_i = 1$
18:    Piggyback c_i, μ_{shift_i}
19:    Check $c_j, \forall j \in one - hop\ neighbor$
20:    **If** $(c_j == 1\ (\forall j \in one-hop\ neighbor))$
21:        Find new frame size:
22:        $F_{shrunk}(t) = \max\left\{\mu_{shift_i}(t), \mu_{shift_j}(t)\right\}$
23:        **If** $(F_{shrunk}(t) == F_{shrunk}(t-1))$:
24:            *Frame Size* $\leftarrow$ *Frame Size* $- F_{shrunk}$
25:            $\mu(t) = \mu(t-1) - F_{shrunk}$
26:            Ignore all collisions
27:        **End If**
28: **Else:**
29:        Do Nothing
30:        Set $c_i = 1$
31:        Piggyback c_i, μ_{shift_i}
32:        Check the value of $c_j, \forall j \in one-hop\ neighbor$
33:        **If** $c_j == 1\ (\forall j \in one-hop\ neighbor)$
34:            Find new frame size:
35:            $F_{shrunk}(t) = \max\left\{\mu_{shift_i}(t), \mu_{shift_j}(t)\right\}$,
36:            *Frame Size* $\leftarrow$ *Frame Size* $- F_{shrunk}$
37:            $\mu(t) = \mu(t-1) - F_{shrunk}$
38:        **End If**
39: **End If**

Algorithm. 1. Defragmented Backshift

This bandwidth redundancy factor plays a significant role in the MAB learning convergence speed. This can be observed from Fig. 8, which shows that for a 20-node mesh network, learning convergence speeds up with larger K. It is because with increase in K, the number of feasible solutions of the MAB problem increases and hence the probability of finding a collision-free transmission strategy increases. Also, the convergence speed is observed to be high with Hysteretic learning as compared with the classical MAB update rule [11, 16]. This is achieved by giving less importance to penalties than rewards in Hysteretic MAB as explained in Section IV.

As observed in Fig. 8, convergence of MAB learning speeds up with increased bandwidth redundancy factor K. However, increased K leads to an increase in frame length which in turn increases bandwidth wastage. This redundancy can be mitigated by the following *slot defragmentation* mechanism after the MAB learning converges.

Slot defragmentation is implemented by discretizing each mini-slot within a frame into 's' micro-slots. After MAB convergence, each node shifts its transmission by one micro-slot back in time till it experiences a collision. Upon experiencing a collision, the node undoes its previous shift action to find a new transmission micro-slot. In this way, the nodes estimate the unused space in the frame and try to reduce it in a coordinated manner. The logic for defragmented backshift executed by each node i is given in Algorithm 1.

This mechanism of defragmentation for a 3-node fully-connected network is shown in Fig. 4 (Stage 2). It shows how the frame structure (with respect to node 1) evolves over 5 iterations of the defragmentation process for bandwidth redundancy factor $K = 1.33$ and 7 micro-slots ($s = 7$). Node 1 does not shift its transmission since it is transmitting at the beginning of the frame. Nodes 2 and 3 backshift their transmissions by one micro-slot per iteration. In iteration 2, nodes 1 and 2 experience collision. Hence node 2 undoes its previous action by shifting by one-micro-slot forward in iteration 3. But node 1 does nothing in iteration 3 since it experienced a collision without any micro-slot shift in its previous frame. Similarly, nodes 2 and 3's packets collide in iteration 4 because of backshift operation of node 3. Node 3 shifts forward its transmission by one micro-slot and knows that it has found its suitable transmission micro-slot. In this example, the new frame size as shown in the figure reduces by 21% because of slot defragmentation. This bandwidth redundancy left after slot defragmentation is due to the time lag existing among the nodes resulting from the lack of network synchronization.

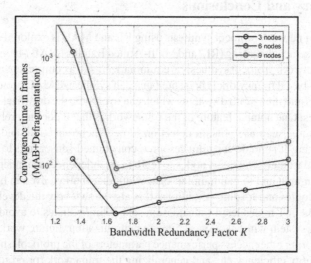

Fig. 9. Convergence time variation with K for fully connected networks

Once a node finds a stable micro-slot, it piggybacks over data packets the information about the number of micro-slots it has shifted (μ_shift) to find its final stable position. Thus, a node i knows that its one-hop neighbors have found stable micro-slots. It then computes the new frame size by subtracting the maximum of the μ_shift values (i.e., received from its neighbors) from its current frame size.

Upon performing slot defragmentation in a 9-node fully-connected topology with the bandwidth redundancy factor K set at 1.67, the bandwidth redundancy goes down from 67% to 3.3%. The bandwidth redundancy of 3.3% at the end of defragmentation is caused primarily by the temporal lags across the frame start times. Similarly, for a partially connected topology shown in Fig. 9, for $K = 2$, bandwidth redundancy after defragmentation reduced from 100% to 7.11%.

Figure 9 depicts the additive time for stage-1 MAB convergence and stage-2 defragmentation convergence. Larger K values speed up MAB convergence while slowing down the defragmentation process. The latter is because with a larger frame length, the number of iterations that a node has to backshift its transmission micro-slot to find a suitable micro-slot increases. Thus, the search space to find the suitable transmit micro-slot increases with K. As can be seen in Fig. 10, the total convergence duration (MAB and slot defragmentation) initially goes down with increase in K, reaches a minimum, and then goes up again. This is because for small K, MAB convergence time is significantly higher than defragmentation convergence and hence the total convergence is largely affected by the MAB learning convergence. However, for larger K values, defragmentation convergence time overpowers MAB convergence time, and thus, total convergence time increases with K. These results indicate that an optimum value of K exists that gives the minimum total convergence time of the proposed learning framework.

7   Summary and Conclusions

The concept of network protocol synthesis using RL and MAB is explored in this article. Here, Reinforcement Learning (RL) and Multi-Armed Bandits (MAB)-based approaches for wireless network protocol synthesis are summarized and a comprehensive distributed RL and MAB-based framework is presented that can synthesize MAC protocols for both random access and time-slotted systems which can overcome the drawbacks of the existing approaches. One notable feature of the framework is that it does not rely on complex hardware features such as collision detection, time synchronization, and carrier sensing, thus making it suitable for ultra-resource constrained sensor and IoT nodes. The learning-based framework allows nodes to learn in an independent manner to maximize network throughput and to maintain fair bandwidth distribution, even in heterogeneous network topologies and loading conditions. It is also shown how the developed mechanism makes the IoT nodes learn transmission scheduling policies to avoid collisions in a time-slotted system without network time-synchronization. Future work on this topic includes exploring other access performance parameters of the protocol, such as, end-to-end delay, energy efficiency etc. and generalizing the framework for protocol synthesis in networks with or without any resource-constraints.

References

1. Leon-Garcia, A., Widjaja, I.: Communication Networks: Fundamental Concepts and Key Architectures, vol. 2. McGraw-Hill, New York (2000)

2. Lee, J.-S., Su, Y.-W., Shen, C.-C.: A comparative study of wireless protocols: Bluetooth, UWB, ZigBee, and Wi-Fi. In: IECON 2007–33rd Annual Conference of the IEEE Industrial Electronics Society. IEEE (2007)

3. Chu, Y., Mitchell, P.D., Grace, D.: ALOHA and q-learning based medium access control for wireless sensor networks. In: ISWCS, IEEE (2012)

4. Lan, Z., Jiang, H., Wu, X.: Decentralized cognitive MAC protocol design based on POMDP and Q-learning. In: 7th International Conference on Communications and Networking, China, pp. 548–551 (2012)

5. Ali, R., Shahin, N., Zikria, Y.B., Kim, B.-S., Kim, S.W.: Deep reinforcement learning paradigm for performance optimization of channel observation–based MAC protocols in dense WLANs. IEEE Access 7, 3500–3511 (2019). https://doi.org/10.1109/ACCESS.2018.2886216

6. Yu, Y., Wang, T., Liew, S.C.: Deep-reinforcement learning multiple access for heterogeneous wireless networks. IEEE J. Sel. Areas Commun. 37(6), 1277–1290 (2019)

7. Lee, T., Shin, O.J.: CoRL: collaborative reinforcement learning-based MAC protocol for IoT networks. Electronics. 9(1), 143 (2020)

8. Galzarano, S., Liotta, A., Fortino, G.: QL-MAC: A Q-learning based MAC for wireless sensor networks. In: Aversa, R., Kołodziej, J., Zhang, J., Amato, F., Fortino, G. (eds.) Algorithms and Architectures for Parallel Processing. LNCS, vol. 8286, pp. 267–275. Springer, Cham (2013). https://doi.org/10.1007/978-3-319-03889-6_31

9. Savaglio, C., et al.: Lightweight reinforcement learning for energy efficient communications in wireless sensor networks. IEEE Access 7, 29355–29364 (2019)

10. BayatYeganeh, H., ShahMansouri, V., Kebriaei, H.: A multi-state Q-learning based CSMA MAC protocol for wireless networks. Wirel. Netw. 24(4), 1251–1264 (2016). https://doi.org/10.1007/s11276-016-1402-0

11. Park, H., et al.: Multi-agent reinforcement-learning-based time-slotted channel hopping medium access control scheduling scheme. IEEE Access. 8, 139727–139736 (2020)

12. Liu, J., et al.: Dynamic channel allocation for satellite internet of things via deep reinforcement learning. In: ICOIN, IEEE (2020)

13. Ahmed, F., Cho, H.-S.: A time-slotted data gathering medium access control protocol using Q-learning for underwater acoustic sensor networks. IEEE Access 9 (2021)

14. Park, S.H., Mitchell, P.D., Grace, D.: Performance of the ALOHA-Q MAC protocol for underwater acoustic networks. In: 2018 International Conference on Computing, Electronics & Communications Engineering, IEEE (2018)

15. Sutton, R.S., Barto, A.G.: Reinforcement learning: An introduction. MIT Press, Cambridge (2018)

16. Dutta, H., Biswas, S.: Towards multi-agent reinforcement learning for wireless network protocol synthesis. In: 2021 International Conference on COMmunication Systems & NETworkS (COMSNETS), pp. 614–622 (2021).https://doi.org/10.1109/COMSNETS51098.2021

17. Dutta, H., Biswas, S.: Medium access using distributed reinforcement learning for IoTs with low-complexity wireless transceivers. In: 2021 IEEE 7th World Forum on Internet of Things (WF-IoT), pp. 356–361 (2021). https://doi.org/10.1109/WF-IoT51360.2021.9595062

18. Dutta, H., Biswas, S.: Distributed reinforcement learning for scalable wireless medium access in IoTs and sensor networks. Comput. Netw. 202, 108662 (2022). https://doi.org/10.1016/j.comnet.2021.108662

19. Matignon, L., Laurent, G.J., Fort-Piat, N.L.: Hysteretic q-learning: an algorithm for decentralized reinforcement learning in cooperative multi-agent teams. In: 2007 IEEE/RSJ International Conference on Intelligent Robots and Systems (2007)

Distributional Reinforcement Learning for VoLTE Closed Loop Power Control in Indoor Small Cells

Sara Koulali[1], Mostapha Derfouf[2], Mohammed-Amine Koulali[3(✉)], and Mohammed Barboucha[4]

[1] University Abdelmalek Essaadi, Tétouan, Morocco
skoulali@uae.ac.ma
[2] University Mohammed V, Rabat, Morocco
mostaphaderfouf@research.emi.ac.ma
[3] Laboratoire de Modélisation et Calcul Scientifique, National School for Applied Sciences of Oujda, Mohammed I University, Oujda, Morocco
m.koulali@ump.ac.ma
[4] Research Center High Studies of Engineering School EHEI, Oujda, Morocco

Abstract. We present a Distributional Reinforcement Learning (DRL) empowered downlink power control algorithm for voice over LTE (VoLTE). We mainly focus on closed-loop power control with small cells serving an indoor environment. We model the power control problem using DRL to efficiently manage the uncertainty in the function approximation process used to evaluate the power control decisions. The proposed DRL-based power control algorithm greatly improves the performance w.r.t. Fixed Power Allocation and Deep Q-Networks-based approaches in terms of voice calls retainability.

Keywords: VoLTE · Distributional Reinforcement Learning · IQN · DQN · Artificial Intelligence

1 Introduction

Network parameterization and tuning precede the deployment of cellular base stations and should be realized continuously as the requirements evolve. Therefore, the performance and faults-related data are monitored to adapt the parameter settings and configuration of the network. These tasks shall take place automatically using intelligent agents to allow radio engineers to reorient their time towards other network operations and maintenance tasks.

Power Control (PC) is a key tuning and parameterization task that ewer generations of telecommunication technologies such as 3G and 4G rely on to cope with network faults/failures and transmission impairments. To this end, two different modes are available. One is Open Loop Control (OLC), and the other is Closed Loop Control (CLC). They differ in the use of feedback for adjusting the transmit power level at the sender to meet operational requirements.

Power control is exploited to provide applications using the wireless network infrastructure with resiliency and minimize packet retransmission. The resiliency is based on the received Signal to Interference plus Noise Ratio (SINR). This is especially crucial for voice and low latency data transfer applications.

The authors of [2] propose a deep learning-based mechanism for power control to manage radio resources in wireless communication. First, they use convolutional time-series prediction to predict future SINRs. Then, power allocation is realized, such as a threshold SINR is maintained to improve total power consumption and energy efficiency. In [6], the authors propose an efficient link adaptive power control and allocation (LaPCA) to address the overused transmission power of the cell. The objective is to balance energy efficiency with maintaining a good QoS level. To realize this objective, they define the portion of cell transmission power to be proportional to the volume of data flows going to be transmitted as indicated by the scheduling process. The studied scenario is modeled as a nonconvex optimization problem.

Two downlink scheduling algorithms using partial information on future channel conditions are proposed in [10]. The scheduling allows power control and channel allocation under an average power constraint.

In [8] a reinforcement learning based closed loop power control algorithm for the downlink of VoLTE for small cells served indoor environment is proposed. They prove that effective SINR due to neighboring cell failure is sufficient for VoLTE power control purposes. Two performance metrics, namely: voice retainability and mean opinion score, are used to prove the efficiency of the proposed approach compared to fixed power allocation. In the same line of research, tuning cellular network performance to face constantly occurring impairments improves end users' network reliability. The authors of [7] formulate cellular network performance tuning using Deep Q-Networks. They propose a closed loop power control algorithm for downlink voice over LTE (VoLTE) and a Self-Organizing Network (SON) fault management one. The VoLTE power control is based on reinforcement learning and adjusts the indoor base station transmit power to meet a target SINR of user equipment. On the other hand, reinforcement learning is also used for SON fault management algorithm to enhance the performance of an outdoor base station cluster.

Femtocells have been proposed to overcome indoor coverage issues and improve macrocell efficiency. However, using femtocells in conjunction with a macrocell introduce co-channel interference and decreases the network's overall capacity. In [11], a decentralized Q-learning algorithm with custom initialization for femtocells sharing with macrocell is proposed. The proposed algorithm's performances are evaluated w.r.t. basic Q-learning algorithm, fixed power allocation, and received power-based PC-both enhanced performance and convergence.

Small cells for indoor coverage are valuable for communication quality improvement but produce intra-layer and inter-layer interference management issues. In [4], Q-learning-based distributed and hybrid power control are investigated based on the communications environment characteristics. Energy efficiency and user experience satisfaction are used as metrics for a benchmark with conventional scheduling methods are compared. Distributed Q-learning performs better than local optimization, and hybrid Q-learning enhances global performance.

Downlink power control is either static or dynamic. In static power control, the Base Station (BS) transmit power parameters are configured on the basis of cell reference power to meet coverage requirements. Whereas in dynamic power control, feedback from the User Equipment (UE) is used to adaptively adjust the BS transmit power.

In this paper, we propose to use Distributional Reinforcement Learning (DRL) as a framework for online tuning of cellular networks when used for voice applications in an indoor cellular network. We use the effective SINR as an input to our proposed indoor power control module to optimize the received power at UEs, as illustrated in Fig. 1. We use a distributional reinforcement learning approach to implement the indoor power control module and test its performance w.r.t. fixed power allocation and standard reinforcement learning used in [8] and prove that it enhances hey performance metrics.

The paper is organized as follows: The studied system model is presented in Sect. 2. We present a primer on Distributional Reinforcement Learning in Sect. 3. Then, the proposed power control algorithm and the adopted performance metric are discussed in Sect. 4. Finally, we show our results and conclusions in Sects. 5 and 6.

2   System Model

The studied system is inspired by [8] and comprises a radio environment where VoLTE capable UEs are served by a base station. The UEs are subject to inter-cell interference from adjacent cells. The second component of the system, is an agent using distributional reinforcement learning to perform closed loop power control to improve effective downlink SINR measured at the receiver.

Orthogonal Frequency-Division Multiplexing (OFDM) technology is used in the studied indoor cellular cluster. The cluster is formed by one cell containing a serving base station and adjacent cells with low-power nodes such as pico, femto, and relay nodes. Each cell is modeled as a square of length L.

Let us denote by N_{UE}, the number of UEs. Then, the received signal y_i^t at time t for an additive white Gaussian noise channel is:

$$y_i^t = h_i^t s_i^t + n^t, \qquad i = 1, 2, \ldots N_{\text{UE}} \tag{1}$$

We suppose that the signal do not suffer frequency selective fading i.e., h_i^t is a single-tap channel coefficient, and n^t is a Gaussian noise with mean 0 and variance σ^2 (i.e., $n^t \sim \text{Norm}(0, \sigma^2)$). Also, UEs are distributed within cells according to a homogeneous Poisson Point Process (PPP) [1] with intensity λ. The state of the cellular cluster could be either normal or faulty. The different faults are summarized in Table 1.

Without loss of generality, we assume that the indoor cluster contains N_{BS} base stations positioned at the origins of the cells. Base station 1 is the serving

Table 1. Network actions

Action ν	Definition
0	Cluster is normal.
1	Feeder fault alarm (3 dB loss of signal).
2	Neighboring cell down.
3	VSWR out of range alarm.
4	Feeder fault alarm cleared.
5	Neighboring cell up again.
6	VSWR back in range

one, and $k_{1 \le j \le N_{BS}}$ is the proportion of users from the adjacent cells j whose signals are transmitted on the same Physical Ressource Block (PRB) as the i-th UE at Transmission Time Interval (TTI) t. The downlink SINR for the UE i at TTI t is given by:

$$\gamma_i^t \triangleq \frac{P_{\text{UE},i}^t}{\sigma^2 + \sum_{j=2}^{N_{BS}} k_j P_{\text{UE},j}^t}. \tag{2}$$

where $P_{\text{UE},i}^t$ is the received power for the allocated PRBs.

Our objective is to optimize the effective downlink received SINR for users in the serving cell at a given TTI t, $\bar{\gamma}^t$ expressed as follows

$$\bar{\gamma}^t \triangleq 10 \log \left(\frac{1}{N_{\text{UE}}} \sum_{i=1}^{N_{\text{UE}}} \gamma_i^t \right) \quad \text{(dB)} \tag{3}$$

To achieve this objective, the proposed downlink power control module keeps the downlink SINR at the receiver at $\bar{\gamma}_{\text{target}}$ when the faults captured in φ_{fault}^t occur. The PC module operates using a power control command c^t and a repetition factor η^t. The optimal values of these two parameters are learned using a distributional reinforcement learning algorithm as illustrated in Fig. 1.

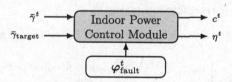

Fig. 1. Downlink power control module.

3 Distributional Reinforcement Learning Primer

We propose using a distributional reinforcement learning-based framework to formulate the VoLTE closed loop PC problem. In this framework, the agent's objective is to maintain SINR at a target effective SINR $\bar{\gamma}_{\text{target}}$ when network faults happen. To this end, at time t the environment (cluster) is in state $s \in \mathcal{S}$, the agent takes action $a \in \mathcal{A}$. As a result, the state of the cluster changes to s' and the agent obtains a reward $r_{s,a}$ as illustrated in Fig. 2.

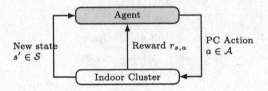

Fig. 2. Reinforcement learning elements.

The set of actions $\mathcal{A} = \{0, 1, \ldots, 4\}$ with the associated power command c and repetition factor η are shown in Table 2.

Table 2. Power Control Agent Actions

Action a	PC action command (c)	Repetition factor (η)
0	0	0
1	-1	3
2	-1	1
3	$+1$	1
4	$+1$	3

The cluster's set of states $\mathcal{S} = \{0, 1, 2\}$ indicates how the BS's transmit power reacts to the action command C. The states are described as follows:

- State 0: Unchanged transmission power.
- State 1: Increased transmission power.
- State 2: Decreased transmission power.

Let $\Delta\bar{\gamma}^t \triangleq \bar{\gamma}^t - \bar{\gamma}^{t-1}$, we define the reward function $r_{s,a}^t$ at time t as follows:

$$r_{s,a}^t \triangleq \begin{cases} r_{\min}, & \bar{\gamma}^t = \bar{\gamma}_{\text{target}} \text{ not feasible or } t \ll \tau \\ -1, & \Delta\bar{\gamma}^t < 0 \\ 0, & \Delta\bar{\gamma}^t = 0 \\ 1, & \Delta\bar{\gamma}^t > 0 \\ r_{\max}, & \bar{\gamma}^t = \bar{\gamma}_{\text{target}} \end{cases} \tag{4}$$

The optimal policy is learned through a proxy mapping that associates to each state-action pair, a real value indicating how good (respectively, bad) is choosing action a at state s in terms of expected return. Thus mapping denoted $Q(s, a)$ is the Q-function. To derive the action-state value function $Q(s, a)$ for all possible state/action pairs, Tabular Q-Learning [12] is used. For problems with large or continuous state/action spaces, the tabular approach fails due to the curse of dimension. Thus, reinforcement learning approaches offer valuable help in learning approximate action state value functions.

Model-free reinforcement learning algorithms can be classified into Policy Optimization, Q-Learning, and hybrid. Q-Learning-based algorithms use experience collected by an agent through its interaction with the environment. The policy mapping action to a state is learned through the maximization of the Q-function $Q(s, a)$ (i.e., state-action value function). The latter indicates the goodness of a state-action pair. This contrasts with on-policy reinforcement learning algorithms, where a policy is updated via data collected by itself. It estimates the return for state-action pairs assuming the current policy continues to be followed.

Standard reinforcement learning algorithms, like Deep Q-Networks [5] (DQN), optimize the expected total returns. However, averaging over randomness to estimate the value has many limitations. One of the major drawbacks is that compressing a probability distribution to its first moment (i.e., expectation) necessarily leads to information losses.

In distributional reinforcement learning [9] the probability distribution of returns is learned instead of simply focusing on its expected value. This significantly improves the agent's performance and allows it to deal with the randomness of the environment more efficiently.

$$Q(s, a) = \mathbb{E}\left[R(s, a) + \gamma Q(s', a')\right] \tag{5}$$

The Bellman equation (5) states that $Q(s, a)$ the action-value of a state s when action a is chosen and the new state is s' is the sum of the immediate reward plus the discounted sum of future action values.

$$Z(s, a) \overset{D}{=} R(s, a) + \gamma Z(s', a') \tag{6}$$

Equation (6) is called the distributional Bellman equation. probability distribution of returns Z is characterized by the interaction of three random variables: the reward R, the next state-action (s, a'), and its random return $Z(s', a')$. Note that the operator $\overset{D}{=}$ stands for the equality between probability distributions.

Implicit Quantile Networks (IQN) [3] was proposed as a distributional reinforcement learning algorithm. It uses quantile regression to approximate the full quantile function for the state-action return distribution. Also, it provides a large class of risk-sensitive policies. IQN provides an effective way to learn an implicit representation of the return distribution by reparameterizing a distribution over the sample space.

To solve the downlink PC problem, we consider an PC agent that chooses a sequence PC commands c (i.e., actions) to face impairments $\nu \in \mathcal{N}$ at each time slot t. Unlike Fixed Power Allocation (FPA), the optimal PC commands are learned through IQN. As a result , the effective downlink received SINR $\bar{\gamma}^t$ is either increased or decreased by a finite quantity $\Delta \bar{\gamma}^t$.

4   Power Control Algorithms and Performance Metrics

We will be using fixed power allocation as a baseline to benchmark reinforcement learning-based PC frameworks (i.e., standard and distributional). FPA is an open-loop PC algorithm that serves as a baseline for comparison. FPA is an open-loop power allocation mechanism that distributes the transmit power P_{TX} equally over all N_{PRB} available PRBs while respecting the cell's maximum transmission power $P_{\text{BS}}^{\max}$. The base station transmit power is expressed as follows:

$$P_{\text{TX}}^t \triangleq P_{\text{BS}}^{\max} - 10 \log N_{\text{PRB}} \quad (\text{dBm}) \qquad (7)$$

When a closed loop PC is used, the base station adjusts its transmit power according to the UEs feedback (i.e., effective downlink received SINR $\bar{\gamma}^t$) at time slot t. The adjustment is simply increasing (respectively, decreasing) the current transmit power P_{TX}^{t-1} using a PC command c^t repeated η^t times.

$$P_{\text{TX}}^t = \min \left(P_{\text{BS}}^{\max}, P_{\text{TX}}^{t-1} + \eta^t c^t \right) \quad (\text{dBm})$$

In episodic reinforcement learning, an agent interacts with an environment in episodes of finite duration. For the PC problem for voice bearers, An episode is a period of time in which an interaction between the agent and the environment takes place. In our case, this period of time is $\tau = 20$ TTIs is the AMR frame duration.

To assess the performance of our proposed Distributional PC agent, We will benchmark it with respect to other approaches using the call retainability metric. Retainability is a function of the effective downlink SINR threshold $\bar{\gamma}_{\min}$ and is computed during the final episode, where the agent has learned the optimal policy:

$$\text{Retainability} \triangleq \frac{\tau - \sum_{t=0}^{\tau} \mathbb{1}_{(\bar{\gamma}^t \leq \bar{\gamma}_{\min})}}{\tau}. \qquad (8)$$

where $\mathbb{1}_{(.)}$ is the indicator function.

5   Simulation Results

We implemented IQN and DQN algorithms using the hyper-parameters summarized in Table 3. We give all faults an equally likely chance of occurrence. Thus the network performs reliably for 45% of the time. The initial effective downlink SINR $\bar{\gamma}_0$ is 4 dB and the desired target effective SINR $\bar{\gamma}_{\text{target}}$ is 6 dB.

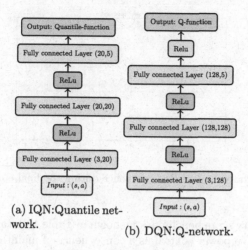

(a) IQN:Quantile network.

(b) DQN:Q-network.

Fig. 3. Neural Networks Architectures.

To learn the optimal Q-function DQN uses the Q-network depicted in Fig. 3b. The network comprises a sequence of three Fully connected layers followed by ReLu activation functions. IQN uses a similar architecture with fewer neurons for its linear layers. As Fig. 3 shows DQN uses 6, 4 folds the number of neurons that IQN requires. Nevertheless, IQN exhibits higher performance as illustrated by the conducted simulations.

Table 3. Reinforcement Learning algorithms Hyper-parameters

Parameter	Value
Number of episodes Γ	707
One episode duration τ (ms)	20
Discount factor ψ	0.980
Learning rate α	0.001

The optimal Q (5) and Z (6) functions are learned after Γ episodes. At this stage, the closed loop PC for both IQN and DQN performs better than FPA. Figure 4 depicts the power command sequence for the episodes $z = 462$ for IQN and $z = 606$ for DQN.

Figure 4 illustrates the power control sequence for the proposed solution and the baselines (DQN and FPA, respectively). Unlike fixed power allocation (FPA), both IQN and DQN-based closed loop power control sent several PCs per transmit time interval (TTI) for the entire VoLTE frame. Also, we notice that the same optimal sequence of PCs is learned by the two algorithms except for TTIs 16 and 17. Nevertheless, IQN achieves higher retainability.

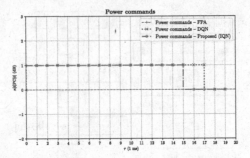

Fig. 4. Power control (PC) sequence during the final episode Γ.

The retainability score benchmark is shown in Table 4. Retainability improves when using adaptive power control as a consequence of maintaining the effective downlink SINR closer to the target one as required by the formula (8). Our proposed IQN-based PC solution enhances the retainability score and manages to outperform the FPA and DQN-based solutions.

Table 4. Retainability for FPA, DQN, and IQN (Proposed).

FPA	DQN	IQN (Proposed)
55.00%	87.19%	**92.22%**

As illustrated in Fig. 5, both DQN and IQN closed-loop PC reaches the target SINR using an optimal learned sequence of PCs. We also notice that the two algorithms maintain the effective SINR at the same level for each TTI until reaching the target SINR at TTI 16.

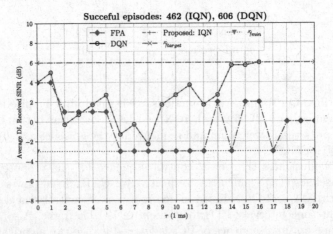

Fig. 5. Downlink SINR improvement vs. simulation time for IQN/DQN closed loop power control and fixed power allocation (FPA)

The proposed algorithm, both for IQN and DQN, reaches the target SINR, while FPA does not. It is noteworthy to mention that while both algorithms (IQN and DQN) reach the target SINR, our proposed IQN-based algorithm performs better than DQN in terms of retainability.

6   Conclusion

We introduced downlink closed-loop power control using distributional reinforcement learning, which improved VoLTE performance in a realistic indoor environment compared to the open-loop fixed power allocation power control and Deep Q-Networks-based solution. The quality of experience was improved, as illustrated by the voice call retainability metric. Indeed, the distributional-based PC allows maintaining the effective SINR closer to the target downlink SINR and consequently prevents a voice call from dropping.

References

1. Baccelli, F., Blaszczyszyn, B.: Stochastic Geometry and Wireless Networks, Volume I - Theory. Now Publishers, Norwell (2009)
2. Biswas, S., Nasir, A.M., Hossain, M.F.: A deep learning based energy efficient downlink power control mechanism for cellular networks. In: 2020 11th International Conference on Electrical and Computer Engineering (ICECE), pp. 343–346. IEEE (2020)
3. Dabney, W., Ostrovski, G., Silver, D., Munos, R.: Implicit quantile networks for distributional reinforcement learning. In: International Conference on Machine Learning, pp. 1096–1105. PMLR (2018)
4. Gao, Z., Wen, B., Huang, L., Chen, C., Su, Z.: Q-learning-based power control for LTE enterprise femtocell networks. IEEE Syst. J. 11(4), 2699–2707 (2016)
5. Huang, Y.: Deep Q-Networks. In: Dong, H., Ding, Z., Zhang, S. (eds.) Deep Reinforcement Learning, pp. 135–160. Springer, Singapore (2020). https://doi.org/10.1007/978-981-15-4095-0_4
6. Madi, N.K., Hanapi, Z.B.M., Othman, M., Subramaniam, S.: Link adaptive power control and allocation for energy-efficient downlink transmissions in LTE systems. IEEE Access 6, 18469–18483 (2018)
7. Mismar, F.B., Choi, J., Evans, B.L.: A framework for automated cellular network tuning with reinforcement learning. IEEE Trans. Commun. 67(10), 7152–7167 (2019)
8. Mismar, F.B., Evans, B.L.: Q-learning algorithm for volte closed loop power control in indoor small cells. In: 2018 52nd Asilomar Conference on Signals, Systems, and Computers, pp. 1485–1489. IEEE (2018)
9. Mnih, V., et al.: Playing atari with deep reinforcement learning. CoRR abs/1312.5602 (2013). http://arxiv.org/abs/1312.5602
10. Nguyen, T.N., Brun, O., Prabhu, B.J.: Joint downlink power control and channel allocation based on a partial view of future channel conditions. In: 2020 18th International Symposium on Modeling and Optimization in Mobile, Ad Hoc, and Wireless Networks (WiOPT), pp. 1–8. IEEE (2020)

11. Simsek, M., Czylwik, A., Galindo-Serrano, A., Giupponi, L.: Improved decentralized q-learning algorithm for interference reduction in lte-femtocells. In: 2011 Wireless Advanced, pp. 138–143. IEEE (2011)
12. Sutton, R.S., Barto, A.G., et al.: Introduction to reinforcement learning. MIT Press, Cambridge (1998)

Reinforcement Learning Aided Routing in Tactical Wireless Sensor Networks

Andrews A. Okine[1,2]($\boxtimes$), Nadir Adam[1,2], and Georges Kaddoum[1,2]

[1] Department of Electrical Engineering, École de technologie supérieure,
University of Québec, Montréal, QC, Canada
`andrews-allotei.okine.1@ens.etsmtl.ca`, `georges.kaddoum@etsmtl.ca`
[2] Resilient Machine Learning Institute, Montréal, QC, Canada

Abstract. A wireless sensor network (WSN) consists of a large number of sensor nodes with limited battery lives that are dispersed geographically to monitor events and gather information from a geographical area. On the other hand, tactical WSNs are mission-critical WSNs that are used to support military operations, such as intrusion detection, battlefield surveillance, and combat monitoring. Such networks are critical to the collection of situational data on a battlefield for timely decision-making. Due to their application area, tactical WSNs have unique challenges, not seen in commercial WSNs, such as being targets for adversarial attacks. These challenges make packet routing in tactical WSNs a daunting task. In this article, we propose a multi-agent Q-learning-based routing scheme for a tactical WSN consisting of static sensors and a mobile sink. Using the proposed routing scheme, a learning agent (i.e., network node) adjusts its routing policy according to the estimates of the Q-values of the available routes via its neighbors. The Q-values capture the quickness, reliability, and energy efficiency of the routes as a function of the number of hops to sink, the one-hop delay, the energy cost of transmission, and the packet loss rate of the neighbors. Simulation results demonstrate that, in comparison to a baseline random hop selection scheme, the proposed scheme reduces the packet loss rate and mean hop delay, and enhances energy efficiency in the presence of jamming attacks.

Keywords: Routing · Wireless sensor networks · Tactical wireless networks · Reinforcement learning · Jamming

1 Introduction

Tactical WSNs are specifically designed for military operations, including surveillance and reconnaissance [1]. For instance, a tactical WSN is usually deployed in a remote area to track the location of troops, monitor deployed systems, and trigger alerts at a command-and-control (C&C) site when certain events occur. The tactical WSN's gateway, or sink, is the bridge between the tactical WSN and the C&C site and serves as the destination for a sensor node's packets. Routing in WSNs refers to the process of finding a path to send packets from a source

© The Author(s), under exclusive license to Springer Nature Switzerland AG 2023
E. Sabir et al. (Eds.): UNet 2022, LNCS 13853, pp. 211–224, 2023.
https://doi.org/10.1007/978-3-031-29419-8_16

node to the destination node, which can be based on the number of hops to sink. Moreover, in network routing, hop count represents the number of intermediary devices, a packet must traverse from a device in the network to the destination node, e.g. a sink.

Tactical WSNs must operate for long periods of time and have adequate network coverage. Besides, a tactical WSN is normally deployed in hostile environments and is a target for adversarial attacks, such as jamming. In addition, packet routing in tactical WSNs is constrained by bandwidth and energy limitations of the sensor nodes. Therefore, to prolong the network's lifetime, routing in tactical WSNs should take into account the residual energy of the nodes [2]. In this context, the energy cost of transmitting packets should be minimized taking into account the distance between sensor nodes. Furthermore, the reliability of routes in tactical WSNs is affected by inconspicuous adversarial attacks such as jamming. Under these attacks, data transmission between the affected network nodes may not be possible. Hence, an efficient routing protocol for tactical WSNs should take into consideration the reliability of paths when forwarding packets to minimize packet loss, frequent retransmissions, and the associated energy cost.

Due to the many-to-one communication nature of WSNs, sensor nodes that are close to a static sink may experience faster energy depletion [3,4]. To avoid this situation and maintain adequate coverage, a tactical WSN may employ an unmmaned ground vehicle (UGV) moving along the periphery of the network as a mobile sink. For tactical WSNs with a mobile sink, the hop count from a device to the sink varies according to the sink's position. Consequently, there is uncertainty regarding the optimal path for data routing due to the varying position of the sink. The dynamic nature of a mobile sink-based tactical WSN creates the need for an adaptive routing policy that finds reliable and energy efficient routes in the presence of changing network conditions (i.e., links' reliability, links' delays, expected number of hops to sink, and energy levels of nodes).

Reinforcement learning (RL) is a class of machine learning (ML) algorithms in which an agent learns to maximize its long-term reward from the actions taken in an environment. In particular, RL allows an agent to observe actions and their rewards to determine its next action [5]. Through trial-and-error, the agent learns from the system responses to previous actions to arrive at an optimal decision policy that optimizes the target reward of the agent. Q-learning is an RL algorithm that does not require a model of the environment and enables the network nodes to adjust their routing strategies, according to the reinforcement rewards (i.e., Q-values), to better adapt to the dynamic network conditions. Hence, it was proposed as a promising routing technique for tactical WSNs [6]. The Q-value can be used as a measure of the usefulness of a routing action, based on the obtained reward signals.

In this paper, we leverage multi-agent Q-learning to design an intelligent routing protocol in which the next-hop selection is influenced by the delay and reliability of a route as well as the energy cost of packet transmission via the route. The neighboring agents (nodes) share knowledge about their locations, residual energies, hop counts to sink, packet loss rates, and one-hop delays of received packets. This allows the learning agents to learn an adaptive routing policy using the Q-values of their neighboring nodes.

2   Related Works

In this section, we present related studies on routing in mobile-sink-based WSNs in addition to RL-enabled routing techniques in traditional WSNs. Afterwards, we discuss the related works on routing in tactical WSNs. We conclude this section by highlighting our main contributions.

2.1   Traditional WSNs

The authors in [7] employed two mobile sinks to distribute the energy consumption throughout the WSN and balance the network load. Additionally, they arranged the network into cells and utilized the mobile sinks to gather the data sensed by the nodes in these cells. Each cell is categorized as a single-hop or a multi-hop cell, where the single-hop cells are one hop away from the anchor points of the sink, and the multi-hop cells are more than one hop away. Their proposed mobile-sink-based routing technique ensures that each half of the network is covered by a sink, by controlling the mobility pattern of the sinks. Similarly, the authors in [8] developed an energy-efficient routing scheme that combines clustering and a mobile sink moving over a predefined trajectory. Firstly, they divided the network area into clusters, where a cluster head (CH) is selected based on its residual energy and the distance between the CH and a source node. Afterwards, the members of a cluster select the routing path with minimal energy consumption for data transmission to their corresponding CHs. Furthermore, intercluster communication is enabled by a greedy algorithm, in which the closest CH to the sink is selected as the leader to communicate with the sink.

An integrated location service and routing (ILSR) scheme was proposed in [9] to address the issues of geographic routing to a mobile sink in static WSNs. Since geographic routing requires knowledge of the location of the destination, there is a need to update and search for the location of the sink. ILSR updates the sink's location to neighboring sensors and sends location update messages to a selected subset of nodes. On the other hand, the authors in [10] developed a green routing protocol that minimizes the energy overhead of updating the sink's location and reduces the data delivery delay using an angle-based approach to routing. The proposed routing scheme creates multiple rings in the sensor field and limits the mobile sink location updates to the nodes belonging to the rings. In a related article [11], the authors proposed a hierarchical routing scheme, in which a virtual ring structure is established to deliver sink position updates to sensor nodes from the ring with minimal overhead. In addition, anchor nodes are selected along the sink path to relay sensor data from the normal sensor nodes to the sink. Moreover, in [12], a virtual grid based hierarchical routing approach was proposed for a mobile-sink-based WSN considering the delay requirements of applications. In this scheme, the data is routed from source nodes to sub sinks and from sub sinks to the mobile sink. A sub sink collects sensed data from its assigned grid and is visited by the mobile sink within a given time period. On the other hand, the unvisited candidate sub sinks send their aggregated sensed data to their nearest sub sinks via the available shortest routing paths. In this scheme, the path to the mobile sink is chosen based on the hop counts and data generation rates of the sensor nodes in order to meet the requirements of delay-bound applications.

Aiming to optimize the network's lifetime, the authors in [13] proposed a Q-learning algorithm where the next-hop selection strategy is based on the link distance between nodes, nodes' residual energies, and the hop count to the sink. In [14], the authors proposed a Q-learning-based energy-aware routing scheme for WSNs involving data aggregation, in which optimal routing paths are selected with regard to the degree of data aggregation of neighboring nodes. Moreover, distributed RL was applied in [15] to optimize the lifetime and energy consumption of WSNs, considering the distance between nodes, available energy, and hop count to the sink. In addition, the authors in [16] presented a RL-based routing protocol to reduce the length of routes and to improve energy consumption in clustered WSNs involving sleep scheduling and controlled data transmissions. Their protocol factored the residual energies of the neighboring nodes, their hop counts to sink, and the distance between the current node and its neighboring nodes into the optimal path selection problem. On the other hand, the authors in [17] implemented a centralized routing protocol in a software-defined WSN, where the sink, acting as the SDN controller, learns the routing table that minimizes the sensor nodes' energy consumption by leveraging RL.

2.2 Tactical WSNs

Due to its critical role, the sink node is a prime target for attackers seeking to destabilize the tactical WSN. To mitigate the vulnerability of the sink node in tactical WSNs, the authors in [18] proposed a technique based on the modified lightweight ad hoc on-demand next-generation reactive routing protocol. They aimed to achieve sink node anonymity, without adding much system complexity by having at least one of the nodes act as the sink node. Moreover, in [1], an energy-efficient routing algorithm with zone clustering, where the nodes are partitioned into specific zones while ensuring the availability of a nearby CH, was presented. The proposed zone routing algorithm tactically controls the network topology to increase the service life of the nodes. This enhances the collection of situational data, which is crucial to tactical decision-making. On the other hand, a shadow zone delay-aware routing (SZODAR) scheme for tactical undersea acoustic sensor networks was proposed in [19]. A shadow zone is an area in a wireless underwater sensor network (WUSN) where the signals from a source cannot be received as a result of refraction. The proposed SZODAR scheme finds reliable routes around shadow zones in WUSNs by changing the depth of acoustic sensors to avoid the shadow zones of neighboring nodes.

The preceding proposals for routing in tactical WSNs aimed at either attack-resilience [18], energy-efficiency [1], or reliability [19]. Although the previous RL-based studies have some relation to our work, they either did not consider the reliability of the routes in their learning frameworks or only considered a static-sink-based WSN. Unlike these past studies, we address energy-efficient and reliable routing in tactical WSNs at the same time. In addition, we take into account the delay of the routes and leverage multi-agent Q-learning to solve the next-hop selection problem in a mobile-sink-based tactical WSN. By sharing information about their packet loss rates, the nodes select neighbors with more reliable forwarding links. Moreover, we demonstrate, via simulations, the ability of our proposed routing scheme to withstand selective jamming attacks in a time division multiple access (TDMA)-based tactical WSN.

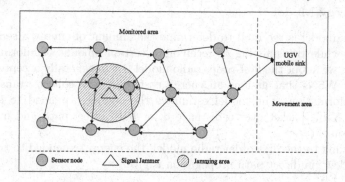

Fig. 1. System model of the tactical wireless sensor network with a mobile sink.

3   System Model

We consider a tactical WSN consisting of sensors and a mobile sink. This network can be represented as a graph $G = (V, E)$, where each node is a vertex $v_i \in V$ and each edge $e_{ij} \in E$ is a bidirectional wireless communication channel between a pair of nodes v_i and v_j. We analyze a single source node $v_0 \in V$ and the mobile sink node D as the destination node. The task is to find the optimal path to send data packets to the sink. Figure 1 depicts the architecture of the tactical wireless sensor network.

We assume the sensor nodes can determine their geographic location using global positioning system (i.e., GPS) and share it periodically using HELLO packets. When the mobile sink changes its position, it broadcasts HELLO packets for neighbor discovery to establish and confirm network adjacency. The transmission range of the sensor nodes is denoted by L. The mobile sink moves around the periphery of the sensor network to gather sensory data. We consider the mobile sink node as a UGV that moves between some pre-defined waypoints to execute the mission. Moreover, the nodes use point-to-point communication links to send sensory data to the sinks, via multi-hop routing [20].

Each node in the network is allocated a fixed time slot based on the time division multiple access (TDMA) protocol [21]. In our tactical WSN model with $|V|$ nodes, the TDMA frame is assumed to have $|V|$ time slots, and each node is assigned a unique slot. Thus, there are no collisions during transmissions. However, a selective jammer can monitor the communication of a potential victim node and detect its receiving time slot, aiming to jam the slot while minimizing the likelihood of being detected, and conserving as much energy as possible. Let $1/\lambda$ denote the time during which the jammer is in the ON state (transmits a jamming signal) and $1/\mu$ denote the OFF state (sleeping) time duration, where μ and λ are the jammer's wake-up and switch off rates, respectively [22].

3.1 Energy Model

An energy model is required to determine the amount of energy a sensor node consumes while transmitting or receiving a certain amount of information. In this study, we adopt the first-order radio model [13], a generally accepted energy model for WSNs that assigns an energy cost-per-bit to collect, transmit, and receive information. The model estimates the energy expended to send and receive a K-bit packet over a distance d for both direct-path and multi-path propagation.

According to the first-order radio model, the energy expended to transmit a K-bit packet via direct path propagation is given by

$$E_{TX}(K,d) = E_{elec}K + \epsilon_{fs}Kd^2, \tag{1}$$

where E_{elec} denotes the energy consumed by the transmitter or receiver circuitry to transmit or receive a unit of data, ϵ_{fs} is a constant corresponding to the energy consumed by the transmitter amplifier to transmit a unit of data over a unit distance. For multi-path propagation, the energy expended to transmit a K-bit packet is given by

$$E_{TX}(K,d) = E_{elec}K + \epsilon_{mp}Kd^4, \tag{2}$$

where ϵ_{mp} is a constant relating to the energy consumed by the transmitter amplifier to transmit a unit of data over a unit distance. Irrespective of the nature of the propagation, the energy expended to receive a message of K bits is given by

$$E_{RX}(K) = E_{elec}K \tag{3}$$

3.2 RL-Based Routing Technique

In this section, we propose a Q-learning-aided routing scheme for tactical WSNs. In the proposed RL framework, the Q-value is an estimation of the goodness of a route, considering the expected number of hops to the mobile sink, the one-hop delay, the energy cost of transmission, and the packet loss rate of the next hop.

3.3   Reward Function

Considering the scenario where sensory data packets are sent from a given source node toward the destination node (i.e., mobile sink) via multi-hop communication, the tactical WSN is viewed as an environment and each node in the network represents an agent. Let H_j be the number of hops from the neighbor node n_j to the mobile sink D. We denote the set of candidate nodes to forward a packet at node i as F_i. The forwarding set F_i is the set of neighbors of node i whose hop-count to the sink is lower than that of node i $(H_j < H_i)$. The reward obtained by a node from the environment, after taking a routing action a_i, is estimated by

$$R(a_i = n_j) = \begin{cases} (1 - P_{jn}^l)R_{ack} - \beta\frac{E_{ij}^{Tx}}{E_i}, & if\ ACK\ is\ received \\ -\beta\frac{E_{ij}^{Tx}}{E_i}, & otherwise \end{cases} \tag{4}$$

where E_{ij}^{Tx} is the energy cost of packet transmission (in joules) from node i to its neighbor node j, and E_i is the residual energy of node i. Moreover, β is a weighting coefficient (i.e., a higher value for β puts more weight on the energy cost), P_{jn}^l is the average packet loss rate of the links between node j and its neighbors (excluding node i), and R_{ack} is given by

$$R_{ack} = \frac{1}{C_{ij} + E[H_{j,D}]}, \tag{5}$$

where R_{ack} is a measure of the route's quickness, $E[H_{j,D}]$ is the expected number of hops from neighbor node $n_j \in F_i$ to the sink D, and $C_{i,j}$ is the normalized one-hop delay cost of the link between node i and its neighbor node j:

$$C_{i,j} = \frac{t_{i,j} - t_{i,min}}{t_{i,max} - t_{i,min}} \tag{6}$$

where $t_{i,j}$ is the estimated one-hop delay from node i to node j. The one-hop delay includes the waiting time for the data packet to reach the head of the transmission queue at node j and the time needed by the medium access protocol to deliver the packet to node j. $t_{i,min}$ and $t_{i,max}$ are the minimum and maximum one-hop delays experienced by node i, respectively. When a node successfully transmits a data packet to a neighbor, it receives an ACK packet containing information about the neighbor's residual energy, the one-hop delay, the number of hops from the neighbor to the sink, and the average packet loss rate of the neighbor's forwarding links. The node uses this information to estimate the rewards obtained from routing actions and to update the Q-values of its neighboring nodes in the neighbor table. Table 1 is a sample neighbor table of a node v_i with neighbors s_1, s_2, and s_3.

3.4   Learning Framework

In the proposed RL framework, a learning agent learns from its routing actions to find the most reliable, quickest, and most energy-efficient paths. Thus, the reward

Table 1. An example of a neighbor table for node v_i

v_i	s_1	s_2	s_3
Location coordinates	(10, 3)	(15, 8)	(20, 10)
Residual energy (joules)	0.4	0.45	0.38
Average packet loss rate	0.02	0.015	0.017
Normalized hop delay	0.13	0.19	0.14
Expected hop count to sink	5	3	4
Q-value	0.9	0.6	0.8

of a routing action is a combination of the speed, reliability, and energy cost of data packet forwarding. At the initial stage of Q-learning, the agent only has knowledge of the location of its neighboring nodes and the number of hops separating them from the sink. Hence, prior to learning, the Q-values are initialized according to Eq. 7:

$$Q_i^0(n_j) = \frac{1}{1 + H_{j,D}^0} \qquad (7)$$

where $Q_i^0(n_j)$ is the initial Q-value of neighbor n_j and $H_{j,D}^0$ is the initial number of hops from neighbor n_j to the sink advertised during the network initialization phase. Subsequently, the Q-value of neighbor n_j is updated according to Eq. 8:

$$Q_{new}(n_j) = Q_{old}(n_j) + \alpha_{ij}\left(R(n_j) + E\left[Q_j(s', a')\right] - Q_{old}(n_j)\right) \qquad (8)$$

where $Q_{old}(n_j)$ is the previous Q-value of neighbor n_j, $E\left[Q_j(s', a')\right]$ is the expected action-value of the next hop n_j, and $R(n_j)$ is the reward obtained by node v_i for routing action n_j. In other words, after choosing the neighbor n_j as the next hop, node i receives a reward and updates the Q-value of n_j in the neighbor table. α_{ij} is the learning rate at which the Q-value of the neighbor n_j is updated.

3.5 Next-Hop Selection

The Q-value captures the benefits (quickness and reliability) and penalties (energy cost) of using a particular route. Thus, based on the Q-values of its neighbors, node i computes a potential next-hop as

$$n_j^{q*} = argmax_{n_j} Q(n_j) \qquad (9)$$

However, selecting the route with the highest Q-value may result in a sub-optimal solution since other routes may yield better rewards as network conditions change. Hence, a good routing policy strikes a balance between the exploitation of best routes and the exploration of the available routes. Secondly, selecting the neighbor with the highest Q-value may cause it to die out faster

---

Algorithm 1: ERG Next-Hop Selection

Input: Q-values Q; Energy values E_{res}; epsilon ϵ; rho ρ
Result: Selected next-hop;
Function SELECT-NEXT-HOP $(Q, E_{res}, \epsilon, \rho)$ **is**
$k \leftarrow$ uniform random number between 0 and 1
if $k < \epsilon$ **then**
$\quad | \quad n_j^H \leftarrow$ random neighbor n_j;
else
$\quad\quad | \quad k \leftarrow$ uniform random number between 0 and (1-ϵ)
$\quad\quad$ **if** $k < \rho$ **then**
$\quad\quad | \quad | \quad n_j^H \leftarrow argmax_{n_j} \, E_{res}(n_j^H = n_j)$;
$\quad\quad$ **else**
$\quad\quad | \quad | \quad n_j^H \leftarrow argmax_{n_j} \, Q(n_j^H = n_j)$;
$\quad\quad$ **end**
end

---

due to the energy consumed to receive and transmit packets. Using the residual energy values of its neighbors, node i may compute a potential next-hop as

$$n_j^{e*} = argmax_{n_j} E_{res}(n_j) \tag{10}$$

where $E_{res}(n_j)$ is the residual energy of node j.

In the search for optimal routes, we build on the ϵ-greedy exploration strategy, which chooses an exploratory action with probability ϵ and a greedy action with probability 1-ϵ [23]. We propose an ϵ-ρ-greedy exploration strategy to accommodate the exploration of routes based on the neighbors' residual energy values. Accordingly, the next-hop selection is given by

$$n_j^H = \begin{cases} n_j^{q*} & with \quad probability \quad 1 - (1 - \epsilon)\rho - \epsilon \\ n_j^{e*} & with \quad probability \quad (1 - \epsilon)\rho \\ \forall n_j & with \quad probability \quad \epsilon \end{cases} \tag{11}$$

where $\forall n_j$ denotes any neighbor in the forwarding set $|F_i|$ and ρ is a probability measure which influences the selection of a neighbor based on the residual energy values. Following the ϵ-ρ-greedy exploration strategy, the probability of selecting the neighbor with the highest Q-value is given by:

$$P(n_j^H = n_j^{q*}) = 1 - (1 - \epsilon)\rho - \epsilon \left(1 - \frac{1}{|F_i|}\right) \tag{12}$$

where $|F_i|$ is the number of neighbors of node i in its forwarding set F_i. Similarly, the probability of selecting the neighbor with the highest residual energy is given by:

$$P(n_j^H = n_j^{e*}) = (1 - \epsilon)\rho + \frac{\epsilon}{|F_i|} \tag{13}$$

Algorithm 1 describes the epsilon-rho-greedy (ERG) next-hop selection procedure for node i.

Table 2. Simulation Parameters

Parameter	Value
Transmit and receive energy constant E_{elec}	50 nJ/bit [1]
Transmit amplifier, multi-path propagation ϵ_{mp}	0.0013 $pJ/bit/m^4$ [1]
Data packet size K	2000 $bits$ [1]
Area dimensions	$250 \times 250 \ m^2$
Number of nodes	150
Nodes' transmission range L	50 m [24]
Maximal velocity of mobile sink v_{max}	20 ms^{-1} [25]
Learning rate α_{ij}	0.9
Exploration rate ϵ	0.075
Probability measure ρ	0.15
Weighting coefficient β	140
Jamming radius J_r	50 m
Jamming switch off rate λ	0.2 s^{-1}
Packets generation rate	2 packets/s
Number of iterations	1000
Number of packets per iteration	100

3.6   Performance Evaluation

Simulation Scenario. The sensor nodes are uniformly distributed in an area of size $250 \times 250 \ m^2$, such that each node's x and y coordinate is a random variable between 0 and 250 m. Each node has an initial residual energy of 0.5 joules. The energy they consume to transmit and receive packets is obtained from the first order radio energy model [13], where the model's parameters are given in Table 2. The location coordinates of the sink node are $((250+\delta x), Y)$, where δx is a small distance (i.e., 10 m) and the value of Y is uniformly distributed over the interval [0, 250] m. The sink node pauses for a time $T = 5$ s, then moves at a uniform random velocity between 0 and v_{max}, where v_{max} is the maximal velocity. For each iteration, a source node is randomly selected from the area, and the location coordinates of the selective jammer are uniformly distributed between 0 and 250 m. In the active state, the jammer randomly selects a receiving node within its radius $J_r = 50$ m to jam its transmission slot. Moreover, the links' delays are uniformly distributed in [0.005, 0.25] s. Following extensive simulations, the optimal parameters for ϵ, ρ, β, and α_{ij} were obtained as 0.075, 0.15, 140, and 0.9, respectively. We compare our proposed ERG next-hop selection scheme against a random selection scheme as a benchmark. The considered benchmark scheme randomly chooses the next-hop from a node's forwarding set F_i.

Results and Discussion. *Packet Loss Rate*: Figure 2 shows the average packet loss results for the ERG and random next-hop selection schemes. The results indicate that ERG can overcome jamming and maintain a relatively low packet loss rate. The ERG scheme penalizes a routing decision that does not yield an ACK due to the signal jamming of the receiver's time slot. Hence, ERG tends to

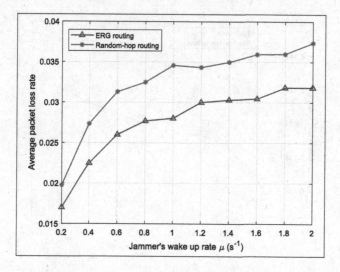

Fig. 2. Average packet loss rate versus the wake-up rate of selective jammer μ for ERG and random next-hop selection.

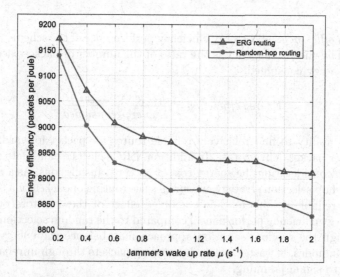

Fig. 3. Energy efficiency versus the wake-up rate of selective jammer μ for ERG and random next-hop selection.

select hops with a higher chance of transmission success. Since all the neighbors of the current node may not be in the jamming area, ERG routes packets to the nodes outside the jamming area, considering their Q-values. In other words, ERG selects the more reliable links for packet forwarding. Meanwhile, random selection does not take the reliability of routes into account in the next-hop selection. Consequently, it is unable to respond to a jamming attack, resulting in a higher packet loss rate.

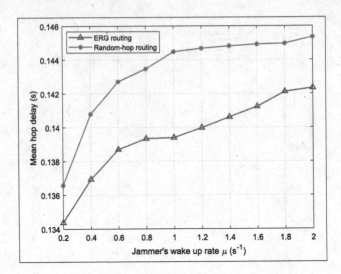

Fig. 4. Mean hop delay versus the wake-up rate of selective jammer μ for ERG and random next-hop selection.

Energy efficiency: The energy efficiency performance of the schemes are given in Fig. 3. The energy efficiency is the ratio of the number of packets delivered to the total energy consumed:

$$Energy\ efficiency = \frac{\Sigma\ packet_{success}}{\Sigma\ energy\ consumed} \tag{14}$$

Due to its ability to find relatively reliable routes for packet forwarding, ERG has a higher packet delivery rate. In addition, ERG selects a candidate next-hop, taking into consideration the energy cost of packet transmissions. As a result, the ERG next-hop selection strategy encourages the routing of packets via the closest and most reliable neighbors. The combined effect of these factors produces a better energy efficiency performance, compared to the random selection strategy. Even though the random selection approach may balance the energy levels of neighboring nodes, it wastes energy by sending packets through unreliable paths subjected to signal jamming.

Hop delay: Figure 4 shows the average hop delay performance for the ERG and random next-hop selection schemes. The results indicate that ERG maintains a relatively low average hop delay, since it learns from the hop delays of previous routing actions, which affect the Q-values of the routes. Hence, ERG tends to send packets through the routes with lower delays. On the other hand, random selection does not take the hop delays of routes into account in the next-hop selection. Consequently, it is unable to overcome the impact of jamming attacks on packet delays, leading to higher average hop delays for routing actions.

4   Conclusion

In this paper, we presented a multi-agent Q-learning-based routing scheme for tactical WSNs in which knowledge, such as the nodes' residual energy, packet loss rates, and the number of hops to the sink, is shared among neighboring nodes. We evaluated the performance of the proposed scheme considering selective jamming attacks in a TDMA-based tactical WSN. Simulation results show that the proposed ERG next-hop selection strategy can adapt to the jamming rate and maintains a low packet loss rate and a low mean hop delay by selecting hops with a high chance of transmission success, and a high energy efficiency by routing packets via the closest and most reliable neighbors.

References

1. Thulasiraman, P., White, K.A.: Topology control of tactical wireless sensor networks using energy efficient zone routing. Digit. Commun. Netw. **2**(1), 1–14 (2016)
2. Mutombo, V.K., Lee, S., Lee, J., Hong, J.: EER-RL: energy-efficient routing based on reinforcement learning. Mob. Inf. Syst. **2021**, 1–12 (2021)
3. Ghosh, N., Banerjee, I.: Application of mobile sink in wireless sensor networks. In: 2018 10th International Conference on Communication Systems & Networks (COMSNETS), pp. 507–509. IEEE, Bengaluru, India (2018)
4. Jain, S., Verma, R.K., Pattanaik, K.K., Shukla, A.: A survey on event-driven and query-driven hierarchical routing protocols for mobile sink-based wireless sensor networks. J. Supercomput. **78**(9), 11492–11538 (2022)
5. Krishnan, M., Lim, Y.: Reinforcement learning-based dynamic routing using mobile sink for data collection in WSNs and IoT applications. J. Netw. Comput. Appl. **194**, 103223 (2021)
6. Keum, D., Ko, Y.B.: Trust-based intelligent routing protocol with q-learning for mission-critical wireless sensor networks. Sensors **22**(11), 3975 (2022)
7. Naghibi, M., Barati, H.: EGRPM: energy efficient geographic routing protocol based on mobile sink in wireless sensor networks. Sustain. Comput. Inform. Syst. **25**, 100377 (2020)
8. Wang, J., Gao, Y., Liu, W., Sangaiah, A.K., Kim, H.J.: Energy efficient routing algorithm with mobile sink support for wireless sensor networks. Sensors **19**(7), 1494 (2019)
9. Li, X., Yang, J., Nayak, A., Stojmenovic, I.: Localized geographic routing to a mobile sink with guaranteed delivery in sensor networks. IEEE J. Sel. Areas Commun. **30**(9), 1719–1729 (2012)
10. Jain, S., Pattanaik, K.K., Verma, R.K., Bharti, S., Shukla, A.: Delay-aware green routing for mobile-sink-based wireless sensor networks. IEEE Internet Things J. **8**(6), 4882–4892 (2020)
11. Tunca, C., Isik, S., Donmez, M.Y., Ersoy, C.: Ring routing: an energy-efficient routing protocol for wireless sensor networks with a mobile sink. IEEE Trans. Mob. Comput. **14**(9), 1947–1960 (2014)
12. Mitra, R., Sharma, S.: Proactive data routing using controlled mobility of a mobile sink in wireless sensor networks. Comput. Electri. Eng. **70**, 21–36 (2018)
13. Guo, W., Yan, C., Lu, T.: Optimizing the lifetime of wireless sensor networks via reinforcement-learning-based routing. Int. J. Distrib. Sens. Netw. **15**(2), 1550147719833541 (2019)

14. Yun, W.K., Yoo, S.J.: Q-learning-based data-aggregation-aware energy-efficient routing protocol for wireless sensor networks. IEEE Access **9**, 10737–10750 (2021)

15. Bouzid, S. E., Serrestou, Y., Raoof, K., Omri, M. N.: Efficient routing protocol for wireless sensor network based on reinforcement learning. In: 2020 5th International Conference on Advanced Technologies for Signal and Image Processing (ATSIP), pp. 1–5. IEEE, Sousse, Tunisia (2020)

16. Abadi, A.F.E., Asghari, S.A., Marvasti, M.B., Abaei, G., Nabavi, M., Savaria, Y.: RLBEEP: Reinforcement-Learning-Based Energy Efficient Control and Routing Protocol for Wireless Sensor Networks. IEEE Access **10**, 44123–44135 (2022)

17. Obi, E., Mammeri, Z., Ochia, O. E.: A Lifetime-Aware Centralized Routing Protocol for Wireless Sensor Networks using Reinforcement Learning. In: 2021 17th International Conference on Wireless and Mobile Computing, Networking and Communications (WiMob), pp. 363–368. IEEE, Bologna, Italy (2021)

18. Haakensen, T., Thulasiraman, P.: Enhancing sink node anonymity in tactical sensor networks using a reactive routing protocol. In: 2017 IEEE 8th Annual Ubiquitous Computing, Electronics and Mobile Communication Conference (UEMCON), pp. 115–121. IEEE, New York (2017)

19. Nguyen, S. T., Cayirci, E., Yan, L., Rong, C.: A shadow zone aware routing protocol for tactical acoustic undersea surveillance networks. In: MILCOM 2009–2009 IEEE Military Communications Conference, pp. 1–7. IEEE, Boston (2009)

20. Altowaijri, S.M.: Efficient next-hop selection in multi-hop routing for iot enabled wireless sensor networks. Fut. Internet **14**(2), 35 (2022)

21. Liu, Lei, Liu, Yiming, Wang, Zhaowei, Liu, Chunxu: Design of dynamic tdma protocols for tactical data link. In: Li, Bo., Shu, Lei, Zeng, Deze (eds.) ChinaCom 2017. LNICST, vol. 236, pp. 166–175. Springer, Cham (2018). https://doi.org/10.1007/978-3-319-78130-3_18

22. Sheikholeslami, A., Pishro-Nik, H., Ghaderi, M., Goeckel, D.: On the impact of dynamic jamming on end-to-end delay in linear wireless networks. In: 2014 48th Annual Conference on Information Sciences and Systems (CISS), pp. 1–6. IEEE, Princeton, NJ (2014)

23. Majumdar, S., Trivisonno, R., Carle, G.: Understanding Exploration and Exploitation of Q-Learning Agents in B5G Network Management. In: 2021 IEEE Globecom Workshops (GC Wkshps), pp. 1–6. IEEE, Madrid (2021)

24. Gao, D., Liu, Y., Zhang, F., Song, J.: Anycast routing protocol for forest monitoring in rechargeable wireless sensor networks. Int. J. Distrib. Sens. Netw. **9**(12), 239860 (2013)

25. Wilson, Graeme N.., Ramirez-Serrano, Alejandro, Mustafa, Mahmoud, Davies, Krispin A..: Velocity selection for high-speed ugvs in rough unknown terrains using force prediction. In: Su, Chun-Yi., Rakheja, Subhash, Liu, Honghai (eds.) ICIRA 2012. LNCS (LNAI), vol. 7507, pp. 387–396. Springer, Heidelberg (2012). https://doi.org/10.1007/978-3-642-33515-0_39

A Green and Scalable Clustering for Massive IoT Sensors with Selective Deactivation

Amine Faid[1(✉)], Mohamed Sadik[1], and Essaid Sabir[1,2]

[1] NEST Research Group, LRI Lab, ENSEM, Hassan II University of Casablanca, Casablanca, Morocco
{a.faid,m.sadik,e.sabir}@ensem.ac.ma
[2] Department of Computer Science, University of Quebec at Montreal (UQAM), Montreal, QC H2L 2C4,, Canada

Abstract. Wireless Sensor Networks (WSNs) play an important role in the advancement of today's internet of things (IoT) solutions. It allows the possibility to overcome different classical challenges in the telecommunication domain with the latest modern solutions. Thus, allowing a smooth technological transformation with unprecedented new use cases. Therefore, fields such as healthcare, environment, and industrial usecases are the most demanding areas for implementing such technology. However, WSN comes with several problems, limitations, and constraints impacting its optimized deployment. The most popular dilemma are data privacy, energy efficiency, and computation capabilities. In this paper, we address the energy performance challenge through the design of an enhanced algorithmic approach. We propose a multi-stage and energy-aware clustering algorithm to enhance the energetic performance of wireless networks. The idea behind the proposed algorithm relies on the continuous on-boarding of wireless sensor nodes in different lifetime phases for the progressive construction of a network. Throughout the phases, we apply a k-medoids and LEACH protocols with a trade-off principle for best network clustering. We compare the algorithm results to LEACH protocol and our previous contributions. The extensive simulations have shown a good energetic improvement in different metrics, such as energy dissipation trends, first dead node, last dead node, network lifetime, and energetic dissipation. The results show an improvement of 379% compared to LEACH and 166% compared to K-medoids in terms of the first dead node, while the network performance was enhanced by 379% compared to LEACH and 166% compared to IHEE and 115% compared EACA.

Keywords: IoT · WSN · D2D · M2M

1 Introduction

Nowadays, the extensive investment in technology's key enablers allows the creation of contemporary new services and new products within different

E. Sabir et al. (Eds.): UNet 2022, LNCS 13853, pp. 225–237, 2023.
https://doi.org/10.1007/978-3-031-29419-8_17

areas. Healthcare, military, environment, and industry are the most demanding domains for the new technologies' applications, a demand that is justified by the continuous increase in terms of complexity and the seamless emergence of new business cases. Therefore, emerging technologies, such as the Internet of things (IoT) have opened a new chapter in the ongoing evolution. IoT solutions become key aspects in today's world as they aren't only guiding the technological evolution path but they exceed that into enabling a smooth digital transformation with significant impacts on human being life However, during the coronavirus disease 2019 (COVID-19) period, the pandemic has shown how the global organizations were unusually impacted based on their internal digital transformation's maturity [1]. Thus, a universal need for a global digital transformation has exponentially emerged on the surface. Schools, companies, hospitals, and governments have accelerated their technological innovation adoption more than ever through new approaches for rebuilding their ways of working in a smart, innovative, and sustainable way. IoT, as smart technology, allows the connection of everything at any time and anywhere [2]. Its idea comprises the deployment of tiny connected devices for day-to-day applications such as wireless sensing, cognitive monitoring, automation, and actuation in respective application areas such as Massive IoT, Broadband IoT, Critical IoT, and Industrial IoT. Meanwhile, IoT, like all other innovation domains, comes with drawbacks in various fields. It presents challenges such as privacy and trust, architecture and standards, and safety and security. Additionally, a standalone IoT device is very limited in terms of capability, therefore limited resources for superior performance is always a complex dilemma to overcome. Thus, the idea of geographical-based sub-networking has captured the interest of different field players like researchers, and engineers. IoT solutions can be deployed on top of Wireless Ad-hoc NETwork (WANET), Mobile Ad hoc NETwork (MANET), or WSN to cover large areas.

WANET or MANET is a type of decentralized wireless network since it does not rely on pre-existing communication infrastructures, such as routers in wired networks or access points in managed wireless networks. Therefore, each standalone node takes part in the overall network's routing by forwarding data to other neighbor nodes. The choice of which node to transmit data to is decided dynamically, which depends on the network connection and routing algorithm in use. Self-configuring and dynamic networks in which nodes are free to roam around are known as ad-hoc networks. Without the complexity of infrastructure development and maintenance, wireless sensor networks allow devices to build and join wireless networks anywhere and whenever they choose. General comparison between WSN and Ad-hoc networks is presented in Table 1.

WSN allows creating wirelessly connected nodes in open areas, which allows the possibility to overcome the most known challenges, such as long distances, restricted mobility, and high infrastructure costs [3]. It comprises a group of different standalone nodes in geographic space. Set of nodes that are heterogeneous with limited hardware (HW) and software (SW) configurations. Although the WSN technology is very popular, however, various limitations constrain the massive deployment of such a network, such as a network's reliability, the return on

Table 1. Comparison between WSN vs. Adhoc networks

Feature	WSN	Ad-hoc
Number of nodes	Massive	Medium
Deployment type	Dense	Scattered
Rate of failure	Very high	Very rare
Network topology	Dynamic	Static
Communication	Mesh	Point to point
Battery	Not rechargeable	Replaceable
Centric mode	Based on data	Based on address
Aggregation	Possible	Not suitable
Computational	Limited	Not limited
Data rate	Lower	Higher
Redundancy	High	Low

investment (ROI), the cost of deployment, etc. Thus, its penetration into developing countries remains very limited. Hence, the technological improvement of this technology will lead directly to a positive economic impact on these countries. For these reasons, topics like wireless communication enhancement, energy efficiency, and routing optimization are among the hot areas where studies are continuously conducted to improve WSN efficiency. Because of the physical constraints, energy consumption remains one of the most challenging aspects of WSN solutions. Various techniques and mechanisms have been presented in the literature dealing with energy consumption on a different scale. Networks clustering is a very well-known field that aims to optimize wireless networks into physical or logical subnetworks.

2   Related Works

Many WSN routing algorithms have been developed to improve network performance. The proposed protocols were based on different approaches and detailed in different surveys. [4,5]. In order to tackle challenges such as localization, deployment, routing, energy efficiency, etc. as depicted in Fig. 1. One of the most used protocols for network construction is the hierarchical approach, which combines cluster-based and grid-based methodologies. In a cluster-based strategy, cluster formation can be centralized in the base station (BS) or decentralized in the cluster heads (CHs). In the centralized approach, the BS performs the clustering based on specified criteria such as Line of sight, quality of service, sensitivity, etc. The centralized approach is particularly successful in terms of energy management, with the added benefit of having a comprehensive view of all network nodes and architecture. While, in the decentralized approach, it is the CHs that perform distributed clustering based on a probabilistic algorithm. Low-Energy Adaptive Clustering Hierarchy (LEACH), as introduced in

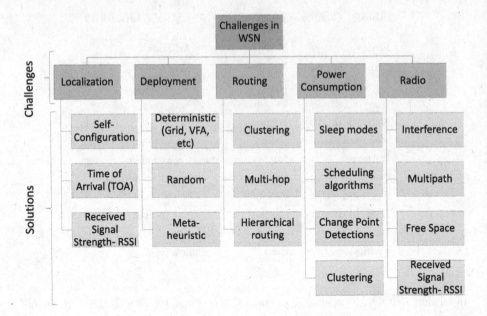

Fig. 1. Wireless sensor network challenges and solutions.

[6], is indisputably the most famous protocol for WSN clustering. LEACH uses low-cost, energy-efficient sensors to produce higher-quality clustering in wireless networks. For a balanced energy distribution in the network, LEACH arranges itself via adaptive clustering, cluster head rotation, and local computation. The set-up phase and the steady-state phase are two crucial phases of LEACH. The set-up phase, which aims to minimize overhead, is shorter than the steady-state phase. The CH is typically chosen first in LEACH before the clusters are generated. Equation 1 illustrates LEACH's overall structure. In LEACH, the cluster is established once the cluster head has been chosen.

$$T(n) = \begin{cases} \frac{P}{1-P\left(r \bmod \left(\frac{1}{P}\right)\right)}, & \forall n \in \mathcal{G} \\ 0, & \forall n \notin \mathcal{G} \end{cases} \tag{1}$$

where p represents the desired cluster heads' percentage within the WSN. r represents the current algorithm's iteration. $\mathcal{G}$ represents the set of nodes that weren't elected as CH in the 1/P round.

In this work, we explore the advantages of using K-means clustering as a non-metaheuristic algorithm for cluster formation. K-means idea is built around forming clusters from the centroids that are selected before the cluster's formation. The K-means algorithm calculates the range between every point in the dataset and every one of the k selected points, then assigns the points to the k point that is closest to them. The mean of all data contributing to the cluster is then used to calculate the k point of the new cluster. The aim function for k-means can be shown in the following equation:

$$J = \sum_{i=1}^{C_k} \sum_{j=1}^{C_i} d\left(x_i, x_j\right) \tag{2}$$

In the literature, a modified k-means technique was suggested by the authors in [7] to determine the ideal centroid and create clusters. They established only 3 clusters because the k value in this literature is 3, which may restrict scalability. After identifying the three centroids, they perform several iterations until they identify the best means. The final CH then chooses two additional CHs that are closer to it to load, share, and reduce the energy consumption of a single CH. The authors of [8] suggested a lifetime-enhanced cooperative data gathering and relaying algorithm (LCDGRA) for event-driven monitoring applications. Since it guarantees that the sensor node's transmission distance and energy consumption are optimized during the clustering phase, LCDGRA adopts Huffman entropy coding in K-means clustering. In addition, the authors in [9] proposed a nonuniform clustering routing technique based on a strengthened K-means algorithm. To lessen the randomness of centroid selection based on a threshold function, a clustering point selection method is included in the suggested approach. To avoid blind iterations and quickly locate the centroid. The threshold function is built using numerous nearby nodes and a few iterations. The K-means method exhibits higher performance in terms of decreased energy usage, balanced network, and increased network lifetime, as shown by the simulations of the aforementioned research. Additionally, by utilizing an upgraded K-Means method, the authors of [10] proposed an optimal Q-learning-based clustering and load balancing technique. By taking into account throughput, end-to-end delay, packet delivery ratio, and energy usage, the suggested Q-Learning-based clustering algorithm maximizes the reward. Existing k-means-based clustering algorithms were examined for performance and compared to the Q-learning algorithm's performance.

3   System Model

Since transmission dominates the WSN, we are particularly interested in how much energy it uses in our work. We are relying on the most widely acknowledged and applied model in the literature, the Radio energy model used in the LEACH. The radio energy model for each sensor node is shown in Fig. 2. Wireless range and energy are typically inversely correlated. The two main phenomena that have a substantial impact on each node's power usage during transmission are free space and multi-path. Equations 3 and 4 are used to present the energy consumption during transmission $E_{Tx}(k, d)$ and reception $E_{Rx}(k)$.

$$E_{Tx}(k, d) = \begin{cases} E_{\text{elec}} \times k + \varepsilon_{fs} \times k \times d^2, d < d_0 \\ E_{\text{elec}} \times k + \varepsilon_{mp} \times k \times d^4, d \geq d_0 \end{cases} \tag{3}$$

$$E_{Rx}(k) = E_{elec} \times k \tag{4}$$

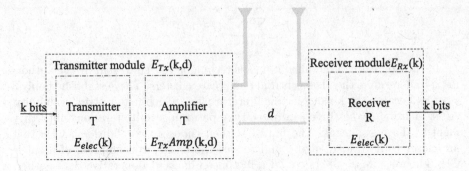

Fig. 2. Energy consumption model.

In our testings, we deploy a WSN with N evenly dispersed heterogeneous nodes that are randomly placed in a 100-by-100 m region. Identical properties, such as GPS modules, battery modules, radio, etc. characterize the nodes. We broke the network up into K clusters. A set of cluster member nodes characterizes each cluster. In the same cluster, the K node, which plays the role of a gateway, is recurrently chosen based on the node's availability and the energy threshold E_t, as presented in Eq. 5. The K-node is considered the only valid gateway for the entire K-cluster toward the BS. As a result, in each round, the K node needs to be permanently connected to LEACH's CHs. The K-cluster's CM nodes are disallowed from engaging other cluster nodes. Within each K-cluster, m CHs are chosen for each round. The CHs make sure that local data is collected from pertinent sensor nodes and sent to the corresponding k node. Only the gateway can exchange messages with the chosen CHs and aggregate the data before sending it to the sink. The BS is situated away from the study space. When data is received, the BS saves it locally before sending it to the cloud for remote management and control.

$$E_t = \frac{\overline{E}}{E_{int}} \times 100\% \tag{5}$$

where E_t is the initial energy of the wireless nodes in Joule. While $\overline{E}$ presents the network's mean energy at the current iteration. The calculated energy ratio in 5 shows how much the cluster mean energy differs from the nodes' initial energy. The result of this ratio serves as the primary parameter to specify the algorithm's energy threshold for choosing the subsequent K-cluster nodes. According to Eq. 6, we suggest four levels of thresholds for our WSN algorithm: E_{th1}, E_{th2}, E_{th3}, and E_{th4}. The levels are allocated to a set of the E_t ranges.

$$E_{thi} = \alpha_i \times E_{int} : \frac{i-1}{100} < E_t \leq \frac{i*25}{100} \tag{6}$$

where α_i is the proportion of the starting energy associated with each E_{ti} range, and E_{thi} is the i_{th} energy threshold.

4   Proposed Algorithm

Our proposed algorithm is based on a multi-stage and energy-aware energy efficiency in WSN for massive IoTs. We broke the algorithm down into 3 main phases
which are the ramp-up phase, the steady-phase, and the ramp-down phase. We
can illustrate the holistic view as in Fig. 3.

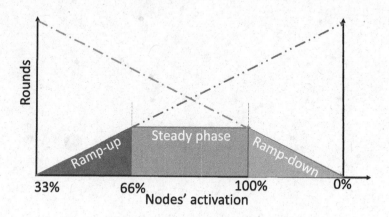

Fig. 3. Network's multi-phases

The purpose behind the activation of the progressive nodes' onboarding is to
limit the energy dissipation within the nodes due to the wireless communication
and to extend the network's life. Deactivating nodes within the same Sensing
range and the continuous onboarding of these nodes will have minimal impact on
the quality of the collected data since the meteorological data is near constant at
the time. In Fig. 4, we can see that the random deployment of nodes may create
a state where several nodes are conducting the same sensing range.

4.1   Ramp-Up Phase

The first stage entails splitting the network into K sub-networks and regrouping
nodes under the K clusters. The procedure is carried out using a calculation
of Euclidean distance. The best K parameter for the network clustering is first
determined using the elbow technique, which forms the basis for the K choice,
and involves calculating the network Sum Squared Error (SSE) to various K
parameters. The following equation is used to determine the SSE:

$$SSE_{\mathcal{K}} = \sum_{k \in \mathcal{K}} \sum_{i \in \mathcal{C}_k} d(x_i, x_k) \qquad (7)$$

K is the number of clusters found throughout each iteration. The set of k-
medoids points is called C_k. The collection of points called C_j is connected to

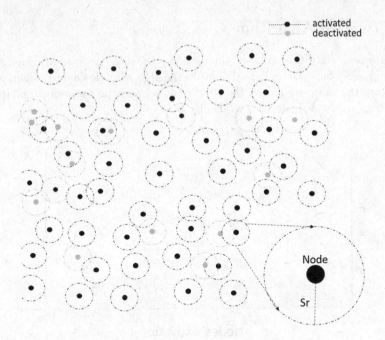

Fig. 4. Random nodes' deployment

each cluster of k. A cluster's medoid point is x_i, and cluster k's x_j is the cluster's $x_t h$ point.

In contrast to K-means, the K-medoids algorithm chooses actual network nodes from the network to serve as the network's centroids. The cluster's nodes are chosen at random, and the distance between the chosen node and them is calculated. The goal of the partition approach is to reduce the distance between the chosen node and the cluster nodes. The equation shown below can express the k-medoids formula:

$$X_{\text{medoid}} = \begin{cases} \sum\limits_{i=1}^{n}_{x=x_1,x_2,\cdots,x_n} d\left(x, x_i\right), \forall x \in \mathcal{G} \\ 0, \qquad\qquad\qquad\quad \forall x \notin \mathcal{G} \end{cases} \tag{8}$$

where $\mathcal{G}$ is the set of nodes with energy $E \; \llcorner \; E_{thi}$

The rump-up phase refers to the stage where the algorithm continuously engages new nodes in the network. According to Fig. 5, the nodes' onboarding is done when the number of dead nodes S_n is reaching 33% compared to the initial nodes.

4.2   Steady Phase

The clusters function as independent sub-networks. Once the network has been divided, the k-medoids serve as a gateway, and LEACH begins grouping the sub-networks into logical sub-clusters at each round. For better k-medoids rotation,

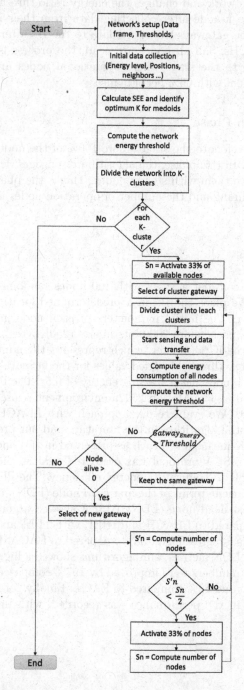

Fig. 5. Flow chart of the proposed algorithm.

the BS scans the network and changes the energy ratio threshold E_t. The CHs transfer data to the k-node after collecting data from their respective cluster members (GW). The gateways transport data to the BS after condensing data from the relevant CHs. Till all nodes are dead, the process is repeated. Thus, steady-phase refers to the stage where operational nodes are stable and the network is operational with 66% performance.

4.3   Ramp-Down Phase

Rump-down phase refers to the stage where 100% of the nodes are operational within the network. In this phase, the algorithm disengages dead nodes without being able to replace them with steady nodes. This is the phase where network performance is declining and the number of operation nodes is on a continuous decrease.

5   Simulations

For simulation, we consider a WSN with 100 nodes randomly placed in a 100 × 100 m2 space. We place the BS in a predetermined location that is outside the WSN perimeter. The initial parameters of each node in the network are the same. The data packets are 2000 bits in size (250Kbytes). According to the elbow's approach, the K parameter, which represents the number of clusters, is fixed to 3. The energy thresholds' fixed values for the network's α_i are 0%, 25%, 50%, and 75%. Each node has a starting energy of 0.5j. The likelihood that CH will be elected is 20%. The Matlab 2022a environment is used to simulate the system performance. We evaluate our approach with LEACH and K-medoids, the primary referential algorithm in the literature and our previously improved hybrid versions of K-means and Leach as presented in [11] and [12].

The suggested MSEA protocol was evaluated against the LEACH, IHEE, and EACA protocols to confirm its energy efficiency. The illustration in Fig. 6 shows the performance in terms of the first dead node (FDN), the half-dead node (HDN), and the last dead node (LDN). MSEA showed a good performance in terms of FDN compared to LEACH and IHEE with 119% and 4% respectively. Meanwhile, it shows a regression of -35% compared to EACA. However, when we compare HDN and LDN metrics, our algorithms showed a high improvement. In terms of HDN, the numbers were improved by 197% compared to LEACH, 36% compared to IHEE, and 12% compared to EACA. Finally, for the LDN, another high improvement in the performance was recorded, with increasing values of

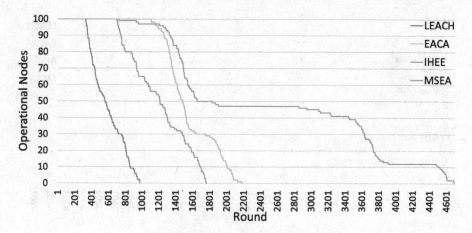

Fig. 6. Operational nodes per transmission.

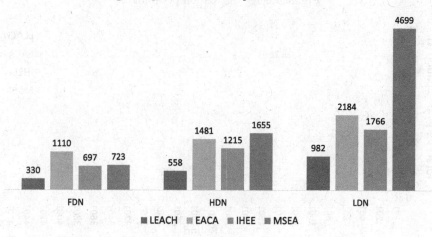

Fig. 7. Rounds of the first, half, and last dead node.

379% compared to LEACH, 166% compared to IHEE, and 115% compared to EACA. The rounds' mapping is presented in Fig 7.

We illustrate energy dissipation and accumulative energy consumption in Fig. 8 and Fig. 9. From the profile's behavior, we can conclude that the proposed approach balanced the energy consumption throughout the rounds, which allows us to expand the network lifetime by avoiding the high consumption of power in the wireless nodes.

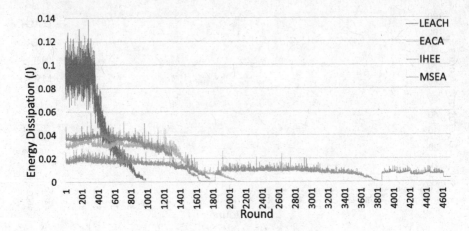

Fig. 8. Energy dissipation per round.

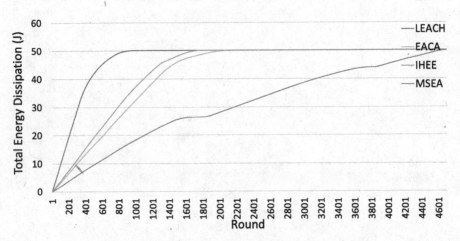

Fig. 9. Accumulative energy dissipation per round.

6   Conclusion

To improve the energetic performance of WSN for IoT, we suggested a multi-stage, energy-aware clustering approach in this study. The principle of our approach is based on integrating a distributed LEACH protocol and an optimized centralized K-medoids algorithm for self-organizing networks. The method deploys a dynamic threshold computation and configuration within the WSN and a continual onboarding of wireless nodes in various life cycle phases for a progressive creation of a network. This approach allows the protection of nodes' resources, such as computation resources, battery, radio, etc. which leads to efficiency improvement. When compared to LEACH and K-medoids, our approach performs well in the simulation. The first dead node, the half-dead node, the last dead node, and the trending of energy usage were used to compare performance. To enhance our results and verify the validity of our methodology in large-scale networks we will include additional metrics like entropy, latency, and throughput in our next work.

Acknowledgment. This work has been conducted within the framework of the Meteorological Station Project funded by the Moroccan Ministry of Higher Education and Scientific Research, and the National Centre for Scientific and Technical Research (Meteorological Station Platform-PPR2).

References

1. Fletcher, G., Griffiths, M.: Digital transformation during a lockdown. Int. J. Inf. Manag. **55**, 102185 (2020)
2. Riahi Sfar, A., Natalizio, E., Challal, Y., Chtourou, Z.: A roadmap for security challenges in the Internet of Things. Digit. Commun. Netw. **4**(2), 118–137 (2018)
3. Lashkari, B., Chen, Y., Musilek, P.: Energy management for smart homes-state of the art. Appl. Sci. **9**(17) (2019)
4. Shahraki, A., Taherkordi, A., Haugen, Ø., Eliassen, F.: Clustering objectives in wireless sensor networks: a survey and research direction analysis. Comput. Netw. **180**, 107376 (2020)
5. Raj, B., Ahmedy, I., Idris, M.Y.I., Noor, R.M.: a survey on cluster head selection and cluster formation methods in wireless sensor networks. Wirel. Commun. Mob. Comput. **2022**, 5322649 (2022)
6. Heinzelman, W.R., Chandrakasan, A., Balakrishnan, H.: Energy-efficient communication protocol for wireless microsensor networks. In: Proceedings of the 33rd Annual Hawaii International Conference on System Sciences, vol. 1, p. 10 (2000)
7. Periyasamy, S., Khara, S., Thangavelu, S.: Balanced cluster head selection based on modified k-means in a distributed wireless sensor network. Int. J. Distrib. Sens. Netw. **12**(3), 5040475 (2016)
8. Agbulu, G.P., Kumar, G.J.R., Juliet, A.V.: A lifetime-enhancing cooperative data gathering and relaying algorithm for cluster-based wireless sensor networks. Int. J. Distrib. Senso. Netw. **16**(2) (2020)
9. Tang, X., Zhang, M., Yu, P., Liu, W., Cao, N., Xu, Y.: A nonuniform clustering routing algorithm based on an improved k-means algorithm. Comput. Mater. Continua **64**(3), 1725–1739 (2020)
10. Sathyamoorthy, M., Kuppusamy, S., Dhanaraj, R.K., Ravi, V.: Improved K-means based q learning algorithm for optimal clustering and node balancing in WSN. Wirel. Pers. Commun. **122**(3), 2745–2766 (2022)
11. Faid, A., Sadik, M., Sabir, E.: IHEE: an improved hybrid energy efficient algorithm for WSN. In: Arai, K. (ed.) FICC 2021. AISC, vol. 1364, pp. 283–298. Springer, Cham (2021). https://doi.org/10.1007/978-3-030-73103-8_19
12. Faid, A., Sadik, M., Sabir, E.: EACA: an energy aware clustering algorithm for wireless IoT sensors. In: 2021 28th International Conference on Telecommunications (ICT), pp. 1–6 (2021)

Pervasive Services and Cyber Security

Threat Mitigation Model with Low False Alarm Rate Based on Hybrid Deep Belief Network

Avewe Bassene[✉] and Bamba Gueye

Université Cheikh Anta Diop, Dakar, Senegal
{avewe.bassene,bamba.gueye}@ucad.edu.sn

Abstract. Most Deep Learning techniques propose solutions against Distributed Denial of Service (DDoS) attacks by leveraging networking enhanced programming abilities. However, all these proposals lack robustness since it struggles to cope with the false alarm rate, which is the amount of normal traffic classified as not being normal. A former work, called DeepDDoS, provides an Intrusion Prevention System (ISP) that detects and mitigates, in real time fashion, DDoS attacks within a healthcare-based IoT environment. However, rather than restricting the access of a single malicious device, the authors define blocking rules according to the entire subnet. In the event of a false positive decision, DeepDDoS will actively interrupt normal activities that may impact real-time patient data monitoring and consequently affect decision-making with respect to critical healthcare IoT devices such as blood pressure, blood sugar levels, oxygen, ECGs, etc. In this work, we take the advantage of an extra pre-training step in Deep Belief Network (DBN) model with a feed-forward backpropagation network to minimize the false positive rate (FPR) in cybersecurity concerns. Our obtained results show the effectiveness of our hybrid proposition, called *soft-DBN*, that successfully reduces FPR lower than 0.30%.

Keywords: Intrusion detection · Internet of Things · Hybrid Deep Belief Network · Self-Security

1 Introduction

There is a blurring line between Intrusion Detection and Intrusion Prevention Systems (*IDS* and *IPS* respectively). In fact, IDS monitors network traffic and alerts security personnel upon discovery of an attack, whereas, IPS actively stops the threat by maintaining an offensive action such as blocking or deletion. In a production environment, an IPS will take initiatives that can cripple the entire network when DDoS attacks occur. A potentially life-threatening event in a medical environment if a bad prediction decision is made.

DDoS attacks attempt to target the server's availability and impede the ability of designated and authorized individuals to access resources. Previous studies such as [1–8] tackle DDoS attack problems. However, the real challenge besides attack detection systems is to maintain a consistently low false alarm

E. Sabir et al. (Eds.): UNet 2022, LNCS 13853, pp. 241–252, 2023.
https://doi.org/10.1007/978-3-031-29419-8_18

rate while performing in a real-time fashion. A state-of-the-art, DeepDDoS [5] IPS, in its build-in mechanism, will block an entire network if ever a false alarm is detected which could result in valuable data loss. A situation that can commonly happen given the consequent false alarm rate of DeepDDoS (nearly 3.33%).

Deep Learning (DL) overcomes many of the traditional multilayer perceptrons/artificial neural networks shortcomings regarding "local minima" that comes from backpropagation. DBN is an important model in deep learning. With it class of Restricted Boltzmann Machines (RBMs) methods, DBN has recently gained popularity thanks to proposed results across a wide range of applications as demonstrated in [9,10]. DBN is a probabilistic generator model consisting of a series of (RBM) units whose training and learning ability has allowed us to reduce false alarms in the detection of DDoS cyberattack types. This paper proposes an approach to reducing the false positive rate based on the hybrid Deep Belief Network (DBN) model between binary RBMs [11] and softmax layer with sigmoid belief networks.

Firstly, RBMs are used to optimize the network parameters of the deep belief network; extract feature vectors of DDoS time series data at the flow scale. Secondly, the RBM stack is combined with a softmax layer for prediction concerns. The weights of the softmax layer are then refined using backpropagation for classification purposes. The contributions of this paper are as follows:

- We propose new deep learning-based models, named soft-DBN, including a hybrid DBN with multiple RBMs layers linked to a sigmoid neural network to classify DDoS attack types.
- The features of the studied dataset are preprocessed mainly in three specific steps for the detection process fluency: Min-Max normalization, Equal Width Discretization, and features extraction using a correlation-based Feature Selection algorithm.
- We provide a performance evaluation and comparative analysis of proposed soft-DBN approach in DDoS attacks performing.
- The model's performance is studied within binary classification type over an up-to-date real traffic, CICDDoS2019.

The rest of the paper is organized as follows. Section 2 reviews related works. Section 3 presents the proposed model architecture along with its practical operation, including the model training and optimization. Section 4 gives experimental environment setup. Section 5 provides a comparative analysis of soft-DBN and discusses obtained results. Finally, Sect. 6 concludes this paper.

2   Related Work

Various motivations have led to numerous proposals to optimize DDoS attack detection efficiency. However, these approaches suffer from a high false positive rate, which means classifying legitimate traffic data as potentially dangerous.

In [12], Ferrag et al. propose three deep learning-based IDS models, including a CNN-based IDS model, a deep neural network-based IDS model, and a

RNN-based IDS model to mitigate DDoS attacks in agriculture 4.0. The binary and multiclass classification performances show that the CNN-based IDS model outperforms with at least 99.92% of accuracy and a poor average false positive rate up to 3, 13% depending on models.

A high accuracy IDS model based on DL is proposed by Manimurugan et al. in [13]. Despite the obtained high-performance value (up to 96%), no false positive rate estimation, which is essential for medical decision-making, is given by the authors. Latah et al. [6] propose an IDS system that achieves a false positive rate of 3.99% while investigating the performance of the well-known anomaly-based intrusion detection approaches over the NSL-KDD benchmark dataset. Furthermore, a hybrid SDN-based approach tries to minimize false positive rate in DoS attack detection [7]. Experimental results exhibit a FPR equals to 0.3% with an accuracy of 91.27%. It is worth noticing that the accuracy rates is very low according to previous work [5].

In [5], the authors propose an IPS, named DeepDDoS, that detects and mitigates DDoS attacks within software-defined healthcare IoT networks. DeepDDoS with a high prediction ability of 98.8%, can forward any suspicious traffic through the SDN control plan for mitigation decisions. However, DeepDDoS suffers from high FPR.

In this work, we aim to minimize the FPR within a given intrusion detection system by combining multiple RBMs layers and a neural network with backpropagation as parts of our new hybrid DBN model. Therefore, we address the false positive rate reduction for DDoS attack types by using a hybrid DBN model that proceeds feature selection and classification in a layer-by-layer fashion.

3 Proposed Hybrid DBN Model

3.1 Theoretical Aspect of DBN Model

The background regarding DBN is to solve "local minima" comes from backpropagation in artificial or perceptrons neural networks. As a solution, DBN adds a pre-trained step to models before backpropagation. This extra step brings closer to the solution's "neighborhood" with some error rate which is reduced by using backpropagation. Thus, DBN is partitioned between multiple layers of RBN to pre-train the network and a fine-tuned process is performed by feed-forward backpropagation network from binary output of RBM stacks.

The RBM mechanism mimics bipartite graph properties where processing data consists of a single visible layer v called the input layer and a set of multiple n-dimension h of hidden neurons where the model attempts to match these entries to minimize system energy. The main purpose of the RBN process is to reduce joint energy between visible and hidden layers based on the Bernoulli distribution described by **Eq.** 1. The RBM admits no link between neurons of the same layer, and thus, neurons of different layers are connected with the weight matrix W that contains weight values between visible and hidden layers. The term weight stands for interconnection between two consecutive input and hidden layers. **Table** 1 gives **Eq.** 1 parameters nomenclature.

Table 1. Key nomenclatures.

m	The dimensions of the visible layers
n	the dimensions of the hidden layers
b	The bias vectors of m
c	The bias vectors of n
W_{ij}	The connection between visible unit i and the hidden unit j
$\sigma(x) = \frac{1}{1+exp(-x)}$	activation function (logistic-sigmoid function)
c_i	e_i link capacity
b_i	Current bandwidth load on e_i
a_i	Available bandwidth on e_i

$$E(v,h) = -\sum_{i=1}^{m} b_i v_i - \sum_{j=1}^{n} c_j h_j - \sum_{i=1}^{m}\sum_{j=1}^{n} w_{ij} v_i h_j \tag{1}$$

Solving this problem amounts to finding an estimate of the conditional probabilities (CP) of the visible and hidden neurons. Hinton's proposal [14], named Contrastive Divergence (CD), allows to estimate the CP of visible and hidden neurons either by using **Eq. 2** or **Eq. 3**. The **Eq. 2** gives the activation probability of the jth neural unit of layer h when v is known, while inversely, **Eq. 3** refers to the activation probability of the ith neural unit of the visible layer v. The parameters in **Eq. 2** and **Eq. 3** are well defined in **Table 1**. Each neuron in each layer will be able to resolve its state value between 0 and 1 with probability p. By using a few cycles of Markov Chain Monte Carlo ($MCMC$) sampling, the Hinton algorithm enables us to: (i) transform our training data (drawn from the target distribution) into data drawn from the proposed distribution; (ii) provide a sense of where the proposed distribution should evolve to better model training data.

$$p(h_i = 1|v) = \sigma(c_j + \sum_{i=1}^{m} w_{ij} v_i \tag{2}$$

$$p(v_i = 1|h) = \sigma(b_i + \sum_{j=1}^{n} w_{ij} h_j \tag{3}$$

3.2 Practical Aspect of the Proposed Hybrid Model

The multilayers RBM that composes DBN are used to train dataset layer-by-layer. The training parameters values are used recursively between layers so that output from the previous layer is refined as input for the next layer. Indeed, DBN acts as a unsupervised learning model. A learning representation of input data is then converted into a supervised prediction. Training RBM layers with a dataset allows us to get model parameters. The training process is approximated based on CD algorithm and it also improves efficiency [15]. This paper first uses DBN to extract the essential features from the CICDDoS2019 [16] by the training and learning of RBM stacks. The abstract features gained from the training are then used as the input to softmax layer. The softmax layer located at the top level of our model is used to optimize RBMs processing results over backpropagation for classification purposes. The proposed hybrid model is depicted in Fig. 1.

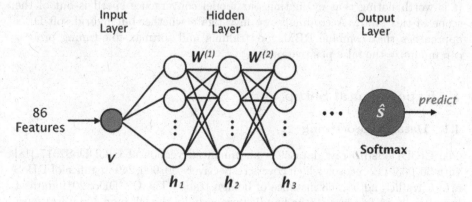

Fig. 1. soft-DBN architecture with 3 hidden layers

Figure 1 shows soft-DBN architecture, with n-dimensions h_x hidden layers connected by the weights matrix $W^{(l)}$ with $l \in [1, L]$. The parameter L stands for the number of hidden layers. According to the soft-DBN training process, the dataset is first unsupervised trained based on a greedy layer-wise approach. Afterward, the supervised softmax layer performs a fine-tuned stage from the DBN layer (upper RBM unit) for labeled sample feature enhancement. The softmax layer is a sigmoid neural network attached at the top of our soft-DBN model to perform classification after the DBN pre-training phase. It fine-tunes the model using ADAM [17] optimization function through with a fixed learning rate for each layer of the sigmoid neural network.

It is worth noticing that the soft-DBN process is twofold: (i) a feature extraction process using DBN pre-training phase; (ii) a DDoS attacks traffic classification with softmax layer. Each of these folds has its own experimental parameters that will be depicted in Sect. 4.2. Moreover, the proposed soft-DBN processing steps are as follows:

1. Determination of DBN learning parameters (RBM layers). Initialize learning rate and the number of iterations.
2. Use of the CD algorithm to pre-train each layer of RBM and find the optimal initial weight of the network model. It prevents DBN from falling into the local optimum during the training process. It also ensures optimal weight values for each layer for features vector mapping. At the end of this pre-training phase, features extraction and therefore, the reduction of the size of the dataset are ensured. A features selection process will be detailed in Sect. 4.1.

3. Determination of the softmax layer parameters. In soft-DBN processing steps, the higher RBM layer output will be used as input to the softmax layer training phase. The softmax layer training phase gives optimal parameters to build our final prediction model.
4. Estimation of the best prediction model to adopt based on specified threshold error rate.

It is worth noting that evaluating our model convergence speed is out of the scope of this study. Accordingly, we investigate whether our hybrid soft-DBN approaches that combine RBMs pre-training and softmax fine-tuning process can minimize the false positive rate.

4   Experimental Setup

4.1   Data Preprocessing

The CICDDoS2019 raw dataset is an enhanced version of CICDDoS2017 [18] with $50,063,112$ records which covers respectively $50,006,249$ instance of DDoS attack traffic and $56,863$ instance of benign traffic. The CICDDoS2019 dataset has globally 86 features. To be handled properly by the DL model, dataset must be presented to the model in a specific form. This data preparation operation is called preprocessing. The preprocessing tends to fit the dataset in the best range within three major actions, each of them has its advantages; data normalization, data discretization, and the features selection process.

Data normalization (known as standardization or feature scaling) is a main step of data preprocessing in any ML model fitting. It transforms data in such a way as to be dimensionless and/or have similar distributions. One of its advantages is that it gives equal weight to all CICDDoS2019 features based on a fixed range. In this work, the Min-Max normalization function is used to process the conversion of our data samples. The Min-Max normalization is shown to be the more efficient normalization approach [8] and it performs based on given **Eq.** 4. It converts each value from σ to σ^* that is suitable in the range of $[A, B]$.

$$\sigma^* = \frac{\sigma - \sigma_{min}}{\sigma_{max} - \sigma_{min}} \tag{4}$$

The discretization transform provides an automatic way to change a numeric input variable to have a different data distribution, which in turn can be used as input to a predictive model. It is also called a binning and can improve the performance of some machine learning models for datasets by making the probability distribution of numerical input variables discrete. Here, Equal Width Discretization (EWD) is performed as a discretization function to transform a continuous field to bins. In EWD, values for the variable are grouped together into discrete bins. Each bin is assigned a unique integer so that the ordinal relation between bins is kept. EWD has divided lines of numbers between $Vmax$ and $Vmin$ at k intervals. The **Eq.** 5 defines the considered interval width in

EWD. In **Eq.** 5, N denotes the interval and A and B are the lowest and highest values of the features.

$$W = \frac{B - A}{N} \tag{5}$$

$$r_{zc} = \frac{k\overline{r_{zi}}}{\sqrt{k + k(k-1)\overline{r_{ii}}}} \tag{6}$$

In the features selection process, irrelevant and redundant features in the dataset are removed. One of the advantages of this operation is the improvement of prediction accuracy and redundancy avoidance, which moderate the computational cost of modeling. While we are performing unsupervised learning (DBN), Correlation-based Feature Selection (CFS) is used to select a subset of the input features from the dataset without considering target features and removing redundant variables (correlation).

According to CFS, the target variable is removed since it keeps a strong relationship with the other features. The evaluation of a subset r_{zc} in CFS is given by **Eq.** 6. Where $\overline{r_{zi}}$ is the mean correlation between a feature subset and an outside feature, and $\overline{r_{ii}}$ is the average feature-to-feature intercorrelation of a feature subset containing k features.

4.2 Experimental Parameters

Soft-DBN is a deep learning model that connects three stacked RBMs and one sigmoid neural network model. The experimental phase is twofold. In a pre-training approach based on DBN layer processing with a batch of size 128, a learning rate of 0.1, the bottommost RBM is trained with the original input data with 50 epochs and 25 epochs for intermediate and top RBM.

After the RBMs training phase, the output of the last hidden layer of the DBN is used for classification. Finally, soft-DBN can efficiently output the predicted probability value according to the softmax layer. In this classification phase, the softmax layer performs a fine-tuning process for 20 epochs. Each of the softmax layers' learning rate is fixed to 0.001. To assess the robustness of soft-DBN, 10 distinct executions of soft-DBN are performed with 10 different DBN networks that differ according to the number of hidden neurons and layers. The testbed results will be described in Sect. 5.

5 Experimental Results

5.1 Results

The experimental study assesses the performance of the proposed FPR minimization system in terms of FPR values and "$Accuracies$" (Ac). The mathematical expressions of Ac and FPR metrics are computed as mentioned in **Eq.** 7 and **Eq.** 8 respectively.

Table 2. Experimental results on different number of neurons and hidden layers

$RBMH_{size}$	Average Accuracies (AAc) (%)	
	Soft-DBN	DeepDDoS
#1. 500;200;50	94	97
#2. 500;200;200;50	98.42	92.57
#3. 500;200;200;200;50	98.67	98.77
#4. 500;500;500;500;50	97.20	98.63
#5. 1000;1000;50	96.33	97.51
#6. 1000;1000;1000;50	97	97.41
#7. 1000;1000;1000;1000;50	98.5	98.80
#8. 2000;2000;50	96.56	97
#9. 2000;2000;2000;50	97.63	98.40
#10.2000;2000;2000;2000;50	98.74	94.57

FPR refers to the number of nonattacking events incorrectly labeled as attacks, or the number of falsely classified normal DDoS traffic instances while the Ac indicates how close our model decision is to the actual true value. Ac measurement is significant since it might be caused by various factors from defective devices to human error [8,19].

$$Ac = \frac{TP + TN}{TP + TN + FP + FN} \qquad (7)$$

$$FPR = \frac{FP}{TN + FP} \qquad (8)$$

According to **Eq.** 7 and **Eq.** 8, TP indicates attack samples that are correctly classified as an attack, whereas TN, the benign samples that are correctly classified as benign. FP refers to the benign samples that are incorrectly classified as an attack; FN indicates the attack samples that are incorrectly classified as benign.

Concerning evaluation, we varied the number of RBM hidden neurons and layers to assess the soft-DBN robustness. We choose 10 random scenarios that are evaluated 10 times. **Table 2** depicts the "*Average Accuracies*" (AAc) values according to the sets of performed simulations. For instance, each scenario is illustrated by considering a fixed line from #1 to #10. In fact, the number of RBM layers increases from 3 to 5 with different numbers of neurons within each RBM layer. For instance, in **Table 2**, the line #1 shows the 3 layers whereas the different values between semicolon's exhibit the number of used neurons within each layer. The minimum, the maximum and the average FPR values were recorded in each of the 10 scenarios.

Figure 2 and **Fig.** 3 illustrate a comparative evaluation between soft-DBN and DeepDDoS based on different scenarios, as illustrated in **Table 2**, and a couple of metrics. Indeed, **Fig.** reffig:minMax(a) (respectively **Fig.** 2(b)) depict the minimum FPR (respectively maximum FPR) obtained by considered 10 simulations series for each scenario. The *X-axis* shows the number of scenarios and the *Y-axis* the min, max, or average FPR according to selected figures (**Fig. 2**, **Fig. 3**).

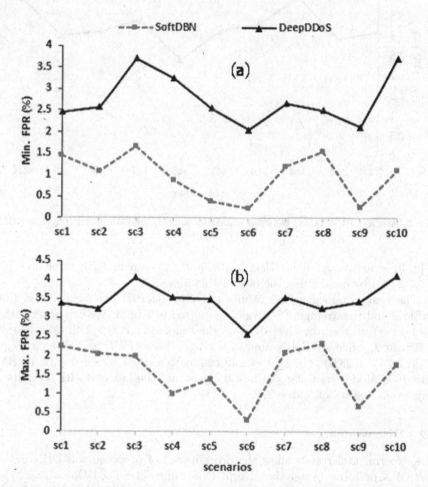

Fig. 2. Min and Max FPR values between soft-DBN and DeepDDoS under different RBMs

Table 2 provides the AAc rate based on hidden RBMs layers and size ($RBMH_{size}$) as well a comparative evaluation between soft-DBN and Deep-DDoS over CICDDoS2019 dataset. Based on results in **Table** 2, **Fig.** 2 and **Fig.** 3, one can observe that soft-DBN detection system achieves the best $AFPR$ (near 0.28%) with a minimum value of approximately 0.22% (**Fig.** 2 (a)) while processing scenario 6. However, soft-DBN records the lowest accuracy values compared to DeepDDoS [5]. Furthermore, DeepDDoS provides the highest accuracy rate compared to the proposed soft-DBN, nonetheless, the max $AFPR$ in

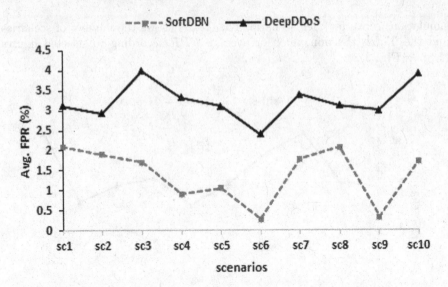

Fig. 3. Average FPR values between soft-DBN and DeepDDoS under different RBMs

(**Fig. 3**) is on average higher than 3.30%, and a maximum FPR value up to 4% (**Fig. 2** (b)) by considering the overall scenarios.

The best obtained mixed results ($ACC - AFPR$) can be deduced from **Table** 2 and the average FPR values reported in **Fig.** 3. We can observe that the best result given by DeepDDoS is the couple (97.41% − 2.40%) in line #6 of **Table** 2, while soft-DBN approach gives a lower FPR as well as a couple of (97.00% − 0.28%). The best overall results were then obtained with 4 RBMs with 1000 hidden units for the first 3 layers and the last one with 50 units as denoted in line #6 of **Table** 2.

5.2 Discussions

The experimental results show the preeminence of proposed soft-DBN model. Soft-DBN performs better than DeepDDoS while detecting DDoS attack types in terms of minimizing FPR. The lines #2 and #4 in **Table** 2 and **Fig.** 3 show best combined ($AAc-AFPR$) results for DeepDDoS, however, either the $AFPR$ is too high (line #4), or either the AAc value is too low compared to soft-DBN. False alarms may be triggered in two ways: from network anomalies or raised from a specific unusual, albeit legitimate traffic. The detection decision of IDS comes from a short time (ms-scale) flow inspection, which can be not enough as an expected batch of data for decision making. That is one of the weaknesses in DeepDDoS [5].

Soft-DBN uses CFS to reduce the data dimension and the redundancy in data. A processing that ensures a low false positive probability in undersampling cases, and accordingly, an optimal size of data that will be needed for decision making. In addition, the pre-training step is the main key that put us in the vicinity of the minimal solution (reducing error surface) and thus avoids overfitting that can be caused by "local minima". Afterward, this error rate is considerably reduced by backpropagation steps.

False alarms can be also caused by the high packet loss rates in network communication. We didn't study this scenario because it assumed that this probability is extremely low [20]. Soft-DBN's best setup seems to be the one with 4 RBMs described in line #6 of **Table** 2. By leveraging this specific implementation under 20 iterations, we note that soft-DBN converges less quickly than DeepDDoS [5] after 8 epochs. DeepDDoS stays the most accurate technique when globally considering all 20 iterations, however its high RPF rate makes it a model to improve.

This paper also highlights the trade-off between obtaining a model with a low FPR value and a model with low converge delay. This is certainly the result of the significant training delay required by the model to concurrently deal with both high sensitivity value and low false positive rate. Whatever, a long training delay is a hindrance to real-time systems deployment.

6   Conclusion

In this paper, we proposed soft-DBN, a hybrid Deep Belief Networks approach based on RBNs layers pre-training for feature extraction combined with a sigmoid neural network attached at the top of RBM stack. Soft-DBN performs DDoS attack prediction with a very low false positive rate. The empirical experimental results over the most up-to-date publicly available dataset, CICD-DoS2019, confirm the preeminence of soft-DBN as an IPS for DDoS attack type detection. By so doing, it is possible to reduce the false positive rate and achieve a high level of accuracy. It is shown that soft-DBN successfully minimized the FPR from 3.33% to 0.28%. In addition, the soft-DBN build-in mechanism allows using it also in classification and recognition problems. Furthermore, we agreed that there is a trade-off between model convergence delay and low FPR, so we believe that trying to break this trade-off is a path towards accurate and real-time detection models.

We plan to estimate the model learning time depending on the number of hidden nodes and different learning rates. It is important to gain insight into the impact of the training phase on the real-time aspect of the detection model.

References

1. Yuan, X., et al.: DeepDefense: identifying DDoS attack via deep learning. In: Proceedings SMARTCOMP, pp. 1–8, China (2017)
2. Elsayed, M., et al.: DDoSNet: a deep-learning model for detecting network attacks. In: IEEE 21st WoWMoM, pp. 391–396, Ireland (2020)
3. Nanda, S., et al.: Predicting network attack patterns in SDN using machine learning approach. In: IEEE NFV-SDN, pp. 167–172, USA (2016)
4. Roopak, M., et al.: Deep learning models for cyber security in IoT networks. In: Proceedings IEEE CCWC, pp. 0452–0457, USA (2019)

5. Bassene, A., Gueye, B.: DeepDDoS: a deep-learning model for detecting software defined healthcare IoT networks attacks. In: Elbiaze, H., Sabir, E., Falcone, F., Sadik, M., Lasaulce, S., Ben Othman, J. (eds.) UNet 2021. LNCS, vol. 12845, pp. 201–209. Springer, Cham (2021). https://doi.org/10.1007/978-3-030-86356-2_17

6. Latah, M., et al.: An efficient flow-based multi-level hybrid intrusion detection system for software-defined networks. CCF Trans. Netw. **3**, 261–271 (2020). https://doi.org/10.1007/s42045-020-00040-z

7. Latah, M., et al.: Levent Toker, towards an effcient anomaly-based intrusion detection for software-defned networks. IETN **7**(6), 453–459 (2018)

8. Agrawal, A., et al.: Autoencoder for design of mitigation model for DDOS attacks via M-DBNN **2022**, 14 (2022)

9. Hassan, M., et al.: Human emotion recognition using deep belief network architecture. Inf. Fusion **51**, 10–18 (2019)

10. Wang, J., et al.: Deep Boltzmann machine based condition prediction for smart manufacturing. JAIHC **10**(3), 851–861 (2019)

11. Hinton, G., et al.: A fast learning algorithm for deep belief nets. Neural Comput. **18**(7), 1527–1554 (2006)

12. Ferrag, M., et al.: Deep learning-based intrusion detection for distributed denial of service attack in agriculture 4.0. Electronics **10**, 1257 (2021)

13. Manimurugan, S., et al.: Effective attack detection in internet of medical things smart environment using a deep belief neural network. IEEE Access **8**, 77396–77404 (2020)

14. Hinton, G.: Training products of experts by minimizing contrastive divergence. NC **14**, 1771–1800 (2002)

15. Yan, J., et al.: A prediction model based on deep belief network and least squares SVR applied to cross-section water quality. Water **12**(7), 1929 (2020)

16. CICDDoS2019 dataset. http://205.174.165.80/CICDataset/CICDDoS2019. Accessed 20 Feb 2021

17. Kingma, D., et al.: Adam: a method for stochastic optimization. Int. Conf. Learn. Representations (2014)

18. Sharafaldin, I., et al.: Developing realistic distributed denial of service (DDoS) attack dataset and taxonomy. In: ICCST, pp. 1–8, India (2019)

19. Bassene, A., et al.: A group-based IoT devices classification through network traffic analysis based on machine learning approach. In: TISDC, AFRICOMM (2021)

20. Orosz, P., et al.: Low false alarm ratio DDoS detection for MS-scale threat mitigation. In: 14th CNSM, pp. 212–218 (2018)

On Feature Selection Algorithms for Effective Botnet Detection

Meher Afroz[1][✉], Muntaka Ibnath[1][✉], Ashikur Rahman[1][✉],
Jakia Sultana[1][✉], and Raqeebir Rab[2][✉]

[1] Department of CSE, BUET, Dhaka, Bangladesh
1605114@ugrad.cse.buet.ac.bd, muntaka@cse.uiu.ac.bd,
ashikur@cse.buet.ac.bd, jakiajyoti@gmail.com
[2] Department of CSE, AUST, Dhaka, Bangladesh
raqeebir.cse@aust.edu

Abstract. The threats posed by botnets are becoming a growing concern as more and more computers are getting infected every day. Although botnets can be detected from their behavioral patterns, the margin in the behavior of the malicious traffic and the legitimate traffic are diminishing with the advancement of the technologies as the malicious traffics have learned to follow the behavioral patterns of benign traffics. The detection of malicious traffic largely depends on the traffic characteristics that are being used to feed the detection algorithm. Selecting the best features for effective botnet detection is still infancy and is the main contribution of this paper. At the very beginning, we iterate different features used for botnet detection process. Then we propose several heuristics to select the best features from this handful set. Some proposed heuristics are flat feature-based and some are group-based yielding different levels of accuracy. We also analyze the time complexity of each heuristic and provide a comprehensive performance comparison. As working with all combinations of a large number of features is infeasible and intractable, some proposed heuristics group the features based on their similarity in patterns and check all combinations within the group of small sizes, eventually improving the time complexity by a large margin. Through experiments, we show the efficacy of the proposed feature selection heuristics. The result shows that some heuristics outperform state-of-the-art feature selection algorithms.

1 Introduction

With the advancement of technology, security threat has become one of the biggest concerns in cyberspace. The loss for Cyber-attack is projected to grow up to USD 10.5 trillion by 2025 [13]. Network traffic generated by malicious entities in all types of networks is one of the major security concerns, and a major research domain of the security community. One such malicious entity–the so-called *botnet*–is a collection of Internet-connected devices used for infecting a computer with malicious code under a common Command-and-Control infrastructure (C&C) [5]. Botnets are used for nefarious purposes such as accessing

E. Sabir et al. (Eds.): UNet 2022, LNCS 13853, pp. 253–266, 2023.
https://doi.org/10.1007/978-3-031-29419-8_19

private sensitive information, spam, click fraud, extortion, identity theft and large scale Denial of Service (DoS) attacks to deny legitimate users from accessing network resources [1,14].

Botnets are becoming sophisticated and diverse which is causing their detection a daunting task. Therefore, researchers and security experts are exploring different approaches and techniques over the past decade. The most popular botnet detection techniques are *behaviour based, signature-based* and *anomaly based*. These detection techniques require detail knowledge of a bot to identify unexpected traffic behavior such as high latency, or unusual port activities while actively monitoring a network. However, these techniques can detect only known botnets [12]. Due to these limitations, machine learning-based techniques have shown much promise to identify the bots. Many studies have found that machine learning-based techniques can detect real-world botnets with a very low false-positive rate [8,16].

Machine learning algorithms create a model by training with a dataset. Once trained, they can decide on new or unseen data making them most appropriate for detecting *zero-day attacks*. There are two popular approaches to ML-based botnet detection, packet content based and network flow statistics based. IRC botnets can be detected based on the packet content. However, if the packet contents are encrypted then this approach becomes ineffective. In recent studies, [19], network flow-based approach has been mostly used to detect botnets.

Machine learning techniques require a large amount of samples for training to be effective. Despite using a quality dataset, the ML-algorithms may not perform well due to the set of features they employ. A naive primary assumption is if one can use more features then the detection rate and classification accuracy might increase. With the reduced number of features it may not capture the abnormal traffics correctly. However, the truth is there are some drawbacks of using a large number of features. In one end, it increases the computational complexity of the classification schemes. Some studies [15] find that in large scale environment it can slow down the performance and optimal defense. In other end, redundant or irrelevant features may reduce the accuracy and yield error-prone results. If a feature set has a high internal accuracy with poor generalization, it suffers with the over fitting problem. That is why feature selection is a very challenging and a core aspect of any machine learning based approach. In order to get more effective results, one need to feed only those features which are really important. Feature selection techniques removes the irrelevant, redundant features and select a better subset. Thus, it reduces the computational cost; the model also becomes less complex and easy to interpret. Therefore, developing a good feature selection algorithm for botnet detection could be extremely useful.

In this paper, we devise several feature selection heuristics to detect botnets using machine learning. At first, we choose the commonly used state-of-the-art suitable features and discuss their relevance, effectiveness and rational behind their selection to detect botnets. We mainly focus on network flow-based features as packets might be encrypted in some protocols. We propose five different heuristics based on feature inclusion-exclusion techniques and perform a comparative analysis of these methods. We experiment these methods on a well-known comprehensive data set. We analyze these methods based on the performance metrics such as accuracy, detection rate and false alarm rate. We also calculate the time complexity of each method. The result shows that the proposed heuristics outperform state-of-the-art feature selection algorithms.

2 Literature Review

The state-of-the-art research works on botnet detection can be broadly classified into two categories. The first stream deals with devising botnet detection algorithms and focus on improving their accuracy. The second stream deals with different aspects of selecting features, devising novel feature selection algorithms for improving the accuracy of the detection process that would run on top of the selected features. Our work falls under the second stream.

Among the works under first stream, Choi et. al. [4] focus on botnet detection using fundamental characteristics of the botnets. Chaudhary et. al. [3] propose a detection model using a clustering algorithm. Stevanovic et al. [16] work with categorizing the network-based and client-based approaches for botnet detection. These works can again be broadly categorized into centralized, decentralized, and protocol-independent approaches.

The centralized approaches mainly work with the packet-based features and has a few real-time applications. Livadas et al. [11] propose an approach for IRC botnet detection and show that the average bytes per second has a significant impact on the results. The decentralized approaches mainly target P2P traffics. Saad et. al. [15] focus on the feature selection for botnet detection and have grouped a total of 17 features into flow-based and host-based groups. They show that the flow based group helps to detect P2P traffics whereas the host-based group is good at detecting C&C communication patterns. Zhao et. al. [23] work with the same feature set but focusing on the machine learning techniques. They show that using first packet size (FPS) and number of reconnect attempts, it is possible to detect the botnets that the model has never seen before. Finally, Protocol independent approaches find patterns in the behavior of bots that are within the same bot network. Clustering analysis for this kind of traffic is performed using BotMiner.

Among the works under second category, Beigi et. al. [2] propose the feature grouping of 16 features and work on selecting one feature from each group and achieve a detection rate of 69%. The proposed algorithm consists of two iterative steps. In first step, the method does the backward group elimination to find out the least contributing group. In the second step, it identifies the most contributing feature with best accuracy from the worst group and adds the feature in the final feature set. Hossain et. al. [7] use a different set of features and increase the detection rate upto 91% with high accuracy. They train a model using Multi-layer Feed Forward Network (ANN). Their feature-set includes a total of 12 features by grouping them into 8 flow-based and 4 conversation-based features.

3 Features Description

The feature selection algorithms devised in this paper are initially fed with 15 relevant flow-based features. Each feature selection algorithm then generates a reduced number of features that are finally used for detecting botnets. In this section, we discuss the rationales behind selecting those 15 flow-based features.

Total Number of Packets Exchanged - (PX). This is the summation of the number of packets exchanged between a communicating pair within a time window. In general case, bot communicates on the network continuously to keep the connection alive like a heart-bit. So, it usually sends uniformed sized packets continuously. Zhao et al. [22], shows that this feature has the higher discriminatory power among the other features.

Number of Small Packets Exchanged - (NSP). Exchanging small packets (typically $63 - 400$ bytes) is a known behavior of botnet communications. Many researches found this behavior useful for detecting botnets [2,10].

Percentage of Small Packets Exchanged - (PSP). In many studies, it is shown that the percentage of small packets is significantly higher in P2P botnet detection [10]. It is calculated as,

$$Percentage\ of\ small\ packets\ exchanged = \frac{NSP}{px} * 100$$

Ratio Between the Number of Incoming Packets Over the Number of Outgoing packets - (IOPR). Some researches have shown that there is a number of significant directional differences found between inbound and outbound traffics [9] and has been used to analyse and detect the botnet behavior [2,15]. IOPR is calculated as,

$$IOPR = \frac{Total\ backward\ packets}{Total\ forward\ packets}$$

Number of Reconnects - (Reconnect). Botnet performs frequent reconnections to disguise their flow behavior such as number of packets exchanged [17].

Flow Duration - (Duration). Duration is one of the most applied characteristics used in machine learning algorithms for botnet detection [11,18] Many malicious communications follow a certain type of flow duration e.g. weasel establishes brief connections, on the otherhand Palevo botnet and IRC botnets are known to be chatty [2] yielding long duration.

Length of the First Packet - (FPS). The length of the first packet in the flow can have an identical behavior in case of malicious communications. Many studies have found this characteristic is useful to detect the botnets [15,23].

Total Number of Bytes - (TBT). Generally, botnet traffic's communication pattern is uniform. Some botnet uses fixed length command such as Weasel [6]. Similarity of the botnet traffics can be found out using this feature [15,23].

Average Payload Packet length - (APL). This is the mean of all the forward packet lengths and backward packet lengths in a flow. It helps to find out the similarity in botnet traffics.

Total Number of Packets with the Same Length Over the Total Number of Packets - (DPL). This feature represents similar communication pattern. Many studies have used this feature to distinguish specific protocols [6]. DPL is calculated as,

$$DPL = \frac{Sum\ of\ the\ number\ of\ same\ length\ packets}{Total\ number\ of\ packets}$$

Standard Deviation of Packet Payload Length - (PV). Many studies use standard deviation of all payload of the packets of a flow as a feature to differentiate IRC traffic and non IRC traffic [22].

Average Bits-per-Second - (BS). Bits per second is a useful characteristic to analyse the network traffic flows. Average bits-per-second has been used in online botnet detection efficiently [21].

Average Packets-per-Second in a Time Window - (PS). In a particular time window, packets per second shows the possibility of malicious communications. This feature is also used to detect IRC and non IRC traffic [11,21].

Average Inter Arrival Time of Packets - (AIT). AIT of the packets in a flow is used to extract the similarity in botnet traffic.

Average Packets-per-Second - (PPS). This feature is also used to find the similar network communications. PPS is calculated as,

$$PPS = \frac{Total\ number\ of\ packets\ exchanged}{\sum Flow\ Duration}$$

4   Dataset

For training and testing our model, the "ISCX-Bot-2014 dataset" [20] has been used. The train data size is 5.3 GB and test data size is 8.5 GB. 43.92% of training data is malicious which contains seven types of the botnet and the remaining 56.08% is benign traffic. Neris (IRC), Rbot (IRC), Virut (HTTP), NSIS (P2P), SMTP Spam (P2P), Zeus (P2P), Zeus control (C & C) botnets are used for training purposes. On the other hand, 44.97% of test data is malicious flows that contain 15 types of botnets and the remaining 55.03% contains normal traffic. Neris (IRC), Rbot (IRC), Menti (IRC), Sogou (HTTP), Murlo (IRC), Virut (HTTP), etc. botnets are used in the test data.

After extracting the features, we removed null values. There were no missing values.

5   Feature Selection Algorithms

Initially, we select 15 potential features for botnet detection. However, all features may not be (equally) useful for building a machine learning model. Increased number of features also increases the complexity of the model and might reduce the overall accuracy. That is why feature selection step is needed to find the best set of features to build a better model. In fact, the feature selection methods eliminates one or more input attribute(s) which are less important for the model, non-informative or redundant.

Algorithm 1. Feature Inclusion

1: **Input**
2:      Final feature set $= \emptyset$
3:      Current feature set $= \emptyset$
4:      Available feature set $= \{f_1, f_2, ..., f_n\}$
5: **Output:** Final feature set
6:      **while** detection rate is increasing **do**
7:          **for** each feature $f_i \in$ *Available feature set* **do**
8:              /* Best feature inclusion step */
9:              Copy final feature set into current feature set
10:             Add f_i in the current feature set
11:             Do experiment using current feature set, calculate accuracy (a_i);
12:         **end for**
13:         Find maximum accuracy, a_{max} which is achieved in the previous step. Suppose f_{max} is the feature yielding the best accuracy, a_{max};
14:         Add f_{max} in the final feature set
15:         Remove f_{max} from the available feature set
16:         Calculate detection rate
17:     **end while**

5.1   Notations Used

In this study we use following notations throughout the paper.

- n = Number of total features in the dataset.
- m = Number of total groups of the features.
- k = Number of the features in the largest group.

5.2   Feature Inclusion Algorithm

This heuristic method (Algorithm 1) is based on forward feature selection. The heuristic picks the first feature from the available features (all features are initially available) that maximizes the detection rate. After selecting that feature, it is deleted from the available feature set and the procedure is repeated with the remaining features but with the first selected feature already included in the set. The process is repeated as long as the detection rate increases.

Complexity Analysis: Initially, all features are in the available feature set. Statement 7 picks one feature at a time from the available feature set. Statements 7–12 runs $\binom{n}{1}$ times. Statement 13 finds the maximum accuracy of previous step which runs n times. Statements 14–16 take constant time to run. After completing first iteration, selected best feature is included in the final feature set and it is excluded from the available feature set. So in the next iteration, Statements 7–12 run $\binom{(n-1)}{1}$ times. Statement 13 also runs $(n-1)$ times. Therefore, the complexity of the,
1st iteration, $n + n = O(n)$

2nd iteration, $(n-1) + (n-1) = O(n-1)$

nth iteration, $(n-n+1) + (n-n+1) = O(1)$

In worst case, the while loop in Line 6 runs n times yielding,

$$(n + (n-1) + (n-2) + ... + 1) = \frac{n(n+1)}{2} = O(n^2)$$

Therefore, the time complexity in worst case becomes $O(n^2)$.

5.3 Feature Exclusion Algorithm

This heuristic method performs backward feature elimination technique. This method is presented in [7]. At first, all the features are included in the available feature set. Then the features are checked one at a time and the feature that minimizes the detection rate most is selected for elimination. Once it is removed from the set of available features, the whole process is repeated with the remaining features. The process is repeated as long as the detection rate increases. Algorithm 2 summarizes the process.

Complexity Analysis: Initially all features are in available feature set. Statement 5 picks one feature at a time from the available feature set. Statements 5–10 runs $\binom{n}{1}$ times. Statement 11 finds the maximum accuracy of previous step which runs n times. Statements 12–13 take constant time to run. After completing first iteration, selected worst feature is excluded from the available feature set. So in next iteration, Statements 5–10 run $\binom{(n-1)}{1}$ times. Statement 11 also runs $(n-1)$ times. Therefore, the complexity of the 1st iteration, $n + n = O(n)$

2nd iteration, $(n-1) + (n-1) = O(n-1)$

nth iteration, $(n-n+1) + (n-n+1) = O(1)$

In worst case, the while loop in Line 4 runs n times yielding,

$$(n + (n-1) + (n-2) + ... + 1) = \frac{n(n+1)}{2} = O(n^2)$$

Therefore, the time complexity in worst case becomes $O(n^2)$. In wrapper method, if we search the entire space of all possible combinations of features then the process becomes almost infeasible if number of features is large. For example, for 15 features, one need to consider 2^{15} or 32768 different combinations. In order to reduce the search space, in next three heuristics, we categorize the features into four groups based on their relevance with each other as in [2]. Following is the list of groups:

- **Byte-based:** TBT, APL, DPL, PV
- **Time-based:** BS, PS, PPS, AIT
- **Behavior-based:** Reconnect, Duration, FPS
- **Packet-based:** PX, NSP, IOPR, PSP

Algorithm 2. Feature Exclusion

1: **Input**
2:    Available feature set $= \{f_1, f_2, ..., f_n\}$
3: **Output:** Final feature set
4:    **while** detection rate is increasing **do**
5:        **for** each feature $f_i \in Available\ feature\ set$ **do**
6:            /* Feature exclusion step */
7:            exclude feature f_i
8:            Do experiment using all remaining features, calculate accuracy (a_i);
9:            Add f_i in Available feature set
10:       **end for**
11:       Find maximum accuracy, a_{max} which is achieved in the previous step. Let's consider f_{max} is the feature yielding worst accuracy, so it is selected for exclusion;
12:       Remove f_{max} from available feature set
13:       Calculate detection rate
14:   **end while**

Algorithm 3. Feature Inclusion with Group Sequencing

1: **Input**
2:    Current feature set $= \emptyset$
3: **Output:** Final feature set
4: **Procedure: getSortedGroup**
5:    **for** each group $g_i \in (g_1, g_2, ...g_m)$ **do**
6:        include all features of g_i in current feature set
7:        Do experiment using current feature set, calculate accuracy (a_i);
8:        Include a_i in current test accuracy
9:        Exclude features of g_i from current feature set
10:   **end for**
11:   /* Best to worst group */
12:   Sort current test accuracy in descending order
13:   Return sorted group set, $g_{sort} = \{g_1, g_2, .., g_m\}$
14: **Procedure: getFinalFeatureSet**
15:    **for** each group $g_i \in g_{sort}$ & detection rate increases **do**
16:        Current features $= \emptyset$
17:        Final feature set $= \emptyset$
18:        C is the set of combination of features of g_i
19:        **for** each combination c_j in C **do**
20:            /* Member inclusion step */
21:            Add c_j to current features set
22:            Do experiment and calculate accuracy (a_j);
23:            Remove c_j from Current features set
24:        **end for**
25:        Find maximum accuracy a_{max} achieved in the previous step. Let's consider c_{max} is the combination of the best feature(s) in group g_i. So, it is added to the final feature set;
26:        Calculate detection rate
27:    **end for**

Algorithm 4. Best Feature Combination from Worst Group

1: **Input**
2:    Initialize all groups
3:    Current feature set = set of all features
4:    Final feature set = $\emptyset$
5:    Detection rate is calculated by applying all features
6: **Output:** Final feature set
7:    **while** detection rate is increasing **do**
8:        **for** each group $g_i \in (g_1, g_2, .., g_m)$ **do**
9:            /* Group exclusion step */
10:           Exclude all features of g_i from current feature set
11:           Do experiment using all remaining features (including final feature set), calculate accuracy (a_i);
12:           Put back all features of g_i in current feature set
13:       **end for**
14:       Find maximum accuracy, a_{gmax} achieved in the previous step. Let's consider g_{max} is the worst performing group so it is selected as the candidate for exclusion;
15:       C is the set of combination of features of g_{max}
16:       **for** each combination c_j of C **do**
17:           /* Member inclusion step */
18:           Add c_j and exclude remaining features of g_{max};
19:           Do experiment and calculate accuracy (a_j);
20:       **end for**
21:       Find maximum accuracy a_{fmax}, achieved in the previous step. Let's consider c_{max} is the combination of the best feature(s) in group g_{max}. So, it is added to the final feature set;
22:       Calculate detection rate
23:   **end while**

5.4   Feature Inclusion with Group Sequencing

This heuristic performs small-scale exhaustive feature selection. At first, features are divided into m groups. Instead of picking groups one by one, we rank the groups based on the detection rate they provide. Then, we select one group at a time from the best to worst performing. Once a group is selected, we run exhaustive feature selection technique by generating all possible combination of features of the group. The best performing combination is added to the final feature set and the process is repeated with the next best performing group until the detection rate can not be increased any more. Algorithm 3 shows the procedure in details.

Complexity Analysis. Procedure getSortedGroup has two steps. Statements 5–10 calculate the accuracy for each group which take m time. Then, it sorts the groups based on the accuracy result which takes $(mlog(m))$ time. So this procedure has a time complexity of $m + (mlog(m))$.

For the procedure getFinalFeatureSet, Statement 18 generates all combination of features of a group. The total combinations is $C(k, i) = 2^k$. Statements 19–24 run 2^k times. Statement 25 finds the maximum accuracy of previous step. So, it runs 2^k times as well. Statement 26 takes constant time. This procedure can run at most m times. So, Statements 15–26 runs m times in worst case as we have m number of groups. Total time complexity of this algorithm is $(m + mlog(m)) + (m * 2^k) = m * 2^k$ Time complexity is $O(m * 2^k)$ where the k is the maximum number of features in the groups.

5.5   Best Features from Worst Group

In this heuristic, we use both backward feature elimination and exhaustive feature selection techniques in two steps. It starts with all features and remove groups one by one to find out the least contributing group in the overall accuracy. After identifying the worst performing group it becomes the candidate for group exclusion. Then next step is feature inclusion which exhaustively searches from all possible combination of features of the candidate group that can provide the best overall accuracy. Thus, a set of the best feature(s) from the least contributing group is selected and included in the final feature set. The process is repeated and the procedure ends as soon as the detection rate gets decreased.

Complexity Analysis: In Statement 8, each time one group is picked from the available group set. So, in first iteration of the while loop, Statements 8–13 run $\binom{m}{1}$ times. Statement 14 finds the maximum accuracy of previous step. If available group set is m then it takes m times. Statement 15 generates all combination of feature sets of a group. In worst case, a group may have k features. Then total features set will be $C(k, i) = 2^k$. Statements 16–20 run 2^k times. Statement 21 finds the maximum accuracy of previous step. So, it runs 2^k times as well. Statement 22 takes constant time. After completing first iteration, selected worst group is excluded from the available group set. So in the next iteration, statement 8–13 run $\binom{(m-1)}{1}$ times. Statement 14 also runs $(m - 1)$ times. Thus time complexity of the:-
1st iteration, $m + m + 2^k + 2^k + 2^k = O(m + 2^k)$
2nd iteration, $(m - 1) + (m - 1) + 2^k + 2^k + 2^k = O((m - 1) + 2^k))$
m th iteration, $(m - m + 1) + (m - m + 1) + 2^k + 2^k + 2^k = O((m - m + 1) + 2^k))$.
The while loop in Statement 7 run at most m times. Statement 7–23 run m times at most. So the algorithm runs $(m * (m + 2^k))$ times at most. Thus the time complexity becomes $O(m * 2^k)$ where the k is the maximum number of features among all the groups.

5.6   Best Feature Combination from Best Group

In this heuristic again two steps are performed, one is the group inclusion and the second is feature inclusion step. The algorithm starts with an empty feature set. At first, forward feature selection technique is applied on the available groups to find out the best performing group. This best group is the candidate group for the next step. Then exhaustive feature selection technique is applied on the features of the candidate group. One by one combination of features of the candidate group is included in the feature set and the overall accuracy is calculated. After completing this step, a set of the best feature(s) from the best group is selected. This selected feature (s) is included in the final feature set. The procedure continues until the detection rate cannot be improved.

Complexity Analysis: In Statement 7, each time one group is picked from the available group set. So, in first iteration, Statements 7–12 run $\binom{m}{1}$ times. Statement 13 finds the maximum accuracy of previous step. If available group set is m then it takes m times. Statement 15 generates the combination of feature set from all features of a group. In worst case, a group may have k features. Then total features set will be $C(k, i) = 2^k$. Statement 16–22 run 2^k times. Statement 23 finds the maximum accuracy of previous step. So, it runs 2^k times as well. Statements 14 and 24 take constant time. After completing first iteration, selected best group is excluded from the available group set. So in next iteration, statement 7–12 run $\binom{(m-1)}{1}$ times. Statement 13 also runs $(m-1)$ times. Thus the time complexity of,

1st iteration, $m + m + 2^k + 2^k + 2^k = O(m + 2^k)$

2nd iteration, $(m-1) + (m-1) + 2^k + 2^k + 2^k = O((m-1) + 2^k))$

m th iteration, $(m-m+1) + (m-m+1) + 2^k + 2^k + 2^k = O((m-m+1) + 2^k))$.

The while loop in Line 6 can run at most m times. Statement 6–25 run m times at most. So the algorithm runs $(m * (m + 2^k))$ times at most. Time complexity is $O(m * 2^k)$ where the k is the number of maximum features of the groups.

6 Experimental Results

In this section, we discuss about performance metrics and performance comparison of the five feature selection heuristics that we propose. Feature vectors were extracted in the 60 s time windows as in Beigi et. al. [2] just to make two algorithms comparable. The feature vectors were then passed to the detection module where the decision tree model was applied

6.1 Performance Metrics

We consider four performance measures namely accuracy, detection rate, false alarm and precision. Using four categories true positive (TP), true negative (TN), false positive (FP), and false negative (FN) the definition of four metrics are as follows:

Accuracy. Accuracy is the ratio of correctly classified data over total input samples. $Accuracy = \frac{(TP+TN)}{(TP+TN+FP+FN)}$.

Detection Rate (True Positive Rate). Detection rate is the proportion of true positive over actual positive data. $DetectionRate = \frac{(TP)}{(TP+FN)}$.

False Alarm. False alarm is the proportion of false positive & actual false data.

$$FalseAlarm = \frac{(FP)}{(FP+TN)}$$

Algorithm 5. Best Feature Combination from Best Group

1: **Input**
2:     Available group set $=\{g_1, .., g_m\}$
3:     Current feature set $= \emptyset$
4:     Final feature set $= \emptyset$
5: **Output:** Final feature set
6:     **while** detection rate is increasing **do**
7:       **for** each group $g_i \in$ available group set **do**
8:         /* Group inclusion step */
9:         Copy Final feature set into Current feature set
10:        Include features of g_i in Current feature set
11:        Do experiment using Current feature set, calculate accuracy (a_i);
12:       **end for**
13:       Find maximum accuracy, a_{gmax} achieved in the previous step. Let's consider, g_{max} is the best performing group. So it is selected as the candidate group for inclusion;
14:       Exclude group g_{max} from Available group set
15:       C is the set of combination of features of g_{max}
16:       **for** each combination c_j of C **do**
17:         /* Member inclusion step */
18:         Copy Final feature set into Current feature set
19:        Add c_j in Current feature set
20:        Do experiment using Current feature set and calculate accuracy (a_j);
21:        Remove c_j from the Current feature set
22:       **end for**
23:       Find maximum accuracy a_{fmax} which is achieved in the previous step. Let's consider $c_{max} = \{f_1, ..f_k\}$ is the set of best feature(s) in group g_{max}. So it is added to the Final feature set;
24:       Calculate detection rate
25:     **end while**

Precision. Precision is defined as, $Precision = \frac{(TP)}{(TP+FP)}$

In Table 1 we summarize the results of the five heuristics and compare their performance with the result of Beigi et. al. [2]. Among the five heuristics, Best Feature Combination from Worst Group (Algorithm 4) generates the best accuracy (80.07%) with least false alarm rate (13.53%) and best precision (80.79%), whereas Feature inclusion heuristic (Algorithm 1) outperforms rest of the heuristics in terms of detection rate (90.07%).

7 Discussion

Mainly, we try to propose different heuristics of selecting features and compare them in term of complexity & performance. Our goal is to improve result than previous work [2]. All of our algorithms outperform Beigi et. al. [2] on the same data set in terms of detection rate. On the other hand feature inclusion yields best detection rate of 90.07% which also runs in polynomial time.

Table 1. Result Analysis of All Five Algorithm

Contributor	Algorithm	Selected features	Accuracy (%)	Detection rate (%)	False alarm rate (%)	Precision (%)
This paper	Feature Inclusion	BS, TBT	74.23	90.07	38.28	65.03
This paper	Feature exclusion	DPL, Duration, FPS, IOPR, NSP, PS, PX	70.16	77.86	35.92	63.14
This paper	Feature Inclusion with Group Sequencing	APL, DPL, IOPR, TBT	65.48	76.52	14.73	77.83
This paper	Best Feature Combination from Worst Group	APL, BS, DPL, Duration, FPS, IOPR, NSP, PSP, PV, PX, Reconnect, TBT	80.07	72.0	13.53	80.79
This paper	Best Feature Combination from Best Group	AIT, APL, DPL, IOPR, TBT	78.58	72.17	16.34	77.73
Beigi et. al. [2]	Group Based Feature Selection	APL, IOPR, BS, Duration	75	69	2.3	unknown

8   Conclusions

Machine learning provides viable solution for botnet detection. A good machine learning-based solution detects botnets more accurately, triggers low false alarm and runs in reasonable time. In this paper, we have considered all of these as our major goals. We have also experimentally analyzed the features to find their relevance in detecting malicious traffics. We proposed several heuristics to select important features from the available feature set which in turn increases the accuracy and reduces the run time of a machine learning model. We have evaluated the performance of the proposed methods and have reviewed other state-of-the-art methods for botnet detection. Our selected feature set performs reasonably well in the machine learning model for identifying the botnets.

Acknowledgement. The author acknowledges Bangladesh University of Engineering and Technology (BUET) for its generous support to make this work publishable by providing *Basic Research Grant*.

References

1. Ahmed, A.A., et al.: Deep learning-based classification model for botnet attack detection. J. Ambient Intell. Human. Comput. **13**, 3457–3466 (2020). https://doi.org/10.1007/s12652-020-01848-9
2. Biglar Beigi, E., Hadian Jazi, H., Stakhanova, N., Ghorbani, A.A.: Towards effective feature selection in machine learning-based botnet detection approaches. In: IEEE Conference on Communications and Net, Security, pp. 247–255 (2014)

3. Chaudhary, P., Sherya, S., Vanshika, V.: Detection of botnet using flow analysis and clustering algorithm. Int. J. Mod. Edu. Comp. Sci. **11** (2019)
4. Choi, H., Lee, H.: Identifying botnets by capturing group activities in DNS traffic. Comput. Netw. **56**(1), 20–33 (2012)
5. Faek, R., Al-Fawa'reh, M., Al-Fayoumi, M.: Exposing bot attacks using machine learning and flow level analysis. In: International Conference on Data Science, E-learning and Information Systems (2021)
6. Garant, D., Lu, W.: Mining botnet behaviors on the large-scale web application community. In: 27th International Conference on Advanced Information Networking and Applications Workshops (2013)
7. Hossain, M.I., Eshrak, S., Auvik, M.J., Nasim, S.F., Rab, R., Rahman, A.: Efficient feature selection for detecting botnets based on network traffic and behavior analysis. In: 7th IEEE NSysS, 2020, pp. 56–62 (2020)
8. Hyslip, T.S., Pittman, J.M.: A survey of botnet detection techniques by command and control infrastructure. J. Digit. Foren. Sec. Law **10**, 1 (2015)
9. John, W., Tafvelin, S.: Differences between in-and outbound internet backbone traffic. In: TERENA Networking Conference (TNC) (2007)
10. Liao, W.H., Chang, C.C.: Peer to peer botnet detection using data mining scheme. In: International Conference on Internet Technology and Applications, pp. 1–4 (2010)
11. Livadas, C., Walsh, R., Lapsley, D., Strayer, W.T.: Using machine learning techniques to identify botnet traffic. In: In IEEE LCN, pp. 967–974 (2006)
12. Miller, S., Busby-Earle, C.: The role of machine learning in botnet detection. In: 11th International Conference for Internet Technology and Secured Transactions (ICITST), December 2016
13. Morgan, S.: Cybercrime To Cost The World $10.5 Trillion Annually By 2025 (2020). https://cybersecurityventures.com/hackerpocalypse-cybercrime-report-2016/
14. Nivargi, V., Bhaowal, M., Lee, T.: Machine learning based botnet detection. CS 229 Final Proj. Report, Comput. Sci. Dep. Stanford Univ (2006)
15. Saad, S., et al.: Detecting P2P botnets through network behavior analysis and machine learning. In: IEEE PST, pp. 174–180 (2011)
16. Stevanovic, M., Pedersen, J.M.: Machine learning for identifying botnet network traffic (2013)
17. Stinson, E., Mitchell, J.C.: Towards systematic evaluation of the evadability of bot/botnet detection methods. WOOT **8**, 1–9 (2008)
18. Strayer, W.T., Lapsely, D., Walsh, R., Livadas, C.: Botnet detection based on network behavior. In: Lee, W., Wang, C., Dagon, D. (eds.) Botnet Detection. Advances in Information Security, vol. 36, pp. 1–24. Springer, Boston (2008). https://doi.org/10.1007/978-0-387-68768-1_1
19. Tariq, F., Baig, S.: Machine learning based botnet detection in software defined networks. Int. J. Secur. Appl **11**(11), 2017 (2017)
20. UNB: Iscx botnet dataset (2014). https://www.unb.ca/cic/datasets/botnet.html
21. Yu, X., Dong, X., Yu, G., Qin, Y., Yue, D.: Data-adaptive clustering analysis for online botnet detection. In: 2010, vol. 1 (2010)
22. Zhao, D., Traore, I., Ghorbani, A., Sayed, B., Saad, S., Lu, W.: Peer to peer botnet detection based on flow intervals. In: Gritzalis, D., Furnell, S., Theoharidou, M. (eds.) SEC 2012. IAICT, vol. 376, pp. 87–102. Springer, Heidelberg (2012). https://doi.org/10.1007/978-3-642-30436-1_8
23. Zhao, D., et al.: Botnet detection based on traffic behavior analysis and flow intervals. Comput. Secur. **39**, 2–16 (2013)

A Novel Hybrid Deep Learning Model for Crop Disease Detection Using BEGAN

Houda Orchi[(✉)] [iD], Mohamed Sadik [iD], and Mohammed Khaldoun

Department of Electrical Engineering, NEST Research Group ENSEM, Hassan II University,
Casablanca, Morocco
{houda.orchi,m.sadik,m.khaldoun}@ensem.ac.ma

Abstract. Crop diseases are a considerable threat in the agricultural sector as they adversely affect the production and quality of agricultural products, resulting in heavy economic losses for both farmers and the country. Therefore, early identification and diagnosis of crop diseases at each stage of their lifespan is critical to protect and maximize crop yields. In this paper, we have proposed a novel deep learning model that utilizes the began to generate synthetic images of crop leaves in order to improve the network generalizability. Thereafter, a hybrid InceptionV3 + RF model is trained on real and synthetic images using transfer learning to classify crop leaves images in ten categories.

Keywords: Boundary equilibrium generative adversarial network · Hybrid InceptionV3-RF model · Classification accuracy

1 Introduction

Agriculture is the pillar of several nations. Due to global population growth, the demand for agricultural production is surging. To meet this pressing need, it is mandatory to boost agricultural productivity and protect cultivated crops. However, cultures are highly susceptible to various diseases owing to numerous pathogens existing in their environment. Some of these agents are viruses, while others are fungi or bacteria (Lucas et al. 1992). The untimely recognition of some viral diseases can have devastating effects on food sustainability and decrease productivity by 10 to 95% (Shirahatti et al. 2018). Therefore, early disease identification is crucial to prevent enormous losses and minimize the overuse of pesticides, which can harm both human health as well as the environment. In most cases, and notably in developing countries and on small farms, farmers still identify crop diseases through the naked eye, relying on visual symptoms. This is very time-consuming, laborious, and requires expertise in plant pathology (Liu et al. 2020). Thus, this visual observation method is not convenient and feasible for big farms and could even provide faulty predictions due to biased decisions (Singh and Misra 2017). To this end, many researchers have developed numerous methods (Afifi et al. 2020; Mugithe et al. 2020) based on computer vision, deep and machine learning to automate the process of disease detection. Deep learning has revolutionized the field of computer vision and is emerging as a mainstream tool for numerous applications. Popularized

E. Sabir et al. (Eds.): UNet 2022, LNCS 13853, pp. 267–283, 2023.
https://doi.org/10.1007/978-3-031-29419-8_20

by supporting frameworks like TensorFlow (Abadi et al. 2016) and PyTorch (Paszke et al. 2019), DL is advantageous as it abolishes the need for manual feature engineering upon unstructured datasets. The classification layer of a deep learning model driven by fully connected layers may lead to overfitting when fed with fewer data or even, in most cases, these models demand needless use of computational power and resources, which is not the case with classical machine learning algorithms. Hence, we leveraged the advantages of DL and ML and mitigated the drawbacks of both techniques to obtain more accurate and lower computational cost solutions by applying deep hybrid learning. Generally, the performance of CNN architectures depends highly on the availability of the training dataset. Collecting real crop leaf disease datasets is an intricate and costly procedure that demands the collaboration of experts from different fields at contrasting levels. Even though public datasets are available, most of them are still limited in size and applicable to specific tasks. The employment of classical data augmentation has been reported in various publications (Perez and Wang 2017) to expand the training set and balance classes. Nevertheless, the diversity that can be obtained from such image alterations (such as translation, rotation, scaling, and flipping) is relatively minor. This drives us to use synthetic data, where the generated samples bring in more variability and can further enrich the dataset, to enhance the accuracy and recognition training process as well as to reduce the imbalance.

Our motivation is to enhance the quality and performance of the identification model as well as to strike a compromise between a low misclassification rate and high accuracy. Therefore, we developed a novel deep hybrid learning-based framework to recognize diseases in crops. This framework would assist farmers in the classification of diseases affecting crops by simply grabbing an image of diseased leaves, rather than going through expensive expert analysis. This hybrid model consists of two main parts; the InceptionV3 as a feature extractor and the random forest as a classifier.

The core contributions of this present study are presented below:

- We address the problem persisting in GANs, WGANs, and C-GANs that consists of the training stability and the visual quality of the generated images. Therefore, we applied a new data augmentation method based on BEGAN that balances the generator and the discriminator during training. This is a new way to control the trade-off between visual quality and image diversity. Indeed, the discriminator used in BEGAN is implemented like an auto-encoder, in a similar way to EBGAN. However, the difference lies in the fact that BEGAN uses the Wasserstein distance to construct the loss function. So, it is a simple combination of EBGAN and WGAN, but it yields a striking outcome. Besides, the networks converge more regularly than earlier.
- The key contribution lies in developing a hybrid InceptionV3-RF model capable of classifying leaf diseases affecting several crops while providing a better trade-off between the highest accuracy and the lowest misclassification rate. It should be noted that a typical InceptionV3 network uses an FC layer to make the final classification decision. However, overfitting occurs, especially with inadequate samples, resulting in an insufficiently robust and computationally demanding system. By using the RF layer instead of the FC layer to make the final decision, the occurrence of overfitting can be effectively mitigated to enhance the accuracy of crop identification further and lessen the misclassification rate.

The rest of this paper is arranged in the following manner: The second section reviews the existing work in this field. Then, the third section reports the methodology and materials needed to perform this study. Subsequently, the fourth section shows the experimental results along with their detailed discussion, and eventually, the work concludes with the fifth section, which addresses potential future directions for the present work.

2 Related Work

Many researchers have encountered the problem of class imbalance owing to the scarcity of disease lesions in real-world settings (Lu et al. 2022). So, in presence of unbalanced data, machine learning-based algorithms tend to deal with minority samples as noise and then produce a heavy bias in favor of the majority class (Johnson and Khoshgoftaar 2019). Moreover, these skewed distributions also result in failure to learn the true minority class features due to the lack of representativeness. In this respect, this issue can be addressed through two approaches, either to tackle it from an algorithmic perspective, by using a heavier weight on the error term inside the loss function when the classifier misclassifies the minority class samples (Zhou and Liu 2005), or by feeding the algorithm with the prior class probabilities beforehand (Lawrence et al. 2012), or to address the problem from a data perspective, by using sampling or synthesis techniques to generate or remove samples for getting a balanced data distribution (Johnson and Khoshgoftaar 2019). We are particularly interested in data-level solutions that perform on the training set and modify its class distribution. As we aim to employ a hybrid deep learning-based model that has the advantage of avoiding manual feature extraction, embracing local connectivity and sharing of parameters, also drastically reducing the parameter number. Despite the impressive results obtained by DL models in the field of modeling and analysis, it has been firmly demonstrated that sourcing large-scale dataset is necessary to ensure the performance of DL models or state-of-the-art machine learning models (Paullada et al. 2021) while preventing overfitting. Some methods can solve overfitting problems, such as dropout (Srivastava et al. 2014), early stopping, data augmentation, etc. Data augmentation seeks to increase the dataset size (Kukačka et al., 2017). It is extensively used in neural network training. There are presently two methods of data augmentation: supervised as well as unsupervised (Shorten and Khoshgoftaar 2019). Unsupervised data augmentation consists of learning the distribution that the data conform through the model and randomly outputting the data that are consistent with the sample set distribution. The generator model is the most crucial technique in unsupervised learning tasks. To date, the most popular models used are directed graphical models such as Helmholtz machines (Dayan 2000), Deep Belief Networks (DBNs) (Hinton 2009) Variational Automatic Encoders (VAEs) (Kingma and Welling 2013), Autoregressive models (AR) and Generative Adversarial Networks (GANs)(Goodfellow et al. 2014). Owing to the GAN's ability to adapt to the high-dimensional data distribution and outstanding performance in generating images, the GAN is currently the leading and most promising method in the generation model. Nevertheless, GANs still encounter many unsolved challenges: generally, they are notoriously tough to train, even with the application of many tricks (Radford et al. 2015; Salimans et al. 2016). Balancing the convergence of the generator and discriminator is a daunting task: the discriminator usually wins much more easily at the beginning of training (Goodfellow 2016). GANs are easily prone to modal collapse, a failure state in which only one image is learned (Dumoulin et al. 2016). The repelling regularizer (Zhao et al. 2016) and heuristic regularizers like Batch Discrimination (Salimans et al. 2016)) have been proposed to remedy this problem with varying levels of success. Then, while the earliest variants of GANs did not have a convergence measure, Wasserstein GANs (Dumoulin et al. 2016; Arjovsky et al. 2017) (WGANs) have recently introduced a loss that also serves as a convergence measure. In their implementation, it does so at the detriment of slow training, but with the advantage of stability and greater mode coverage. Indeed, WGAN uses the DCGAN deep convolutional architecture, which is proposed by (Radford et al. 2015). This model is employed as the base architecture for many subsequent approaches to ensure stable training across most settings.

3 Material and Methods

The following section will present the proposed method and discuss it. The functional block diagram of the proposed method is illustrated in Fig. 1.

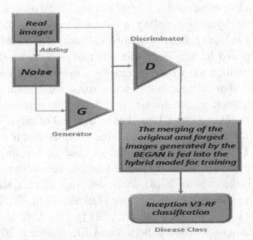

Fig. 1. Functional block diagram of BEGAN and hybrid InceptionV3-RF model.

Our proposed approach can be split into two parts: In the first one, synthetic images have been produced by using BEGAN for data augmentation. In the second one, a novel hybrid model has been developed for crop leaf disease classification in order to improve classification accuracy and lower the misclassification rate. An in-depth description is provided in the upcoming subsections.

3.1 Dataset

We opted for the PlantVillage open dataset (Hughes and Salathé, 2015), which contains 54,306 images of 14 crop leaf species and 38 disease kinds. We selected 13 types of crop leaves that exhibit a significant imbalance in the disease classes compared to the healthy classes. The crop species on which we have worked are: blueberry, apple, corn, cherry, grape, pepper, potato, peach, squash, raspberry, soybean, orange, and tomato. These crop leaves are adversely affected by fungal, viral, and bacterial diseases. All leaf images are taken on a similar grayish background. The size of the leaf images is 256 × 256 pixels in RGB colors, which were captured under different weather conditions with a standard camera. Therefore, contrast adjustment and background removal are necessary to prevent any potential bias. It is noteworthy that the distribution of the images is uneven, posing a problem of data imbalance, which we addressed by using the BEGAN model.

3.2 Addressing Unbalanced Data Problem by Generating Synthetic Data with the Use of BEGAN

For the sake of preventing the network from overfitting, the Boundary Equilibrium Generative Adversarial Network (BEGAN) is used as a data augmentation technique to expand the dataset size. In GAN, conventional convolutional layers are employed to build an image matrix using random noise. The GAN is made up of a discriminator and a generator model. The generator's work consists of producing fake images and the discriminator's work consists of distinguishing real images from fake ones. Both the generator and the discriminator train simultaneously and attempt to outperform each other. The discriminator ensures that the fake images generated by the generator are as close as possible to the real ones. In our method, we employ an auto-encoder as a discriminator as pioneered in EBGAN (Zhao et al. 2016). Considering that typical GANs try to directly match the data distributions, our approach aims to match the loss distributions of the autoencoders through a loss derived from the Wasserstein distance. For this, we use a typical GAN objective with the insertion of an equilibrium term to balance the discriminator and the generator. Our BEGAN model has a much easier training procedure that uses a simpler neural network architecture than typical GAN techniques.

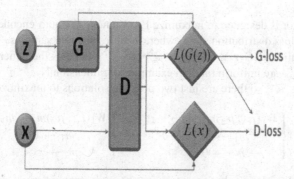

Fig. 2. Dataflow chart of the BEGAN model.

As shown in Fig. 2, we denote the generator by G with parameter θ_G, and the discriminator by D with parameter θ_D whose input can be the real or generated samples from G and z stands for the initialized uniform random samples. For each training epoch, the modeling goal is to minimize the error functions of D and G as well as to maximize θ_D and θ_G. Also, BEGAN introduces as γ an equilibrium term to trade off the effort allocated to the discriminator and generator. It is also denoted as the diversity ratio. Smaller values of γ result in better sample quality but poorer diversity, because the discriminator tends to focus more on the autoencoding of the real samples.

Lower Bound of the Wasserstein Distance for Autoencoders

We are interested in studying the effect of matching the error distribution instead of directly matching the sample distribution. Firstly, we introduce the autoencoder loss, followed by the computation of a lower bound of the Wasserstein distance between the autoencoder loss distributions of forged and real samples. In the first instance, we introduce the loss $\mathcal{L} : \mathbb{R}^{N_x} \to \mathbb{R}^+$ for training a pixelated autoencoder as:

$$\mathcal{L}(v) = |v - D(v)|^\eta \text{ where } \begin{cases} D : \mathbb{R}^{N_x} \mapsto \mathbb{R}^{N_x} & \text{is the discriminator function} \\ \eta \in \{1, 2\} & \text{stands for the target norm} \\ v \in \mathbb{R}^{N_x} & \text{is an example of dimension } N_x \end{cases}$$

Consider $\mu_{1,2}$ as two autoencoder loss distributions, let $\Gamma(\mu_1, \mu_2)$ be the coupling set of μ_1 and μ_2 as well as let $m_{12} \in \mathbb{R}$ be the ir corresponding means. The Wasserstein distance is expressed as the following: $W_1(\mu_1, \mu_2) = \inf\limits_{\gamma \in \Gamma(\mu_1, \mu_2)} \mathbb{E}_{(x_1, x_2) \sim \gamma}[|x_1 - x_2|]$

From Jensen's inequality, we are able to derive a lower bound to $W_1(\mu_1, \mu_2)$:

$$\inf \mathbb{E}[|x_1 - x_2|] \inf |\mathbb{E}[x_1 - x_2]| = |m_1 - m_2| \tag{1}$$

Note that we seek to optimize a lower bound of the Wasserstein distance between the loss distributions of the autoencoder and not between the distributions of the samples.

GAN Objective

The discriminator is designed to maximize Eq. 1 among the auto-encoder losses. Consider μ_1 as the loss distribution $\mathcal{L}(x)$, where x represents real samples. Then let μ_2 be the loss distribution $\mathcal{L}(G(z))$, where $G : \mathbb{R}^{N_x} \to \mathbb{R}^{N_x}$ denotes the generating function and $z \in [-1, 1]^{N_z}$ are uniform random examples of dimension N_z.

As $m_1, m_2 \in \mathbb{R}^+$ so there are just two possible solutions to maximize $|m_1 - m_2|$:

$$(a) \begin{cases} W_1(\mu_1, \mu_2) m_1 - m_2 \\ m_1 \to \infty \\ m_2 \to 0 \end{cases} \quad or \quad (b) \begin{cases} W_1(\mu_1, \mu_2) m_2 - m_1 \\ m_1 \to 0 \\ m_2 \to \infty \end{cases}$$

We choose the solution (b) for our purpose because minimizing m_1 naturally results in auto-encoding of the real images. Given the generator and discriminator parameters θ_G and θ_D, each being updated by minimizing the L_G and L_D losses, we state the problem as the GAN objective, where z_G and z_D represent samples from z: θ_G and θ_D, each being updated by minimizing the L_G and L_D losses, we state the problem as the GAN objective, where z_G and z_D represent samples from z:

$$\begin{cases} \mathcal{L}_D = L(x; \theta_D) - L(G(z_D; \theta_G); \theta_D) & \text{for}\theta_D \\ \mathcal{L}_G = -\mathcal{L}_D & \text{for}\theta_G \end{cases} \tag{2}$$

Throughout the following, we employ a shortened notation: $\mathcal{L}(.) = \mathcal{L}(.; \theta_D)$ and $G(.) = G(.; \theta_G)$. Although this equation is similar to WGAN, it contains two significant differences:

Firstly, we fit the distributions between losses, rather than samples. Secondly, the discriminator is not explicitly required to be K-Lipschitz because the duality theorem of Kantorovich and Rubinstein (Villani 2009) is not used. For approximating functions, it is also necessary to consider the representation capabilities of each function D and G.

Equilibrium

Practically, it is very essential to keep the losses of the generator and the discriminator in balance; we deem them to be in equilibrium when:

$$\mathbb{E}[\mathcal{L}(x)] = \mathbb{E}[\mathcal{L}(G(z))] \tag{3}$$

In case we generate samples that are indistinguishable from true samples by the discriminator, the distribution of their errors must be the same, along with their expected error. Through this concept, we can strike a balance between the effort allocated to the generator and the discriminator so that neither gain against the other. To ease the equilibrium, we can introduce a new hyper-parameter $\gamma \in [0, 1]$ defined as follows:

$$\gamma = \frac{\mathbb{E}[\mathcal{L}(G(z))]}{\mathbb{E}[\mathcal{L}(x)]} \tag{4}$$

The discriminator in our model has two concurrent objectives, to auto-encode the real images as well as discriminate the real images from the spawned images.

Boundary Equilibrium GAN

BEGAN's objective is:

$$\begin{cases} \mathcal{L}_D = L(x) - k_t \cdot L(G(z_D)) & \text{for}\theta_D \\ \mathcal{L}_G = L(G(z_G)) & \text{for}\theta_G \\ k_{t+1} = k_t + \lambda_k(\gamma \mathcal{L}(x) - \mathcal{L}(G(z_G))) & \text{foreachtrainingstep}t \end{cases}$$

We use the theory of proportional control to keep the equilibrium $\mathbb{E}[\mathcal{L}(G(z))] = \gamma \mathbb{E}[\mathcal{L}(x)]$. This is realized by using a variable $k_t \in [0, 1]$ to monitor the importance given to $\mathcal{L}(G(z_G))$ during the gradient descent. By default, we initialize $k_0 = 0$. λ_k equals the proportional gain for k; in terms of machine learning, it refers to the learning rate for k.

We employed k = 0.001 in our experiments. During the early stages of training, G is prone to generate data that is easy for the auto-encoder to reconstruct because the generated data is near 0 and the distribution of the actual data has not yet been accurately learned. This results in $\mathcal{L}(x) > \mathcal{L}(G(z_G))$ at the beginning and this is maintained for the entire training process by the equilibrium bound.

3.3   Crop Foliar Disease Detection Using the InceptionV3-RF Hybrid Model

Our driving motivation is to enhance the quality and performance of the detection model. Indeed, the particularity of our study compared to other works is that we are not only seeking a high accuracy but also investigating if the model has been able to identify the disease successfully, i.e., the classifier may provide high accuracy, but at the same time, the misclassification rate is also very elevated and unacceptable. For this reason, we resort to the confusion matrix and we strive to lessen the false negative (FN), i.e. the leaves that were classified as healthy but are actually diseased.

1) InceptionV3 architecture: Inception vN was first introduced in the GoogLeNet architecture by (Szegedy et al., 2016) with N referring to the version number. (Szegedy et al., 2016) proposed the InceptionV3 architecture, which provides updates to the Inception module to similarly increase the accuracy of ImageNet classification. This Inception module consists of convolutions, maximum pooling, medium pooling, dropping, fully connected layers, and concatenations. Batch normalization is widely used in the inceptionV3 and applied to the activation inputs. We used the InceptionV3 model with pre-trained weights on the ImageNet dataset for comparison purposes.

2) Random Forest (RF): (Liu et al. 2012) is part of machine learning techniques for solving classification and regression problems. It allows combining the concepts of random subspaces and bagging and also performs training on multiple decision trees trained on slightly different data subsets.

3) Our proposed hybrid model: Accordingly, our hypothesis is to combine the inceptionV3 and random forest models, to take benefit of the high accuracy offered by the InceptionV3 network and the lower FN afforded by the random forest model Figure 3 displays the InceptionV3-RF architecture in detail, including convolutional layers, pooling layers, fully connected layers, and dropout. The network implementation has one extra linear layer for linear activation. Inception's convolution layers employ rectified linear activations. The InceptionV3 features a receptive field of size 229 *229 in RGB color space with zero average. This paper investigates a customized deep learning method of pixel-based crop disease classification, which is constrained by the number of bands, so the convolutional filter width was set to 2. Subsequent 2 * 2 continuous convolutional kernels were chosen to substitute the largest convolutional kernel to assure the enhancement of the network depth under the same insight. In the InceptionV3 network structure combined with the random forest algorithm, we tested the hyperparameters as well as picked the optimal values of the hyperparameters for the network training. The first convolution layer channel numbers were measured equal to 32, 64, and 128, The optimal value for the first convolution layer is 64. Throughout the training process, the pooling layers were set to "max-pooling" using a window size of 2 * 2. Dropout is a regularization technique in which some neurons are randomly discarded. The proportion of eliminated neurons was fixed at 50%. The InceptionV3 contains three fully connected layers at the output. The FC layer output feature vector was pulled and placed into a random forest (RF) for classification. The hybrid InceptionV3-RF model used the high-dimensional features extracted by Inception V3 and combined the advantages of RF to substitute the fully

connected layer (FC) so as to make the ultimate decision. The model is trained on 40 epochs and yields an accuracy of 96,68%, as shown in Fig. 7.

4 Experimental Results

The present section covers the implementation details of our proposed method and the analysis of the results. Two experimental sets have been conducted. Under the first set of experiments, the BEGAN model has been trained on the training set for 10000 epochs to generate synthetic images of crop leaves for each category. The generator and discriminator model weights were updated after each epoch so as to produce forged images as closely as possible to the real images. At the completion of the network training, we generated 9000 synthetic images of crop leaves from the BEGAN model. Under the second set of experiments, the InceptionV3-RF hybrid model was trained on both the original and synthetic training set.

4.1 Experimental Setup

The experiments were performed on Google Colaboratory and on a local HP pavilion machine with 16 GB of RAM. The Colab gives access to speedy TPUs and runs on Ubuntu 17.10 64-bit and is consisted of an Intel Xeon processor along with 13 GB of RAM. It is powered by an NVIDIA Tesla K80 processor, 12 GB RAM, and 2496 CUDA. We ran the experiments in Python, using the PyTorch library, which carries out automatic differentiation on dynamic computational graphs. Additionally, we used the Colaboratory accelerated runtime TPU which is adequate not only for accelerating operations such as deep learning but also for handling other GPU-centric apps. TPUs are also deemed faster than GPUs, and each TPU brings up to 180 teraflops of floating-point performance and 64 GB of memory with high bandwidth on a single card.

4.2 The Hyperparameters Selection for the BEGAN Training Aimed at Data Augmentation

To obtain better performance, the hyperparameter choice is crucial. As such, the parameter values that we chose are based on either documented value in the published literature or on our empirical study. Due to the model's ability to learn the features of low-resolution images, we scaled the RGB images to 64 × 64 for computational cost reduction. We trained the BEGAN model for 10000 epochs according to the loss function convergence, we experimented with different learning rates and 0.001 seems to be a local optimal value. A similar empirical investigation prompted us to select 0.2 as the dropout rate. The synthetic images generated by the BEGAN model are displayed in Fig. 4.

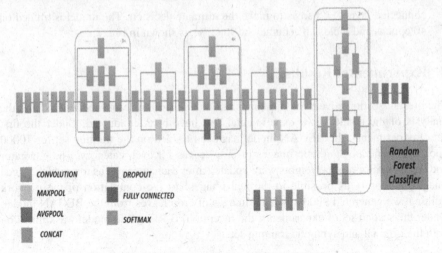

Fig. 3. Synthetic images generated by the BEGAN model.

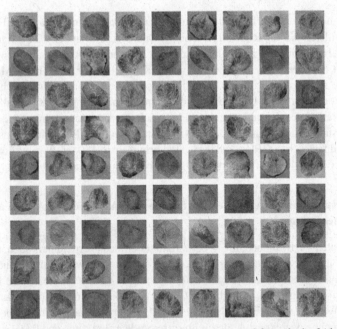

Fig. 4. Sample input image (left) and background removal from the leaf (right).

4.3 Hyperparameters Selection for Training the Inceptionv3-RF Hybrid Model

Once the synthetic images were generated using BEGAN, we merged the two datasets to feed our hybrid model for disease classification purposes. It should be noted that in this study, we are dealing with a multi-classification task, which means that the model can classify the disease species of each crop class. To speed up the network training, we preprocessed the images before introducing them to our hybrid model, by scaling down the image size, and removing the leaf background as shown in Fig. 5. Then, we introduced these images to both the hybrid model and the InceptionV3 architecture. For benchmarking purposes, we have trained the InceptionV3 network and assessed its performance to pinpoint its weaknesses, which we subsequently overcame by combining this architecture with the RF, allowing us not only to improve the accuracy but also to reduce the error rate in classifying diseased leaves. We have selected the SGD optimizer with a learning rate equal to 0.001 and for the loss function, we have chosen cross-entropy loss, which measures the performance of the model. Regarding the choice of the batch size, we selected a batch size of 16, 32, 64, 128, and 256 to elaborate an experimental comparison, since a small batch size enables the network to converge faster by updating the parameters more frequently, but using a large batch size, we obtain higher gradient confidence. Consequently, we adopt a batch size equal to 64 because when we tried other batches, we found that the network loss oscillation fluctuated more. For classifier training, we found that the classifiers converge after 40 epochs.

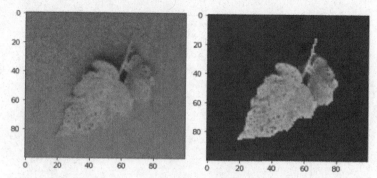

Fig. 5. Curve representing the accuracy value for the InceptionV3 architecture.

Therefore, we reported the performance of the trained classifiers over 40 epochs. So, this configuration gave us an accuracy of 94.71% for InceptionV3 and 96.68% for the hybrid InceptionV3-RF model as shown in Figs. 6 and 7 on our test set.

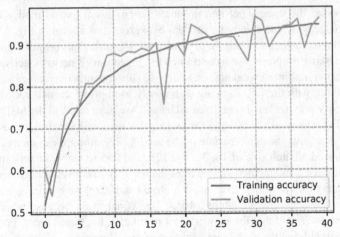

Fig. 6. Curve representing the accuracy value for the hybrid InceptionV3-RF model.

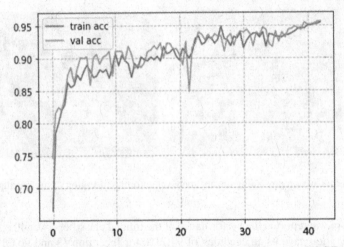

Fig. 7. Curve representing the accuracy value for the hybrid InceptionV3-RF model.

4.4 Performance Measures

In this work, the confusion matrix was employed to thoroughly assess the results obtained by the hybrid model. This confusion matrix data depicts the actual class in the samples and one predicted by the InceptionV3-RF model. Generally, the four metrics comprise true negatives (TN), true positives (TP), false positives (FP), and false negatives (FN). The model performance was assessed based on certain statistical parameters of the confusion matrix, such as accuracy, precision, precision, and F1-score. The performance evaluation was done by running images from the validation set with their respective labels, which had not previously been used for training. Table 1 provides the performance evaluation formulas and the results attained by the models. According to Table 1, we can clearly observe that the measurements of our proposed hybrid model have all been significantly improved to the InceptionV3 architecture. Note that we are extremely concerned about the recall that calculates the ratio of true positives, meaning that if an infected leaf is predicted to be healthy, then the consequences will be extremely severe if the leaf disease is contagious. The values of all tested measures were greater than 94.34% To gain a better grasp of the classification results, we have used the confusion matrix. Figures 8 and 9 present the confusion matrix graphs of the two models. The abscissa in a confusion matrix plot represents the predicted label and the ordinate represents the actual label. The diagonal of the confusion matrix includes the correctly classified instance data, while the values above and below the diagonal contain the incorrectly classified instances. It is then possible to visually assess the models' performance. By examining Fig. 9, we can notice that several crop classes are generally correctly classified, however, the InceptionV3 network failed to classify a few classes, where we observe soaring values in the matrix, respectively: 173 images of squash leaves affected by powdery mildew are predicted as healthy potato leaves, 128 corn leaf images affected by Northern leaf blight are predicted to be of the class of corn leaf affected by Cercospora spot,115 images of healthy potato leaves are classified as the cherry leaf affected by powdery mildew, 94 images of healthy blueberry leaves are predicted as the pepper leaf class, and 93 images of healthy cherry leaves are predicted as being from the class of healthy pepper leaf and finally, 60 images of healthy cherry leaves are predicted as images of orange leaves affected by Huanglongbing. So, with the aim of minimizing the error rate, we combined this architecture with the Random Forest algorithm. According to Fig. 9, the misclassified classes of 173, 128, 115, 94, 93 and 60 are respectively dropped to 15, 9, 0 (no misclassified image), 6, 0 and 0. Moreover, the confusion matrix in Fig. 9 reveals the success of the proposed hybrid model for the majority of classes by showing outstanding discrimination.

Table 1. The test set performance of the two models considered in this study.

Metrics	Formula	InceptionV3	InceptionV3-RF
Accuracy	$\frac{No of correct predictions}{Total no of predictions}$	94.71%	96.68%
Recall	$\frac{TP}{TP+FN}$	94.34%	96.47%
Precision	$\frac{TP}{TP+FP}$	94.47%	96.50%
F1-score	$2 * \frac{Precision*Recall}{Precision+Recall}$	94.35%	96.48%

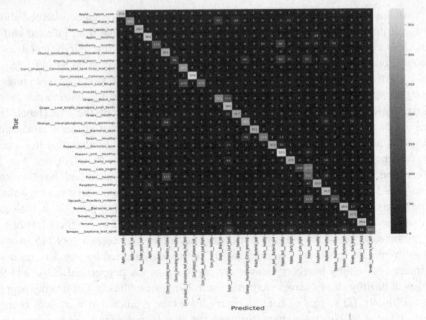

Fig. 8. Confusion matrix of InceptionV3.

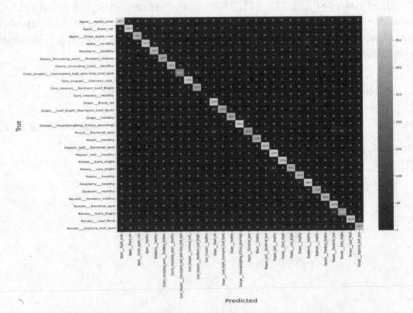

Fig. 9. Confusion matrix of the hybrid InceptionV3-RF model.

5 Discussion

In the present work, we conquered the class imbalanced dataset issue by generating synthetic images through BEGAN network. This model balances the discriminator and generator throughout the learning process. Moreover, it succeeds in striking a compromise between visual quality and image diversity. Despite the progress made by BEGAN in terms of image quality and convergence measurement, many problems remain and need to be optimized. At lower γ values, the produced images appear uniform and have many noisy regions, while at higher γ values, the generated images become more diverse but the quality degrades. Another shortcoming of BEGANs is that the generator is unable to learn features with low probability. We can proceed in our forthcoming work, by appending denoising loss to the discriminator in order to mitigate the noisy regions in the generated images as well as to further improve diversity, we will introduce batch normalization. Our results show that the BEGAN-based data augmentation method has been able to attain a decent result in the PlantVillage dataset. Also, the effectiveness of synthetic data augmentation using BEGAN can be tested on a large range of datasets facing data scarcity and imbalance, i.e. when collecting a high number of data samples is a daunting task. Nevertheless, the network capability remains insufficient when it concerns images with intricate backgrounds. Consequently, our future work will concentrate on expanding the network parameters to enhance the fitting capacity, lower the computational resources and produce images with higher resolution.

Besides, the experimental findings demonstrate the superiority of our proposed hybrid model over the existing DL model, indeed, the combination of BEGAN with hybrid deep learning has improved both the overall model accuracy, recall, and F1-score and has decreased the miss-classification rate of diseases. The proposed approach provides a better generalization.

6 Conclusion

In this study, a novel hybrid model was proposed by combining the InceptionV3 network and random forest that utilizes BEGAN to generate synthetic images of crop leaves in order to improve the network generalizability and accuracy as well as to lower the mis-classification rate. The obtained results are very promising and largely demonstrate the dominance of the DL method, in particular our proposed model, over the classical ML algorithms. Nevertheless, the DL method also has some constraints, namely, it is mandatory to have a very powerful GPU/TPU for training since the CNN models take a long time to be trained and can take from hours to days depending on the size of the dataset. Therefore, to shorten the training time, we used a pre-trained InceptionV3 architecture. Furthermore, combining the deep network and machine learning approaches requires far fewer CPU resources and consumes roughly half of the memory bandwidth while producing better models. So, in the future, a web application could be deployed with a complete system consisting of server-side components containing a trained model with features such as a display of recognized diseases in crops that can be applied in the field for validation and testing. Furthermore, the application could provide a discussion forum for agronomists and farmers to discuss treatments and pre cautions for the diseases they have encountered. Besides, we will endeavor to reduce the learning time, computational complexity, and size of deep models for running them on embedded or mobile platforms.

Acknowledgment. This work was done within the framework "Agrometeorological Stations Platform" project funded by the Moroccan Ministry of Higher Education and Scientific Research - National Centre for Scientific and Technical Research (NCSTR) (PPR2 project).

References

Abadi, M., et al.: {TensorFlow}: a system for {Large-Scale} machine learning. In: 12th USENIX Symposium on Operating Systems Design and Implementation (OSDI 2016)

Afifi, A., Alhumam, A., Abdelwahab, A.: Convolutional neural network for automatic identification of plant diseases with limited data. Plants **10**, 28 (2021). In: s Note: MDPI stays neutral with regard to jurisdictional claims in … (2020)

Arjovsky, M., Chintala, S., Bottou, L.: Wasserstein generative adversarial networks. International Conference on Machine Learning (2017)

Dayan, P.: Helmholtz machines and wake-sleep learning. In: Handbook of Brain Theory and Neural Network, vol. 44, pp. 1–12. MIT Press, Cambridge, MA (2020)

Dumoulin, V., et al.: Adversarially learned inference. arXiv preprint arXiv:1606.00704 (2016)

Goodfellow, I.: Nips 2016 tutorial: Generative adversarial networks. arXiv preprint arXiv:1701.00160 (2016)

Goodfellow, I., et al.: Generative adversarial nets. Adv. Neural Inf. Process. Syst. **27**(2014)

Hinton, G.E.: Deep belief networks. Scholarpedia **4**(5), 5947 (2009)

Hughes, D., Salathé, M.: An open access repository of images on plant health to enable the development of mobile disease diagnostics. arXiv preprint arXiv:1511.08060 (2015)

Johnson, J.M., Khoshgoftaar, T.M.: Survey on deep learning with class imbalance. J Big Data **6**(1), 1–54 (2019). https://doi.org/10.1186/s40537-019-0192-5

Kingma, D.P., Welling, M.: Auto-encoding variational bayes. arXiv preprint arXiv:1312.6114(2013)

Kukačka, J., Golkov, V., Cremers, D.: Regularization for deep learning: a taxonomy. arXiv preprint arXiv:1710.10686 (2017)

Lawrence, S., Burns, I., Back, A., Tsoi, A.C., Giles, C.L.: Neural network classification and prior class probabilities. In: Montavon, G., Orr, G.B., Müller, K. (eds.) Neural networks: Tricks of the trade. LNCS, vol. 7700, pp. 295–309. Springer, Heidelberg (2012). https://doi.org/10.1007/978-3-642-35289-8_19

Liu, L., et al.: A disease index for efficiently detecting wheat fusarium head blight using sentinel-2 multispectral imagery. IEEE Access **8**, 52181–52191 (2020)

Liu, Y., Wang, Y., Zhang, J.: New machine learning algorithm: Random forest. In: International Conference on Information Computing and Applications (2012)

Lu, Y., Chen, D., Olaniyi, E., Huang, Y.: Generative adversarial networks (GANs) for image augmentation in agriculture: a systematic review. Comput. Electron. Agric. **200**, 107208 (2022)

Lucas, G.B., Campbell, C.L., Lucas, L.T.: Causes of plant diseases. In: Introduction to Plant Diseases, pp. 9–14. Springer, Boston (1992). https://doi.org/10.1007/978-1-4615-7294-7_2

Mugithe, P. K., Mudunuri, R. V., Rajasekar, B., Karthikeyan, S.: Image processing technique for automatic detection of plant diseases and alerting system in agricultural farms. In: 2020 International Conference on Communication and Signal Processing (ICCSP)

Paszke, A., et al.: (2019). Pytorch: an imperative style, high-performance deep learning library. In: 32nd Proceedings on Advances in Neural Information Processing Systems (2019)

Paullada, A., Raji, I.D., Bender, E.M., Denton, E., Hanna, A.: Data and its (dis) contents: a survey of dataset development and use in machine learning research. Patterns 2(11), 100336 (2021)

Perez, L., Wang, J.: The effectiveness of data augmentation in image classification using deep learning. arXiv preprint arXiv:1712.04621(2017)

Radford, A., Metz, L., Chintala, S.: Unsupervised representation learning with deep convolutional generative adversarial networks. arXiv preprint arXiv:1511.06434 (2015)

Salimans, T., Goodfellow, I., Zaremba, W., Cheung, V., Radford, A., Chen, X.: Improved techniques for training GANs. In: 29th Proceedings on Advances in Neural Information Processing Systems (2016)

Shirahatti, J., Patil, R., Akulwar, P.: A survey paper on plant disease identification using machine learning approach. In: 2018 3rd International Conference on Communication and Electronics Systems (ICCES) (2018)

Shorten, C., Khoshgoftaar, T.M.: A survey on image data augmentation for deep learning. J. Big Data 6(1), 1–48 (2019)

Singh, V., Misra, A.K.: Detection of plant leaf diseases using image segmentation and soft computing techniques. Inf. Processing Agric. 4(1), 41–49 (2017)

Srivastava, N., Hinton, G., Krizhevsky, A., Sutskever, I., Salakhutdinov, R.: Dropout: a simple way to prevent neural networks from overfitting. J. Mach. Learn. Res. 15(1), 1929–1958 (2014)

Szegedy, C., Vanhoucke, V., Ioffe, S., Shlens, J., Wojna, Z.: Rethinking the inception architecture for computer vision. In: Proceedings of the IEEE Conference on Computer Vision and Pattern Recognition (2016)

Villani, C. (2009). Optimal Transport: Old and New, vol. 338. Springer, Heidelberg (2009) https://doi.org/10.1007/978-3-540-71050-9

Zhao, J., Mathieu, M., LeCun, Y.: Energy-based generative adversarial network (2016). arXiv preprint arXiv:1609.03126

Zhou, Z.-H., Liu, X.-Y.: Training cost-sensitive neural networks with methods addressing the class imbalance problem. IEEE Trans. Knowl. Data Eng. 18(1), 63–77 (2005)

Multivariate Skewness and Kurtosis for Detecting Wormhole Attack in VANETs

Souad Ajjaj[1(✉)], Souad El Houssaini[2], Mustapha Hain[1], and Mohammed-Alamine El Houssaini[3]

[1] ENSAM, Hassan II University, Casablanca, Morocco
SOUAD.AJJAJ-ETU@etu.univh2c.ma
[2] Department of Computer Science, Faculty of Sciences, Chouaib Doukkali University, El Jadida, Morocco
elhoussaini.m@ucd.ac.ma
[3] ESEF, Chouaib Doukkali University, El Jadida, Morocco

Abstract. Vehicular ad hoc networks (VANETs) represent an emergent variant of mobile ad hoc networks (MANETs) where nodes are intelligent vehicles characterized with high mobility, open and shared communications. In VANETs, routing security attacks represent a real threat to the safety of passengers and materials. Hence, the aim of this work is to present a novel approach for detecting malicious behavior in VANET routing protocols based on multivariate statistical method namely: the Mardia multivariate normality test. Our detection approach is as follows: first, we monitor the network traffic in real time by simulating two scenarios of AODV routing protocol, one normal AODV without attacks and a second with AODV Wormhole attack. The collected data is modeled by multivariate data sets sampled at different times of the simulation and consisting of three main parameters: throughput, packet drop ratio and routing overhead. The mardia's multivariate skewness and kurtosis are then computed to assess the normality assumption of the multivariate datasets. Indeed, we compare multivariate skewness and kurtosis values against theoretical values. The measurement of these statistics will allow identifying the Wormhole attacker's presence whenever these coefficients fall out of the normal ranges. Simulations of both network and realistic mobility model are ensured by the two simulators NS-3 and SUMO.

Our approach, which is implemented in the Matlab environment, provides a real-time detection method that uses multivariate data to identify anomalous behavior. As per our humble knowledge, our proposed approach is the first to use multivariate normality tests to detect attacks in VANETs. It can then be applied to any VANET routing protocol with no additional changes to the routing algorithm.

Keywords: VANETs · AODV · Wormhole attack · Mardia test

1 Introduction

Vehicular ad hoc networks (VANETs) are a sub-category of mobile ad hoc networks (MANETs) where nodes are intelligent vehicles characterized with highly dynamic

E. Sabir et al. (Eds.): UNet 2022, LNCS 13853, pp. 284–295, 2023.
https://doi.org/10.1007/978-3-031-29419-8_21

environment, open and shared communications. VANETs are currently one of the most intensively studied domains in intelligent transportation systems (ITS) used to enhance the traffic management systems. VANETs are deployed for various reasons including minimizing the risk of car accidents, optimizing vehicle flows by reducing travel time and avoiding traffic congestion situations. VANETs can also provide information and entertainment applications to road users [1, 2]. However, their deployment is subjected to a lot of vulnerabilities and security attacks because of the open and decentralized communications. In this context, Wormhole attack is considered among the potential threats to the network performances and safety of both lives and equipment [3, 4]. Hence, the purpose of this study is to provide a novel solution for mitigating routing security attacks in VANETs particularly the occurrence of the Wormhole attack against the AODV routing protocol [5] by applying multivariate statistical techniques, namely the Mardia normality test [6, 7]. The first step in our detection approach is to create the input data by monitoring network traffic over time and measuring three main parameters namely throughput, dropped packets ratio, and overhead traffic ratio. The second step is to model the collected data using multivariate data sets and fed them to the detection step. The detection step distinguishes between normal and attack situation by continuously checking the dataset's conformity to the multivariate normality assumption. We used Mardia's multivariate skewness and kurtosis to assess the normality assumption of the multivariate datasets. Indeed, we compute multivariate skewness and kurtosis values and compare them against theoretical values. For skewness, the sample is from multivariate normal distribution if the statistic value is less than critical value, while for kurtosis, the sample is from normal distribution if the statistic value is between lower critical value and upper critical value. The measurement of these statistics will allow identifying an attacker's presence whenever these coefficients fall out of the normal ranges.

To illustrate the practicability of the proposed approach, we implemented two scenarios of AODV routing protocol: one normal AODV with no attacks and a second with AODV under Wormhole attack. VANET Simulations are carried out by considering two simulators: the SUMO (Simulation of Urban Mobility) [8] road traffic generator and the NS-3 network simulator [9]. SUMO is used to generate mobility trace files from real-world maps extracted from OpenStreetMap. The network simulator NS-3 then uses these trace files as input.

The results show that our approach, which is implemented in the Matlab [10] environment, can detect Wormhole attack in real time by considering multiple network traffic characteristics simultaneously. It can further be applied to any VANET routing protocol without making any additional changes in the routing algorithm. The simulation results show that our approach requires fewer computational requirements while still being capable of analyzing multiple network traffic characteristics simultaneously. As per our humble knowledge, our proposed approach may provide a new solution for the detection of routing security attacks in VANETs.

The remainder of the paper is organized as follows: the Wormhole attack against AODV routing protocol is presented in Sect. 2. Recent state-of-the-art solutions to ensuring secure AODV routing protocol against Wormhole attack are given in Sect. 2. Section 3 describes the proposed approach, while implementation details and evaluation results are provided in Sect. 4. Ongoing research issues and future research directions are released in Sect. 5.

2 Wormhole Attack Against AODV Routing Protocol

2.1 AODV Routing Protocol

Ad hoc On Demand Distance Vector (AODV) is one of the reactive protocols wherein routes are created only when demanded. The details of AODV functioning are explained in [11]. AODV is based on three concepts which are the route discovery mechanism, the route maintenance and the sequence number. In the route discovery process, the source node broadcasts an RREQ (Route Request) message to all its neighboring nodes, this message is relayed by the intermediate nodes until reaching the destination or an intermediate node that has a valid route, then an RREP (Route Reply) message is unicasted to the source node in the reverse path. The routing tables of each node are updated after each retransmission of RREQ and RREP messages. In AODV route maintenance mechanism, nodes maintain only active routes, indeed a route is considered active as long as packets are transmitted between nodes. Furthermore AODV uses the HELLO messages to check connectivity of the routes. AODV employs the sequence numbers which are time stamps that indicate the freshness of a route.

2.2 Wormhole Attack

Wormhole attack is another most severe attack that may occur against AODV routing protocol in VANETs. It is carried out in a cooperative way, where a pair of attacker nodes forms a private and virtual tunnel between them (at distant location) representing themselves as neighbors. The goal is to change the network topology and misguide the network traffic. There are two ways to implement the wormhole tunnel, either using an out of band channel, such as a high power transmission signal, or an in band route between the compromised nodes by incorporating other network nodes. The wormhole's operation is depicted in the diagram below (Fig. 1).

At the first end of the tunnel (E1), the malicious node captures the control packets, encapsulates them and forwards them to the other colluding node at the second end of the tunnel (E2). The latter opens the encapsulated packet and spreads it. The hop count cannot be updated because of encapsulation, regardless of the number of hops between them. Hence, attackers are directly connected with each other and can communicate at a fast speed with less number of hops and less time in comparison to the other nodes. This impacts the route chosen between source node S and destination node D (see Fig. 1). Node S receives two route replies, one with a path of 5-hops, D-N4-N3-N2-N1-S, and another with a path of 3-hops, D-E2-E1-S. S and D choose this shortest path for communication. As a result, the routing can be affected by the Wormhole nodes in a multitude of ways: forward data packets back and forth to each other; drop, modify, or send data to a third party for malicious purposes.

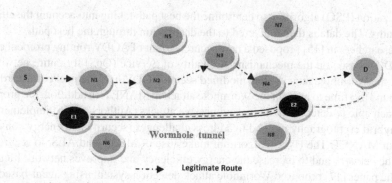

Fig. 1. Description of the Wormhole attack against AODV routing protocol.

3 Related Works

Numerous solutions in the previous literature were designed to detect and mitigate the Wormhole attack. For instance, researchers of [3] proposed a hybrid Wormhole attack detection (HWAD) algorithm to detect Wormhole attack based on round trip time (RTT), its corresponding hop count, and packet delivery ratio (PDR) for in-band type of worm hole attacks. Additionally, a solution for detecting out-of-band Wormholes is also presented based on transmission range between successive nodes. Further, the K-Means clustering algorithm was performed to identify the threshold value in packet delivery ratio employed for detection.

In the paper [12], a new version of AODV routing protocol labelled AOMDV (Ad hoc On demand Multipath Distance Vector) is proposed. This version is based on RTT (Round Trip Time) mechanism. Indeed, RTT is computed for each path connecting a source to a destination. The presence of Wormhole attack is detected whenever the RTT values exceeds a threshold value determined by incorporating the corresponding hop count.

Authors of [13] suggested an approach based on Artificial Immune System (AIS) to countermeasure Wormhole attack. The proposed approach is divided into two stages. The first stage evaluates the safety of candidate routes using by employing a test packet sent for each route and the destination is required to send a confirmation packet upon receiving the test packet. As a result, if the route contains Wormhole nodes, the packet will not arrive at its destination and the validation packet will not be received. In the second stage, Wormhole attacks typically have a lower hop count when compared to actual nodes. Hence, having a low hop count in a route increases the likelihood of pollution. In terms of dropped packet count, packet loss ratio, throughput, packet delivery ratio, and end-to-end delay, the proposed approach is compared to other previous approaches.

In the paper [14] a new method against wormhole attack in MANET is suggested based on the generation of multiple paths between source and destination called 'K' using Ad-hoc on demand Multipath Distance Vector (AOMDV) routing protocol. The source node determines the Wormhole attacked route by checking from the destination two types of packets namely: the detection packet (DP) and feedback packet (FP). After figuring out the attacked paths by Wormhole, the source node will use the particle swarm optimization (PSO) algorithm to determine the best path taking into account the attacker free paths. The data is then delivered to the destination through the best path.

Researchers in [15] proposed a new secure variant of AODV routing protocol called MSADOV based on the mechanism of Quality of Service (QoS) for entire network to detect the Wormhole attacks. The modified secure AODV uses the packet forward ratio and round trip time to prevent the Wormhole attack in MANET. In addition, the proposed approach able to detect both active and passive attacks. Authors of [16] implemented a new hybrid cryptography method to address challenges (security and energy consumption) in MANET. The Hybrid algorithm makes use of MRSA and AES, to secure data over the network and to increase the energy efficiency and improves network lifetime.

The paper [17] proposed Wormhole attack detection system using agent-based self-protective method for unmanned aerial vehicle networks (ASP-UAVN). The source node will initiate route request (RREQ) to the destination to detect the existing routes. Then as soon as the route reply (RREP) is received, a self-protective technique based on agents and the knowledge base is employed to pick out the most secure route amongst different routes and identify the attacking UAVsThis mechanism will protect the network against Wormhole, selective forwarding and sink hole attacks.

4 Proposed Work

The current study aims at proposing a new method for detecting Wormhole attack in VANETs by applying the multivariate normality test used mainly in statistics to test whether the distribution of an observed dataset follow a multivariate normal distribution and calculating the probability that a random variable underlying the dataset is normally distributed. The most widely used multivariate normality tests include the Mardia test, the Henze-Zirkler test and the Royston [6]. In our study, we employed the Mardia test which makes use of two measures: multivariate skewness and multivariate kurtosis.

Consider a set of observations denoted by X, where each observation is described by a row vector of p variables. The data set is thus represented by a matrix Xn × p (Eq. 1).

$$X = \begin{bmatrix} x_{11}\ x_{12}\ \cdots\ \cdots\cdots\ x_{1p} \\ x_{21}\ \cdots\ \cdots\ \cdots\cdots\cdots \\ \cdots\cdots\cdots\cdots\ \cdots\cdots\cdots \\ x_{n1}\ \cdots\cdots\ \cdots\cdots\ x_{np} \end{bmatrix} \tag{1}$$

Consider the matrix of centred data:

$$X_C = (I_n - \frac{1}{n}1_n)X \tag{2}$$

And varaince covariance matrix:

$$S = \frac{1}{n}X_C{}^t X_C \tag{3}$$

Let:

$$M = X_C S^{-1} X_C{}^t \tag{4}$$

$$M = \begin{bmatrix} m_{11} \dots & \dots m_{1n} \\ \dots \dots & \dots \dots \\ \dots \dots & \dots \dots \\ m_{n1} \dots & \dots m_{nn} \end{bmatrix} \tag{5}$$

Mardia (1970,1974, 1980) [7] defined multivariate skewness ($\gamma_{1,p}$) and kurtosis ($\gamma_{2,p}$) measures of a p-variate normal distribution as follows:

$$\gamma_{1,p} = \frac{1}{n^2} \sum_{i=1}^{n} \sum_{j=1}^{n} m_{ij}^{3} \tag{6}$$

$$\gamma_{2,p} = \frac{1}{n} \sum_{i=1}^{n} m_{ii}^{2} \tag{7}$$

The test statistic $\frac{n}{6}\gamma_{1,p}$ for skewness, is approximately chi-square distributed with. p(p + 1)(p + 2)/6 degrees of freedom.

$$\frac{n}{6}\gamma_{1,p} \sim \chi^2(df) \tag{8}$$

$$df = \frac{p(p+1)(p+2)}{6} \tag{9}$$

For small samples (n < 20), Mardia (1974) introduced a corrected skewness statistic $(n*k/6)\gamma_{1,p}$, where:

$$k = \frac{(n+1)(n+3)(p+1)}{n(n+1)(p+1) - 6} \tag{10}$$

This statistic is also distributed as chi-square with degrees of freedom p(p + 1)(p + 2)/6.

$$\frac{nk}{6}\gamma_{1,p} \sim \chi^2(df) \tag{11}$$

Similarly, the test statistic for kurtosis, $\gamma_{2,p}$ is approximately normally distributed with mean p(p + 2) and variance 8p(p + 2)/n.

$$[\gamma_{2,p} - p(p+2)]\sqrt{\frac{n}{8p(p+2)}} \sim N(0, 1) \tag{12}$$

Our proposed detection approach allows identifying legitimate behavior from malicious one by following the steps explained below and described in Fig. 2.

The first step in our method includes building the input data by monitoring in real time the vehicular network traffic. This monitoring system is deployed in every receiving node and consists of the measurements of three key traffic metrics namely throughput, dropped packets ratio and overhead traffic ratio. The output data gets updated continuously over a certain time interval. The generated data is modeled by multivariate data sets sampled at different times. The Mardia's multivariate skewness and kurtosis is used to assess

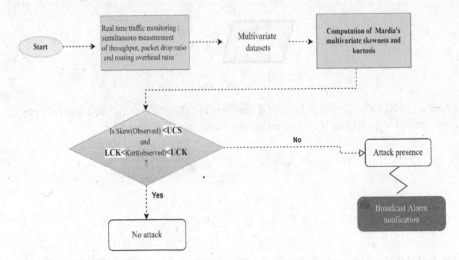

Fig. 2. Flow chart of the proposed Wormhole detection method

the normality assumption of the multivariate datasets. Indeed, we compute multivariate skewness and kurtosis values and compare them against theoretical values. For skewness, the sample is from multivariate normal distribution if the statistic value is less than Upper critical value (USC), while for kurtosis, the sample is from normal distribution if the statistic value is between lower critical value (LKC) and upper critical value (UKC). Based on these measured statistics, a Wormhole attacker is detected whenever these coefficients fall out of the normal ranges.

The values of both skewness and kurtosis will allow determining the probability that an attacker is present or not, so that observations with skewness and kurtosis values that fall out of the normal ranges representing the normal critical value will identify an abnormal behavior. The critical values for skeweness and kurtosis are given in the study[18].

If $Skew_{calculated} \leq USC$ and $LKC \leq Kurt_{calculated} \leq UKC$. where:

USC, LKC and UKC are respectively the Upper Skewness Critical, the Lower Kurtosis Critical, the Upper Kurtosis Critical, so the assumption of normality is approved and consequently we can conclude the absence of malicious behavior. Otherwise, the normality assumption is rejected and we detect the existence of Wormhole attack. A notification is generated as soon as the multivariate skewness and kurtosis are not in the normal critical ranges.

Our proposed approach has numerous advantages. First, the network traffic is monitored in real time using small time intervals which very useful since time is a critical factor in detecting incidents in the VANET networks.

Further, our approach lies on the multivariate concept, which is very useful in the context of our study. The VANET network traffic must be characterized by more than one parameter rather an individual one. In that regard, our approach has the capability to identify legitimate behavior from malicious one based on multiple network characteristics simultaneously. We involved three main important network metrics that have not been previously combined for Wormhole attack detection namely the throughput, the dropped packets ratio and the overhead traffic ratio.

5 Implementation and Results

5.1 Simulation Setup

In our study, realistic VANET scenarios are simulated using two simulators: the road traffic generator SUMO (Simulation of Urban Mobility) and the network simulator NS-3.

SUMO is a free, open and microscopic simulator implemented in C++. It is destined to simulate unlimited network size and number of vehicles. SUMO provides the ability to configure vehicle types, traffic lights, speeds, and multi-lane roads. It also supports model lane changes and automatic traffic light schedule generation. SUMO also supports the import formats, such as OpenStreetMap. We executed a set of Python command lines on SUMO in order to generate realistic vehicle trace files that are then used as an input by the network simulator, NS-3.

In our study, we extracted the simulation zone from OpenStreetMap, which is a map of the city of El Jadida in Morocco, as shown in Fig. 3. The generated.osm file is connected to SUMO to generate the mobility.tcl file with details of each node (vehicle), including the number of vehicles, position, speed, and direction.

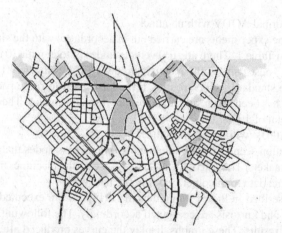

Fig. 3. XML file of the Simulation zone from El Jadida city edited by SUMO

Based on Linux, the system is set up and configured in an Ubuntu environment. The simulation parameters are shown in Table 1.

Our simulations are implemented using the version 3.29 of the simulation environment NS-3. The 802.11p standard is used on the MAC/PHY sub-layers, and the channels are modelled using the YansWiFiChannel with friisLoss propagation model. The transmit power is fixed at 33 dBm and the simulation runs for 100 s, distributing a total of 100 vehicles to the imported simulation zone. Ten source nodes simultaneously generate traffic with fixed size packets of 1024 Bytes. Packets are routed using AODV routing protocol. Further, User Datagram Protocol (UDP) is used as the transport layer protocol.

Table 1. Simulation settings

N	Parameter	Value
1	Network simulator	NS3.29
2	Mobility simulator	SUMO-0.32.0
3	Propagation model	Friis loss model
4	Number of vehicles	100
5	Wifi channel	YansWifi
6	Mac and physic layer	IEEE 802.11p
7	Transmission power	33 dbm
8	Simulation time	100 s
9	Packet size	1024 bytes
10	Routing protocol	AODV

5.2 Results and Discussion

In this part, we consider two different scenarios of the AODV routing protocol (scenario 1 and 2):

Scenario 1: normal AODV with no attacks

In this case, the experiments are carried out in accordance with the simulation specifications shown in Table 1. There are 100 vehicle nodes in total with 10 random source-destination pairs. These pairs simultaneously produce CBR traffic with 1024-byte fixed-size packets. The standard AODV routing protocol is used to route packets. Thus, no Wormhole nodes has been taken, and all nodes are normal vehicles. The simulation was set to run for a total of 100 s.

Scenario 2: AODV with Wormhole attack

In this simulation scenario, we implement two malicious nodes that act as two.

Wormhole attackers. The rest of the nodes are trustworthy machines that act normally and send legitimate data to the other nodes in the network.

The steps described in the previous flowchart (Fig. 2) are executed and the multivariate skewness and kurtosis are computed accordingly. The following figures (Figs. 4 and 5) depict the results. These graphs display the curves produced after implementing the suggested detection method in both scenarios 1 and 2.

Figure 4 depicts the results of applying our detection method to scenario 1(the absence of Wormhole attack). This figure shows the plots of the calculated multivariate skewness and kurtosis Thresholds used for attack detection corresponding to the critical values of the Mardia's multivariate skewness and kurtosis are also plotted.

From this figure, it is noticed that the multivariate skewness and kurtosis values start with lower values in the then first seconds of the simulation. These values are logical since the ODV routing protocol uses the route discovery mechanism before launching the data transmission. As the simulation advances, it can be seen that the overall skewness and kurtosis of the multivariate data fall in the normal ranges at various times of the simulation. For skewness, the values (Skew normal) are less than the upper critical value

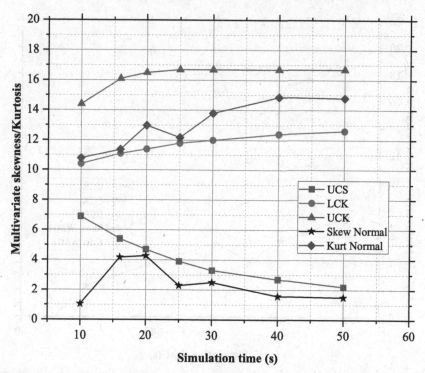

Fig. 4. Results of the multivariate skewness and kurtosis in the normal scenario (**scenario 1**)

(UCS), while for kurtosis, the values fall between the lower critical value (LCK) and the upper critical value (UCK). These outcomes suggest that the multivariate skewness and kurtosis without Wormhole attack confirm the multivariate normality assumption.

On the contrary, when the Wormhole attack is initiated in the network (scenario 2), the computed values of the multivariate skewness and kurtosis fall out of the normal ranges at various times of the simulation. The Fig. 5 bellow shows the results of these calculations.

Based on Fig. 5, we note that in the beginning of the simulation, the values of both multivariate skewness and kurtosis are approximatively very close to the normal critical values. However, as we progress in the simulation, these values increase noticeably and the overall skewness values exceed the upper critical values (UCS). Similarly, the overall kurtosis values exceed the Upper Critical values (UCK) and fall below the lower critical values (LCK). These results show that the data traffic collected at different times including the three variables namely the throughput, dropped packets ratio and overhead traffic ratio doesn't follow a multivariate normal distribution. These findings imply the rejection of the multivariate normality assumption and therefore prove the existence of malicious behavior.

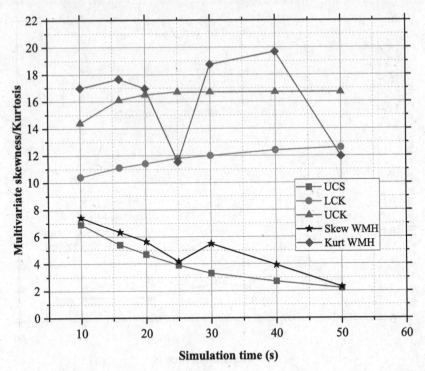

Fig. 5. Results of the multivariate skewness and kurtosis with Wormhole attack (scenario 2)

6 Conclusion

In this paper, we suggested a new efficient and simple method to detect Wormhole attack that affects the AODV routing protocol in VANETs by employing the concept of multivariate normality tests particularly the Mardia's multivariate Skewness and Kurtosis. The basis of our proposed approach is that malicious activities have traffic characteristics that are significantly different from the normal ones. Thus, our approach is based on the real time monitoring of the network traffic through the measurement of multiple network characteristics simultaneously. We integrated three key network traffic parameters that have not been previously considered simultaneously for Wormhole attack detection mainly the throughput, the dropped packets ratio and the overhead traffic ratio. These measurements are used to compute the Mardia's skewness and kurtosis used for attack detection. The values of these statistics will allow identifying the Wormhole attacker's presence whenever these coefficients fall out of the normal ranges. For skewness, the normal values should be less than the upper critical value (UCS), while for kurtosis, the values must fall between the lower critical value (LCK) and the upper critical value (UCK).

To test the efficiency of our detection method, we simulated realistic scenarios using SUMO and NS-3. Our approach implemented in the Matlab environment is capable of identifying the abnormal behavior in a real time by involving multivariate data. It can also be applied to any VANET routing protocol without requiring further modifications to the routing algorithm. The proposed detection method can be enhanced by integrating other performance metrics and implementing a reaction scheme to countermeasure the Wormhole attack.

References

1. Lee, M., Atkison, T.: VANET applications: past, present, and future. Veh. Commun. **28**, 100310 (2021). https://doi.org/10.1016/j.vehcom.2020.100310
2. Ajjaj, S., El Houssaini, S., Hain, M., El Houssaini, M.-A.: Performance assessment and modeling of routing protocol in vehicular ad hoc networks using statistical design of experiments methodology: a comprehensive study. Appl. Syst. Innov. **5**, 19 (2022). https://doi.org/10.3390/asi5010019
3. Tahboush, M., Agoyi, M.: A hybrid wormhole attack detection in mobile ad-hoc network (MANET). IEEE Access **9**, 12 (2021)
4. Ajjaj, S., El Houssaini, S., Hain, M., El Houssaini, M.-A.: A new multivariate approach for real time detection of routing security attacks in VANETs. Information **13**, 282 (2022). https://doi.org/10.3390/info13060282
5. Saini, T.K., Sharma, S.C.: Recent advancements, review analysis, and extensions of the AODV with the illustration of the applied concept. Ad Hoc Netw. **103**, 102148 (2020). https://doi.org/10.1016/j.adhoc.2020.102148
6. Rencher, A.C.: Methods of Multivariate Analysis. John Wiley & Sons, Inc., New York (2002)
7. Mardia, K.V.: Mardia's Test of Multinormality. John Wiley & Sons, Inc., New York (2006)
8. Documentation - SUMO Documentation. https://sumo.dlr.de/docs/index.html. Accessed 21 Sep 2021
9. ns-3 | a discrete-event network simulator for internet systems. https://www.nsnam.org/. Accessed 21 June 2022
10. Build MEX function or engine application - MATLAB mex. https://www.mathworks.com/help/matlab/ref/mex.html. Accessed 14 Apr 2022
11. Das, S.R., Belding-Royer, E.M., Perkins, C.E.: Ad hoc On-Demand Distance Vector (AODV) Routing. https://tools.ietf.org/html/rfc3561. Accessed 20 Dec 2020
12. Amish, P., Vaghela, V.B.: Detection and prevention of wormhole attack in wireless sensor network using AOMDV protocol. Proc. Comput. Sci. **79**, 700–707 (2016). https://doi.org/10.1016/j.procs.2016.03.092
13. Jamali, S., Fotohi, R.: Defending against wormhole attack in MANET using an artificial immune system. New Rev. Inf. Netw. **21**, 79–100 (2016). https://doi.org/10.1080/13614576.2016.1247741
14. Tamilarasi, N., Santhi, S.G.: Detection of wormhole attack and secure path selection in wireless sensor network. Wirel. Pers. Commun. **114**(1), 329–345 (2020). https://doi.org/10.1007/s11277-020-07365-4
15. SankaraNarayanan, S., Murugaboopathi, G.: Modified secure AODV protocol to prevent wormhole attack in MANET. Concurr. Comput. Pract. Exp. **32**(4), e5017 (2020). https://doi.org/10.1002/cpe.5017
16. Aswale, A.B., Joshi, R.D.: Security enhancement by preventing wormhole attack in MANET. In: Saini, H.S., Singh, R.K., Tariq Beg, M., Sahambi, J.S. (eds.) Innovations in Electronics and Communication Engineering. LNNS, vol. 107, pp. 225–237. Springer, Singapore (2020). https://doi.org/10.1007/978-981-15-3172-9_23
17. Fotohi, R., Nazemi, E., ShamsAliee, F.: An agent-based self-protective method to secure communication between UAVs in unmanned aerial vehicle networks. Veh. Commun. **26**, 100267 (2020). https://doi.org/10.1016/j.vehcom.2020.100267
18. Mardia, K.V.: Applications of Some Measures of Multivariate Skewness and Kurtosis in Testing Normality and Robustness Studies. 15 (2021)

Author Index

© The Editor(s) (if applicable) and The Author(s), under exclusive license
to Springer Nature Switzerland AG 2023
E. Sabir et al. (Eds.): UNet 2022, LNCS 13853, pp. 297–298, 2023.
https://doi.org/10.1007/978-3-031-29419-8

Printed in the United States
by Baker & Taylor Publisher Services